Undoing Empire

Undoing Empire

Race and Nation in the Mulatto Caribbean

José F. Buscaglia-Salgado

University of Minnesota Press
Minneapolis • London

Published by the University of Minnesota Press
111 Third Avenue South, Suite 290
Minneapolis, MN 55401-2520
http://www.upress.umn.edu

Library of Congress Cataloging-in-Publication Data

Buscaglia-Salgado, José F.
    Undoing empire : race and nation in the mulatto Caribbean / José F. Buscaglia-Salgado.
        p.   cm.
    Includes bibliographical references and index.
    ISBN 0-8166-3573-0 (HC : alk. paper) — ISBN 0-8166-3574-9 (PB : alk. paper)
    1. Caribbean Area—Race relations.   2. Racially mixed people—Race identity—Caribbean Area—History.   3. Racism—Caribbean Area—History. 4. Self-determination, National—Caribbean Area—History.   5. Spain— Relations—Antilles, Greater.   6. Antilles, Greater—Relations—Spain. I. Title.
    F2190 .B87   2003
    305.8'040729—dc21   2003004997

Printed in the United States of America on acid-free paper

The University of Minnesota is an equal-opportunity educator and employer.

12 11 10 09 08 07 06 05 04 03   10 9 8 7 6 5 4 3 2 1

Para Maüi, mi rudí.
Y por Javi.

Contents

Acknowledgments

First I wish to thank one who has always been my teacher, Arcadio Díaz-Quiñones. Without his guidance and support over the years this project would not have been possible. Shaun Irlam, David Johnson, and Mary Elizabeth Perry provided invaluable comments to various manuscript versions of this work. Both Thomas F. Glick and Jorge Cañizares Esguerra offered good critical insights to earlier versions of the first chapter. Jorge Guitart helped me in the challenging task of translating José Martí's prose, and Sami Hanna was kind enough to go over my transcriptions of Arabic texts. Thanks also to Marilyn Martin, who did a delicate and very thoughtful job of editing the final manuscript.

This work would not have been more than a disorganized collection of notes were it not for the many conversations I have had with good friends who share my concerns and whose work and ideas have inspired me in great measure. My most heartfelt thanks to Rosa Alcalá, Antón Arrufat, José Antonio Baujín, José Julio Balmaceda Bravo, Antonio Benítez Rojo, Amaury Boscio, Mike Brill, Ana Cairo Ballester, Felicia Chateloin, Alma Concepción, José E. Crespo Badillo and the Chavalotes, Zoila Cuadras Sola, Alfonso Díaz Concepción, Alicia Díaz Concepción, Antonio John DiMarco, Alexis Esquivel, Santiago Fernández Stelley, Rodolphe Gasché, Nathan Grant, Jorge Guitart, Reinaldo Gutierrez, Andrew Hewitt, Irvin Massey, Licia Fiol-Matta, Sandy Flash, Luz Merino Acosta, Walter Mignolo, Francisco Fuentes Millán, Reinaldo Funes Monzote, Miguel Antonio García Bermúdez, Oreste Gil, Ena Harris, Magaly Hernández, Juan A. Horta Merly, Michael King, Jean LaMarche, Margarita Mateo

Palmer, Lázara Menendez, Bonnie Ott, Francisco Pabón Flores, Nick "the Captain" Papagni, María de los Ángeles Pereira, Lorna Pérez, Reinier Pérez Hernández, María Luisa Pesquera Salvá, Mario Piedra, Deborah Ponjuan, Aníbal Quijano, Jack Quinan, Ricardo Quiza Moreno, Elio Rodríguez, Reina María Rodríguez, Rogelio Rodríguez Coronel, Eugenio Rodríguez Rodríguez, Luis R. Rojas Buscaglia, Jane Gregory Rubin, Timothy Rutenber, Francisco Enrique Salgado, Ana Serra, Ernesto Sierra, Edwin Smart, Ada Suárez Díaz, Daniel Taboada, Henry Louis Taylor Jr., Sørentius Thomas, Decio Torres, Carlos Venegas Fornias, Aida Vergne Vargas, Wolfgang Wolck, and Yolanda Wood Pujols.

I have also benefited greatly from my discussions with students, especially with those who, since 1997, have accompanied me to Cuba in the summers and who, like so many other friends, have shared in the vision of a Greater Caribbean.

Julia María Rodríguez, Barbara Stelley, and Santiago Fernández García provided guidance and very valuable assistance while I was conducting research in Spain.

I am grateful to the personnel at the Archivo General de Indias in Seville, the Archivo Histórico Nacional and the Museo de América in Madrid, the Museo del Hombre Dominicano in Santo Domingo, and the Office of the Architect of the Capitol in Washington, D.C. My work in these institutions could not have been possible without generous assistance from the University at Buffalo. I am thankful to the vice provost for international education, Stephen C. Dunnett, and the dean of the College of Arts and Sciences, Kerry S. Grant, who contributed money to the cause and granted me a research leave so that I could work exclusively on the manuscript.

Finally, I never could have started what I have now finished had it not been for the support of my family, especially my parents, Inés y José, and of Eloísa Salvá, Nenenó y Papito, Rafi, Gian Carlo, Gina, and Piero. I have also enjoyed the love and encouragement of my wife, María Luisa, and my son, Javier, who asked me every weekend when I was going to be finished with the book. Well, Javi, the work is not done, but the book is finished.

Introduction

> I refused to belong to a race, I refused to accept a nation.
> —Jamaica Kincaid, *The Autobiography of My Mother*

On 30 January 1891, the Mexican newspaper *El Partido Liberal* published an article under the title "Nuestra América" (Our America), written by José Martí, who was then living in exile in New York City. The Cuban essayist, poet, and political activist made an eloquent appeal for a radical new approach to the problems of what we today call Latin America, emphasizing the need to develop creative and critical solutions born of a direct and comprehensive understanding of the societies in question. "Neither the European book nor the Yankee book gave the key to the enigma of Spanish America,"[1] he wrote, pointing to the epistemological insufficiencies of imported models and schools of thought. The essay identified some of the principal problems inherited from the colonial experience and stressed the inherent potential of the region's peoples. Above all, it was an urgent call to get the region's house in order before "Yankee" interest came knocking at the door. Martí warned his readers to beware of the threat posed to Nuestra América by "an enterprising people who do not know her and disdain her."[2] No doubt, "Nuestra América" was a powerful exhortation to share in a program of political renovation of hemispheric proportions: "It is the time of reckoning and of marching together, and we shall walk in closed formation, tight as the veins of silver deep within the Andes."[3] But there are moments in the text where, moved by the sense of urgency, Martí asks his readers to take great leaps of faith; in those moments the essay reads more as a last-minute invitation to board the train of national redemption, an invitation that would seem to require passengers to leave behind all the baggage that could impair, contradict, or otherwise detract from the goal of reaching a happy destination.

In the opening paragraph Martí claims that "barricades of ideas are stronger than barricades of stones,"[4] and indeed, reading the piece one gets the sense that Martí set out to construct precisely such an ideological parapet, laying one statement on top of another while moving along with careful footing but at a frantic pace. Invariably, however, the strongest walls are weakest at the top, and Martí's is no exception. The last paragraph is capped with a keystone that cannot possibly hold: "There is no racial hatred, because there are no races."[5]

Martí's position concerning the total inadequacy and arbitrariness of racial classification systems was undoubtedly radical for his day. But as a political stance it was not new. At least in the Caribbean, the struggle against what he called the "textbook races"[6] had been part of a concrete political program that began to take shape during the Haitian Revolution a century before Martí's article went to press. And, as Martí readily admitted, those textbook races had always been mocked by the practices of everyday life of what he called the "Natural man." What was new, however, was Martí's assertion that there was no racial hatred. But it was one thing to debunk the myth of racial difference and quite another to attempt to erase the very real history of oppression and genocide carried out in the name of such arbitrary demarcations. Doing so would be the stuff of the most deranged utopian dream, for it would amount to eradicating all memory of what Aníbal Quijano has called "the most visible expression of the coloniality of power during the last 500 years."[7] Quijano defines *coloniality of power* as "that specific basic element of the new pattern of world power that was based on the idea of 'race' and in the 'racial' social classification of world population" and whose "most significant historical implication is the emergence of a Eurocentered capitalist colonial/modern world power that is still with us."[8]

The method to such apparent madness in Martí is to be found in the sense of urgency that is so latent in the time of reckoning announced in "Nuestra América" and that also propelled his project for making Cuba a nation-state through the creation and nurturing of what he called *patria*, or the fatherland. There is no question that his concept of *patria* was broad, inclusive, and built around the notion of giving power to the historically disenfranchised (though Martí thought only in terms of the males). Louis A. Pérez describes it as a "promised salvation, to all, of course, but especially to the dispossessed and displaced—*los humildes* (the humble), as Martí was wont to say: an entirely plausible formulation because *patria* implied a source of community and membership, something real and important, something that suggested a far more inclusive definition of nationhood than had been previously imagined."[9] But for Martí *patria* was also an unassailable ideal "for whose defense he tolerated excesses that in almost every other context he denounced."[10] *Patria* was the reason for Martí's racial mythomania. Because the nation-state held the promise of the erasure of all differentia created by the systems of racialization—the coloniality of power—joining the movement that would lead to its constitution required the a priori setting aside of all racially based claims and animosities.

The dispassionate observer might reply to Martí's "There is no racial hatred, because there are no races" by acknowledging that there are, indeed, no races but that there is a racial problematic that affects in rather terrible ways all societies, not just in what Martí called Nuestra América, but in the rest of the continent and beyond. In fact, it would not be difficult to argue precisely that which Martí seems to have feared. That is, that as long as the hatred among "the races" remains the common *non possumus* of all these societies, American states can be considered nothing but impossible nations. And it may also be necessary to question what Martí understood by "racial hatred," at least with regard to the apparent impossibility—or undesirability—of making nations out of colonial American societies. Maybe what he termed racial hatred was the perceived mistrust and animosities between supporters of competing ideas of the nation as they responded to different understandings of freedom and of the possibilities for independence and justice. Moreover, there are reasons to be suspect of certain creole projects of national liberation as being possibly quite contrary to the historical experience and claims to freedom of Martí's Natural man, and as these might have essentially favored the creation of "postcolonial" regimes that, ideologically speaking, were dependencies of what Quijano calls the "Eurocentrist perspective of knowledge."[11]

Perhaps nowhere else can this be pointed out more clearly than in the Caribbean, being as that region is the historical epicenter of the coloniality of power and, more important, the place where that category of knowledge first encountered a practice of everyday life that ran contrary to, around, and through it. This book is an attempt to present that practice as the constitutive movement of Caribbean aesthetics.

Tracing such a movement requires us, in turn, to circumvent two of the basic tenets of Eurocentrist knowledge as outlined by Quijano. First, we need to bridge the artificial temporal division that confined the "non-European" to a past that is in contrast to European modernity. Modernity and coloniality are coeval and codependent. Second, we must reject the Cartesian-based notion that divides the world between "non-Europeans" as objects of study or of domination/exploitation/discrimination" and European "rational subjects."[12] In what I term the mulatto world of the Caribbean such divisions are not practicable, because the body of the mulatto in the fullest spatial sense and the body politic of mulatto societies are the sites of convergence of and resistance to precisely that which the coloniality of power aims to keep apart. If, as Quijano points out, the coloniality of power attempts to relegate the "non-European" to the condition of a "non-Body"[13]—and, I might add, also of a no-body—the body of the subject of Caribbean coloniality, in its fullest spatial memory and practice, must be understood as a most welcome site of modern experience.

Having set aside these two basic tenets of Eurocentrist knowledge does not, however, eliminate the historical reality that gave rise to and sustained the Eurocentrist organization of experience in the coloniality of power. Believing as much would amount to assuming Martí's mythomaniac position with regard to racial hatred. The fact is that, though the Eurocentrist position is indefensible, the world of coloniality has always revolved around a notion of quasi-mythological proportions that I call the European Ideal. In the history of the Caribbean, every-body that wanted to be some-body has had to measure itself to that ideal.

Metaphorical Subjectivity

In measuring up or measuring down, running through or dancing around, being obsessed by or altogether dismissing the European Ideal, the subject of coloniality in the Caribbean established an aesthetic universe parallel to that established by the practice of knowledge expressed

in the coloniality of power. Half a century ago, the Cuban poet and intellectual José Lezama Lima developed a now mostly forgotten critical approach to what he termed "the American expression." I believe that the
Lezamian approach, which is more poetic than historicist, is quite possibly the best way to move through that world of Caribbean subjectivity.

Lezama was interested not in pursuing the formulaic derivatives of
dialectic logic in search of the Hegelian objective spirit, but rather in
the movement of what he called the *sujeto metafórico,* or metaphorical
subject.[14] The metaphorical subject does not try to make sense of history and participates in a narrative that "makes sense" only through the
most engaging interaction, or *contrapunteo,*[15] with the imago, which is
the idea(s) mysteriously and representatively embodied in the image.
This movement of counterpointing implies that the metaphorical subject is both imaged and imagined through a spatial experience that is
altogether real and that could best be described through what Ackbar
Abbas calls a politics of space, "where experiences, perceptions, and
affects take on some of the character of events."[16]

The metaphorical subject, Lezama pointed out, is the agent that pre-
vents natural and cultural formations from becoming frozen pieces of
the historical imaginary,[17] the one who reminds us of "an obligation almost to relive what can no longer be ascertained."[18] In this sense the
metaphorical subject is the custodian of the silent ruin, the one who,
moving in and out of it at will, inhabits a place long deserted by the historical memory of later arrivals. Such places always contain the traces of
previous movement. These are the events that the metaphorical subject
brings to life by moving through space creating a long concatenation of
related sites whose contrapuntal positions in reference to each other are
always shifting. Lezama's imago is thus a spatial entity in the fullest sense
and, in the best of cases, can also be considered an architectural event.
Guillermo Cabrera Infante has stated that "aside from a few books, architecture is the only possible form to history."[19] As he notes, architecture is
a "silent but eloquent witness: a building is worth a thousand words
because it is a hard image that endures."[20] Here is the imago at its most
concrete, as a movement that can be confirmed in real space.

Yet the metaphorical subject is more than just a custodian of the long
forgotten. It is also a prankster of the imago. Aristotle described the
metaphor as "giving the thing a name that belongs to something else,"[21]
not only in the analogical sense of transferring meaning from species to

species and from genus to genus, but, more important, in the true transgression of moving from genus to species and from species to genus. This
is the movement of the metaphorical subject, which, far from residing
in a motionless—and arguably placeless—state of objective and objecti-
fying contemplation, makes sense of the world as does the one who moves
through the scene of the crime picking up objects at will and contaminating the evidence. Contrary to placing value in the differentia that
validates the differentiator's position as the master interpreter of signs
and as chief appraiser and brander of all bodies—that is, contrary to
the "objective spirit" of the coloniality of power—the metaphorical subject, to borrow once again from Aristotle, can be said to have "an intuitive
perception of the similarity in dissimilars."[22] The metaphorical subject
moves freely across otherwise impermeable boundaries, leaving behind
a trail of formidable complicities while establishing "a sort of retrospective causality" that responds to what Lezama called the *sorpresa de los
enlaces,* or the pleasure of the unsuspected connections.[23]

In this sense my reading of Lezama is not altogether unrelated to what
Edouard Glissant finds in what he calls the "strategy of trickery"[24] in Creole language and in the "subterranean convergence" that "brings to light
an unsuspected, because it is so obvious, dimension of human behavior: transversality."[25] Glissant thinks of this transversality as a movement
of becoming that, contrary to the belief in what he calls "the universal
transcendence of the sublime," is a deeply rooted spatial practice in Caribbean aesthetics: "We have the good fortune of living, this shared process
of cultural mutation, this convergence that frees us from uniformity."[26]

Mulataje as Metaphorical Movement

Metaphorical movement responds to, describes, and informs a politics
of space that undermines and transcends the perspective of knowledge
that sustains the claim to the "universal transcendence" of the coloniality
ity of power. This much can be corroborated in a long array of events
revolving around the Caribbean world. More precisely, since the origins
of coloniality there has been a constant contrapuntal relationship between an evolving notion of the European Ideal and a movement of
what I call *mulataje,* which responds to the very essence of metaphorical
subjectivity. The first is a progression that goes from a notion of geometric perfection and of analogical projections emanating from an Ideal
Body to a reductive concept of socioracial exclusivity that accompanied

modern imperial projects and helped secure national utopias. The second is the movement of the metaphorical subject in the mulatto world, a movement that can be traced to a geography of ever-shifting boundaries, to a sort of Ishmaelite memory, and to a practice of being where bodies respond to a subjective trilogy that is a kind of permanent triangulation of the imago that is altogether not that different from what Antonio Benítez Rojo describes in the "wandering signifiers" that converge and run through the image of the Virgen de la Caridad del Cobre.[27] This triangulation is less dialectical than purposefully open and ambivalent, as in "the precision of the imprecise" that Arcadio Díaz-Quiñones finds in the movement of *bregar*,[28] a term, difficult to translate, that is widely used by Puerto Ricans to describe an action that is informed by wisdom and cunning and carried out with great (social) skill, thus describing a sort of Caribbean savoir faire that points to a way of being— in all its vagaries and possibilities—rather than to the more technical and reductive notion of know-how. Here I am reminded of Aldo Rossi's reflection: "Whenever I draw a triangle I always think not only of the difficulty of closing it, but of the richness implicit in the error."[29]

As metaphorical movement, the movement of *mulataje* is informed not so much by the production of difference that nurtures the coloniality of power, but by "an intuitive perception of the similarity in dissimilars."[30] In fact, the mulatto subject, as the embodiment of metaphorical subjectivity, can be thought of as the very prankster of the imago, always escaping reduction and definition. In every case, the mulatto always moves beyond, not by being *alter* but by being *ultra*. Indeed, in a curious antidote to conquest and reduction, the mulatto subject describes a movement of reverse colonization of the Ideal that is always more, not less, always additive and forever seemingly shifting. The mulatto subject is the true *plus ultra* of the Atlantic world.

Let me clarify here that my use of the term *mulatto* is not an idealization or a categorical imperative in the sense of José Vasconcelos's "cosmic race."[31] Throughout the text the term will come up in its historical context and will be used to describe the racial station in the coloniality of power that alludes to the offspring of Europeans and Africans, or their descendants. However, when speaking of *mulataje,* and of the mulatto subject within that context, I will not be pointing to marked bodies or racial categories, but rather to a history of subversion of those categories through the metaphorical movement that I attempt to uncover in the historical record and to describe in a performative way throughout the text. If *mestizaje* is commonly used to refer to the mixing of "races," my use of *mulataje* is intended to point to the possibility that Martí wished to see fulfilled in the *patria* as the ultimate realization of all potentiality in the erasure of racial difference.[32] Accordingly, when I refer to the mulatto subject as the receptacle of the essence of *mulataje* I am thinking of a social and historical agent that, although inevitably inscribed within the world of the coloniality of power in the most infinitely tortuous ways, nevertheless represents the very possibility and describes the vectorial intention of the nonracialized. My perspective, however, is less utopian than aporatic. I am not betting on the abolition of race but rather seeking out the pleasures of double-crossing the coloniality of power at every possible turn, in an attempt, as Glissant would put it, "to link a possible solution of the insoluble to the resolution other peoples have achieved."[33]

Mending the Sails

In order to move against the coloniality of power in such a fashion, I will first need to question some of the principal Eurocentric claims to the Caribbean made in the European and the Yankee books. Accordingly, I have chosen to begin the work with the "Usonian"[34] rapture of the originary Columbian rape. During the first half of the nineteenth century the myth of Columbus became one of the foundational building blocks of Usonian national ideology. This was the result of a calculated manipulation whereby the United States came to bequeath to itself a civilizational pedigree through a process of historical shoplifting directed against the peoples of Spain and of "Spanish" America. The claim to the Columbian legacy was a heist that required Usonian ideologues, in a contrived and roundabout way, to sever Columbus's ties to a world that was deemed too tenebrous, both religiously and racially. The work of Washington Irving was at the center of this movement, and it occupies the pivotal place that marks and facilitates the transition from republic to empire in the United States. In fact, together with his new and improved—and sanitized—version of Columbus, Irving gave Usonians a taste for the acquisition of things Spanish, a craving that would soon take the U.S. Army all the way to Mexico City.

Irving also gave his readers something far more important that was overlooked then as it has been to date. I believe that at the outset of the Usonian imperial era Irving had a strange premonition about the inevitable end of the nascent empire. His civilizational insecurity responded to a profound fear of the unknown and uncontrollable variance of subjectivity among the peoples who inhabited the lands against which the Usonian claim to hemispheric hegemony was to be staked out. Irving's own uneasiness with Spain's Moorish past confirmed his prejudice. It was as if somehow the civilizational pedigree he was claiming through Columbus carried an incurable virus. Irving took drastic measures against this perceived threat by attempting to separate the figure of Columbus from that of his crew and drawing the line between romance and history—and between Moors and Christians—in 1492. The first chapter of this book is thus an invitation to revisit Irving's premonitory prejudice by considering precisely that which he most feared, returning to a "circa 1492" peninsular frontier world that was to contribute significantly to the cultural formation of New World societies. There, at the embryonic stage of the first national-imperial project of Christian Europe, I find the basic incongruence between analogical and metaphorical movement as the Ideal Body of universal projections—well formed, male, Christian, and European—came to be measured against practices of space and of everyday life that, to put it in Irvian terms, were thought of as debased and dependent on superstitious fancies.

Irving's fears were nothing new. In fact, they had already been expressed three centuries before by Bartolomé de las Casas, whose apocalyptic visions at the outset of the Spanish empire in the Indies are well known today. What is, however, not generally emphasized is that Las Casas's vision of the end of empire did not relate to the genocide of the native populations as much as to the mounting threat posed by the ever-increasing numbers of blacks and mulattoes that came in their stead. To Las Casas's crusading spirit the *morenos,* as blacks and mulattoes came to be known, could potentially represent a greater threat to Christianity in the New World than the Moors ever did in the Old. In the second chapter of the book I explore the possible basis for Las Casas's premonitions. In the process I present a preliminary assessment of a phenomenon that has systematically been occluded in the history of America, that is, the irrevocable Moorish presence in early New World societies. This historical restoration would not be complete without making a case against a similar occlusion on the other side of the Atlantic, where the important presence of the *morenos* during the period of the "Golden Age" of Spanish civilization has been seldom given the importance it deserves.

Due to the scarcity of written records on the subject, in the second chapter I look at the built environment of early colonial Santo Domingo as it evolved in an ambitious but short-lived building campaign centered around the construction of the first cathedral of the New World (1521–44). There, perhaps as in no other place at the time, the production of imperial ideology at a symbolic level was prodigiously checked at every point by a practice of space that has been overlooked by critics and historians alike to this day. Simply put, the construction of the cathedral—and of the city—during what I call "the period of the *alarifes* (master builders)" was a unique moment in the formation of American societies and the very first great *sorpresa de los enlaces,* as the old peninsular rivalries between Christians and Moors came to be played out in Hispaniola on a highly symbolic level. As it turned out, the conquistadores soon moved on to Mexico and Peru in search of riches, and the island that had been the theater of the early colonial enterprise was practically abandoned. But behind that official exodus is the story of peoples who stayed behind and who "vanished" behind the otherwise official symbols of Christianity triumphant, going beyond the frontiers of the colony in search not of plunder, but of land and asylum.

The politics of space in the first decades of the colonial enterprise in Hispaniola was a prelude to things to come on a broader continental scale, as the *moreno* subject replaced the Moor as the site of European alterity, thereby coming to embody the colonizer's greatest fear. This was the origin of the legend of the "black Other" in the "American expression" or, as I prefer to put it, of a movement against the coloniality of power that was organized around a mulatto subject who for the authorities was ever harder to figure out, to control, and to dismiss.

The first one to enunciate this fear, although arguably still in a rather cryptic and veiled—and censored—way, was Las Casas. He had been an early witness to what Lezama called the *contraconquista,* or counterconquest,[35] a movement that at the original sites of colonization in the Indies produced an interesting overlap of disparate traditions of resistance to and accommodation of the European Ideal, some of which, as happened with the Moorish and the *moreno* phenomenon, managed to traverse the Atlantic. Nowhere was this more clear than in Hispaniola, where opposition to conquest, reduction, and slavery soon gave way to alternative economies that emerged along and beyond the frontier of the first colonial settlements and that were organized around a polyphonic and contrapuntal movement of social—and also bodily—fugue and subterfuge. Gone were the early hopes Las Casas had harbored for the Indies as the site of a world of Christian love and fraternity. The third chapter of this book invites the reader on a tour of the tragic vision Las Casas expounded at the end of his life as he came to reflect on the circumstances that had led to the destruction of the Indies. It is a visit to a world that the old friar surmised would remain forever on the verge of chaos and catastrophe.

Las Casas's vision was enunciated following the logic of inevitability, and as such it can be understood as the originating site of and as the oldest precedent to a discourse of creole[36] legitimacy that has always been conceived as being in permanent opposition to a perceived "*moreno* threat*.*" With the Indians gone, the New World would be forever disputed between the *indianos,* or Europeans from the Indies, and the blacks and mulattoes. Ultimately Las Casas would argue that the only course of action for Europeans and their descendants in the Indies would be to impose their will on the *morenos* by all means necessary. Failing to do this would result in the defeat of the Christian enterprise and in the emergence of what could only be described as a new Granada in the Indies.

Las Casas's work was censored by the Inquisition before it could be circulated. But the visions contained in his reflections turned out to be a silent augury of the first planned genocide in the history of coloniality. At the start of the seventeenth century most of the island of Hispaniola was forcibly depopulated in accordance with royal instruction in an effort to stamp out the sinful ways of the inhabitants of what already could be called a mulatto world. That was a classic example of the most decadent Habsburg prepotency. But it was too late. As it was already evident in a small town called San Cristóbal de La Habana, the walls erected to protect the coloniality of power had already been breached.

In the fourth chapter I look directly at the first programmatic enunciation of the creole will to power, in the work of the Mexican intellectual Carlos de Sigüenza y Góngora. In the Indies the Baroque was the imaginary era par excellence, and it is there that we find for the first time an American subject whose image was not just being promoted to a level of universal relevance, but also projected into a space of authority and certain political coherence within colonial society. This was done through the narrative medium, in the story of a young man from San Juan de Puerto Rico who was the first subject of coloniality to take the place of the European in the saga of circumnavigation. Sigüenza entitled this work the *Infortunios de Alonso Ramírez* (The misfortunes of Alonso Ramírez), and as the title implies, it was a log of terrible trials and continuous setbacks. But it was also a voyage of metaphorical displacement through the troubles and anxieties that plagued the creole imagination at the end of the seventeenth century, describing the rite of passage of an entire world that was seemingly in crisis. Neither a work of direct contestation nor a planned attempt at subverting the colonial order, the *Infortunios* questioned the fundamental premises that supported the imperial armature by merely visiting and moving through its contradictions and revealing its weak points.

The *Infortunios* also marks the first major instance when a creole subject took the liberty to speak on behalf of the colonial populations of the empire. This was a precarious position, informed by what I call a sense of the "being unbecoming," and buttressed through the parallel development of a system of socioracial organization that came to be known as the *sistema de castas,* or caste system. The fourth chapter ends with a discussion of this system and of the so-called *castas* paintings that were developed to explain it. As I will show, the *castas* paintings came to coincide with the original Lascasian premonitions, pointing to the mulatto subject as the keystone in the arc of the colonial and the protonational equilibrium of forces, as the unknown quantity that could upset all social balance and lead to the undoing of the colonial and creole orders.

On the eve of the Haitian Revolution the Spanish authorities and the creole planters in Santo Domingo tried to reimpose a close hierarchical system of socioracial organization over a people who, for three centuries after the island had been practically abandoned by the imperial authorities, had been living in a world where the boundaries that separated "whites" from "nonwhites" were lax if not altogether unkempt. Fashioned at this time, the Spanish Negro Code described a movement of terror specifically directed against the body of the mulatto as the site of all markings and demarcations. But plans for reinvigorating the plantation economy in Santo Domingo were cut short by the start and spread of the revolution against slavery in the neighboring French colony. The fifth chapter focuses on the significance of the revolutions for freedom and political emancipation that took place in the French and Spanish colonies in Hispaniola throughout the course of the nineteenth century. From a rereading of C. L. R. James's *The Black Jacobins,* and particularly of his characterization of Toussaint L'Ouverture, I suggest a reinterpretation of the historically protagonistic role played by the mulatto subject and that much too often has been dismissed by ideologues and historians alike. Then I revisit the discursive practices of *mulataje* by reading the life and works of the nineteenth-century Cuban mulatto poet known as Plácido and by taking a new look at the revolutions of the peoples of the Cibao as they fought against the perceived threat of the reimposition of slavery as the logical consequence of the annexation of the Dominican Republic to the Kingdom of Spain (1861–65).

I argue that in the Haitian Revolution the European Ideal was programmatically and symbolically unmasked and turned around, a movement that later acquired graceful and complex aesthetic form in Plácido's verses. This process was further promoted through the enunciation of a mulatto political position in Santo Domingo that was weary of the creole project of national independence and its authoritarian tendencies and that was able to approach the European Ideal with confidence, dexterity, and a healthy dose of irreverence as evidenced in the position taken by the peoples of the Cibao Valley toward the person of the queen of Spain during the War of Restoration. Nevertheless, the mulatto movement of freedom proved unable to sustain itself due in part to its apparent inability to produce a sense of group solidarity and to the recurring claim of the European Ideal on the Caribbean imaginary.

The epilogue, chapter 6, deals with the last three decades of the nineteenth century, when the revolution that had started in Santo Domingo spread through Spain's last remaining colonies in the Antilles. During that time the Puerto Rican poet Lola Rodríguez de Tió, referred to Puerto Rico and Cuba as "two wings of the same bird."[37] But the fact is that this allegorical bird had, at best, a double set of wings and that the real significance of the war for the independence of Cuba and Puerto Rico cannot be fully appreciated without taking into consideration the Haitian and Dominican precedents. This has been an error commonly and intentionally committed by traditional creole historians who have tended to look at the respective national projects of the different island states in insularist isolation. The connections, however, are rather obvious, if only poorly documented and studied. As I will point out in a preliminary way, these connections all came to revolve around a project for Caribbean confederation that was the mulatto alternative, on the one hand, to creole caudillismo and the foreseen persistence of colonial institutions of racial differentiation in the nationalist programs and, on the other, to the mounting threat posed by the Usonian hegemonic claim to the Caribbean. In every case, the rising tide of creole nationalism seems to have been perceived as a treacherous current by peoples whose geographic memory had always reached, as it still does today, well beyond the shores of insularist discourses and practices of power.

Finally I offer a few thoughts on the significance of the war of 1898, in which Spain and the United States came to transact an imperial succession whereby a creole republic was able to lay claim to a respectable civilizational pedigree through the acquisition of overseas colonies. This was a curious relay of sorts, as the United States came to wear the caesarian laurels and to think of itself as the alpha and the omega of American civilization. But the imperial expansion carried with it, as it always does, the possibility of the undoing of the imperial order. The everexpanding margins of the mulatto world were already latent testimony to the unsuitability and ultimate indefensibility of creole national projects in the Caribbean and beyond.

Careening and Sailing On

Because all inquiries by colonial subjects into the world of coloniality always yield, in some way, a measure of the elusive possibility of decolonization, the process of writing this book has helped me understand in a more critical way the perils and the vices of nationalist thought. In the "would-be nation" that Ada Ferrer correctly identifies as the ideal pursued in one way or another by Cuban insurgents during the independence wars, the "would-be" is a synonym for *raceless*.[38] But the problem of race in a Caribbean context—and in an American one, too—is that moving away from racial differentiation must also by necessity be a moving beyond the nation as the truest programmatic depository of the Eurocentric perspective of knowledge. In the creole world, race and nation are one and the same.

As a native of Puerto Rico, I originally undertook my research with the purpose of explaining to myself the reasons for the continuous and systematized colonial subjection of Puerto Ricans and for what I perceived as our relative acquiescence to the whole process. Although I am still not sure I can explain all of that, I have come to the realization that many of those questions require extraterritorial answers. For all too long, Puerto Ricans have neglected to look beyond the shores of San Juan or

Manhattan and into the broader Caribbean experience. Even worse, when looking at their own misfortunes they have tended to position themselves insolently above their island neighbors. This, by the way, is the result of a generalized malaise of the peoples of the region, not just of Puerto Ricans. I have come to understand, and I hope I will be able to demonstrate, the fallacy of such approaches and the centrality of the history of Haiti/Hispaniola in a world that—as many are fond of thinking these days about the Caribbean, and I believe wrongfully so—lacks clear contours and a center.

This narrative moves through the history of a discourse of racial difference that was in many ways an antecedent of and an indispensable counterpoint to similar ideological manifestations in the United States. In fact—why not say it—this discursive practice might also be a window into the fundamental transformations that may already be taking place as Usonian society comes to think of itself in less racially bipolar terms. In this sense, the text also engages Spanish and Usonian history in a movement of reverse colonization that claims and restructures those worlds and traditions from the point of view of peoples who were supposed to be subservient to their dominant discourses. In the measure that I may have been successful at this, I will have paid tribute to the long-standing search for a route of escape from the colony, the plantation, and their nation.

I have chosen to be faithful to the original spelling, punctuation, and accentuation of all texts taken from primary documents in Spanish, including most of those in the notes. Unless otherwise noted, all the translations are mine. In the case of nineteenth-century poetry I have chosen to do not a literal translation, but rather one that I hope preserves both the original meaning and the rhythm of these works. These give us, I believe, a valuable insight into the movement of mulatto subjectivity and limited access to a world that would completely elude us if I were to have translated the poems word by word.

In the interest of undermining the movement toward officializing and validating the categories of racial difference, I have chosen to put all racial descriptors, including *black, white,* and *mulatto,* in lowercase letters.

CHAPTER ONE

Tales of the Alhambra

Washington Irving and the Immaculate Conception of America

"Woe! woe! woe! To Granada!" exclaimed the voice, "its hour of desolation approaches. The ruins of Zahara will fall upon our heads; my spirit tells me that the end of our Empire is at hand!"
— Washington Irving, *A Chronicle of the Conquest of Granada*, 1831

In 1481 the King of Granada, Abû-l-Hasan 'Alî,[1] broke the uneasy truce with the Kingdom of Castile by launching a surprise attack on the mountain village of Zahara. Perched atop a jagged rock and defended by a castle, this small frontier outpost was said to be inexpugnable, a condition that according to tradition had also shaped the character of its people. The ruins of the castle stand today above the town of Zahara de la Sierra in the province of Cádiz, halfway between Málaga and Seville. The reputation of the place and of its ancient inhabitants remains intact in the term *zahareño*, which, beside naming the people of the town, is also, as Washington Irving noted in his chronicle, the Spanish term for that which cannot be brought under control, a synonym for *contemptuous*, and thus a marker of opposition and resistance.[2]

Abû-l-Hasan 'Alî launched his surprise attack a few days after the Christian feast of the Nativity. In his romantic account Irving tells of a stormy night when the inhabitants of the frontier outpost woke to find the blades of the infidels' scimitars at their throats.[3] The survivors were forcibly marched to Granada and paraded in rags through the streets of the city along with booty and captured Christian banners. To the people of Granada, who knew that they were living under siege, the entire spectacle was unbearable, as they saw in the despair of the Zaharenians the reflection of their own misfortunes to come. Just then a soothsayer ran through the streets of the city decrying: "Woe! woe! woe! to Granada! its fall is at hand! desolation shall dwell in its palaces; its strong men shall fall beneath the sword, its children and maidens shall be led into captivity. Zahara is but a type of Granada!"[4]

This is the beginning of the end in Washington Irving's version of the fall of Granada, which he wrote under the pseudonym of Friar Antonio Agapida, a fictional character who was, according to the author, the "incarnation of the blind bigotry and zealot extravagance of the 'good old orthodox Spanish chroniclers.'"[5] The fictional narrator was to make the story more believable to Irving's English-speaking readership by appealing to common Protestant stereotypes of Catholic bigotry and obscurantism. In other words, the closer the Spanish chronicler was to the Protestant view of Catholic orthodoxy, the more believable the story would seem. After all, how could a person like Irving, who at the time was beginning to be recognized as a talented writer but certainly not as a historian, write about such contextually remote events with any degree of authority? By recounting this story through the eyes of good old Friar Agapida, not only was he hoping to get away with being the first English-speaking author to "uncover" the story of the conquest of Granada, but he was skillfully placing himself in a superior moral position to that of his narrator and above the world he had been created to embody.

Like the monkish writers who had originally chronicled the events and whose texts he had been granted special royal permission to study, Irving was to orchestrate the swan song of the tragically unruly world of Moorish Granada as it was overrun by a vibrant and confident Christian civilization fulfilling its God-given destiny. In the process he would quietly steal the historical protagonism of Spain, raising his position and that of his own people one step above her and ever closer to the divine. This time around, the story of the conquest of Granada would wield a double moral. It would no longer be exclusively a story of the triumph of a Christian nation over Moorish tribalism. Now, through Irving's eyes and in the context of his broader work at the time, it was to include a corollary story about the coming of age and the civilizational pedigree of the newly born United States of America. Only by understanding Irving's version of the story in such a way can we understand how the contesting traditions of Catholic and Protestant Christianity establish such a curious rapport in the text as anonymous writer and fictional narrator set aside all differences and come together as one to face the absolute Other in the Moor. As Earl N. Harbert has noted, "Agapida was introduced into Irving's account as a useful literary device, to help eliminate the gap between the ancient past and the literary present; he was expected to erase the commonsense boundaries between fact and fiction, reality and romance."[6] He was also invented to test the permeability of the boundary separating Protestants from Catholics in the broader context of a world that was increasingly conceived as being divided between the forces of civilization and those of barbarity, where any claim to the civilized had to be made from Europe or had at best to show proof of both European and Christian origins. Through this authorial tandem the distance between Enlightened Usonia and Inquisitorial Spain is closed in the text, and the gap between the profession of Liberty and the auto-da-fé[7] is bridged by the urgency of avenging the rape of Zahara.

From that point Irving's epic moves directly to the birth of a Spanish state triumphantly unified under one monarchy and one god. Traditionally the most celebrated moment in the chronicle is the famous "last sigh of the Moor," the fateful instant when on his way to exile the king of Granada is said to have contemplated the end of history. In Irving's retelling of the Spanish legend, Abû' Abd Allâh Muhammad XII (known to the Christians as Boabdil) faces the end of Islamic civilization in al-Andalus when from the foothills of the Sierra Nevada mountains he takes a last look at the city of Granada and hears the faint sounds of cannons announcing the Christian celebration of her capture. "Allâh u Ackbar," he is said to have muttered as if seeking refuge in faith by proclaiming the greatness of God. Immediately the king began to cry, at which point Irving cites the words of his mother, the Sultana Ayxa, who "was indignant at his weakness. 'You do well,' said she, 'to weep like a woman, for what you failed to defend like a man.'"[8] In one sentence the tragic Abû' Abd Allâh is stripped not only of his kingdom, but also of his pride and honor, and his God and his manliness are presented as less than adequate. The book, however, does not end with the absolute humiliation of the Moor and the defeat of his all-but-powerful God. The final moment chronicled is the ceremony through which the Christian monarchs take possession of Granada. It is there where, dressed in the monastic garb of Friar Agapida, Irving joins Cardinal Mendoza, King

Ferdinand, and Queen Isabella for one of the most representationally charged moments in the history of early European nationalisms. In a pompous passage Irving tells how the ensigns of the state were placed atop the highest tower in the Alhambra, the former palatial citadel of the Nasrid kings: "At length they saw the silver cross, the great standard of this crusade, elevated on the Torre de la Vela, or Great Watch-Tower, and sparkling in the sunbeams. . . . Beside it was planted the pennon of the glorious apostle Saint James, and a great shout of 'Santiago! Santiago!' rose through the army. Lastly was reared the royal standard by the king of arms, with the shout of 'Castile! Castile! For king Ferdinand and queen Isabella!'"[9]

Inventing Tradition: Retracing the Origins of "Great Nations" to 1492

As it turns out, Irving's work subscribes to the basic assumption that has sustained most standard histories of Spain to this day. For Irving, as for so many other historians and ideologues, the conquest of Granada was simply the last chapter in the Christian saga that had begun eight centuries before with the first signs of organized resistance to the Arab-Berber armies that conquered the Iberian Peninsula at the beginning of the eighth century. That process is called by the official name of Reconquista, or Reconquest, and it is supposed to have resulted in the creation of the Spanish nation.[10] But what was Irving doing imploring the name of Saint James the Moor-slayer and heralding the triumph of Castile for King Ferdinand and Queen Isabella? After all, the Anglo-American writer was a citizen of a young republic that had just emancipated itself from tradition, especially the monarchical one. Let us not forget that independence did not significantly alter the cultural mores that the first generation of Usonians inherited from their Dutch and English forebears, especially with respect to a shared and deep-seated contempt for Catholic Spain.[11]

To understand how Washington Irving got himself entangled in the romantic history of Spanish nationalism we need to remember that he was part of a larger group of early Usonian intellectuals who were looking to create a tradition for a country that had just attempted to sever all connections to the past in exchange for "the promise of the present."[12] More important, we need to see the *Conquest of Granada* as part of the complex assemblage of the Irvian oeuvre, a literary machine that worked not only to manufacture tradition but also to bring forth the promise of a "*novus ordo saeclorum.*" In his *History of New York* (1809) and in his two most famous short stories, "Rip Van Winkle" and "The Legend of Sleepy Hollow," which were part of *The Sketchbook of Geoffrey Crayon, Gent.* (1819), Irving anchored Usonian tradition in the history and fictive memories of the "old" Dutch families of New Amsterdam. The young republic might have been a country without ruins, but at least, thanks to Irving and others, it had a history—and even the beginnings of what could be considered a modern mythology—that predated the recent English past. Still, the United States was a less-than-European country, a creole society with an "anomalous self-image" that looked to its former colonial master for approval and recognition of its claim to national adulthood.[13] Even when the publication of *The Sketchbook* in 1819 led the English to proclaim Irving the first truly talented Usonian writer, the United States was still an oddity to Europeans, a country located somewhere on the margins of civilization—a country, after all, of only one writer. A broader and deeper claim to tradition had to be made on behalf of the young republic.

Soon literary projects and national priorities came to revolve around Irving's newfound European reputation. In 1826 he was invited by the U.S. minister to Spain, Alexander H. Everett, to go to Madrid as an honorary attaché entrusted with translating a recent work on Christopher Columbus written by the Spanish historian Martín Fernández de Navarrete. Irving had been waiting in England for Everett's invitation. When it arrived, he had before him the opportunity to write the first chapter of the saga of "American civilization" in its English version, a situation of primacy he would revisit in his later years when he set himself the task of writing the first major biography of George Washington, which, in turn, would amount to the first major work on the national history of the United States. Immediately he set out for France and across the Pyrenees, entering a country that had not figured in the fashionable grand tour of Europe that he had taken as a young man between 1804 and 1806.

The Iberian Peninsula captivated Irving's melancholic nature from the start,[14] thrusting him into a spiral of the most complicated regression in the reenactment of the life of the subject of his writings. Soon after his arrival in Madrid, his voyage in search of Columbus took him to the "Spanish labyrinth of history and literature that linked the fall of the Moorish kingdom of Granada, the rise of the Catholic Kings, and the dawn of the Spanish Empire in the New World."[15] After all, Columbus had been a witness to the rendition of Granada in January 1492, arriving, as Irving writes, at the moment when "Spain was delivered from its intruders, and its sovereigns might securely turn their views to foreign enterprize."[16] However, the task of putting the work together soon became daunting, and Irving began to have considerable doubts about his ability as a writer and, more important, as a historian.[17] At the same time, he had begun to write the *Conquest of Granada,* delving into a subject that seemed to pick up his spirits, helping him to combat his melancholia with a good infusion of passion.[18] All signs point to his enthusiasm and belief in his work as he became every day more immersed in the vagaries of the world he intended to capture. As an inventor of tradition he was seduced by a people whose everyday life seemed to be firmly grounded in the oldest historical experiences. In a letter written from Granada to Antoinette Bolviller he expressed how he was torn between the duty of the historian as a collector of antiquities and the realities of a people who, albeit unbeknownst to themselves, were the embodiment of history: "I am continually awakened from my reveries by... the song of a pretty Andalusian girl who shows me the Alhambra, and who is chanting a little romance that has probably been handed down from generation to generation since the time of the Moors."[19]

In Spain Irving faced a landscape where history and myth were inseparably intertwined, and he was able to trace this condition all the way back to what he called the "storm of Moslem invasion that swept so suddenly over the peninsula."[20] By all accounts, the author's "association" with the monk Agapida, in itself one of the major sticking points presented by critics as proof of his historical disingenuousness, was a way both to excuse himself and to indulge the "wild extravagancies of an Oriental imagination" he quickly came to fancy.[21] Irving had contracted "Arab fever." This by itself was not necessarily significant. After all, this had been standard practice among Christians in the Iberian Peninsula since the early Middle Ages, and in Irving's time all of Europe was dreaming of the Orient. In fact, three years before Irving left England for Spain, the prince of Wales had just built himself a pleasure palace in Brighton, known as the Royal Pavilion, which was an architectural synthesis of all Oriental and imperial desire.[22] What was important was that the Orient that Irving found in Spain was disorienting to him. So much was confirmed as soon as he arrived in Granada: "I shall remain here very probably for three or four weeks perhaps longer if I find I can pass my time profitably. I find literary materials multiply upon me so much in this country, that I am almost bewildered, and find it difficult to extricate myself from it."[23] For Irving, the history of Granada had become a Zaharenian story of sorts insofar as it was a narrative that proved difficult to bring under control.

By August 1826 he could no longer keep himself from his Granadian project, and he put off finishing the book on Columbus, a sign perhaps of a historian who felt the need to master the complexities of the world that had given birth to his subject of study. As with so many others before and after him, the year 1492 quickly became a watershed for Irving. On one side, the romantic memories of the Alhambra and the glory of the birth of Spain fed his Orientalist, religious, and nationalist fancies. On the other, the epic enterprise of the discovery and conquest of the New World called him to the task of depurating the Spanish precedent so that it could be safely claimed by the Usonian creoles.[24] Sent out to capture and bring back Columbus, Irving was increasingly enamored of the romantic history of the banished peoples of Granada while identifying redeeming qualities in the nation-building gest that had required their banishment before Columbus could be given permission to depart. Irving's entire enterprise was becoming irreconcilably bifurcated as he began to jump from one side to the other of 1492, that thoroughly ransacked historical site that lies somewhere between the fall of Granada (2 January 1492) and the birth of the Spanish empire (12 October 1492) and into whose placeless temporality the idea of Spain is often driven as a wedge to separate what some consider the tragic historical accident that led to the establishment of an Islamic foothold within the geographic confines of Europe from whatever claims to nationhood could be put forth after the last king of Granada was sent into exile and the arms of Castile were raised above the Alhambra and across the Ocean sea.

Irving adopted the imaginary demarcation of 1492 as a convenient roadblock. Using it as the line separating the stories of the Moors from the history of the Christian nation helped him set a limit on how far Usonians could go in claiming a civilized pedigree in good old Spain. In his retrogressive search for the origins of a Usonian civilization Irving set his ne plus ultra right between the last sight of the Moor and the raising of the royal standards over the Great Watch-Tower. He saw the

entire history that had led from the eighth century to Abû' Abd Allâh's
final gaze at Granada as just a cute story, a sort of Arabian tale that he
hoped would sell back home. It was one thing to be related to the Castilian Catholics and their chivalrous quest, and quite another to consider
any sort of kinship with the followers of Mohammed. The subsequent
publication of his Spanish works demonstrates that Irving was unable,
if not unwilling, to reconcile both sides of 1492. Instead he ended up al-
ternating between two moments in one and the same movement, clearly
distinguishing between Columbian histories and pre-Columbian romances in the writings he produced: *A History of the Life and Travels of
Christopher Columbus* (1828), *A Chronicle of the Conquest of Granada*
(1829), *Voyages and Discoveries of the Companions of Columbus* (1831),
and *The Alhambra* (1832). The problems Irving encountered in separating history from myth—and turning history into myth—in Spain force
the critic to see these four works as one. This is even more imperative
when one considers that, through a difficult interplay between these
very different but complementary texts, Irving was able to selectively
rescue from the peninsular past elements that would come to play an
important part in the making of Usonian national culture and mythology, elements that remain at the foundations of that tradition to this
day. Chief among these, as we will see, is the belief in what I call the immaculate conception of Usonian America as a European-based or creole
civilization that came into being without any major degree of "racial
mixing" or corruption of the "white race" through miscegenation.[25] As
was clearly enunciated by Irving and his contemporaries, it follows from
this precept of Usonian nationalism that the United States holds the
claim to hemispheric dominance over the bastard children of the Spanish empire in all their dubious racial provenance and moral degenera-
tion. As I will soon demonstrate, by the end of the nineteenth century
these principles would already be consecrated and set in stone in the
holiest shrines of the Usonian nation.

Thus, Irving was the first to be given the opportunity of presenting to
an English-speaking audience the claim of the Usonian creoles to the
foundational moment of civilization in the New World,[26] a claim that,
in all fairness to the English and their North American descendants,
and judging by the role played by the United States in hemispheric
affairs since Irving's times, should have been built around the figure of
Francis Drake rather than Columbus. Having conquered Britain with

his pen, Irving was to take one more step back in the genealogy of colonial relations to claim Columbus for "America" in the same bold way that Columbus had once laid claim on behalf of Christendom to all the lands he found on the other side of the Ocean sea: by simply assigning to them his own religious—and, in the case of Irving, moral—nomenclature and descriptors.[27] The United States was staking a claim to what Peter Antelyes calls "the panorama of sacred universal history."[28] This was an operation carried out with surgical precision in the *Life of Columbus*. Irving did it by stressing Columbus's Christian piety and his alleged innocence in the treatment of the native inhabitants, both of which principles Usonian creoles had inherited as self-descriptors from their English masters as they set their imperial projects, albeit rhetorically if never effectively, in contraposition to the systematic mayhem conducted by the Spanish in the New World. The new Usonian Columbus was to be extricated from what the detractors of Spain had come to know as the Black Legend.[29]

More to the point, Irving set out on what amounts to a very selective historical search-and-rescue operation whereby he carefully brought back Columbus while leaving his followers abandoned to their fate at sea. Irving's text concludes with his "observations on the character of Columbus," in which he states that in "this glorious plan he was constantly defeated by the dissolute rabble which he was doomed to command; with whom all law was tyranny, and order restraint."[30] In the work Columbus's crew is the antithesis of science and reason, of progress and civilization.

Irving levied two principal accusations against the men who followed in the footsteps of the admiral. First, their minds were diseased insofar as they were unable to acknowledge and comprehend the significance of Columbus's enterprise. Second, their depravity led them straight into perdition and to the corruption of the body that is the result of *mestizaje*. Of the men who accompanied Columbus on his first voyage Irving wrote: "The minds of the crews however had gradually become diseased. They were full of vague terrors and superstitious fancies: they constructed every thing into a cause of alarm, and harassed their commander by incessant rumors."[31] Later, he accused the mutineers in Hispaniola under the leadership of Roldán of being "men of idle and dissolute habits,"[32] as they were "captivated by the naked charms of the dancing nymphs of Xaragua,"[33] men whose only objective was to "lead a life of perfect freedom and indulgence."[34] Set apart from the ignorance of that dissolute rabble who were soon to set themselves to rape and pillage, and from the official practices of the Spanish authorities, this Usonian Columbus was the most romantic personification of the civilizing spirit. His plan, in Irving's view, was to colonize and cultivate the land, to conciliate and civilize the natives, to ascertain the geography and its resources and possibilities, and to lay the foundations for "regular and prosperous empires."[35]

In the end, Irving's Columbus came to be a Jeffersonian character, better qualified to lead Lewis and Clark's expedition than to be the predecessor of Cortés or even Las Casas; he was, as Martin would argue, an image "of exactly what made America what it wanted to be."[36] It can also be said that the process of separating Columbus from his crew—and from what Roland Greene calls Columbus's own "Romance figure"[37]—created an image of precisely that which Usonia was coming to reject on the eve of empire, for the descriptors used by Irving to characterize Columbus's crew would soon be used without much variation to describe the people of Mexico. As the United States was to set its sights on transcontinental expansion, Irving's Columbus became the model for that glorious if difficult plan of bringing order to the dissolute rabble of Spanish America, the peoples whom, in this English creole Columbiad, the United States was doomed to command and for whom, it seemed, all law was tyranny, and order restraint. The weight of the work upon the Usonian imaginary was to prove unprecedented: 175 editions of the *Life of Columbus* were to be published before the century was over.

Irving's work matured considerably as he was torn between history and romance, and although the *Life of Columbus* has tended to receive more attention from critics, the *Conquest of Granada* presents a more interesting challenge, as it remains to this day an "unclassifiable text" within the Usonian tradition.[38] It was as if somehow during his search for tradition in Spain Irving came to realize that a national project could not depend solely on the collection of historical artifacts but must of necessity also include the recollection of historical possibilities. Joining in the blind bigotry and zealot extravagance that in large measure characterized the ideology of the Reconquista, Washington Irving found in the conquest of Granada proof that successful national projects must of necessity be framed within the larger context of Christian civilization unified and triumphant against an external threat or heresy. José Ortega y Gasset said as much when he pointed to the fact that "great nations have been made not from within but from without."[39] In the case of

Spain, he argued, the unified nation as an idea responded not to a concrete reality, to a reality at hand, but to a vision of "an abstract ideal
which could be made to exist."[40] In a way, Ortega y Gasset proposed that
"great nations" are organized around an ideal of possibility that expresses,
at the same time, the possibility of the ideal. Ideal and possibility are
thus fused to produce "great nations" out of an imaginary future that
organizes the present "as the bull's-eye pulls the arrow and draws the
bow."[41] Ortega y Gasset made no distinction between early national phenomena and the age of empire in which he lived, jumping in one and
the same paragraph from the Reconquista to a consideration of the birth
of Rhodesia as the possibility of creating an empire "in the savage heart
of Africa."[42] Just as much is evident in Irving's Spanish stories, as they
claim for the United States in Columbus and in the Reconquista a distant but exemplary parentage in the epic lore of Christian civilization
and in the ideal and its possibility as they were inseparably fused together in 1492, the year that the first "great national" empire of the early
modern age came into being, that is, the moment when the national
imaginary began to emerge out of the dream of empire.[43]

Indeed, Irving's Spanish work was also an omen—and even perhaps
a warning—about the coming of the Usonian empire. Certainly, as no
other literary work before it had done in the history of the young country, his books also were a catalyst for a project that would soon assume
continental proportions. In his search for "appendable" traditions and
in his selective colonization of the Spanish imaginary, Irving began to
set the aesthetic agenda for the acquisition of things Spanish. Barely a
decade before the war with Mexico and the U.S. conquest of Texas and
California, the first major Usonian writer was giving his readership a
taste for what President Polk was soon to call Manifest Destiny. As it
turns out, Irving was the most important member of the first generation
of Usonian Orientalists, a proselyte of the exotic who had no qualms
about or difficulties in installing himself as potentate of the places and
traditions he came upon.[44] In Spain he found a people living in the ruined palace of their most memorable antiquity. Then he literally asked
for the keys and moved in, obtaining permission to live in the ruins of
the Alhambra.[45] When in 1831 he was called back to republican duties
through an appointment as Secretary of the U.S. Legation in London
and his *revelement* in the aristocratic traditions of good old Spain came
to an abrupt and unwelcome suspension, a demoralized Irving was

compared to the last Nasrid ruler of Granada by one of his biographers: "The King of the Alhambra was on his way to exile."[46] But unlike Abû' Abd Allâh, who had left never to come back again, Irving was to return to the Alhambra a decade later, just as his large readership back home would seek to appease its newly acquired taste for the exotic in Mexico, in that Orient that for Usonians has since lain not in the Far East but to the south, in the Columbine lands inhabited by the descendants of "the dissolute rabble" who followed Columbus to the Indies.

Columbian Quarantine: Between Civilization and Human Scoria

Spain was to change Irving's life forever, and his experiences there were to carve a place in the Usonian imagination for the figure of the "adventurous American abroad," ultimately leading to the romantic mystique that in the eyes of many Usonians has since accompanied the process of expansion of U.S. cultural and military hegemony beyond its borders. In Usonian literature, Irving's Spanish sojourn influenced every subsequent generation of writers and some of the major literary figures of the country. His legacy can be traced from the quixotic foreign adventures recounted by Twain to Hemingway's Spanish memoirs.[47]

By the time Irving returned to the United States he had been abroad two decades. He had become, in a sense, the embodiment of a national tradition that is constructed from without. He was to provide a link between the romantic memories of a mythical past and the expansionist agenda of the new nation. Immediately after his return from Spain he published *Astoria* (1836) and the *Adventures of Captain Bonneville, U.S.A.* (1837), two stories on the entrepreneurial spirit of Usonian expansion into the Far West and the Rocky Mountains, respectively. Just then his work experienced a sort of aesthetic transformation that nevertheless did not alter his role as a producer of national mythologies and as an early and important ideologue of empire. As Antelyes explains, a new appreciation of the forces of the marketplace led Irving to exchange the romanticism of his Spanish adventures for a more practical commitment to the entrepreneurial venture. Antelyes reminds us of Ortega y Gasset when he writes: "*Astoria*'s American trappers and their foreign competitors, for instance, play out the drama of enterprise in a period of the past that is emblematic of both the sacred origins of the nation and its potential future."[48] Essentially, however, the basic direction of

Irving's work did not change. As Antelyes argues, Astor, the protagonist of *Astoria*, became an "American Columbus" with his own sacred mission to liberate "the promised land of the Far West."[49] If anything, the national agenda for Irving became tied to the expansion of the Usonian marketplace—at the time the underlying justification for empire building—into the Western wilderness. Concurring once more with Ortega y Gasset's vision of the mechanics that support the coupling of "great" national projects and imperial ones, Antelyes concludes by noting that Irving "had found a meeting place between business and culture, producing within it both an imagination of the marketplace and a marketplace of the imagination."[50]

So it was that Irving's initial claim to the Columbian legacy developed into a much broader—though equally selective—project that was to appropriate, actualize, and reenact the history of conquest and colonization that followed the Columbian discoveries. Irving had become the national troubadour, and his romances heralded the coming of the imperial age. In 1845 the United States declared war on Mexico, opening up a process of expansion—and, thinking of the nation as a marketplace, also of historical and territorial shoplifting—one that was to culminate with the U.S. victory over Spain in the war of 1898. As the great despoiler of the Spanish Main, Drake would have been a more appropriate model for the English creoles than Columbus. But the role of ideology has always been to conceal the obvious and to justify the most obscure, especially in times of war when the ideal is wielded as the very dagger with which to procure all possibility. And so as Irving went from his programmatic interest in Columbus to setting up shop in the Alhambra, his fellow countrymen would go from reading Irving's exotic tales of Spanish valor and Columbian vision to bursting into the halls of Montezuma at bayonet point. And just as in the *Conquest of Granada* Irving had taken his readers up the Alhambra for the raising of the banners of the unified Christian nation, U.S. soldiers went to Mexico with copies of William Prescott's *History of the Conquest of Mexico* (1843), pretending to follow in the footsteps of Cortés as they raised the Stars and Stripes atop Chapultepec Hill. Historical romances were no longer just the analogical simulacra of the national ideal. They had also become the guidebooks to the very possibility of its attainment: if Irving's books had given readers a taste of empire, Prescott's work became a manual for its construction.[51]

Like Christians laying siege to Granada, Usonians had found their moral and political Other in the peoples of "Spanish" America, in the descendants of Columbus's crew whom Irving had so emphatically dismissed and carefully separated from the admiral's own recyclable legacy. And it was through the sanitized version of Irving's Jeffersonian Columbus that the young republic was to insert itself into the imperial tradition of European nations, picking up, so to speak, where Spain had left off when two decades before she had been expelled from the mainland following the independence wars in her continental colonies. The entire process would be almost complete half a century later with the final expulsion of Spain from the hemisphere following the Usonian intervention in the Cuban War of Independence and the U.S. capture of the remaining Spanish colonies in the Caribbean and the Pacific. The great feat of imperial expansion would be iconographically synthesized in an eloquent photograph (Figure 1) that would appear in a grandiose and celebratory book entitled *Our Islands and Their Peoples,* a telling title for a book that, in a throwback to Irving's *Life of Columbus,* comes to separate the object of imperial desire from the despicable subjects over whom the U.S. was now doomed to rule. In this picture two U.S. soldiers pose at ease, mission accomplished, in front of the entrance to the Morro Castle in Santiago de Cuba. They stand directly under the royal Spanish coat of arms that hangs above the entryway. It is a telling example of careful ideological posturing similar to the claims made by Irving through Friar Agapida. Official and extra-official justifications for the war, its purpose, and its significance spoke of avenging the crimes of Spanish barbarity, from the Inquisition to the blowing up of the *U.S.S. Maine,* and of expelling the last major European imperial power from the New World in the name of Liberty and Humanity.[52] But in reality, just as when Irving joined with Agapida to face the absolute Other in the Moor, all distance—and old grudges—between the United States and the imperial traditions of Europe had collapsed. The caption under the photograph simply reads: "Past and Present,"[53] as if declaring the United States the new guardian of Civilization on the American continent.

When all was said and done, the United States had become a "great nation" according to Ortega y Gasset's definition. The republic had claimed for itself, exclusively, the imperial traditions of Europe in the New World, picking carefully among the ruins of Spanish civilization, from Granada to Mexico City to Havana, and boldly snatching the last

Figure 1. Photograph captioned "Past and Present," from *Our Islands and Their Peoples, As Seen with Camera and Pencil,* edited by William S. Bryan (1899).

crumbling pieces of her empire, from the Philippines to Puerto Rico. Along the way, as if being rewarded for conjuring up and making popular the image of the imperial nation, Irving and Prescott were immortalized next to each other in Randolph Rogers's monumental bronze doors (1861), known as the *Columbus Doors,* which were placed at the central east front entrance of the United States Capitol in 1871 and moved thirty-two feet east when the east front of the building was extended in 1961. Arguably this is the most important threshold in the catalogue of Usonian national sites, as it is the entrance to the Capitol's Rotunda, which itself was conceived as the architectural marker of the symbolic heart of the nation. It is there we must go to understand the full impact of the Irvian legacy.

Proceeding through the doors and into the building, we come to stand under Constantino Brumundi's *The Apotheosis of George Washington* (1865), a monumental fresco painted on the canopy of the Rotunda's inner dome (Figure 2). At the base of the dome, a frieze painted in grisaille so as to resemble sculpture, begun by Brumundi and completed in 1953, tells the story of the nation, starting, in Irvian fashion, with Columbus's landing. The entire frieze, which is a celebration of the birth of "American civilization," can be read as the history of imperial expansion from 1492 to 1898.[54] In the Rotunda the project of Irving's generation has come full circle:[55] the personification of the republic is dressed in imperial regalia beneath the caesarian representation of Washington in a Christlike ascension into the heavens, where he presides over nineteen scenes that celebrate the coming of age of "America" and its self-investiture as a member of the exclusive club of the "great" civilized nations.[56]

In a detail from the Rotunda's canopy fresco (Figure 3) Washington can be seen sitting like the first person of the Trinity, flanked by figures representing Liberty and Victory. Directly under him is the first of six allegorical compositions, entitled *War,* which heralds the triumph of the young republic over Tyranny. With a bald eagle representing strength through unity at her side, a female representation of "America" as a warrior charges toward two of the figures below. They are representations of Kingly Power (depicted holding a scepter and covering himself with the royal cloak of ermine) and of what Irving called "zealot extravagance": a monk holding the torches with which books were censored and the souls of those judged guilty were set to burn at the stake of the Inquisition. Behind these two figures a pensive man beholds the entire

Figure 2. Constantino Brumundi, *The Apotheosis of George Washington*. Courtesy of the Architect of the Capitol, Washington, D.C.

scene. His is an image of intrigue and conspiracy, the obverse of the ideal of republican fraternity. It seems to me, however, that this figure could represent Washington Irving contemplating his own doubts while looking at "America" standing above the king and the Catholic Church, much as he had done when he adopted the pseudonym of Agapida. Above this scene, George Washington's figure drifts ever closer to the vanishing point, the abstract representation of infinity and, by analogy, of all divinity. In the Usonian Pantheon, that is the placeless site where the "spirit" of the Founding Fathers—Irving's Columbus included—resides.

Below the frieze are eight large mural paintings, one of which (Figure 4) is the oldest of the major works of art in the Capitol to treat the subject of the Columbian enterprise. John Vanderlyn's *Landing of Columbus at the Island of Guanahani, West Indies, 12 October 1492* (1847) was

Figure 3. Detail from Constantino Brumundi, *The Apotheosis of George Washington*. The composition at the bottom of the detail is entitled *War*. Courtesy of the Architect of the Capitol, Washington, D.C.

commissioned in 1837 and set in the Rotunda during the course of the war with Mexico, the year of the Usonian conquest of California. The work is a mise-en-scène that is taken almost verbatim from the first chapter of book 4 of Irving's *Life of Columbus*.[57] The tripartite composition, derived from Benjamin West's *William Penn's Treaty with the Indians* (1771),[58] highlights a heroic central group in the foreground, with Columbus at the head holding an unsheathed sword in his right hand and planting the flag of Castile into the ground of Guanahani with his left. The admiral, now also viceroy, is followed closely by a carefully choreographed group of notables among whom we can distinguish the two other leaders and financiers of the expedition, Martin Alonso Pinzón and Vicente Yañez Pinzón; the royal notary, Rodrigo de Escobar; the inspector general of the armament, Rodrigo Sanchez; and Alonso de Ojeda.[59] All of these men are mentioned by Irving at the end of book 2 of his *Life of Columbus,* "together with various private adventurers, several

Figure 4. John Vanderlyn, *Landing of Columbus*. Courtesy of the Architect of the Capitol, Washington, D.C.

servants, and ninety mariners."[60] Symbolic yet anonymous figures in the group include a friar bearing a cross, a soldier keeping guard as he faces the natives, two other soldiers covering the rearguard, and three supplicant figures who are kneeling and facing Columbus: a sailor, a cabin boy, and a repentant mutineer. In Vanderlyn's attempt to capture the most dramatic instant of Columbus's landing, he has depicted the entire central group in a histrionic revisitation of the well-known academic model of Leonardo da Vinci's *Last Supper,* directly alluding to the image of Christ the Savior and his disciples. Indeed we are looking at Columbus as the Christlike leader of twelve men whose condition as the chosen ones immediately becomes evident when we compare the central group to the lateral groups.

At the right side of the canvas, in the darkest section of the painting and behind the central group, are natives approaching "the Spaniards with great awe; frequently prostrating themselves on the earth, and making signs of adoration."[61] There is a man bowing before Columbus, one hiding behind a tree, and behind them three native nymphs dancing in a circle. In the tree above their heads a red parrot sits on a branch as a disturbing symbol equating the natives to the speaking beast. To the left of the central group, in the background by the water's edge, is the crew, whose "feelings . . . now burst forth in the most extravagant transports."[62] With impeccable resolution Vanderlyn captured the essence of the Irvian Columbiad as an epic whose margins of deviation and most perilous contours are marked on the one side by the seemingly submissive native element and on the other by the dissolute rabble who had accompanied the admiral to the Indies. These are the Zaharenian extremes of Irving's imperial epic, the two clienteles that must be brought under control for the national-imperial project to succeed. Here, neatly depicted, is the triumvirate of contesting interests that have formed the basic building blocks of all creole societies in the New World. In this particular work, the Usonian creole adopts the figure of Columbus to place himself over the native and, to use Irving's terminology, over the extravagant elements that populate the lands he has come to claim in the name of Christian civilization.

Through Irving and Vanderlyn alone, the will to power of the Usonian creoles is furious on this level, presenting little contrast to the religious bigotry and zealot extravagance that Irving had chosen as defining traits of his fictitious Friar Agapida. Of the natives whom Vanderlyn depicted hiding in the darkness of the primeval forest, Irving wrote, "Once they had still further recovered from their fears, they approached the Spaniards, touched their beards, and examined their hands and faces, admiring their whiteness. Columbus was pleased with their gentleness and confiding simplicity, and suffered their scrutiny with perfect acquiescence; winning them by his benignity."[63] In contrast to the image of the most "benign conquest," the crew is the representation of the unruly and the treacherous: "Many abject spirits, who had outraged him [Columbus] by their insolence, now crouched at his feet, begging pardon for all the trouble they had caused him, and promising the blindest obedience for the future."[64] Here the image of the thankful crew speaks to the renunciation, repentance, and profession of faith that is associated with forced conversion, as if the success of the admiral's enterprise had also been a triumph of the faith in line with the conquest of Granada. Rising above these two representational moments, the central figures of Columbus and his Christlike group of twelve chosen followers represent Christianity triumphant. Here are the Christian saviors, the colonizers bringing the light of civilization—which in Vanderlyn's mural shines on the horizon behind the ships—to a world of darkness. These are the forefathers of all creoles, symbolically staking a bipartite claim to the land, first against the peoples of the forest, and second against the abject Columbian rabble, whom Vanderlyn, following Irving's prescriptions, correctly placed at the shoreline or still at sea, conveniently getting to land too late to lay claim to anything and reduced to a condition of prostration and devotion, like some who already "begged favors of him."[65]

In contrast to the solemnity of the central group, the crew at the water's edge is disorganized and noisy, almost the representational obverse of the image of the young nation that Emanuel Leutze was to exhibit in New York in 1851, which presents George Washington at his most Columbian. Far from being an image of a ship of fools, Leutze's *Washington Crossing the Delaware* is an image of unity of purpose and of perseverance against all odds. In this depiction of an Odyssean feat there is no sign of dissent or mutiny; we see only absolute focus. If the men taking General Washington across the Delaware River in Leutze's work symbolize the spirit of the Usonian nation, the crewmen behind Columbus in Vanderlyn's work represent the essence of the antination or, at best, the pariahs of nations who are condemned to live at sea or at the shoreline, at the very edges of the civilized world. Already in the early process of developing a Usonian nationalist ideology, or Usonianism, a conscious manipulation had taken place whereby an entire group of people had been abandoned at the shore and forsaken as unfit to travel on the new Columbian venture. Here are the roots of the tradition of contempt and paternalism toward the peoples who inhabit the lands on which Columbus actually set foot. This much of U.S. history is already well documented,[66] and it may be studied as Usonianist dogma. Vanderlyn's painting was elevated to the status of a national icon on the five-dollar U.S. bank note of 1875, on the fifteen-cent postage stamp from the 1869 series, and on the two-cent stamp from the Columbian series of 1893. By 1898, when the war with Spain over Cuba began, Usonians were accustomed to putting their money where their mouths were, and also literally their mouths where their money was, as more than one billion of these stamps had already been licked.

Mindful of such ideological manipulations, it is important to note that Leutze's masterful work hides the fact that at the time of Washington's crossing of the Delaware his army—and his entire national project—was on the verge of collapse.[67] Similarly, in the careful hijacking of the figure of Columbus by the Usonian creoles the segregation of the chosen ones from both the natives and the pariahs of nations was a delicate ideological moment that had to be presented in the most stable and clear way. In the Columbian epic the Usonian creole would claim the land and its peoples from an aesthetic position where his civilizational paternalism would be divorced from any claim to paternity of or consanguinity with either the natives or the human scoria of the Columbian experience.

This representational moment of historical and territorial shoplifting is made even clearer in the tympanum of the *Columbus Doors* (Figures 5 and 6), where Randolph Rogers sculpted a version of Vanderlyn's earlier painting. This one is entitled *Landing of Columbus in the New World*. Because this is a semicircular relief whose location above the doorway almost by definition promotes the center to a position of prominence and, in the neoclassical aesthetic tradition practiced by Rogers, required perfect compositional equilibrium and symmetry, there is no doubt as to who is the leader. Rogers further abstracted Vanderlyn's Irvian vision of Columbus by elevating the central group well above the lateral ones and by placing the vanishing point in the figure of Columbus, as if the

Figure 5. Randolph Rogers, *Columbus Doors.* Courtesy of the Architect of the Capitol, Washington, D.C.

entire scene emanated from the admiral's navel. Thus the central group stands aloft on terra firma, while below them the crew is still at sea and the natives seek refuge behind a large tree.

But the claim regarding the immaculate conception of Usonian America was made in a scene that appears in the uppermost panel of the right-hand door (Figure 7), which Rogers entitled *Columbus's First Encounter with the Indians* and which is based on book 4, chapter 6, of Irving's *Life*

Figure 6. Randolph Rogers, *The Landing of Columbus in the New World* (tympanum of *Columbus Doors*). Courtesy of the Architect of the Capitol, Washington, D.C.

of Columbus. There a cross stands atop a hill as a sign of the Christian conquest, while in front of it Columbus is flanked by a priest holding a Bible, a soldier clutching the handle of his sword, and a royal official. They are finely attired as embodiments of the principal institutions of the ideal state (the prince, the Church, the army, and the administrative curia), and as such they stand in a square formation. Below them a single crew member rows a small boat toward a shipmate who, walking along the shoreline, is carrying a captured native woman on his shoulder. The woman is naked, and the men are barefoot and shirtless. A palm tree separates the figures of the crew member and the native woman from Columbus's group and, as Fryd has rightly observed, the "palm tree divides the composition between the right wilderness, where the captor and captive are interlocked, and the central, civilized zone, in which Columbus stands under the protection and inspiration of the cross."[68]

Compositionally and programmatically this scene varies little from the one in the tympanum. In fact, it can be considered an addendum or

Figure 7. Randolph Rogers, *Columbus's First Encounter with the Indians.* Courtesy of the Architect of the Capitol, Washington, D.C.

footnote to the *Landing of Columbus.* The admiral and his chosen group stand on terra firma, while the sea and the forest are at the sides of the panel. In this panel contact has been established between the two clienteles that contest the authority of the admiral's enterprise and, through his figure, also that of the Usonian creoles. This panel depicts the rape of the Arawak women, arguably the foundational moment of American civilization. But in this Irvian interpretation Columbus stands in disapproval of such an act. With a firm gesture the admiral orders his sailor to put down his prey. This is the moment when Columbus is finally consecrated and enters the pantheon of the Founding Fathers of Usonia and most definitely removed from his role as enslaver of the native populations that he encountered. If to nineteenth-century Usonians Washington was to be the image of virtue, Columbus would be the personification of dignity and good Christian decorum: if Washington never told a lie, Columbus never took an Indian woman. Thus this Columbus is cleansed of all guilt and separated from his abject followers, from people like Vasco Porcallo, one of the admiral's men who is reported to have had more than two hundred children with Arawak women. To put it simply, this is a Columbus who will have nothing to do with the Black Legend of Spain or, for that matter, with the "prostration and prostitution of Human Nature"[69] in Spain, or with the "blackness" and institutions of sexual exploitation that were set in place through the enslavement of the native peoples and of the millions of Africans who would soon be forcibly brought to the New World. This was a Columbus who was far removed from the man who upon his *entrada,* or invasion, of the Vega Real—the Cibao Valley—in 1494 would give four hundred men and a few dozen man-eating dogs to Alonso de Ojeda under orders to strike terror into the Indians. This was the action that led to the terrible famine of 1495–96 and to the holocaust of the Arawaks, whose population, by some estimates, decreased from close to four million in 1496 to half a million by 1500.[70] Irving's Columbus had nothing to do with this. To paraphrase Marx, the Usonian creoles not only had a caricature of the old Columbus, they now had the old Columbus himself, caricatured as he would inevitably appear in the middle of the nineteenth century and, we might add, at the start of the Usonian imperial era.[71]

The Irvian story of the Usonian civilizational pedigree had come full circle, segregating Columbus from his dissolute crew and placing the romantic origins of the nation in the Christian conquest of Granada and the expulsion of the Moor from Europe. Through Irving the United States inherited a civilized tradition at the expense of Spain and against the peoples of "Spanish" America. Later his literary inventions acquired concrete manifestations in the symbolic architecture of the empire and in the national dogma promoted thereby. In the mechanics of imperial propaganda the call to liberate Zahara would have its echoes in the battle cries "Remember the Alamo!" and "Remember the Maine!" The coming of age of Usonia as a "great nation" was idealized by Irving through a series of curious couplings where the archetype nation-empire was first established in the authorial tandem Agapida-Irving and symbolically represented in the mutually referencing images of Washington and Columbus. Both depictions created violent dislocations in the historical narrative. The first resulted in a romantic vision of the expulsion of the

Moor that hid what was in fact a devastating history of terror. The second led to the separation of the Columbine crew from any claim to hegemony in the Americas, a manipulation that situated the Usonian creole as the undisputed master of the continent. All of this was done within the framework of a discourse of impermeable contact whereby the evils of Spanish conquest and colonization were summarily condemned and rejected, together with the practice of *mestizaje*, while the archetypal image of the Founding Father, forged in the smelting of the personae of Columbus and Washington, had the effect of making an undisputed claim to European parentage in the civilizational gest now commandeered by the Usonian creoles. With time, this discourse would be adopted almost verbatim by other creole elites south of the border.[72]

As we know, Irving would have serious doubts not only of his abilities as a writer and a historian, but also of the national imperial project that he had helped imagine through his work. In an age that, as Ortega y Gasset said, was to produce empires "in the savage heart of Africa,"[73] Irving was among the first Usonians to suspect the hazards that empire, real or imagined, posed to the "heart of the civilized nation." As we have seen, such are the contradictions supported by his texts, contradictions that descended through the levities of the symbolic universe to acquire concrete form and gravity from the Capitol's Rotunda to the Halls of Montezuma. At the time Irving could not put his finger on it, but he sensed that the stories he was collecting ultimately possessed a certain Zaharenian character that made them impossible to bring completely under control. As the parading of the Zaharenians through the streets of Granada had led the soothsayer to foretell the end of her empire, Irving's capture and display of his Spanish stories could have also made him realize the ultimate impossibility of controlling the production of meaning. The historical loot that Washington Irving had brought with him from Spain contained within it the curse of Zahara, the curse of the end of empire.

Incorporeal Modernities: Looking into the Irvian Oblivium

To explore the Zaharenian character of Irving's story is to reveal what has remained forbidden and inaccessible by returning some historical protagonism to those who were overlooked or deemed unfit to travel in his Columbiad. This can be done by questioning the integrity of 1492 as a boundary that separates history from romance and by moving back from the raising of the royal standards of the Christian kings above the Alhambra in search of a world that was to contribute significantly to the foundations of coloniality and modernity at large. Considering, however briefly, the complicated "politics of identity" in medieval Iberian societies can shed light on the practices of *mestizaje*—and of what I call *mulataje*—in the New World and on their immediate antecedents in the Old, as well as on the condemnation of such practices by the likes of Irving and others before and since. This is the indispensable prelude to the history of colonization of the Indies and to the history of the body as the site of the most devastating ideological battles in American civilization. Such a process would entail searching for the not-so-romantic history of those who stayed behind when, a week to the day after Columbus's departure on his second voyage, the king of Granada sailed to North Africa with his knights and horses.

When Granada fell to the Christians at the end of the fifteenth century, the history of Islam in the Iberian Peninsula was already seven centuries old. During that time, and almost from the start, al-Andalus had been the most complex society in the western Mediterranean as far as the heterogeneity of its people was concerned.[74] Located in the westernmost confines of Dar al-Islam and enjoying almost complete independence from the major centers of power in the Islamic world, al-Andalus was in fact one of the richest "contact zones"[75] of the Mediterranean world during the Middle Ages, occupying over two-thirds of the Iberian Peninsula south of the *limes hispanicus*.[76] The first two hundred years of Andalusi history witnessed the difficult rise of a centralized state that almost immediately came undone. The Córdoba Caliphate, which became the most powerful state of the High Middle Ages in Europe, experienced its Golden Age between 929 and 1031. Shortly thereafter an institutional breakdown led to the dictatorship of the Amirids, which was, in turn, quickly followed by a cataclysmic collapse of the state and a period of political dismemberment, known as the Taifa Kingdoms, that resulted in three successive invasions of al-Andalus. The contact zone was first claimed by two Berber dynasties from the Maghrib,[77] the Almoravids (1055–1147) and the Almohads (1147–1269). With the retreat of the Almohads, Granada remained the last bastion of Muslim power in the Iberian Peninsula until its conquest by Castile at the end of the fifteenth century.[78] However, not until the beginning of the seventeenth century would Spanish monarchs take the last measures to implement the forced removal of all the Andalusis from their ancestral lands.

With the Christian advance an entire glossary of political vassalage came into usage in the (re)conquered lands, especially after the late eleventh century, when large numbers of Muslims and a much smaller number of Jews came under the rule of Christian lords who did not have at their disposal enough subjects to colonize the vast territories captured. Most of the population in the lands captured from the Muslims came to be labeled mudejars, from the Arabic *mudajjanun,* meaning those who are permitted to stay. These were peoples who had chosen to remain in their lands instead of retreating behind the frontiers of the Muslim states. At that time those who chose to leave their lands and communities behind sought refuge in Granada, and those who had sufficient means searched for permanent escape from Christian aggression by crossing over to the Maghrib. For the most part the peoples of the Guadalquivir Valley, who inhabited the most bountiful land in the heart of al-Andalus, were quite dissatisfied with their lot following conquest. But this was not the case with the generally more accommodating mudejars of Castile and Aragon.[79] There Muslim serfs of a Christian lord came to be known as *exáricos,* from the Arabic *as-sharik,* meaning partner.[80] Initially a small minority, those Muslims who chose to convert to Christianity came to be known as *cristianos nuevos,* or new Christians. Some Andalusis came to refer to the new Christians as *dawa'ir,* or those who turn around, and were accordingly described by ibn al-Kardabûs as "wicked Muslims, despicable, perverse and degenerate."[81] The same people were called *tornadizos* by the Christians, a term equivalent to the English *turncoat.*

There were many more ambiguous categories, such as that of the *enanciados,* subjects of Christian kings who for a number of reasons had close ties with Muslims of other kingdoms and thus acted as agents in the contact zones. The *enanciados* were, of course, fully bilingual, and it is safe to assume that their loyalties shifted according to circumstance. Those who were not moros (Moors) either by blood or religion but who could be considered culturally moros were called *amoriscados,* that is, people who looked like Moors or preferred the ways and customs of the Moors. Indeed there were many Christian princes who belonged to this category and who dressed, spoke, and rode their horses as did the so-called moros. Among them was one al-Sayyid Ruy Díaz, known also as El Cid (from the Arabic *al-Sayyid,* or lord), whom many herald to this day as the symbol of Christian chivalry and of a legendary Spanish nationhood.

The twelfth-century Romance poem *Cantar del Mío Cid,* which has been used most notably by Menéndez-Pidal as a historical document showing the validity and depth of the concept of the Reconquest as a link between pre-Islamic times and the ascendancy of Christian kingdoms during the eleventh century, was based on the life of one Ruy Díaz de Vivar, a Christian captain of lesser nobility who in 1094 took the city and Kingdom of Valencia.[82] But the life of the famous El Cid, also known as el Campeador or al-Kanbayatur (Arabic for lord of the countryside) was more typical of the Taifa period in Andalusi history than of the romantic ideal of the Reconquista.[83] While a vassal to Alfonso VI of Castile and León, Ruy Díaz de Vivar fought in defense of al-Mu'tamid, king of Seville. In 1081, his loyalties to the Castilian crown in question, he was exiled by Alfonso. Al-Sayyid then served al-Mu'tamid ibn Hud, king of Zaragoza, against the Christian lords of Lleida, Aragon, and Barcelona. After a brief reconciliation with Alfonso during which Ruy Díaz was placed at the service of the Taifa king of Valencia, he was again exiled in 1089. Thereafter al-Sayyid waged war on his own behalf, capturing Valencia and ruling over it until his death in 1099, when the city quickly fell back to Almoravid control. Far from the romantic notions that have presented the life and legend of El Cid as the embodiment of the ideal of a single unified and Christian nation, the life of Ruy Díaz de Vivar/El Cid/al-Kanbayatur seems to have been marked by political ambiguities, shifting loyalties, and divided cultural and religious allegiances.

Perhaps the most *amoriscado* of all Christian kings was Pedro I of Castile (1350–69), who recruited the best builders and craftsmen of Granada and Seville to build for him a royal palace, the Reales Alcázares, in the most exquisite Mudejar style, as all Moorish and Moorish-inspired art and architecture has come to be known in the Hispanic world. But he was not the only one. In the former Kingdom of León, Pedro's father, Alfonso XI, had built the Mudejar Palace of Benimarín for his mistress Leonor de Guzmán in the town of Tordesillas. The complex included the most exquisite Arab baths, parts of which are still standing, which leads us to believe that in its day the palace must have been the finest residence in all of Castile. The Benimarín Palace was converted into a convent in 1362. Since then it has been known as the Convent of Saint Clare of Assisi. In the mid–fifteenth century the nuns adorned the vault above the sanctuary of the church with an exquisite Mudejar polychrome timber ceiling that is a testimony to the cultural *amoriscamiento* of peninsular Christians. Separating the sanctuary from the nave of the church, a beam supports the three wooden polychrome statues of the Virgin Mary, a crucified Christ, and Saint John (Figure 8). Superimposed against the Mudejar ceiling, the Gothic-style Calvary scene heralds the triumph of Christianity over Islam. But this architectural palimpsest also speaks to the politics of cultural transgression and of the profound transculturation that characterized the Iberian contact zone at the dawn of the Columbian age.

By far the most interesting category of political vassalage—and vacillation—in the Iberian contact zone was that of *tagarino*, from the Arabic *tagri*, pertaining to the frontier (and originally from *thughur*, or front teeth). It literally meant the person who inhabits or belongs to the frontier, and it was a term used by Christians to refer to those Andalusis who lived under Christian rule and who spoke both the Christian language(s) and Arabic so well that it was impossible to determine whether they were Muslims or Christians.[84] The *tagarinos* were by definition an unknown quantity, peoples whose allegiances shifted according to the situation as they negotiated their immediate survival in a world where stringent laws came to be passed against the conquered Andalusis, forcing them to live in *morerías,* or particular sections of towns, forbidding them to speak Arabic or to show outward signs of their faith, such as making the call to prayer, and even forcing them to wear particular colors and sometimes even the emblem of the crescent moon so they would be clearly identifiable. The fall of Granada, which Irving so gloriously portrayed, only aggravated these conditions, as the Christian kings systematically disregarded the terms of the Nasrid surrender.

It is important to note that even when these new political categories were inscribed within religious and ethnic contexts they were mainly descriptors of possible locations in the psychosocial continuum of loyalty and contempt for the new masters. The social geography of this world where loyalties were always in question, and the complex cultural universe it produced, was to contribute in good measure to the political and

Figure 8. Sanctuary ceiling of the church in the Convent of Saint Clare of Assisi in Tordesillas. Photograph by the author.

cultural foundations of the New World. It was that pre-1492 world that produced Todorov's Cortés and the politics of the calculated contradiction that made him the great manipulator of signs.[85] It is not difficult to see why Columbus, who was not socialized into that world of the Iberian contact zone, was judged by Todorov to be so different from Cortés and to be "closer to those whom he discovered than to some of his own companions."[86] It is also easy to see why, when it came to the clear demarcation of the origins of Usonian civilization, Irving was so eager to

separate the admiral's legible enterprise from the seemingly uncontrollable production of meaning carried on as a practice of everyday life by
his crew, especially when it came to the sexual politics of *mestizaje* and
to the actual production of Columbian bodies and subjects. Is it not
possible to assume that Irving was as "mestizophobic" as the image of
Columbus he helped to create?

In order to have a clean slate on which to work on his rewriting of
the history of civilization in the New World, Irving needed first to clean
house in Spain. As we know, he would accept no connection between the
two sides of 1492, least of all between the tragic and magical Moorish
tales and the history of the Indies. That is why he could feed his melancholia with romantic tales of the aloof Nasrid court, but could not accommodate in his Orientalist fantasies the real plight of the thousands
of Granadians who had stayed behind and who were to suffer the most
devastating persecution.

On 30 March 1492 Ferdinand and Isabella, who were by then residing
at the palace of the Alhambra, ordered the removal from their kingdoms in a space of four months of all Jews who refused to convert to
Christianity. Those who apostatized became known as *conversos*. After
1502 the mudejars of Granada were given the choice of converting or
going into exile. Following papal advice, Charles V extended the practice
to the entire peninsula, setting forth in an edict of 1525 that all Muslims
in Aragon, Valencia, and Catalonia had one year to convert to Christianity or face exile. Officially, then, there were no Muslims in Spain after
1526. Those who agreed to be baptized in order to remain in their country came to be known as *moriscos*. There was even a very particular category, legalized by the Inquisition after 1499 as part of an attempt to
identify those "infidels" whose conversion was a higher priority. The
elches (from the Arabic *ildj*, or renegade), as they were called, were supposed to be descendants of Christians who had converted to Islam in
the fourteenth and fifteenth centuries. There were many of them in Granada, and the Church "wanted them back." Finally, the *monfíes* (from
the Arabic *munfa*, or exiled) were those Muslims who had remained in
Spain after 1492 but who had refused to submit to Christian rule. The
establishment of these three categories came to codify the rituals of inclusion and exclusion that have since universally defined the limits of
the national in terms of varying degrees of assimilability of certain "alien"
populations and the identification of the inassimilable ones.

In 1566 Philip II forbade the use of the Arabic language in written or spoken form, ordered the destruction of all books in that language, and prohibited anyone from dressing in non-Christian fashion, including banning the use of the *almalafa,* the veil worn by all Moorish women. All music forms, customs, ceremonies, and of course religious practices associated with Islam were outlawed. All baths were destroyed, and nobody could be called by an Arabic name. The drastic character of the imperial decrees turned all *moriscos* into potential *monfíes.* However, these measures proved insufficient to eliminate all infidelity, which is why the Christian ideologues came to argue that all *moriscos* were really moros. In his *Memorable expvlsion ylvstrissimo destierro de los Morifcos de Efpaña,* Marco de Guadalajara y Xavier wrote of the *moriscos* of Valencia and of all of Spain:

> The state in which the *moriscos* of the kingdom of Valencia find themselves is the same as that of the *moriscos* of Aragon and of all those in the kingdom of Spain, so that whatever might be said about these can also be said about the others; because they all equally begrudge and resist the Catholic faith, and they all hate and despise their natural king, and would want to see him come under the rule of the Turk or of any other tyrant who would let them live freely in their sect. So it is that, when it comes down to it, there cannot be any difference or accident, whether they dress as Christians or like moros; whether some speak Arabic all the time, whether some of them live in remote places where there are only *moriscos* or whether they live among the old Christians; we know and have moral proof that all these people are moros, and that they follow Mohammed's sect, keeping and observing (whenever possible) the teachings of the Koran, and putting down the holy laws of the Catholic Church; so that, to be frank, we should call them not *moriscos* but rather moros.[87]

According to Friar Marco there were never any *moriscos;* there were only people who pretended to have converted to Christianity in order to remain in the country. But who and where were these moros? In the geography of the nation to be, he tells us they were everywhere and that everywhere they were the same in their refusal to accept the Catholic faith and in their hatred toward it, in their disregard of their natural king, and in their desire to be ruled by the Turk. Here we find a most important moment in the birth of Spain. There could be no unity—and no "great nation"—without an external enemy, no need to defend the faith without a threat, and no need to use violence without a treacherous culprit. The Turk became the enemy without, as the *morisco* had become the threat within. If the expulsion of the *moriscos* had made the dream of Spain possible, the Turkish threat would sustain it.

Moros were ubiquitous, and indeed, judging from the description given by Friar Marco, many of them were essentially *tagarinos*. It was impossible to tell them apart: some of them dressed as Christians, some as Moors; some of them lived among the old Christians, while some lived in distant and isolated places where none other than moros lived. This was the world that had to be reduced so that the Christian house could be put in order. As Miguel de Cervantes Saavedra, the author of *Don Quixote,* would put it two decades before the final expulsion of all Spanish Muslims, the *moriscos* were the essence of the antinational. In the voice of Berganza, his dog interlocutor, in the *Coloquio de los perros* he wrote: "They are her [Spain's] hidden money box, her termites, her magpies, her weasels: they take everything, they hide everything and they eat everything up."[88] Cervantes' words characterizing the Muslims as the termites of Spain would reverberate down through the ages and in the centuries to come would be used repeatedly on the other side of the Atlantic to refer to other antinational types.

In 1568 a major uprising of Spanish Muslims got under way when the *moriscos* took the town of Cadiar in the Alpujarras Mountains near Granada. The Morisco Uprising was eventually crushed, but not before it resulted in the forced removal, in a sort of death march, of thousands of Andalusis, who were sent to Castile and Extremadura. Finally, in 1609 Philip III ordered the banishment of all *moriscos*. By 1614 close to one million people had been expelled from the former lands of al-Andalus. In a way they were pushed out by a wave of migration that took place throughout the sixteenth century and that saw large numbers of Castilians move south to Andalusia in search of what at the start of the seventeenth century Sebastián de Covarruias would call "the most fertile province of Spain and the most abundant in everything that can be desired, by land or by sea."[89] As J. H. Elliott has said, "For all those Castilians who could not themselves cross the Atlantic, Andalusia became the El Dorado."[90]

The Conquest of Granada and the subsequent Castellanization of Andalusia resulted in the reduction of the contact zone and of its vibrant culture, a process that was systematized by the Inquisition. But in this general movement toward the erasure of difference there was yet another agent that is often disregarded. Placed at the service of the imperial project and brought into the Iberian Peninsula by the Habsburg dynasty under Charles V (1517–56), the aesthetic imperatives of the Italian Renaissance came to play an important role at the representational level in the taming of the contradictions and ambiguities that had sustained the frontier culture of the late medieval period in the peninsula. The best evidence of this imposition from above can be found on the grounds of the fortified palatial citadel of the Alhambra, where Charles V ordered the construction of a building from which he might rule the world, a building that would in turn impose its own geometry upon the first empire upon which the sun never set. Nasrid aesthetics, given full expression in the spaces conditioned by an architecture of mystical escapism, of light and lightness, and of a sensual exquisiteness that teases the body with the possibility of the physically insubstantial, was now to be confronted with a concept of the built form that proposed the possibility of endowing the abstract ideal with the ancient Roman concept of *firmitas* as it referred to the tangible and to that which is built on stable terrain, rising solidly upon secure footings.[91] This was a drama that would also reach the New World, where it would ultimately come to frame the discourse on the body, pitching to one side the everyday practice of *mestizaje,* with its roots in the culture of the Iberian contact zone, and, to the other, the myth of the absolute integrity of the European body as an ideal of subjectivity and, more important, as a practice of subjection.[92]

To this day the complex amalgamation of buildings and courtyards that forms the Nasrid palace of the Alhambra, built for the most part during the fourteenth century, conditions a space "whose subtle effect it is difficult to analyze."[93] A brief description of some of the spaces in the complex should give the reader a sense of just how divergent are the moods of the Alhambra when compared to Charles's palace. Keep in mind that modern architectural tradition descends almost directly from the model enunciated in the Habsburg palace. Thus the apparent difficulty in analyzing the subtle effects of the Nasrid Alhambra remains to this day a testament to the contrast and difference I shall attempt to capture here.[94]

The profusion of minute and delicate ornamentation throughout the interior surfaces of the buildings (Figure 9) may speak of a certain horror vacui that was characteristic of both Christian and Islamic architecture in the Iberian contact zone during the Late Middle Ages. But this

Figure 9. Detail of colonnade in the Court of Lions of the Alhambra. Photograph by the author.

was not just an epidermic treatment along the lines of the symbolically discursive art of the Christian Late Gothic style or Isabelino. Rather the desire to attain harmony through the most subtle contrasts and gradations of light resulted in surface treatments that tease our senses, as if trying to force us to retreat into the intangible. There are no hard physical edges, no clear boundaries separating one body, surface, or substance from another. Against this background bands of inscriptions run across the walls, repeating in the most fluid Arabic script lines from the

Koran and from the verses of courtly poets. It is as if the words were trying to fill the void of space while endowing with movement all the lifeless abstraction of the surfaces. Light and sound further condition every major space, giving the overall sense that everything in the Alhambra is in flux and in a constant state of transformation and becoming. How different this all is to the Christian architecture of the time, with its emphasis on verticality, its figurative discursiveness, and the typical heaviness, severity, and darkness of much of the peninsular Late Gothic. But the contrast to the Renaissance architecture of the Hapsburg court, characterized above all by its *firmitas* and its geometric transparency, would turn out to be even greater.

The residence of the kings of Granada was built around a series of smaller palatial dependencies organized around courtyards, or *riyads*. The largest and most solemn of these is the Comares Palace, whose name probably derived from the Arabic *qamariyya,* meaning "light from above."[95] The palace is organized around the Alberca Court, which, in turn, encloses a central pool that is roughly five times as long as it is narrow (34.7 meters by 7.5 meters) and during the day serves to reflect light under the arcades that frame the courtyard on its northern and southern sides. On each end a spout gently releases fresh water into a round and shallow basin. The water then flows through a short channel and into the pool in such a way that the perfectly still surface of the water in the pool is seldom disturbed. Amid this calm one can dip the tip of a finger into the pool, drawing with it a figure upon the surface of the water at a corner of one of the pool's shorter sides, and watch as the ripples float thirty meters down to the other side, then come back over themselves forming the most complicated and evanescent of patterns.

At night one can occupy this space with particular solemnity. Lying on the floor (as the Nasrids did when they occupied this space), as if supported by cushions of thick brocade, facing the fountain under the two-storied arcade of slender columns, one can witness the drama in which the still water seems to invite the moon and the stars to come down from the heavens. The entire courtyard, with its arcades and walls of intricate *yesería,* or lacelike patterns of plaster relief, is reflected, skies and all, upside-down on the water's surface. At times the reflection seems clearer and more real than the world above. Its air seems cleaner, lighter, and easier to breathe. Down there the night is darker and the stars shine brighter. It is a world that seduces us even as bats fly impossibly through the water in curves that resemble ripples caused by a gentle breeze. As we sit there we are sure to discover the secrets of the place and to become one with the timeless movement of the recurrent event the *riyad* has hosted for the past six hundred years. The Alberca Court presents us with a perfect world that is perfectly uninhabitable in the corporeal sense of dwelling in a place; it extends an exquisitely sensual invitation to enter the realm of the metaphysical not by projecting our bodies into it through geometric abstraction, but by accepting the impossibility of leaving our bodies behind.

The most majestic of the Alhambra's *riyads* is a symbolic representation of Paradise in line with Koranic descriptions. The Court of the Lions is thus quartered by four channels that move water toward a central fountain. Once there, the water rises up to a basin and is spilled through the maws of the twelve sculpted lions that support and guard the fountain. An inscription running along the upper edge of the fourteenth-century marble basin demands the most profound meditation: "It appears as if water and marble were entangled so that we cannot tell which is in truth the one that flows."[96]

The high points of all illusions in the Alhambra lie off to the north and south of the Court of Lions in the Halls of the Two Sisters and the Hall of the Abencerrajes. Both these rooms have magnificent honeycomb domes that seem to hover above the walls as light filters in through the eight delicate grilled windows at their base. These carefully illuminated cavelike interiors respond to an architecture of lightness and levitation where masses appear as though they could be unmade by blowing softly against their seemingly evanescent intricate surfaces. Both rooms are ordered according to the most important geometric principle and arguably also the most important philosophical principle of Andalusi civilization as summarized in the icon of the octangular star, also known as the Mudejar star. The Mudejar star describes a movement in which a square seems to rotate on its center an eighth of a turn, thereby creating the eight-pointed shape. But I believe that this rotation describes a movement of metaphorical proportions whereby the seemingly planar condition of the originating square undergoes an axial shift that results in the explosion of the star into a third dimension and also in the creation of two octahedrons that share a common epicenter and are locked in a relation of perfect correspondences and equilibrium. Yet the Mudejar star must be seen as the description of a movement and not of a body in space. The locked octahedrons represent a frozen moment in that movement. In fact, as the domes in the Hall of the Two Sisters and the Hall of the Abencerrajes attempt to show, the movement described by the Mudejar star explodes to colonize space through the most vertiginous prismatic breakdown of all essence, just as the domes manage to do with the light that comes into the rooms of the Alhambra. The Mudejar star represents the union of—and the erasure of the boundary between— the Earth and the heavens, the body and space, the real and the imagined. In the Hall of the Abencerrajes the progression from the quadrangular floor plan to the polygonal vault is a literal spatial enunciation of all metaphorical possibilities as darkness gives way to a moving spectacle of light and the perfect geometry of the square explodes into the vastness of space, leaving behind, as a trace of the initial movement, the seemingly unreadable complexity of a dome where the central star is said to break down into five thousand prisms. Standing under these domes one can bear witness to the crowning architectural achievement of Andalusi civilization and perhaps also to the best solution to the puzzle of how to create a floating dome, a recurring theme in Islamic architecture. This is architecture as an expression of a philosophy of space and of being.

Unlike official Christian architecture, built almost exclusively of stone, the Alhambra was primarily constructed using wood and plaster, brick and tile. It was not meant to last forever. But it seems that it was built to have the last word. In fact, the Alhambra complex was built as a sort of trap. Throughout the walls of the buildings one recurrent inscription claims the surface of every wall: "*wa-lâ ghâlibu illâ'llâh*" (and there is no victor but Allah). This was the heraldic motto of the Nasrids and of the ten knights who are depicted in a painting that adorns the oblong vault above the central alcove of the Hall of Kings. Magnificently attired, they all appear to be sitting around a room with their mouths closed and paradoxically engaged in what seems to be the most engrossing of discussions. All except one are gesturing with one hand while holding firmly to their swords with the other. Keep in mind that in Islamic and southern Mediterranean cultures, then as now, hand gestures have been seen as being as eloquent as words and often as a substitute for words. The tenth figure, possibly that of the king, holds his sword with both hands, firmly and with authority. Nearly nothing is known about the characters depicted or the nature of their commission. But the painting conveys a powerful sense of urgency, as the figures seem to frantically discuss important matters of state. We may never know what these men are depicted as doing in that most militant of silences. But their hands on their swords betray the uneasy sense of impending doom.

The Nasrid world reached its most splendorous moment of cultural expansion under the most difficult of circumstances. Granada was a tributary kingdom, cornered, isolated, and under siege. Yet the delicate walls of the Alhambra remain defiant, as in their repudiation of the Christian Trinity in the living quarters of the Torre de la Cautiva, whose inscriptions proclaim: "In the name of the merciful Allâh. Say: He is God, alone, God, through and through. He has neither begotten, nor is he begotten. And none is His equal."[97] Sometime after the raising of the silver cross and the royal standards over the city of Granada, on the same day that Irving cried out through Agapida the name of Saint James the Moor-slayer, Ferdinand and Isabella walked into the inner sanctum of the Alhambra, where the writing on the walls proclaimed the ultimate failure of their otherwise glorious Christian victory: they had captured the city, but they had failed to conquer the Moor.

More than three decades later, in 1528, Ferdinand and Isabella's grandson Charles V ordered the construction of a new palace in the Alhambra complex directly adjoining the Alberca Court on its southern side (Figure 10). Charles had been raised in the court of Burgundy in Flanders, and although he was favorably impressed with the climate and architecture of Granada, he did not know the Andalusi ways. In other words, he was by no means an *amoriscado,* and at that he was unlike any previous Christian ruler in the Iberian Peninsula since at least the ninth century. Thus he ordered the construction of an imperial palace where he could hold court while in Granada. To build this palace it was necessary to demolish the winter residence of the sultans. Charles had earlier stamped his imperial coat of arms over the walls of intricate *yesería* in the Court of Lions as if trying to bring all movement and flow across the surfaces of the former Nasrid palace to a halt. Now, in true Italian Renaissance fashion, he placed his planometric stamp on the site. The structure was designed by Pedro Machuca, who is thought to have been a disciple of Raphael and Michelangelo, but whose work is closer to that of Bramante.

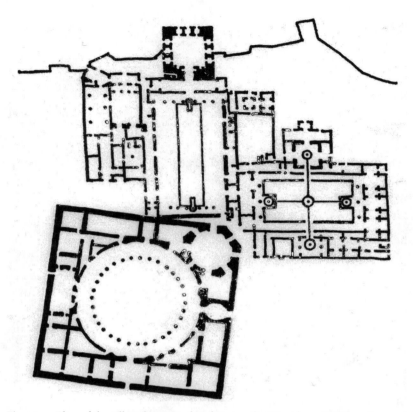

Figure 10. Plan of the Alhambra complex showing the Nasrid courts (above) and the palace of Charles V (below). Line drawing by the author, after Owen Jones, 1845.

The palace is a literal architectural enunciation of the Renaissance theoretical model that equated beauty with proportion and this, in turn, with the human body as the ideal example of the analogical principle of the perfect correspondence of the parts to the whole. The palace of Charles V in Granada is the representative embodiment of the old Roman dictum turned Renaissance ideal, "Man is the measure of all things." This ideal, postulated in Vitruvius's *Ten Books on Architecture,* was based on the claim that the human body held the promise of achieving all potentiality in the pursuit of beauty, a principle that was dependent on the system of proportions whereby, as in the body of a "well-formed man," all parts correspond perfectly to the whole. This principle was supposed to be to some extent verifiable in real space. Arguably it was simply a matter of laying a well-formed man on his back with his four limbs stretched out and the point of an imaginary compass anchored to his navel. From the "center of the body" a circle could then be drawn so that the tips of his toes and fingers would touch its edge. Thereafter a square with sides measuring the distance from head to toe of the same well-formed man standing up could be circumscribed within the circle.[98]

Thus, generated through an analogical movement of self-reproducing linkages or forced concatenations of forms and meaning, the Renaissance concept of beauty found its representative embodiment in the Ideal Body of the well-formed man. Encapsulated within a closed eurythmic system, the Ideal Body would become the standard against which every other body—or everybody else—would be measured. Contrary to the geometric representation of metaphorical movement in the Mudejar star, the Renaissance model appropriated the human body, trapping it, as it were, in a bubble.

That notion of impermeable perfection was to produce a terrible regime of violence, mutation, and amputation. In reality, such manipulations are not possible, since the navel is not the geometric center of the body, supposing, that is, that the human body could be defined in geometric terms to begin with. Thomas Noble Howe has noted that "the arms and legs of a human body have separate pivots, and hence when rotated form four arcs with four centers, not a single circle with the center at the 'umbilicus'-navel."[99] Thus, in order to draw a circle with an umbilical center, either the legs of the well-built man needed to be shortened or the arms needed to be extended through some sort of monstrous surgery. The real violence, however, would be carried out as this idea of analogic perfection encapsulated within a system of eurythmic geometry came to be enunciated in the will to power of the Habsburg dynasty and given concrete form in the architecture of empire. Now the Ideal Body, unitary, stable, and self-contained, would be thought of also as male, Christian, and European, and it would become the standard against which all other peoples and things would be measured.

Following this ideal, the palace of Charles V was built as a two-story portico framing a circular court inside a quadrangular block structure whose four façades were all strictly symmetrical along a central vertical axis. It was the first time that the Vitruvian dictum had been set to stone in such a literal way and, more important, the first time that the Ideal Body of humanist utopia had been associated with the idea of universal rulership. But it would not be the last. Perhaps the most recent enunciation of such subjugatory geometries is Gordon Bunshaft's Hirshhorn Museum (Skidmore, Owings, and Merrill, 1974) of modern and contemporary art, which is part of the Smithsonian in Washington, D.C.[100]

Many of the contemporaries of Charles V saw him as the great hope of Christianity, the great prince who could both check the Turkish advance and unify the entire world of Christendom. The idea of building his palace on top of the Alhambra, the last bastion of Islam in Europe, was symbolic enough. But the confidence and ambition of the monarch, whose aspirations were nothing short of universal governance,[101] were further emphasized in the styles selected and in the iconography of the work. If the use of elements of both the Doric and Tuscan orders conveys a sense of virility and heroism, the references to Hercules on the Western façade further point to the triumphalist spirit of the age. Here was the first truly imperial building of modern times, a building from which to rule the world. Here was the navel of the *imperium*, the place whence all order and power would emanate. Following the analogical logic of the perfect correspondence between the parts and the whole as exemplified in the idealized body of Vitruvian conventions, the building stood for Charles V as Charles stood for the world.

The geometry of Charles's palace, resumed in the ideogram of the circle inscribed within the square, came to clash with the eight-pointed star of the Andalusi peoples and with the notion that the ideal was an insubstantial entity and not a corporeal form capable of being conjured up in real space. From exile in Naples the Sephardic doctor León Hebreo had already refuted "the common view . . . which proves beauty to be the property of bodies and to exist only by analogy and not as a property in incorporeal substances."[102] In a sharp critique of the prevailing ideas of his day, Hebreo added that "every beautiful thing . . . is not proportionate, nor every proportionate thing beautiful, as these moderns imagine."[103]

An object of such gravity and colossal presence forced upon the changing moods and flows of the Alhambra served to confirm that a foreign conception of the body as a concrete and absolute entity, and of space as a singular and comprehensive unit, had come to claim and reduce the internal frontier of the Iberian kingdoms. The building would prove to be an invitation to violence. Befitting Renaissance neoclassic claims to universal design, the palace of Charles V was forced upon Andalusian geography without regard to historical, climatic, or cultural contexts. It is an abstract model, responding to the tenets of Italian design, that was thrown rather forcefully on top of the Alhambra as a symbol of the victory of Christianity over Islam.[104] As such, it marked a most severe departure from the architecture of the Alhambra, which had evolved out of an almost obsessive concern with the climate, the place, and the traditions of the land. How ironic that the palace of Charles V was paid for by the *moriscos* of Granada, who were taxed and paid under the threat of losing the right to keep and practice their traditions. When their descendants rose up against the Christians for the last time in the Morisco Uprising of 1568, construction of the palace was indefinitely suspended. This was a sign of things to come. If the last sigh of the Moor had served to punctuate the Christian conquest of Granada, the last stand of the *moriscos* was to make the Habsburg claim to universal dominance an impossible dream, even if only on account of the truncated symbolic projections that were ascribed to a single but important building that was left unfinished. Almost like Spain herself, the palace of Charles V was to become a ruin before it had time to see realized its claim to universal rulership.

Perhaps there is no other place where the omen of the end of empire can be read so clearly. Is it not fitting that it occurs as an architectural palimpsest where the two sides of 1492 are inseparably locked to each other in an Alhambra that was never fully reduced and in an imperial palace that became the symbol of the impossibility of realizing the Renaissance ideal?

This contest of ideals would be played out under a new set of circumstances in the Indies, where the "Humanist" project of the European Ideal, under which all other idealized notions of spatiality, temporality, and corporeality would be subsumed, would eventually become the overriding basis of all discourse and the guiding principle of the most terrifying practices of human devastation under the coloniality of power. Seen in this light, Irving's despite of the Columbian crew was but a later chapter of the same saga. Indeed, in the case of Irving himself the historical lesson could not have been more ironic. When he lived in the Alhambra he did not reside in the Nasrid palaces in the manner of the Moorish kings whose melancholic spirits he so much fancied. Quite the contrary; his creole need to confirm his civilizational paternity seems to have taken him straight to the source: he lived in the rooms that Charles V had built for himself while he waited for his palace to be completed. There, as if in anticipation of the soon-to-be-proclaimed manifest destiny, this pioneering Usonian ideologue could dream of himself as the new Holy Roman Emperor of all Christendom.

CHAPTER TWO

Contesting the Ideal

From the Moors of Hispania to the Morenos of Hispaniola

Everyone expects to find Christopher Columbus' mausoleum in the metropolitan cathedral of Santo Domingo but, far from it, only tradition supports the idea that his remains are there. In truth, the English invasion of 1586, under the command of Francis Drake, resulted in the sacking of the city and in the burning or destruction of the ecclesiastical archives so that no documents prior to that date are there to be found. Even the oldest documents do not go farther back than 1630, with the exception of an old registry that contains the deliberations of the Cabildo from 1569 to 1593, and even that one has been mostly destroyed by time and by the termites.

—M. L. Moreau de Saint-Méry, 1794

The origins of coloniality during the early Columbian age are marked by the confluence in the Caribbean of three related processes of terror: the spillover from the persecution and deportation of the officially inassimilable Moors of Castile and Aragon; the enslavement and genocide of the native populations of the islands; and the enslavement, deportation, and genocide of Africans during the early stages of the transatlantic slave trade and before. These were, of course, the means to the end of a process that was to produce the first empires or "great nations" of modernity. In the Indies, however, the same process engendered a complex and fragile society whose imaginary was deeply grounded in a common if not always shared experience of displacement and violent loss.[1] This was the world that Washington Irving would discard together with the scoria of the Columbian venture, the world of the pariahs of nations that he would relegate to the fringes of American civilization. But the Irvian ostracism, which as we know responded to his own personal and civilizational insecurities, is only one more index in a long-standing and deeply rooted historical movement of censorship and disappearance—forced, and at times even self-inflicted—that has resulted in the almost complete obviation of the early contributions to New World societies of peoples who did not fit into the romantic formula of the Christian conqueror triumphant against Indian idolatry and Old World heresy. Nevertheless, Irving's Columbiad carries the germ of the Zaharenian curse, and therein rests the value of his vision, however fabulous it may otherwise be. The task now, it would seem, is to validate the historical protagonism and spatial corporeality of what in Irving's work is just a faceless mob at the margins of law and order.

This is much easier said than done. Of the three processes of terror outlined before, only the second—the enslavement and genocide of the native populations of the Indies—has been satisfactorily studied. The Moorish presence in the early stages of conquest—and, most important, of colonization in the New World—has been thoroughly ignored and only euphemistically touched upon by scholars who timidly speak of the undeniably significant "Andalusian" contribution to the first expeditions and settlements.[2] Although an impressive corpus of scholarship has been produced on the subject of the transatlantic slave trade, until recently there were few studies of peninsular slavery and of the cultural institutions relating to it. These studies are of course indispensable to anyone interested in considering the way in which official institutions and common cultural practices in the pre-1492 Iberian world affected the subsequent parallel and complementary development of the economy and the politics of the trade on both sides of the Atlantic. The fact is that when we think of the Atlantic contact zone as the place whence the world of modernity/coloniality emerged, it is possible to say, at least with regards to two of the components of the constitutive triumvirate, that there was a contact zone in the Old World before there was contact in the New World. In this sense, as I will argue, and contrary to commonly held beliefs and long-standing prejudices, the mulatto world predated and conditioned what would later become known as *mestizaje*.

The absence of scholarship is only compounded by the absence of official records. The Martinican creole Moreau de Saint-Méry sadly acknowledged the fact when he visited Santo Domingo at the end of the eighteenth century. His testimony, quoted at the beginning of this chapter, is unequivocal. If Columbus himself has disappeared and the possession of his "true" remains is still being disputed today among the cities of Santo Domingo and Seville, could we not expect that people who were not supposed to be there in the first place, as was certainly the case with *moriscos,* would have been condemned to the farthest confines of official oblivion, whether by the action of time, of termites, or of the privateers of history?

It is my intention to show that right from the start of the Columbian venture, from Seville to the neighborhoods of the first major colonial settlements and the posts on the fringes of colonial jurisdiction, from the first plantations to the runaway enclaves in the mountains, alternative economies began to develop establishing a network of regional and transatlantic connections that came to rival the nascent structures of what at first was an equally fragile imperial order. In most cases, unless forced or provoked, the peoples who inhabited these alternative spaces seem not to have openly contested imperial institutions. Perhaps the memory of terror was too immediate. Instead they chose either to nurture a difficult process of constructive engagement, sometimes emulating the *tagarino* practices of the Iberian contact zone, or to retreat beyond the frontier to an alternate if precarious existence in the countercolony/counterplantation world of the early Caribbean. In all cases, as Ángel Quintero Rivera states, what moved them was the desire "to be left alone by the authorities."[3] Accordingly these were people who purposefully left few records of their whereabouts.

In a sense, to borrow James Clifford's terminology, these were peoples whose culture followed a movement of "dwelling-in-traveling"[4] that was fundamentally the site of their running away. This is what Quintero Rivera calls a culture of *cimarronería* (from the Spanish *cimarrón,*[5] or runaway), describing the constitutive movement of this world in the following terms: "The fundamental characteristic of social action in runaway culture is camouflage as it helps to avoid conflict while sustaining the values of spontaneity and freedom."[6] It is my contention that the first American subjects came into being following this practice of social camouflage as it spilled over from the *tagarino* world of the Iberian contact zone into the larger Atlantic one, coming in contact with the native element and negotiating the vagaries of loyalty through a practice of the simulacrum that had both psychological and physical manifestations. In early colonial society everyone had to appear to be a good Christian in both *genio* and *figura,* that particular Iberian take on the body-mind split that pertains almost exclusively to the performative aspects of an individual's character and bodily expression as they come to describe his or her personality. The idea is summarized in the old Spanish saying "genio y figura, hasta la sepultura," literally meaning that a person will take his or her character and mannerisms to the grave. The saying is usually applied to the stubborn and the nonconformist, implying that a particular person will never change what in English would be summarized as his or her demeanor.[7] In every case this was a simulacrum that responded to a culture whose every expression was a function of the veiled contestation and active eschewing of officialdom.

This particular modality of dwelling-in-travel was thus the performative obverse of Charles V's ideal of universal dominance, the same ideal the emperor had tried to set in stone in his palace at Granada by making the building the representative axis of imperial majesty. Let us remember that the building was imagined to lay claim to the world through a process of analogical reasoning by means of which was projected through it a close geometric system based on the (hu)man body as the ideal of the perfect correspondence between the parts and the whole. If, as noted in the preceding chapter, the navel is the originating point of all perfect geometries in the Vitruvian Greco-Roman model adopted by the Habsburg Court, the well-formed body (of the European) came to be seen by "these moderns," as León Hebreo called them, as the *tableau vivant* of the analogic principle whence all ideal order and beauty emanate.[8] True to these conventions, the Habsburgs saw themselves as the *axis mundi.* But they would go even further in their representational claims to universal rulership by placing in their service the arsenal of linear perspectival construction, a technique through which real space is submitted to a formidable regime of geometric abstraction and that, during the Renaissance, was the primary system used to order space and to erase the boundary between the real and its representation. Thus, the Habsburgs would come to portray themselves as the source from which all meaning and power were derived by claiming to inhabit the abstract mathematical site where all the lines of sight in linear perspectival constructions converge: the vanishing point.[9] In contraposition to this all-encompassing system of representative embodiment, to

this mise-en-scène of imperial power, the intention of those who simply wanted to be left alone was to remain out of sight, socially veiled or
camouflaged—if not to vanish altogether—in order to avoid further
persecution. Curiously, the ideal of the body constructed at the Habsburg court was a representational illusion, while the body of the "vanishing" subject dwelled in real space.

It could be argued that metaphorical movement has always been the
nemesis of analogical order. But in the very real space of early American
coloniality this would explain little. The fact is that the "great national"
or imperial project, when translated to the other shore of the Ocean sea,
came to face a new type of challenge that was, in a way, also a new form
of heresy. Such were the views expressed in the cataclysmic visions of
Fray Bartolomé de las Casas, which I will critique in the next chapter.
Las Casas saw in this new heresy disturbing structural parallels with the
old Moorish threat. At least etymologically, Las Casas's views were corroborated by official practices of power, as the name given to the new
terror of the Indies was that of *moreno*. Derived from *moro*,[10] the term
was originally used, as it is still, to describe a black horse. In the sixteenth
century *moreno* became the general term used to refer to blacks and
mulattoes alike,[11] or to those whom Girolamo Benzoni called the Mori
di Guinea,[12] the Moors of Guinea and their descendants. The transition
from Moro to *moreno*, however, was less factitious than it may seem,
and it was not the product of a transmutation that took place during
the Atlantic crossing. In fact, the existence of important populations of
blacks and mulattoes in cities like Seville and Valladolid is well known
and was significant decades before the Columbian voyages. In any event,
the presence of both moros and *morenos* in the Indies points to the possibility that, from its inception, that which could be called American
civilization possessed strong divergent elements that would influence its
development away from the core values—and ideals—around which
the national and the civilizational were later to be defined by creole historians and ideologues.

Looking for this movement, however tentatively, requires not only
the analysis of document sources and related studies but also the search
for certain traces of the movement in real space, especially on account
of the almost otherwise nonexistence of the *morisco* in official docu-
mentation. This search will involve looking for markings left in the common memory of the body that is nothing but the inheritance of certain

practices of space, in *genio* and *figura,* of some Caribbean peoples. The fact that the techniques of representative embodiment of imperial power were at best fragile and untested in the early days of conquest and empire building, most notably in Santo Domingo, the first city in the colonial world, also means that the architecture that survives from the period should hold the record of that discourse as well as of its contestation.

Allâh u Ackbar: Could the Last Cry of the Moor Have Been Echoed in the Indies?

Peter Boyd-Bowman estimates that from 1493 to 1519, 39.7 percent of immigrants to the Indies were from Andalusia and that Seville gave more of her *vecinos,* or residents, to the New World during the initial period of conquest and colonization of the Greater Antilles than did all other Iberian cities combined. During the second stage identified by Boyd Bowman, which ran from 1520 to 1539, the primacy of Andalusia and of Seville and its hinterland was maintained, if slightly diminished in favor of Extremadura and Castilla la Nueva.[13] Though the data for this period, when available, are generally unreliable, it is nevertheless accepted that Andalusian, and more specifically Sevillian, emigration had a tremendous and disproportionate effect on the foundational stages of American coloniality well into the sixteenth century.[14] This is explained in large measure by the fact that in 1503 Seville obtained the monopoly on all trade with the Indies through the establishment of the House of Trade, or Casa de la Contratación, which regulated and, in principle, was to oversee all movement of peoples and goods between Seville and the New World. Through this royal concession the city beside the Guadalquivir River became the center of the rapidly expanding Habsburg commercial empire and the principal stage of what is often referred to as the Golden Age of Spanish civilization. By the middle of the sixteenth century Seville had become the major urban center of the Atlantic contact zone and the first cosmopolis of early modern times.

   At least initially, the promotion of Seville to the position of gateway to the Indies did not result in a population explosion. During the first three decades of the sixteenth century, large migrations to the city were offset by the considerable exodus of peoples to the Indies and by large-scale epidemics, causing the number of inhabitants to remain at the same level as at the end of the fifteenth century, around 50,000. Only in the 1530s did the city's population begin its dramatic expansion, doubling to around 100,000 by the 1560s and reaching a peak of 129,000 by the 1580s.[15] However, even then Seville must have been sending out many more people than it was receiving. If we take into consideration the number of emigrants to the New World during the entire century—estimated to be around the quarter million mark—and compare it to the population of the city through which the majority of them embarked, it soon becomes obvious that Seville continued to be more of a threshold than a receptacle well into the first decade of the seventeenth century.

The news was out, and people from all over the Christian world were flocking to Seville. But not everyone was going to Seville in search of the treasures of the Indies. If it is true that to many Christian fortune-seekers from all over the peninsula, as well as to mariners and merchants from Genoa to Flanders, the Seville of the Golden Age was the gateway to El Dorado, it is also true that the city became a shelter for countless numbers of landless peasants and religious refugees who flocked to its slums in search of the sanctuary that could be provided by the largest city in Castile at the time. For some of these people Seville was to be the end of the line, the last station before their definitive expulsion from the peninsula. For others Seville held the promise of a new life in the Indies if they were lucky and skillful enough to elude the authorities and obtain passage. Soon the noble families of Seville, many of which traced their lineage to the *gest* of the Christian conquest of the city in 1248, came to see their city overrun by what Ruth Pike calls "the hordes of beggars and unemployed who roamed the streets in search of food and who were often undistinguishable from the substantial criminal elements."[16] These were the people who would contribute to making Sevillian emigration to the Indies "all the more plebeian"[17] when compared to that of the other peninsular regions.

Among the "hordes" of landless peoples who went to Seville in the sixteenth century were more than four thousand *moriscos* who had been forcibly expelled from Granada following the unsuccessful uprising of 1568. The great majority of these people were married and arrived with their children,[18] joining a dwindling population of Sevillian *moriscos* and swelling the ranks of the outcasts, among which there were many Gypsies, who together with the *moriscos* and the *conversos* were thought to be ultimately inassimilable into Castilian society. Following the dismantling of the Adarvejo, Seville's traditional *morería,* or Moorish neighborhood, in 1483, most of the *moriscos* were settled to the east of the city

in the parish of San Marcos. However, by the time of their definitive expulsion in 1609, the largest population of *moriscos* resided to the west of
the city, across the river in the Triana neighborhood, which throughout
the century had contained the largest sector of Seville's floating population. More than any other neighborhood in the city, Triana was where
the great majority of the sailors of the Carrera de Indias, or Route to the
Indies, were recruited.[19]

A look at the geographic location of the *morisco* population of Seville
suggests a series of questions that have yet to be tackled directly by
scholars. It seems that by 1609 the *moriscos* of Seville were concentrated
in two very distinct and separate areas of the city. The first group was
located in the easternmost neighborhoods, behind San Marcos, in the
parishes of San Lorenzo, San Julián, Omniun Sanctorum, San Gil, and
Santa Marina. The second and most numerous group lived in the westernmost districts of the city, along the harbor, in the parish of Santa
María La Mayor and in Triana.[20] At least fifteen parishes and a good half
of the entire city stood between these two nuclei. Without further research little can be said to characterize this dramatic separation of a
population that otherwise is supposed to have been fairly homogeneous,
primarily endogamous, and otherwise forced through persecution to
close ranks and fight for its very survival. But the spatial politics of Seville
seem to have confirmed two distinct urban, historical, and even political attitudes. On the one side of the city, the *moriscos* residing behind
San Marcos lived literally up against a wall, having retreated or been relegated to the districts that were farthest away from the centers of power
and from the most important economic areas of the city. Their urban
attitude seems to confirm their retreat into what could be labeled an internal exile, a sort of ghettoification that, like any such reduction, ultimately points to the possibility of total extermination. It may be argued
that the residents of this unofficial *morería,* like the tragic Boabdil of
Irvian tales, had resigned themselves to living at the end of history. On
the opposite side of the city, more than one-third of all *moriscos* lived in
the vicinity of the mercantile center and the harbor. They were at the
threshold of the door to the Indies, on what could have been to some of
them the last step in a voyage of no return that would grant them the
possibility of starting life anew, far away from Spain and from Christianity. In his well-documented study *Spain's Men of the Sea,* Pablo E.
Pérez-Mallaína shows that persecution and discrimination were two of

the principal factors that encouraged men to enlist and risk their lives at sea, noting that there were at times complaints about the presence of mulattoes and *moriscos* who had even been admitted to the Carrera de Indias as pilots.[21]

Given the incompleteness and unreliability of records, it is reasonable to agree with Pike that "exact numbers of these groups can never be determined, and all figures for them are largely guesswork."[22] However, we know that the *morisco* community, hovering at a number around seven thousand, amounted to about 5 percent of the total population of Seville at the height of the city's growth in the 1580s.[23] Of these, females outnumbered males, though there were more free male *moriscos* than females. The majority in both cases were above the age of twenty and under that of sixty.[24] Such demographics, added to what we know were the tight living conditions *moriscos* were reduced to through poverty and discrimination, makes us wonder about the fact that their overall population seems to have stagnated in the last three decades prior to their expulsion in 1609. No doubt, as a poor and marginalized people they were more susceptible to epidemics than other groups. But integration into the larger society and emigration to the Indies must also have played a role in keeping the official count almost unchanged for three decades.

When considering the *morisco* contribution to the colonization and settlement of the Indies it is even more important to take into account the much larger number of people who were not counted as *moriscos* but who were thoroughly *amoriscados*. They formed the largest group among the peoples who went to Seville as part of the massive migration from the rural areas where, ever since the conquest of the city in the thirteenth century, the mudejars had been relegated as part of a clear policy to make Seville a predominantly Christian city. This was precisely the trend that was dramatically reversed in the sixteenth century as the descendants of the Mudejar peasants who inhabited Seville's hinterland gave the city a markedly Moorish flavor.[25] The impact of this migration on Seville was significant, and among other things it graced the Castilian spoken in Seville with an undeniably Moorish accent that was carried over to the other side of the ocean. We have reports from several contemporary observers who lamented the fact, pointing with disgust to the corruption of the old Castilian pronunciation—a trademark of the city during the previous century—by the increasing use of Moorish speech patterns, most prevalent among which was the *seseo,* or pronouncing the *c* or *z* as an *s*. It should be noted that at any time the number of clearly identifiable *moriscos* was much smaller than the number of those who for some reason or another were able to pass as old Christians or were never counted. There were also instances where people who were counted as *moriscos* could hardly be recognized as such, as was the case of the Moor Fernando Muley, known by the *morisco* name of Fernando Enríquez. Muley was the alleged leader of a *morisco* uprising that was being planned in Seville in 1580. Documents from the time reveal that he was regarded as a *tagarino*, as it was supposedly impossible to tell him apart from Old Christians on account of his good Castilian pronunciation.[26]

There are no figures available to allow one to quantify the extent of *morisco* emigration to the Indies. How could there be if the *moriscos* were not supposed to be there in the first place? Since 1522 emigration to the Indies by *conversos* and *moriscos* had been forbidden, but they were supposed to have been excluded from the beginning according to the instructions given by King Ferdinand to the governor of Hispaniola, Nicolás de Ovando, in 1501. In addition, starting in the middle of the sixteenth century, anyone wishing to travel to the Indies legally had to prove purity of blood, a cumbersome procedure that required people to document that they were not the descendants of *moriscos, conversos,* or people condemned by the Inquisition for the past two generations.

But the Moorish contribution to the foundation of New World societies is undeniable, even if it will never be quantified with any degree of scientific certainty. At best only circumstantial evidence can be presented in an attempt to demonstrate the significance of a migration that, although it was supposed to have never taken place, seems to have been occurring from the beginning of the colonization period. As early as 1503, Juan de Ayala, one of the original conquerors and settlers of Hispaniola and the commander of the fort of Concepción de la Vega (built in 1495), was already asking the king that "it not be permitted that there go there any turncoats *[tornadizos]* or suspects who have been pardoned by the Inquisition, or any Moorish or Jewish slaves, but only gentlemen [hidalgos], so that they may not befoul the land, which is the best and richest of all discovered."[27] Apparently Ayala had reasons to be afraid of the competition *tornadizos* could pose to the hidalgos. Concepción de la Vega was the place where the first sugar mills were erected in the New World, giving birth to an economic activity that would soon come to displace the mining interests that men like Ayala had helped set up. Carlos Esteban Dieve argues that in all probability *morisco* mechanics operated the first such facilities in La Vega.[28]

Legal emigration to the Indies was a cumbersome, time-consuming, and expensive process. For this reason large numbers of emigrants must have found ways of circumventing the official requirements. It is difficult to quantify extraofficial emigration, but we know that it was considerable right from the beginning. On Columbus's second voyage alone, about 150 people—10 percent of the total crew—are thought to have been stowaways. Later it would be easier to buy false documents or to pay crew members for unofficial passage and protection during the long voyage. In addition, enlisting as a soldier or seaman and deserting once on the other side of the ocean was the easiest way to circumvent the bureaucratic requirements, and it seems to have been the preferred way, well into the eighteenth century, for male immigrants who had neither the money nor the interest to purchase legal documents. In some years, the number of soldiers and seamen who deserted in the Indies surpassed the number of legal immigrants.[29] More often than not, captains who were given royal authorization to recruit soldiers for the galleons had to resort to forced conscription. Understandably, not too many questions were asked when volunteers came forward. Occasionally even the Crown would build incentives into the deal made with recruits, as when in a royal decree signed at Medina del Campo on 18 June 1532 it ordered "that it may be cried out on the steps of the Cathedral (of Seville) that all those who may wish to go to Hispaniola, up to a number of two hundred men, to wage war on Enriquillo and on other rebellious Indians, shall be given free passage and victuals and, among other things, shall be fed during the course of the war."[30]

It is impossible to know how many *moriscos* answered the call to go fight the rebellious Indians led by Enriquillo. But it should be noted that it was not at all uncommon to recruit them for such military purposes. Pizarro, for one, is known to have taken some two hundred *morisco* soldiers to Peru.[31] Among the most fascinating objects recently uncovered during archaeological excavations in Puerto Real, one of the early settlements of Hispaniola, is an enameled medallion possibly dating back to the twelfth century. It conforms to the geometry of the eight-pointed star that was so characteristic of Islamic and Mudejar design. In its central disc a Cufic inscription reads "Allâh-u-ackbar" (God is great). Kathleen Deagan writes: "It is not difficult to imagine that this object came to Puerto Real with one of the [Christian] warriors who had engaged in the sack of Alhama or Málaga, or that it came with the very first settlers on the Plain of Limonade."[32] The small size of the icon and the succinctness of its inscription suggest the no less likely possibility that this object could have been the most essential and secret souvenir brought by a moro to the Indies. An entire world is contained in that medallion, a world that to its original owner must have seemed all but impossible to hold onto on account of the terrible reduction of the moriscos at the time. How appropriate, then, that the medallion came to be buried in the originary clays of the American landscape in Hispaniola, like a seed that was to plant in us the idea of the very possibility that there once were Moors in the Indies or, to recall Benzoni's characterization of the sub-Saharan Africans, moros de Indias.

At any rate, knowing that a Moorish presence at the foundation of early New World societies cannot be concretely quantified, I propose that the impact of such a phenomenon may be ascertained first by looking into the broad cultural and social phenomena that it nurtured, into the memory of the body as such, and second by searching for the actual traces it left in real space, in the architecture of the first colonial settlements of Hispaniola, which, as Boyd-Bowman has discovered, was "the most Andalusian region of the New World" at the time.[33] If everything that was to be called Sevillian in the sixteenth century—including the prevalent pronunciation of Castilian in the Indies—had a markedly Moorish resonance, and if, as Comellas argues, due to the overwhelming presence of Sevillians in the New World it was possible for non-Sevillians to become Sevillianized there,[34] it must then be true that the Sevillianization of the Indies resulted in an equally significant amoriscamiento of the first colonial societies.

One of the clearest outward signs of this profound process of transculturation was the female custom of wearing a sort of almalafa, or Moorish veil that covered most of the face. This custom was maintained until relatively recently by women in some of the oldest colonial cities of the New World. In Santo Domingo, where in the seventeenth century a creole woman who could afford to still carried to church a rug and a set of silk pillows to sit on,[35] the custom of using the Moorish veil in the streets was still in existence well into the eighteenth century, when mulatto women wore them in open defiance of decrees that had made the use of mantos, as they were called, the exclusive privilege of white women.[36] In 1838 Flora Tristán described the same type of *manto* as part of the outfit, or *saya,* worn by all the women of Lima, Peru, as a unique costume of unknown origin and different from any sort of Spanish dress of the day. According to her description, the *manto* was exclusively black and covered the entire bust, shoulders, arms, and head so that "only an eye is left visible."[37] Almost a century later, Richard Halliburton was able to photograph women in Lima still wearing *mantos.* He was told that the women were wearing a *tapada* or "Turkish veil which covered the head and shoulders, and was drawn across the face so as to leave only the right eye visible. Every woman wore one, rich and poor, high and low, each looking exactly like the other. Disguised this way they went everywhere, to mass, to balls, to every public place."[38] The *manto,* in Lima or in Santo Domingo, was the most precious resource in the art of camouflage. Covering the body in both *genio* and *figura* and upholding the anonymity of every woman who wore one, the *manto,* according to Tristán, made Lima the "place on earth where women are more free and have more influence."[39] The origins of the *manto* remain unknown, but the truth is that there is little difference in appearance between the women photographed by Halliburton in the Convent of Santo Domingo in Lima in 1928 and those carved into the altar of the Capilla Mayor in Granada, which depicts the forced baptism of Moorish women in the sixteenth century.

Quintero Rivera has alluded to this profound phenomenon of transculturation in the case of Puerto Rico, pointing to what he calls the historical *media morería,* or half-Moorishness, of the societies of runaway peasants there and to the conflictive and confused Hispanicity of what he terms the "mulatto plebeianism" of the Puerto Rican people.[40] Quintero Rivera reminds us that, for almost the entire duration of the Spanish continental empire in America, the island of Puerto Rico was the first stop for the galleon fleets of New Spain.[41] For all those traveling without licenses, for sailors and soldiers alike, the island provided the first opportunity to jump ship. Because the Spanish colony was primarily and for the first three centuries confined to the presidio or military garrison of San Juan, the dense forests of the island's mountainous interior offered deserters the opportunity to flee to a place where, officially, they would never be seen again.

To this day in the Spanish-speaking Caribbean the movement of *irse al monte,*[42] or fleeing to the mountains, is one of the principal markers of resistance and one of the fundamental spaces of culture and mythology. On the rocky northern shores of the inlet where the old walled quarter of the city of San Juan de Puerto Rico is located, battered by the waves of a fierce Atlantic, lies a small stone guard post. It is the lowest and most inaccessible point of the massive Castle of San Cristóbal, which was built during the eighteenth century to defend the city from English attack. It is also, more than any other place, the most prominent and dramatic marker of the edge of town. Because of this, the guard post was infamous from the start. It seems that many of the men sent down to keep watch there were never seen again, leading to the popular christening of the post as the Garita del Diablo, or Devil's Garret. Even today the place manages to live up to its reputation, as anyone who visits it quickly finds out. To get there one must descend from the highest point in town along a rugged cliff to the edge of the water. Once there, a strange feeling of precariousness overcomes the visitor, as one feels wedged between the tall escarpment and the mighty ocean and abandoned, experiencing a solitude that can be increased to the point of vertigo by the howling wind and the thundering waves. One feels as if standing at the edge of the world, on a Caribbean Finisterre,[43] facing the great unknown.

Behind the quaint religious superstition that the name of this guard post bespeaks and the consequent dismissal of any natural explanation for the sentinels' disappearances through the years, the Devil's Garret is above all an important site of desertion and escape. In a city that came to be completely walled in, its three gates closed at nine in the evening and under curfew by ten, the popular imagination turned the Devil's Garret into the Gate of Hell. Somehow the little guard post came to symbolize the weak link in the chain that separated the colonial outpost from the officially "unholy" opportunities that lay beyond.

This much of the legend of the guard house was the inspiration for Cayetano Coll y Toste's nineteenth-century story entitled "La Garita del Diablo." In it Coll y Toste tells that it was from that desolate outpost that a beautiful young mestizo (light-skinned mulatto) woman by the name of Dina escaped into the mountains with her lover, an Andalusian soldier known by the nickname of Flor de Azahar.[44] Curiously, the name Azahar comes from the Arabic al-zahar, or white flower, and it refers more specifically to the flower of the orange tree, which was the most ubiquitous tree in the gardens of Nasrid Granada and the tree most often planted in the atria of of Andalusi mosques, as in the Patios de los naranjos (Courtyards of the Orange Trees) at the mosques of Córdoba and Seville. Thus, in the story the name Flor de Azahar is a marker of Moorishness. Granted that the legend was embellished by Coll y Toste, its allure and the place of prominence it occupies within the Puerto Rican imaginary may be explained by the way it invokes the memory of the basic foundational elements of runaway culture, that is, the coming together of the Moor of Hispania and the *morenos* of the New World.

There, up in the mountains, these deserters would come in contact with other peoples—fugitives, escapees, and runaways of different sorts— some of them former slaves and others who were descended from the native inhabitants of the island who had been first to adopt the life of the maroon, or *cimarrón*. In Quintero Rivera's terms, it was a "running away that made possible the coming together"[45] of a counter-Plantation society that soon developed its own rituals and institutions. Foremost amongst these, as evidenced to this day in Puerto Rico and Cuba, was the custom of holding a communal pig roast on the most special occasions of the year. According to Quintero Rivera, this tradition was born out of the need to avoid persecution through a ritual simulacrum that was intended to demonstrate the Christianity and Spanishness of the members of the community. He writes, "One could very probably have some Moorish or Jewish ancestry [peoples who, we must recall, did not eat pork], but one had the desire to be 'left alone' by the authorities, of not wanting to be persecuted. Now one was Christian—Spanish—and it was important to show it."[46] As always, one thing was intentionally shown and quite another showed through. To this day the people of Cuba and Puerto Rico wait for the pig to roast while dancing to African rhythms and singing romances that are prefaced by melodic formulae that closely follow the patterns of old Andalusi music.

There are, of course, no documented accounts of actual *moriscos* taking their songs with them up into the mountains of central Puerto Rico. But there is one historical figure of importance during the early years of the sixteenth century whose story illustrates what Quintero Rivera alludes to in a broader context. He was known to the Christians as Gonzalo de Guerrero, and the path he chose in the New World led some of his contemporaries to question his Christianity. His story includes the first substantially troubling account of *mestizaje,* that is, of a union between a Christian and an Indian that produced offspring.[47] To be sure, there

had already been hundreds if not thousands of these unions by the time
Guerrero got lost in the Yucatán, because taking Indian women as *criadas,*
or "maids," had been the common practice of Christians in Hispaniola
from the days of Columbus and the infamous Vasco Porcallo. Guerrero's
story survives, however, not because of the uniqueness of the union but
because it is the first case in which a Christian turned his back on his
former comrades in defense of his mestizo, or "mixed," children. Guerrero had been captured by the Mayans and had apparently adopted
their ways, language, and religion, whereupon he was made a *cacique,* or
lord, became a military leader among them, and married and had three
children with a high-ranking Indian woman.

Bernal Díaz del Castillo, a *converso* who had the rank of captain under Diego Velázquez and who fought next to Cortés, tells in his *Historia
verdadera de la conquista de la Nueva España* that Gonzálo de Guerrero
was one of the two survivors—the official imperial chronicler Gonzalo
Fernández de Oviedo speaks of seven—of a shipwreck that occurred
along the Yucatán coast in 1511. The other was Gerónimo de Aguilar, who
would eventually be rescued and sent after Guerrero. Asked by Aguilar
to rejoin the Spaniards, Guerrero declined, arguing that he would never
be understood and accepted by his former comrades, that in his assimilation into the Mayan culture he had, so to say, passed the point of no
return. Bernal Díaz del Castillo paraphrased Guerrero's words to Aguilar:
"Brother Aguilar, I am married and have three children and I am a chief
and a captain among these people; go with God for my face is tattooed
and my ears are pierced; what are those Spaniards going to say when
they see me like this?"[48]

Here Guerrero skillfully navigates the currents of ambiguous identity
that I have identified before in the *tagarino* subject of the peninsular
frontier. He treats Aguilar as a fellow Christian and tells him to go with
God; however, he chooses to remain with the Mayans. Guerrero knew
that he would never be accepted by "those Spaniards," who would most
probably look down upon him for having allowed his face to be tattooed
and his ears to be pierced. Here was a man who chose to separate himself from the idea that Spaniards were creating of themselves as good
Christians, an idea that was to be the basis of Spanish nationalism. At
the same time, Guerrero distanced himself from the Vitruvian-based
ideal of the European body by mutilating his face and going with people
judged to be incapable of reason or understanding.[49] But had he ever

been a Spaniard to begin with? Denouncing Guerrero's treason, and that of five others, Fernández de Oviedo was quick to point out that Guerrero and the others were not Spaniards: "Since they were married to Indian women, and had acquired their vices, and had children with them, they had distanced themselves from the Catholic faith, they now lived like Indians, and did not want to accept the only true faith and would not return to the company of the Spaniards. It is safe to assume that they must have been nothing but people of a vile cast and despicable heretics."[50]

In Fernández de Oviedo the discourse of *mestizaje* already included that movement toward vilification of the pariahs of nations that would later be assumed by Irving and Usonian creoles as part of their discourse on the origins of American civilization. There was thus, from the start of the colonial experience, a direct association between the Indian of the new contact zone, who was seen as incapable of reason, and the vile casts of the old. This was a dangerous association for the Christians, who would see in this particular movement of *mestizaje* a conflation of the Indian will to resist with the connivance of the old vile races of the peninsula. Here are the discursive antecedents of Irving's vile rabble and of a practice of *mestizaje* that would be perceived not just as a threat to the integrity of the European body but to the very stability of the colonial order and, eventually, the national one.

From the beginning of the voyages to the New World, desertion was equated with heresy and with the "vile casts" of the Jews and Muslims. If Fernández de Oviedo felt it was safe to assume that these men were not good Christians, was he not also willing to accept that precisely because of this they must have come to the New World to escape Spain altogether? That a statement like this was put forth with such confidence and nonchalance, especially by Fernández de Oviedo, who was the official imperial chronicler, also speaks to the possibility that these incidents were not all that uncommon at the time. Fernández de Oviedo increased suspicions even further, telling of how Francisco de Montejo, *adelantado* or conqueror of Yucatán, wrote to Guerrero asking him to come back to the Spanish side and offering him a position of importance in the expedition. Guerrero is said to have written, very appropriately on the back of the letter sent by Montejo, that he still remembered God and that he was still a friend of the Spaniards but that he would not go back because he was a slave and thus had no freedom to do as he pleased and that, besides, he was married and had children. This was indeed the *tagarino* way of saying no. But it was unacceptable to Fernández de Oviedo, who wrote of Guerrero: "This unfortunate man must have been raised from the beginning among low class and despicable people, and must not have been well instructed and indoctrinated in the ways of our Holy Catholic faith, and there is the chance that (as it should be suspected) he could have been of a vile caste and so his Christianity must be put into question."[51] In the mind of Fernández de Oviedo the fugitive Guerrero was quite possibly a neophyte Christian and, as such, no Christian at all. In the words of an old saying used to this day in the Spanish-speaking islands of the Caribbean to refer to those whose ingrained habits will never change: "Moro viejo, mal cristiano" (an old Moor makes a bad Christian).[52] The saying is no doubt a throwback to the days of Fernández de Oviedo and to the days, we might conclude, when there were Moors in the Indies.

Although Fernández de Oviedo's repudiation of Guerrero's actions was a rabid condemnation of the sort to which Spaniards of the day commonly resorted, there is no reason to doubt that many of the people who deserted did so on account of the fact that they were not "Spanish" in the sense that "Spanishness" was being defined at the time, first and foremost as a function of a subject's Christianity. Bernal Díaz, whom I have said was of Jewish lineage, was never as severe as Fernández de Oviedo in his criticism of Guerrero. He limited his explanation of Guerrero's actions to stating that the man was a sailor, implying that jumping ship and going native was a common practice of the day. After stating that Guerrero had declined all possible enticements and offerings to come back to the Spanish side, Díaz del Castillo made a rather cryptic remark: "And apparently Gonzalo Guerrero was a man of the sea, a native of Palos."[53] Fernández de Oviedo, who mentioned that Guerrero was from the county of Niebla, repeatedly called him a sailor in a more militant tone: "That bad Christian, that sailor" or "that traitor and renegade sailor called Gonzalo."[54] Here heretic and neophyte became descriptors of the renegade sailor. How many sailors were such turncoats? How many of them were truly men of the seas, people who had been cast out and who were in search of a new land?

Gonzalo de Guerrero gave a final response to Aguilar: "And just look how pretty these three little children of mine are."[55] There was no going back; the outcast had found a new home on the other side of the Ocean sea. Guerrero, the most important renegade Spaniard reported to have jumped ship in the New World, would live as a Mayan until his death in battle at the hands of his former comrades in 1528. With him we have the first significant instance of a type of *mestizaje* that from its inception was problematic from the Spanish point of view, because the mestizos produced by such unions were the final and conclusive reason given by Guerrero for not returning to the Spanish side. The term is even more problematic if we factor in the possibility that Guerrero could have been a neophyte and that, regardless of whether he was indeed of *morisco* origin, he was, as a result of his desertion, seen and condemned as such by his contemporaries. In the union that produced Guerrero's "three pretty little children" we see the first instance in which the "running away that made possible the coming together" of which Quintero Rivera speaks produced a New World subject who could claim a right to the land on the matrilineal side while holding onto a tradition of resistance to socioreligious persecution and to the institutions of the new Spanish-Christian state on the patrilineal side. Through this modality of *mestizaje* an alternate claim to the Indies had been put forth, one that contested both peninsular and nascent creole discourses of Indian possession.

It is important, however, to distinguish between what I call the *mestizos guerreros*—the warring or runaway type, after Guerrero himself—and the *mestizos conquistadores*. The latter were the children of the Christian conquerors. They were among the first colonial subjects of modernity and the ideal of the subject of coloniality insofar as they became the primary agents of conquest. By all accounts, the practice of *mestizaje* assumed vertiginous proportions within a few years of the initial contact. Numbers are hard to come by for the island populations, but we know that in Asunción (Paraguay), by 1575 there were five thousand mestizo males, three thousand of them younger than eighteen years of age, and some five thousand mestizo females. In comparison, "the Spanish were no more than two hundred eighty, and of them, a hundred were useless and the rest were old."[56] The settlement of Asunción had been in existence for less than forty years, and there were already thirty-five mestizos for every Spaniard; that is, the conquistadors and their "legitimate" nonmestizo descendants accounted for only 2 percent of the total population. When talking about the second half of the sixteenth century, when the conquest had proceeded south of Peru and over the Andes, we can hardly speak of native-born Spaniards per se. Juan de Garay founded Santa Fe

(Argentina) in 1573 accompanied by seven Spanish-born settlers and sixty-nine settlers who where not Spaniards.[57] Not surprisingly, as the initial moment in the production of the hybrid type in the context of the coloniality of power, the mestizo came to stand for all hybridity, describing in essence the process of production of one who came to be the child of empire, the modern colonial subject. In contrast to what I have called the *mestizo guerrero,* the "official" mestizo, or the *mestizo conquistador,* became both subject and subjector, victim and victimizer, conqueror and conquered.

The Period of the *Alarifes*

The Moorish presence in the New World was an issue in Hispaniola from its earliest days. In 1512 the advantages of taking to the colonies *esclavas blancas,* or white female slaves of *morisco* or Berber origin, was discussed as a way of avoiding unions between colonists and Indian women, who were judged to be "people far removed from Reason."[58] Thus unions between Christians and Muslims produced some of the first colonial subjects in the Antilles and served to safeguard the body capable of reason—as the depository of the Renaissance ideal—from the corruption to which it was susceptible in the Indies. The plan, like so many other early experiments in the New World, quickly got out of hand and apparently led to the appearance of small "Berber" communities in cities such as Santo Domingo, where male Berber and *morisco* servants, artisans, and builders already resided.[59] In 1531 Charles V forbade the taking of white slaves of Berber origin to the Indies without royal permission,[60] and in 1543 he ordered that all Berber slaves who had passed to the Indies in contradiction of his earlier edict were to be expelled.[61] The emperor's orders seem for the most part to have been disregarded, forcing him, on 13 November 1550, to reiterate in a royal provision to the principal colonial authorities of the Indies what he had ordered in the provision of 1543, adding that all Berber converts who might have been recently freed were also to be returned to Spain.[62]

The presence in the Indies of skilled workers of *morisco* origin can be traced back to the founding of the city of Santo Domingo in 1503 under Nicolás de Ovando, who had taken with him to Hispaniola a large number of craftsmen and builders from the southern regions of the Iberian Peninsula as part of an expedition composed of some twenty-five hundred people. We can suspect that many of these master builders, or *alarifes* (from the Arabic *al-ari*, or knowledgeable one), were in fact of non-Christian origin, as were most of the masons and carpenters at the time in the regions of Extremadura and Andalusia, where Ovando recruited his men. What is indisputable is that these people, and those like them who would follow, soon came to be an important group in the early colonial society of Santo Domingo. A document written two years after the expulsion decree of 1543 emphasized the importance of such skilled laborers to the welfare of the colony: "Without counting the ones who live inland, there are about a hundred male and female Berber slaves in this city... and they have come here with licenses bestowed upon them by Your Majesty and they are married and have children and those among them who are freemen are masons and carpenters and have other occupations of great utility to the people of this land."[63]

This account suggests several important things. First, we know that a number of these Berbers were in fact free and were employed and indispensable to the economic well-being of the colony. Second, many of them, free and slave, were already married and having children, thus contributing to the growth of the colonial population and displaying a certain commitment to the land. Third, there were still others who lived inland, away from the city—and from Spain—and thus closer to the internal frontiers of the colony. It is possible to assume that most of these "inland Berbers" settled in Concepción de la Vega, which was the second most important town in the colony and had a Mudejar-style fortress built entirely of brick.[64] This is of the utmost significance, because it testifies to the kind of people who might have first decided to make their home in the New World. Unlike many of the Christians who had gone to the Indies in search of riches, hoping to strike gold and go back home as rich men, the Berbers and *moriscos* who immigrated to Hispaniola might be considered the first true immigrants of the American Columbiad. They planned to stay, for they had no country to which to return.

The tumultuous history of Santo Domingo during its first decades and the architectural record left behind further corroborate this point. In contrast to the makeshift character of the first Columbian villages of Hispaniola, most notably Isabella, which was begun in 1494, Santo Domingo was the first settlement in the New World to be laid out with ruler and compass. When Alessandro Geraldini, the first resident bishop, arrived in 1520, he found the streets of the city "long and straight in such a way that not even the streets of Florence could in any way be compared to them."[65] As the base of operations of the House of Trade in the colonies, it was the overseas counterpart to Seville. In 1509 it became the seat of the viceregal court under Diego Columbus and, starting in 1511, also the seat of the Real Audiencia, or royal court of appeals, which was instituted to reinforce regal authority over the affairs of the island.[66]

Although the importance of Santo Domingo as the nesting ground of the institutions of coloniality as well as a precedent for the modern city is paramount, the time of its growth and expansion was relatively short. By the time Hernán Cortés entered Mexico City in 1519, the native inhabitants of Hispaniola, whose numbers are calculated to have been close to four hundred thousand in 1492, amounted to fewer than three thousand. Having run out of Indian slaves and engulfed in interminable feuds between competing factions, the great majority of the Christians decided to follow in Cortés's footsteps.[67] By 1526 there were fewer than a thousand colonists in Hispaniola. Though technically still the center of the colonial enterprise in the New World, Santo Domingo had virtually been abandoned. Nevertheless, the amount of construction that went on in the city during the second quarter of the century was impressive. The work was financed by the Church and the Crown by means of the treasures found and pillaged in Mexico and Peru. But it was carried out by the "Berber" masons and carpenters who had stayed behind when the majority of the Christian population fled the city. This is why I deem it appropriate to name the entire period between 1526 and 1544 as the period of the *alarifes*.

These two decades marked the end of the first major period of American colonial history and also the end of Hispaniola as the base of operations of the imperial venture in the New World. During this period the colony of Hispaniola experienced a slow recovery brought about through a change from mining to sugar cultivation and cattle raising as the main economic activities. This, in turn, led to a dramatic change in the composition and distribution of the population, which increasingly became concentrated around the sugar mills—called *ingenios* or *trapiches,* depending on whether the mill mechanism was powered by water or animals—and was composed of Africans brought to the colonies to work as slaves. By the middle of the century there were some seventeen thousand people living in Hispaniola, twelve thousand of whom were slaves of African origin called *bozales* or their black or mulatto American descendants.[68]

In 1543, the year when the walls of Santo Domingo were begun, there was already plenty in the city worth protecting from the increased menace of pirate attacks. During the period of the *alarifes* a number of monumental structures had been built or come close to completion, including a fortress; the three church-monastery complexes of the Franciscan, Dominican, and the Our Lady of Mercy orders; the cathedral; the viceregal palace; the casas reales, or government houses; the cabildo, or city hall; the atarazanas, which was a shipping warehouse under the jurisdiction of the House of Trade; a jail; and the Hospital of Saint Nicholas of Bari, which was the twin of the monumental Hospital de la Santa Cruz in Toledo, Spain. In addition to all these large-scale stone and masonry structures there were a good number of private residences that were equally well built and occupied large lots within the city grid. Most of them stood along two main thoroughfares running on a north-south axis for six city blocks. Under all that there was a sewer system, built of brick, that would have been the envy of most European cities of the time.

The principal monument of the period was the cathedral, a building that is rather unspectacular both in order and in scale, but majestic in the complexity of the contradictions that gave rise to it and that it records. At first glance the Cathedral of Santo Domingo, built between 1521 and 1544, seems a rather modest example of European architecture in the Indies. The building marks the transition between the late medieval and the Renaissance periods. Signs of the temporal and spatial coexistence of the styles of two periods are everywhere, from the chapels that were started in Gothic style and finished with neoclassical vaults to the contrast between the Gothic north entrance and the Plateresque façade. Indeed, the entire early colonial city of Santo Domingo is a showcase for this stylistic transition, as it was mostly built in a relatively short period during the second quarter of the sixteenth century, which coincided with the reign of Charles V and the introduction of Italian neoclassicism into the Iberian Peninsula, a period which architecturally was framed between the highly symbolic and ornament-rich late Spanish Gothic, or *Isabelino,* style and the *estilo desornamentado,* or disornamented, style that had been officialized during the reign of Phillip II.

But a closer look reveals that the purely transitional stylistic exemplarity of the cathedral was secondary in importance to the extraofficial stylistic and formal particularities that the building records, which resulted from the dramatic transformation of colonial society at the time.

Work on the cathedral was started in earnest in 1521, during the first years of the conquest of Mexico, an event that, as we know, almost immediately triggered the exodus of a great part of the Christian population from the island. Before that time, the lack of progress on the first cathedral of the Indies can be directly attributed to the fact that because most of the Christian colonists of Santo Domingo did not plan to die there and, consequently, to be buried there, they were not inclined to contribute to the building effort. As the conquistadors embarked for Mexico, the peoples who had decided to establish themselves on the island, like the Berberiscos mentioned above, stayed behind. It was then that Bishop Alessandro Geraldini, a man of the most refined Renaissance sensibilities who came to be the loneliest person in Hispaniola, willed the Cathedral of Santo Domingo into existence. He did so in the most idealized of ways, by erecting the edifice through his verses:

> May the columns gracefully rise
> Like prayers to the sky;
> And may the ribs interlace,
> Holding up the vaults with grace.[69]

Tragically, Geraldini died in 1524 before his poetic dream could be turned into stone. Quite appropriately, perhaps, he was buried there, so the church came to be built around his remains. His grave, capped by a stone that bears a full-scale likeness of his body, remains one of the biggest curiosities in a city that is full of them. Granted, the image does not have the dynamism of Vitruvian projections. Nevertheless it is a souvenir of a somewhat luminous side of the Renaissance, which for a fleeting moment graced Santo Domingo with its presence.

The cathedral has the plan of a basilica, without a transept. The nave is fifty-four meters long and has eight bays of quadripartite vaults. It is flanked by two aisles of almost the same height (about sixteen meters) but of half the width of the nave. Together the nave and aisles measure twenty-three meters across. The aisles, in turn, open into a series of seven lateral chapels placed between the buttresses on each side in typical Isabelino fashion. On the outside, the unpretentious simplicity of the surfaces and the relative ease with which large volumes are massed speak of Andalusi moral and aesthetic preferences and building practices. At the same time, the building conveys a sense of heaviness that is characteristic of late Spanish Gothic sensibilities. The dark interior is also typical of the Isabelino Gothic, a historicist aesthetic movement that in its effort to create a uniquely Spanish Christian style of architecture borrowed freely from the Mozarabic and Romanesque forms of early Christian times, trying to recreate the sober mood and the simplicity of those earlier structures.

Altogether the structure is modest in size for a cathedral. But what it lacks in size the building makes up for in the universalistic claim it puts forth on behalf of imperial majesty, a claim that it makes more clearly and strongly than the triumphalistic choreography of the palace of Charles V in Granada. Indeed it was in this, the first major city of the colonial world, where the claim to universal rule was most directly and unmistakably made. This representational tour de force occurs in the main façade of the church (Figure 11), located on its western end, which was the last part of the building to be completed. The façade is decorated with Plateresque details, and, as Erwin Walter Palm points out, it is organized following models of the Italian Quattrocento.[70] The entire composition is organized around the entrance, a set of twin doors crowned by a pair of arches. The arches, which are oblique to a central vertical plane and foreshortened, were constructed using a forced perspective and recede toward two disparate points along the central axis of a composition that is otherwise symmetrical. In 1536 Diego de Siloé, who is credited with introducing Renaissance architecture into the Iberian Peninsula, had built a similar façade for the Salvador Chapel in Úbeda, Andalusia. In each work the entrance is flanked by the protruding walls of the nave, which in the case of the cathedral are stylized into massive pilasters terminating in an equally exaggerated cornice. Because of the temporal proximity of the works and the geographic distance that separates them, neither could have been a precedent for the other. What is likely is that they were both based, as we know is indeed the case of the chapel at Úbeda, on Siloé's Portal del Perdón of the Cathedral of Granada. In Granada, as in Úbeda and Santo Domingo, the entrance with its twin doors is flanked by twin columns guarding niches in the manner of a Roman triumphal arch. The single most important connection between the works is the elaborate and exquisite Plateresque decoration in the entablatures.

Aside from these connections, the façade of Santo Domingo's cathedral is unique and without precedent in terms of the overall intent of the composition. At the farthest frontiers of the Christian world, in what

Figure 11. Façade of the Cathedral of Santo Domingo. Photograph by the author.

at least symbolically remained the principal city of the Indies, the façade of the cathedral was conceived so that it would lay claim to the ideal of universal governance on behalf of Charles V. Here, in the first colony of the modern world, the imperial ideal was announced in the most unambiguous symbolic language. Above the entrance and between the arches is the royal coat of arms of Charles V, which was originally supported by the two-headed eagle of imperial iconography. (The present-day sculpture is a reproduction of the original eagle, which was destroyed by the

Haitians when they took the city of Santo Domingo in 1801.) At the time it was common for structures built under royal patronage to sport such emblems; examples are seen in the Bisagra Gate in Toledo and in the façades of the University of Alcalá de Henares and the Alcazar of Toledo. Ecclesiastical buildings were also thus emblazoned, as was the case of the Cathedral of Almería and the Churches of Santiago in Guadix and Saint Sebastian in Antequera. In all these cases the coat of arms was an adornment, the product of a simple albeit representationally charged exercise of power. In those buildings, as in the Alhambra, Charles had simply stamped his seal upon a flat surface. In the Cathedral of Santo Domingo, however, the coat of arms was part of a more complex composition that, through the perspectival manipulation of the twin arches, was intended to burst into real space. The arches, which emanate in forced perspective from a mathematically calculated place in space— the vanishing point—open into the world in opposite directions: one facing toward the septentrional (northern) and the other toward the meridional (southern) regions of the globe. They are thus a representation of the two hemispheres that were the object of all imperial desire. At the time Charles V had what was known as the Padrón general (General Pattern), a map of the world where all the new discoveries were carefully noted. This arguably contained the most sensitive and secret information of the day, and it was most jealously kept by the Habsburg king in an analogic gesture of exclusivity that confirmed his dream of universal domination: own the map and you will own the world. In the façade of the cathedral this will to power was set in stone, as the Habsburg imperial eagle faces in both directions, jealously guarding the two hemispheres under its wings. Because of this continuous vigilance the composition was also the most confident expression of imperial hegemony and stability, as the arches are also a plastic metaphor of the rising and the setting sun. Thus Charles was declared to rule over the Orient and the Occident, and to Spain belonged the first empire in which the sun never set.[71]

In the colonial version of the Ideal City of the Renaissance, the Cathedral of Santo Domingo was erected on the main central square, or Plaza Mayor, of the city. But Santo Domingo was far from an ideal city. Behind the representational montage of the cathedral's façade, the axis that runs across the nave through the north and south portals of the cathedral used to unite the two institutions that marked the alpha and

the omega of colonial life. It was in the south portal where the Ecclesiastical Tribunal met and where those wanted by the authorities could
claim asylum. On the other side of the church, in the middle of the
Plaza Mayor, was the wooden block where hands were cut off and pris-
oners beheaded. Therefore, the bicephalic eagle also reigned over the
genio and the *figura* of colonial subjectivity, as the limits to the first were
decided by the Church and the punishment for transgression was ad-
ministered by the executioner's blade upon the second. This was the eagle
that claimed to rule over the dexter and the sinister, over the legitimate
and the illegitimate body, over the European Ideal and a metaphorical
movement that always transcended it. In this, the first of the planned
cities of the colonial world and the site of many of the mechanisms that
made the urban machine a formidable weapon of conquest and colonization, the national imperial project had not only been enunciated in
clear representational terms, but it was also expressed in the full measure
of its spatial dimensions. In other words, both the plus ultra of Spanish
imperial projections and the ne plus ultra of colonial delimitations came
to revolve around the central longitudinal axis of the first cathedral in
the New World. If it is true, as is commonly accepted, that it was on the
island of Hispaniola (La Española or the Spanish island) where the disparate cultures of the peninsular kingdoms first came together under
the name of a hypothetical Spanishness,[72] it is equally true that it was in
the "navel" of the colonial space where the ideal of empire was most
clearly and forcefully imagined. But as in the palace of Charles V in
Granada, there too the possibility of the realization of the ideal of universal rule would be haunted by the Zaharenian curse that heralded the
ultimate end to empire. In this case, also as in the Alhambra, the writing
was quite literally on the walls of the cathedral.

Perhaps the imprecision of the perspectival construction of the reced-
ing arches over the cathedral entrance should have given us a clue that
the "ideal" in Santo Domingo was wrought with certain otherwise impossible imperfections. This was a place where things were never quite
what they pretended to be, a place where even the most official architecture had been quietly infiltrated by the discursive practices of the
counter-conquest. Nowhere is this clearer than in the point of the cathedral farthest away from the façade, in the eastern end of the building,
where in the center of the apse above the altar a horseshoe window typical of Islamic and Mudejar architecture presides over the longitudinal

Figure 12. Horseshoe window above the altar of the Cathedral of Santo Domingo. Photograph by the author.

axis of the nave (Figure 12). Certainly there were important Mudejar elements in the Isabelino Gothic. But the use of this type of fenestration was infrequent, especially in such a place of prominence. In fact, the placement of the horseshoe window at the culminating point of the building most central to its program reminds us of the use of the horseshoe arch at the entrances to the mihrabs—the prayer niches indicating the direction of Mecca—in peninsular mosques, which had become standard in al-Andalus in the ninth century with the construction of the Great Mosque of Córdoba.[73] The basilica in Hispaniola is oriented on the typical East-West axis of Christian churches, but could it be merely a coincidence that the horseshoe window above the altar also points in the direction of Mecca?

As an architectural palimpsest this symbolic moment is the representative obverse of what we saw in the sanctuary of the church of the Convent of Saint Clare in Tordesillas. If the superimposition of a Calvary scene over the Mudejar ceiling made the latter a discourse on the triumph of Christianity, the placing of the horseshoe window over the main altar in the Dominican basilica is a testament to the tenacity of the Moorish resistance to conquest, subjugation, and disappearance. This is a window to the Granada of the Indies, and it is also an example of architecture as "the only possible form to history."[74] Perhaps, as in the Alhambra during Nasrid times, the *alarifes* of Santo Domingo, thinking of themselves as living at the end of time, also hoped to have the last word.

In the horseshoe window, as in the design of the façade, we see that the cathedral of Santo Domingo was not so much a diminished copy of peninsular architectural models as a building that used the same models in new and unique ways. These architectural models have neither direct peninsular precedents nor clear American progeny. The same is true of the Church of San Lázaro, which was built in a poor neighborhood in the interior periphery of the walled precinct of Santo Domingo that, curiously enough, occupies the same area in relation to the city and its harbor as did the *morisco* neighborhood of Seville behind San Marcos. The modest east façade of the Church of San Lázaro (Figure 13) is decorated with a delicate Mudejar-style brick parapet. It is crowned with merlons in typical Andalusi fashion. A belfry in the corner is a recent addition. The single door of the entrance is capped by a rounded or neoclassical arch. This, in turn, is decorated with a simple *alfiz* (from the Arabic *al-hayyiz*), the rectangular frame for a door or window that is typical of all Islamic architecture. Above the *alfiz* a floral geometric motif is enshrined in a niche that would normally hold the figure of a saint. This is perhaps the closest thing to a Koranic inscription that may be found in a colonial building in the New World, and, together with the parapet and the *alfiz,* it makes the eastern façade of the Church of San Lázaro the entrance to a mosque more than to a church.

To be sure there are other areas in the Caribbean and on the continent, most notably in Mexico, Peru, Cuba, and Colombia, where Mudejar architectural influences are more in evidence than in Hispaniola.[75] There are even instances, as in the *capilla real* (royal chapel) of the church-monastery complex of San Gabriel in Cholula, where the Franciscans built churches that closely resembled mosques.[76] But in the majority of these cases the use of Mudejar forms responded primarily to aesthetic predilections and, more important, to practical necessities, as Mudejar structures were less expensive than typically Gothic or Renaissance ones and were faster to build using materials that were readily available almost anywhere. In Santo Domingo the penetration and the projection of the

Figure 13. Façade of the Church of San Lázaro in Santo Domingo. Photograph by the author.

morisco influence seems to have been the result of negotiation with or even of a careful subversion of the will of colonial authorities.

Perhaps this difficult process of negotiation also explains the imperfect resolution of forces in the Gothic ribbing of the Cathedral of Santo Domingo. All through the nave massive columns are capped by rings instead of capitals. Molded ribs rise from these rings, coming into being in an originary movement that is wholly disassociated from structural connotations. The disjunction between structural vocabulary and form, so atypical of Gothic architecture, is even sharper in the base of the arch that opens into the apse (refer again to Figure 12), where the column is replaced by a compound pier capped by a polyhedral abacus. From the vaults the ribs and arches descend toward the capitals and crash into each other in a terrible and confused rivalry for dominance that results in the overlap and disappearance of major structural elements. There is no apparent hierarchy; there is only the marvelously entangled and un-differentiated forms of the West Indian Gothic, forms that to purists are nothing more than terrible errors because the basic tenets of Gothic construction seem to have been completely and fundamentally dis-regarded. In the end, it would seem, the will to graceful form of Bishop Geraldini never materialized.

Beyond these possible "errors," the cathedral was exquisitely put to-gether in accordance with the best stone- and brick-building techniques of the time by *alarifes* under the supervision of competent master builders.[77] But how could the *alarifes* have practiced sound building tech-niques while disregarding the strict conventions that characterize Gothic construction? Could the builders of the cathedral have forgotten the Gothic forms? Not likely. It is more plausible to suspect that at least those among them who were of Berber and *morisco* origins had never prop-erly known them. They were competent builders, but not of churches. In all its confused Gothicness—which is also the sign of a certain con-fused Christianity and Hispanicity—the arch that opens into the apse of the cathedral serves as a perfect frame for the horseshoe window.[78] The window, in turn, is an early and very unique plastic enunciation of that half-Moorishness which, together with confused Hispanicity, Quin-tero Rivera places at the roots of mulatto plebeianism. Here, behind the imperial façade of the church, a *sorpresa de los enlaces* acquires concrete material form, giving shape to a discursive practice that placed official signs in check to such a degree that it reached the inner sanctum of early colonial society.

The Other Black Legend, or the Legend of the Black Other

The subversion of the national-imperial sign by the *moriscos* of the Indies was a movement that ran parallel to the destabilization of the Re-naissance ideal of the body, which served as the ideological foundation of the European Ideal. This movement of destabilization would propitiate

the most effective contestation of analogical space, exquisitely foment-
ing paradoxical moments of ideological instability by facing the Ideal
Body in both *genio* and *figura*. This is what I call *mulataje*, a movement
that from the earliest stages of modernity has tended to undo all the
calculations of the coloniality of power.

Contrary to common perceptions, the mulatto world also has its origins in the Iberian contact zone. In fact, the practices and realities of
mestizaje in the New World were so far predated by the more ancient
practice of *mulataje* in the Old World that when Esteva-Fabregat refers
to the Spaniard as a "Euro-mestizo"[79] he should really be speaking of a
Euro-mulatto instead. There is no need here to retrace the history of
what could be called a proto-*mulataje* in the Iberian contact zone to the
time of the Córdoba Caliphate or to the invasion of the peninsula by
the sub-Saharan Almoravids in 1086. Suffice it to say that even when
what we would call interracial unions were common in al-Andalus—a
society where tribal and religious differences were the ones that ruled
social relations—it was in the Christian kingdoms, as a direct consequence of the slave trade conducted by Castilians, Portuguese, and Genovese in North and West Africa, where the mulatto phenomenon was
first identified and named. The etymology of the term *mulatto* is not altogether clear. Some have argued that it comes from the Arabic *muwallad* (offspring of an Arab and a non-Arab), an old theory that has never
been entirely ruled out.[80] The consensus today is that *mulatto* more than
likely derives from the Latin or Romance term *mula*, meaning mule,
which in any case is similar to the definition of the Arabic *muwallad*,
which originally referred to a hybrid animal. What is clear is that *mulatto* is yet another term in the long list of descriptors applied to the
subjects of the Iberian contact zone, where years before the fall of Granada it was already used to describe the offspring of a black and a white
parent.

The introduction of skin color into a world ruled by religious differences made the social category of mulatto an unstable locus of subjectivity from the start. In more than one sense, the mulatto became that
which was difficult to locate. In terms of skin color alone, *mulatto* was
related to terms such as *pardo* (someone with skin any shade of brown)
and *loro* (a reddish- or darker-skinned mulatto), which were sometimes
used interchangeably in an attempt to name a difference that was always
relative, and thus never stable or fixed. *Moreno*, as we know, was used to

name both blacks and mulattoes. But it was also used to describe the darker among the mulattoes as well as the "darker" of whites, that is, those who would be considered the lightest of mulattoes.[81] In this sense, following the opposite tendency of the coloniality of power, the term *mulatto* has never been used to describe a specific color of skin. At "best" the term describes an epidermic range in color and the corresponding variable hindrance upon the subject's social *figura* that is imposed at every stage of any of the "racial" continua that respond to the Eurocentric perspective of knowledge. The condition in terms of the person's *genio* is no less terrible, as the mulatto is caught in an existential conundrum that is a coupling of two divergent tendencies within one and the same movement. Within the coloniality of power the mulatto can alternatively practice the movement of being-toward-the-black and being-toward-the-white while at the same time being neither. Back then, however, religious differences superseded protoracial ones, a reality that at least in principle tended to favor the *morenos* over other marginal groups.

In the two centuries that preceded the Columbian expeditions, blacks and mulattoes shared the streets of Seville with Jews, Muslims, Gypsies, foreigners, and of course Castilians. In fact, the oldest surviving religious brotherhood in Seville, the *cofradía* (confraternity) of Nuestra Señora de los Ángeles, dates to the last years of the fourteenth century and was exclusively composed of blacks from the time of its inception until well into the eighteenth century.[82] The brotherhood had originally been organized for the veneration of the Virgen de los Reyes, or Virgin of the Wise Men—the three sages who are said to have offered gifts to the Christ Child and who in Spanish are referred to as the Three Holy Kings, the Tres Santos Reyes or Reyes Magos. As Isidoro Moreno points out, the Virgen de los Reyes (Magos)[83] symbolized the Christian ideal of universal happiness by virtue of the fact that the figures of the kings that accompanied the image of the Virgin represented the stages of life (youth, adulthood, and old age) and the peoples of the three continents known to Christians at the time (the "yellow" people of Asia, the African "blacks," and the "white" Europeans).[84] The Virgen de los Reyes (Magos) was thus, as Moreno rightly points out, the direct iconographic antecedent of other such images of Mary as the symbolic depository of the ideal of social unity and racial peace. Well-known examples of these are the Virgin of Guadalupe (Mexico) and the Virgin of Charity of el Cobre (Cuba), images that were produced by the ideologues of the Church centuries later in the New World. But even before that, marking the origins and early development of the modern slave trade, the Sevillian Virgen de los Reyes (Magos) became the preferred image of worship of most of the black and mulatto brotherhoods of the Iberian Peninsula and of the New World.[85] The attributes of the Virgin were also symbolically conferred upon slaves, as was the case of the mulatto Baltasar de los Reyes, named after the *moreno* "king" of the Epiphany who, by the way, was worshiped in Seville as a *moro*.[86]

During the middle of the fifteenth century the Portuguese penetration into the Gulf of Guinea produced a significant intensification of the slave trade. The business was run from Lisbon, but Seville became the main Castilian depot for slave purchase and distribution. In the following century the slave traffic and the population of blacks and mulattoes in Seville grew considerably, as did the city's role as the purveyor of slave labor to the Spanish Empire. In fact, the rise and fall of Sevillian slavery coincides with the otherwise Golden Age of Spain. In 1565 about 7 percent of Seville's residents were slaves.[87] At the time there was also a significant population of free blacks and mulattoes in the city. Isidoro Moreno has estimated that, free or enslaved, the *morenos* comprised about 10 percent of Seville's population in mid-century.[88] By the end of the sixteenth century the blacks and mulattoes of Seville were not only many but highly visible. By then there was yet another black religious brotherhood and also a mulatto one. In the most important days of religious observance the three brotherhoods of *morenos* took to the streets, marching with their holy images and banners and sharing the streets of Seville with the many other brotherhoods of the city. On account of its seniority, and when allowed to by the authorities, the *cofradía* of Nuestra Señora de los Ángeles always marched in front, ahead of the brotherhoods formed by the well-to-do and the potentates. Descriptions of the day tell of how people would gather to wait for the procession of the black brothers so they could mock and insult them, throwing things at them and even, in some cases, poking them with needles. Christians or not, blacks and their descendants in sixteenth-century Spain were scorned as being naturally vicious and barbaric, prone to engage in criminal activity, and driven by passion and not by reason.[89] The *morenos* might have been the objects of mockery in the procession, but they were pious and their blood was pure, meaning that they were probably the only Sevillians who could claim to have no Muslim or Jewish ancestors. It was in such moments of public ridicule that the brothers of Nuestra Señora de los Ángeles responded to both insult and injury by calling their detractors Jews.[90]

Clearly, in the transition from moros to *morenos* that, as I have alluded, ushered in the period of European modernity and American coloniality, the old foes of the Christians and the new pariahs of Spain had come to occupy the contestatorial role in very different paradigms. Unlike the *moriscos* or the Jews, the blacks and mulattoes of Seville did not belong to a religious minority. Due to their equatorial origins, the blacks of Seville could not be accused of being Jews or Muslims, and the mulattoes were for the most part the children of blacks and Old Christians. In addition, unlike the Gypsies, Jews, and *moriscos,* they seem not to have had a strong sense of ethnic identity. Moreno points out that the Sevillian blacks of this time "did not have sufficient economic or social power to create fear or envy [among the whites], since they were for the most part slaves or belonged to the lower socio-economic strata of the population, nor did they have a strong sense of ethnic identity capable of contesting the dominant groups in society… because, in reality, the *blacks* were not an ethnic group."[91] Nevertheless, they seem to have kept to themselves, preferring or being forced into endogamous marriages in almost as high a proportion as the *moriscos:* three-quarters of blacks married other blacks.[92] In an age when purity of blood was established as a function of one's own distance from Jewish or Muslim ancestors, the black brothers of the *cofradía* of Nuestra Señora de los Ángeles were reminding the rest of the Christians in the city of their own ethnic, cultural, and religious *mulataje.* If having Jewish blood was incompatible with Spanishness, then what should be done with the pious blacks of Seville, who were the most sanguine example of uncontamination? What sort of claim to Spanishness did they have? Were not the insults and vituperations they suffered during the holy feasts—and no doubt throughout the rest of the year—a sign of the uneasiness that "white" Spaniards felt toward a group that, playing by the rules, had obtained a certain processional preeminence while remaining otherwise disenfranchised?

But the real contestation of the national ideal would not come from the blacks who seemed to have kept to themselves. As Cires Ordóñez, García Ballesteros, and Vílchez Vitienes have shown, endogamy sustained marginalization regardless of whether the members of couples were free or slaves. Blacks who kept to themselves, like the *moriscos* in the *morería,* were living at the end of history. After an initial boom in the slave trade that lasted into the early part of the seventeenth century, the presence of blacks in Seville diminished dramatically until it became statistically insignificant by mid-century.[93] It was the mulattoes, who demonstrated a 60 percent tendency to marry outside their group,[94] who would undermine the ideal of the Christian nation and of the Ideal Body. Capable of assuming or negotiating all markings and demarcations of identity, the mulatto body became the site that proved the futility of all demarcation, be it religious, national, political, or protoracial. After all, if the Virgen de los Reyes (Magos) could be all things to all people, why could not the mulattoes who worshiped her image strive for the same ideal? In 1561 Francisco de Cárdenas obtained a license to take a servant to the Indies. The man was described as being "a slave, mulatto, Spaniard, old Christian."[95] The mulatto thus became the embodiment of the metaphorical subject, the prankster of the imago, and the master manipulator of signs of identity.

Here again the differences between moros and *morenos* would be significant. When speaking of the mulatto we are no longer speaking of the conquest and reduction of a well-known religious Other. The mulatto would pose a greater danger than the moro ever had. First, because the mulatto could never be seen as an absolute Other. Second, because the mulatto was from the start—and to some degree has always remained— an absolutely unknown quantity. Finally, in the end, it was also a simple matter of numbers. In an age of terrible human devastation on both sides of the Atlantic, the mulatto simply became the best adapted and the ultimate survivor: the mulatto was the first child of the modern age.

The arrival of the mulatto in early modernity was no cause for celebration. Between the romance of the Reconquest and the heroic spirit of the early imperial age, the birth of the mulatto was barely recorded. At the time Spanish slavery was still centered around the medieval fantasies of crusading knights in armor: while the state was chasing out the infidel Saracens, Spanish nobles, merchants, high-ranking clergy and military men, and even craftsmen were chasing Moorish women in the sort of idealized practice of terror that follows the vanquishing of an old adversary. Although the great majority of slaves sold in Seville were of West African origin, there were also, as we know, many Berbers and *moriscos* who were sold into bondage.[96] In fact, these were the most expensive among the human chattel, especially if female, because the purchase of Muslim women represented the fulfillment of the ultimate and most twisted desire expressed in the medieval romances of the Reconquista. Making the Berber woman his concubine by force, the Christian master could dream of his slave as the captive Mora who abandoned her people and her religion for the love of the chivalrous knight. Fulfilling this terror-filled desire for the Other, a movement that could be seen as the ultimate humiliation of the Moor, was rather costly, however, since a female Berber or Granadian slave would fetch almost twice as much as a black slave from Guinea.[97] In any case, slavery always implies the most oppressive form of sexual exploitation regardless of the religious or psychological pathology of the slave owner. In the transition from Mora to *morena* the romance of the captive Mora came to occupy a place in the mechanics and sexual politics of modern slavery, eventually contributing to the romantic image of the Spanish *mulata* (mulattress)—and to that of the "mulatto Belle" of the Usonian Antebellum South—as the object of all creole desire.

Romance of possession or not, the fact was that many more black women were sold in Seville than Berber ones and that these women produced mulatto slave children for their masters. Vicenta Cortés Alonso has found vivid examples of this practice in Palos de la Frontera, a town in Huelva that was tied to the Columbian enterprise and the slave trade. It was from Palos that Columbus sailed on his first voyage. But the town should be better known for what began to take place there once the admiral came back with news of land to settle on the other side of the Ocean sea. In fact, Palos de la Frontera seems to have become a human factory of sorts: during the second part of the sixteenth century 20 percent of births in Palos were by slave women, and out of ninety slaves in the records, eighty-five were female.[98] To cite only one example, a slave named Teresa gave her master six slave sons between 1570 and 1578![99] If the children were able to survive beyond infancy, they would add not only to the economic resources and social status of the slave owner but also to the mulatto population of the town and, in turn, to the population of nearby Seville, where many of the mulattoes would flock in search of work or passage to the Indies. Based on the record of one Sevillian parish, it is possible to point to what must have been the norm: 90 percent of all slave children were born out of wedlock, and the great majority of them were mulattoes, that is, the offspring of the masters and their black female servants.[100] Such was probably the case of the two Sevillian mulatto children of a black female slave who was the property of one Francisco de Orozco Villaseñor, a creole resident of Mexico City.[101] In 1559 Orozco Villaseñor was granted royal permission to take the three of them as personal servants to New Spain,[102] to which he returned from Seville accompanied by his wife, Leonisa García.

So it was that the mulatto, who was not thought of as a religious Other, was able to claim the right to be a descendant of Old Christians. Furthermore, by marrying outside of their group they also made it possible for their own children to escape slavery altogether. Here, for the first time, was a group that claimed no allegiance to itself. Far from being an ethnic or religious community of their own, the mulattoes of Seville were a group only insofar as they were all in a process of securing the promise of full integration into Sevillian society, a process that arguably would take a few generations to complete. Acceptance was always a relative matter for most mulattoes. Occupying the space between black and white, slave and free, meant that they were also exposed both to the possibility of being accepted as "part of the family," as Christians and good servants, and to the possibility of receiving the cruelest of punishments. Foremost amongst these was the *pringamiento,* the practice of pouring boiling lard over the genitals and the wounds resulting from a whipping.

Understandably, for the mulattoes, too, the New World was a land of promise, especially as the numbers of mulattoes in the islands began to rise considerably during the sixteenth century. Official records indicate that although there were specific prohibitions against transporting mulattoes and *loros* to the Indies, many mulattoes made it there and were in fact highly mobile, passing back and forth from Spain to the New World and traveling within the New World among Peru, Hispaniola, and Mexico. Catalina de Zayas, an unwed mulatto from the town of Ecija, the daughter of an Old Christian by the name of Juan de Zayas and a black woman by the name of Magdalena Hernández, was granted passage to Tierra Firme in 1561.[103] So was Rufina, also a single mulatto, the daughter of a white Spaniard and a black woman from Guinea.[104] There were countless others like them, unmarried single women for the most part, who were given passage mainly as domestic slaves and who went to the Indies to make up for the scarcity of Christian women, thereby reproducing in the New World the dynamics of the human factory already observed in Palos.[105] There were also many cases in which mulattoes who had been born in the Indies obtained licenses to move throughout the empire. There was Ana Martin, a mulatto from San Juan de Puerto Rico, who in 1598 obtained in Seville a license to go to Peru as the domestic slave of Juan Bautista Ortiz.[106] Three years later, Albino de Aureta, a mulatto from Santo Domingo, was granted a license to return to Santo Domingo as a settler.[107]

Meanwhile, parallel to the Sevillian model of domestic slavery that had produced the first mulattoes of the Atlantic world—a *mulataje* that was predominantly urban—there was the *mulataje* of the plantation and the counterplantation. In Hispaniola the increase in the importation of African slaves that followed the economic shift toward the early plantation system produced a new scenario. We know that by the middle of the sixteenth century there were two blacks for every white on the island. The number of licenses given in Seville for the importation of black and mulatto slaves to the Indies ranged anywhere from one to as many as fifty at a time.[108] The sudden increase in the slave population also meant that the blacks were predominantly *bozales*, or African-born slaves of recent capture, and thus people who were hardly socialized into Spanish society and for the most part completely ignorant of Christian practices. Far from pursuing a path of assimilation, these people often found that the most direct way to freedom was to fill the ranks of the runaways by fleeing to the mountains. There they came into contact with other renegades and began creating a culture that was far removed from the will to order of the national imperial project, a culture that Las Casas would define as *montaraz*, or wild.

This is not to say that the predominantly urban-based mulattoes in domestic service were all predisposed to assimilation and patient enough to "wait" generations for the fulfillment of the promise of "Spanishness," a promise that in any event would never be available to those born in the New World. At some point many among the urban mulattoes must have fled to the mountains or had close contact with the runaway communities, as evidenced by the devotion to the Virgen de los Reyes (Magos) in the rural communities of Puerto Rico to this day. This devotion must have been generalized through the Spanish Antilles, but as far as I have been able to tell, it has been maintained only in Puerto Rico, where Quintero Rivera has traced the adoption and subversion of the image of the Black King to "a world characterized by ethnic heterogeneity and amalgam," where it was important "to establish that a black could be Christian and could be a king; and that kings and Christians could be people of unknown origins."[109]

The early penal codes of Hispaniola that relate to slaves and runaways, the Ordenanzas of 1528 and 1533, furnish us with an indirect view of what must have been the very complex world of heterogeneity and amalgam that Quintero Rivera began to describe in his work. It is evident that from the start early runaway society was a space of reunion for moros (referred to in the laws as white slaves) and morenos. The very first article in the Ordenanzas of 1528 clearly makes this connection through the following provisions:

> That all black and white slaves who take leave from service to their masters by fleeing to the mountains shall be forced to return to said service within a period of fifteen days, and that if they should be brought back against their will thereafter, they shall be given one hundred lashes and an iron ring weighing twenty pounds placed on them for a period of one year; that for a second offense, after being absent for twenty days, a foot shall be cut off; and for a third offense, having been absent for fifteen days, they shall be put to death, excepting from such sentence those who come back voluntarily.[110]

The Ordenanzas of 1533 also allude to the connection between certain sectors of the urban population and the monte or runaway culture up in the mountains. Article 8 demonstrates official concern with those black and "Spaniard" residents in the colonial settlements who might aid and abet runaway black and Berber slaves, decreeing: "That no black man or woman shall dare uproot, or help uproot, or help free from prison, any black [or] Berber slave, under penalty of having the right foot cut off; for the same offense, if the accused should be a Spaniard, he shall be given one hundred lashes and forced to pay the owner for the slave."[111]

But the most problematic subject for the authorities at the time was the ladino, that is, the black, moreno, or Berber—whether slave or free—who was reasonably fluent in Spanish and knowledgeable of Christian ways. The ladino was the counterpart to the bozal in the official nomenclature of servility and submission to the European. In fact, the Ordenanzas of 1533 started by establishing a clear distinction between the two conditions,[112] emphasizing that the ladino was the most dangerous element of the two. Fear of this subject of questionable loyalties had moved the authorities to curtail the entry of ladinos de Castilla (ladinos from Castile, i.e., mainly from Seville) to the island since 1528, requiring that a certificate from a ladino's masters be signed by two witnesses who could testify to the ladino's character as not being a criminal, an evil person, or a trouble-maker.[113] It was as if somehow, in a way similar to that I have pointed out in the case of Gonzalo de Guerrero, the *ladinos de Castilla* brought to the Indies with them the politics of the Iberian frontier world. They were the new *tagarino* subjects, who came to be seen by the authorities as a contaminating factor that could ruin the process of reduction and Christianization of the Indians and of the *bozales.* The ladinos initially sent from Castile were well versed in the ways of the Old World and were as such well equipped to influence the metaphorical movement that gave rise to the culture of camouflage in the Indies. Because, unlike Guerrero and others belonging to the "vile casts," the ladinos were considered Old Christians, they came to pose a more insidious threat than the mestizos. They were harder to figure out and to dismiss. In this sense, the ladinos inaugurated the site that most effectively contested the European Ideal in the New World, a site that would soon be inherited by the mulattoes of the Indies.

All this was evident barely a century into the colonial experience in the New World when the king of Spain was forced to pay attention to a group of some forty Spanish-speaking mulattoes and close to five hundred Indians who held claim to a vast stretch of land in the province of Las Esmeraldas, a rich and strategic area on the north coast of Ecuador. Although they probably were the type of *moreno* that would later be called *sambo* or *lobo,* that is, the offspring of black and Indian, they were known as the mulattoes of the Esmeraldas, and their leader was Francisco de Arobe, a mulatto ladino who was referred to in official documents as the governor of the "warring mulattoes and Indians."[114] Arobe was indeed the leader of a *palenque* or *quilombo,* an independent community of Indians who had resisted Spanish rule and over the years welcomed *morenos* and other Indian runaways to their jungle enclaves. At the end of the sixteenth century, mindful of the wealth of the land and wary of it falling into the hands of the English—the privateer Richard Hawkins had been captured in the vicinity of the Esmeraldas in 1594— the Spaniards dispatched a royal emissary, a judge of the Audiencia of Quito by the name of Juan del Barrio de Sepúlveda, and a Mercedarian missionary named Diego de Torres to pacify and convert the rebels.[115] Apparently in 1597 Arobe's people accepted Christianity and agreed to lay down their arms. Two years later, Arobe was invited to Quito, whereupon, for the king's pleasure, his portrait was painted posing next to his son Pedro and another young man by the name of Domingo (Figure 14). Presently housed in the Museo de América in Madrid, this group portrait, known as the *Mulatos de Esmeraldas,* is the oldest existing signed and dated American painting. Its author was an Indian from Quito by the name of Andrés Sánchez Gallque.

The work is a masterful pictorial enunciation of social camouflage. Indeed, it is social camouflage as art. The men are all attired in a combination of dress and ornament that makes them the representative embodiment of the land and its people, as well as of the limits and possibilities of the colonial world in which they lived. The most striking features of the portrait are the gold adornments that pierce their faces. Like Guerrero, these mulattoes have been "tattooed." They had gone to live among the Esmeraldeño Indians and, in the process, had become Indians themselves. Different from Guerrero, however, the mulattoes of Esmeraldas were able to move back and forth between cultures, aptly avoiding the point of no return. In the painting each is wearing a buttoned shirt with *gorguera* and *puñetas,* the ruff and sleeves that were fashionable adornments in the attire of Spanish gentlemen at the time. Although they are men of the coast, as evidenced by the necklaces of seashells they wear, their shirts are covered with the *ruanas,* or ponchos, that were typical of the Andean highlands. On top of these they have rich and colorful cloaks of Chinese silk that give them the status of potentates and that, as references to trans-Pacific trade, imbue their persons with an air of universal projections and proportions.

In a detail that reminds us of the painting in the Hall of Kings in the Alhambra, the three mulattoes are holding their hats in their left hands as a gesture of deference and respect to the Spanish monarch while holding onto their spears with their right hands. These men were kings, too, and although it is possible to see, as William B. Taylor and Thomas B. F. Cummins propose, that "the three black gentlemen are trophies, stuffed and mounted on a wall of blue,"[116] it is perhaps more important to pay attention to the powerful gaze that is outwardly projected from the picture plane of this perspectival construction, a gaze that, once the painting was back in Spain, penetrated to the very center of imperial majesty. There is a triangulation of gazes in the painting, as Don Pedro and Don Domingo, standing behind Don Francisco, channel the energy of their gaze through him and out toward the Spanish king. In a way,

Figure 14. Andrés Sánchez Galque, *Mulatos de Esmeraldas*, 1599. Courtesy of Museo de América, Madrid.

this is a portrait that deactivates the mystery of the Habsburg representative order, as Don Francisco's gaze projects itself, with a certain amount of distrust but no apprehension, out of the picture plane, passing through the point where all lines of sight were supposed to converge: the vanishing point, whence all claims to universal rulership emanated. Don Francisco de Arobe looks out into that placeless site with the certainty of knowing that there is nobody—and no body—there. Following the movement of the metaphorical subject, this work by the hand of an Indian master contests all official demarcations and attempts to recruit every image to its service. These are the three Reyes (Magos) of the Esmeraldas, the Moors of the New World, and they are posing in all their metaphorical regalia, as *moreno* Indians, as Indian kings, as Spanish gentlemen, as African warriors, knowing full well that theirs is no Epiphany and that the King of the Jews—the ultimate ideological underpinning that sustained the coloniality of power—is nowhere to be found, especially not on the other side of the picture plane.

In this sense these mulattoes of the Esmeraldas carried on with the tradition of Iberian *mulataje,* clearly understanding that the European subject was not a mystery or a far-removed, even sublime, presence (or absence, as the case may be), but rather a human subject of flesh and bone occupying a space that was transitable and that these men were very capable of appropriating and redefining at will by commanding a metaphorical movement of transgression that defied all analogical practices of space. The defiance of the three Ecuatorian kings followed in the tradition of the challenge to the national imperial project as it was first organized in Hispaniola. In a sense, these men came to embody Las Casas's greatest fear.

CHAPTER THREE

Bartolomé de Las Casas at the End of Time; or, How the Indies Were Won and Lost

> It should be our duty to remember that we found this island very much full of people whom we killed and plucked from the face of the Earth and we have filled it with dogs and beasts, and by divine judgment, forcibly by force, these shall be harmful and troublesome to us.
>
> —Bartolomé de Las Casas, *Historia de las Indias* (1527–66)

Perhaps no early settler understood the perceived threat of *mulataje* better than Bartolomé de las Casas, whose truly visionary outlook on the destruction of the Indies emanated not necessarily from his condemnation of the genocide perpetrated against the natives of the land (a condition that was self-evident by the time he sat down to write about it) but from his sense as to the very dangerous direction the societies of the Indies could take if they moved away from Christianity and created a new kind of Granada in the Indies, which this time around would be ruled not by moros but by *morenos*. Las Casas's *Historia de las Indias* was never finished, and the parts he did write were censored by the Inquisition and remained unpublished until 1876. Therefore, few in his day heeded the cryptic warnings he put forth in the text. But as often happens in the case of great visionaries, or people like Las Casas who are able to distill a prediction out of the most careful observation of a particular situation, Las Casas's premonitions were to come true, especially concerning his call for the most decisive action against this perceived threat. Almost a century after the island of Haiti was claimed and settled by Christians, the Crown ordered the depopulation of large tracts of land, resulting in what is commonly remembered as the *devastaciones,* or the devastation of Hispaniola. It was to be the first major calculated genocide in the history of coloniality, and it was intended to stamp out an entire way of life that had grown beyond the confines of official imperial jurisdiction as an excrescence that threatened the very integrity and universal validity of those ideal geometries that sustained the myth of the well-formed European body. But the true value of Las Casas's thought lies in the fact that he was able to tap directly into the source of a nascent creole subjectivity, giving it a voice that we can now reconfirm in retrospect as having been the very essence of what later came to be— as it nearly was already in Las Casas—a full-blown discursive practice. Creole discourse would grow, practically oblivious to Las Casas's warnings yet following his premonitory words practically to the letter. Here is the story of one man's most terrible foreboding and of the world that followed in the wake of his predictions.

Bartolomé was born and raised in Seville by a family that was probably of *converso* (Jewish) lineage. He was eighteen years old when Granada fell to the Christian armies and twenty when his father, Pedro de las Casas, a merchant from Tarifa who accompanied Columbus on his second voyage, brought back from the Indies an Indian slave as a present to his son, then a student at the University of Salamanca. From that moment on, as the history of his life of sin and penitence would confirm, Bartolomé's world became quite complex. To be sure, he was a man of the times who believed in the "reconquest" of Jerusalem. For him there was no question as to who was the enemy of Christendom. The Indians could be redeemed from their state of ignorance, but nothing could be done against "the stubborn blindness of the Jews and the cruel infidelity of the Muslims who knowingly attack the Gospel."[1] However, he was also a Sevillian and, as such, he knew how to navigate through a world that was full of ambiguities and contradictions.

Young Bartolomé had to give his slave up to be repatriated in 1500. Two years later the former master went to visit the lands from whence his slave and companion had come. He arrived in Hispaniola with Nicolás de Ovando and participated as a soldier in the punitive expeditions against the Arawaks, for which services he was given a *repartimiento,* that is, land and Indian slaves to work for him. Twelve years later, in 1514, influenced by the preachings of the Dominican friars, Las Casas experienced his "first conversion." Echoing the words pronounced by Fray Antonio de Montesinos in his celebrated sermon of 30 November 1511, he wrote: "We have thrown so many innocent people into Hell, without instructing them in the faith and without administering the sacraments to them . . . that all we are doing and have done is contrary to the intentions of Christ and to the teachings on charity he left for us in his Gospel."[2] The decimation of the native population had gotten to him. Apparently having lived in close quarters with an Arawak for more than five years had long ago led him to accept the basic humanity of the Indians. Now, with the help of a good friend from Extremadura, Pedro de la Rentería, he was to travel back to Spain to speak to the king on behalf of the natives.

Rentería had come from Jamaica with a caravel full of cassava bread and pigs. With these Las Casas's trip was to be financed, and very symbolically so, since the pig was the meat of the Christian—Jews and Muslims were forbidden to eat pork—and cassava was the bread and staple of the Arawak diet. Made from the roots of the yucca plant, cassava was also related to the death and extinction of the native Arawaks. Unless burned and boiled, the juice of the yucca is highly poisonous. Once the Indians realized the inescapable consequences of their devastating oppression, entire villages would gather on a fateful night to hear the stories of their ancestors retold for one last time before drinking the raw juice of the yucca, thereby choosing death over slavery.

Back in Spain, Las Casas met King Ferdinand in Plasencia. He brought a new project to an old man who was still thinking of liberating Jerusalem. A year later, Ferdinand would be dead, buried as the self-appointed Christian King of Jerusalem. Las Casas, in turn, would be given the title of Procurador de los Indios, or universal protector of all the Indians, by Cardinal Cisneros. By this time the Indies had become a political battlefield primarily disputed between *conquistadores* and *predicadores*, that is, between bearers of the sword and the cross. Las Casas was the champion of the latter cause, and he envisioned a victory of faith through sheer numbers. He saw in every native of the Indies a potential Christian and in the conversion of the Indians a triumph of the Church over Islam and heresy that would lead to nothing short of the universal imposition of Christianity. From now on he would wage a crusade of conversion, gaining the enmity of most Spaniards in the New World and securing the support of the new emperor, Charles V, and of his Flemish counselors, all of whom were particularly ill disposed toward the *conquistadores*.

Las Casas's plans were truly heroic, including a proposal to disembark in the Gulf of Cumaná (present-day Venezuela) with fifty unarmed Castilian men wearing white tunics with red crosses painted on them in the fashion of the Spanish crusading Order of the Knights of Calatrava. They would set up villages where Spaniards and Indians would live together in harmony and love. Three years down the line, and every year thereafter, the settlements would send the king a tribute of fifteen thousand ducats. This proposal was accepted by the Habsburg court, and Las Casas was given 260 leagues of the Cumaná coastline on which to try out his utopia. That was less than the *procurador* was hoping for, since his real plan was to colonize a thousand leagues of coastline and eventually to extend the project from Santa Marta (present-day Colombia) to the South Seas, covering the entire coastline, from Venezuela across the isthmus, and all the way down to Chile. Las Casas was proposing a crusade the magnitude of which had never been imagined before, as he was in effect dreaming of conquering most of South America with a handful of well-meaning *predicadores.*

Needless to say, the project turned out to be a complete failure.[3] The crusaders Las Casas left behind in Cumaná while he reported to the Audiencia of Santo Domingo were massacred, requiring the assemblage of a punitive expedition that in turn led to the massacre of hundreds of Indians. As if that were not enough, two hundred Andalusian farmers he had brought from Seville and left in Puerto Rico as back-up decided to desert: they fled to the mountains, never to be seen again. Peaceful colonization and utopian societies based on Christian love had clearly proved unworkable.

At this point Las Casas experienced his "second conversion." Having failed in the religious conquest of Cumaná, he joined the Dominican Order as a friar in 1523. He wrote extensively thereafter. He also played a key role in the passing of the Nuevas Leyes (New Laws) of 1542, which were intended to—but never did—dismantle the *encomienda,* the system of labor exploitation that had supplanted the *repartimiento* and through which the *encomendero,* or lord of the *encomienda,* was "entrusted" with lands and people, originally for the term of two successive generations. In exchange for the free land and labor the *encomendero* was obligated to provide the Indians with a Christian upbringing. In 1544, having been named Bishop of Chiapas, Las Casas embarked on yet another voyage to the New World. Three years later, he was practically expelled from Mexico by the *encomenderos* and sent on his way back to Spain. At seventy-three, he was never to come back to the Indies. But he was to continue his fight in defense of her native peoples and of the principle of conversion through peaceful means, a precept he had carefully argued in 1537 in *Del único modo de atraer a todos los pueblos a la verdadera religión* (Of the only way to bring all peoples to the true religion) and defended even before in his *Apología*. He had always been preoccupied with what he saw as the "heretical" behavior of the Spanish conquistadors in the New World. Many years before in his *Apología*, he wrote: "War should not be used as a way of capturing the souls of the infidels or to uproot idolatry. . . . Military armies are the ones that the pseudo-prophet Mohammed called for, as he used to say that he acted through the terror of the sword."[4]

When Las Casas recovered from his failure in Cumaná, he began the most important project of his life. In 1527 he undertook to write the *Historia de las Indias,* an ambitious project in which he would eventually aim to cover the history of the first six decades of European conquest and colonization of the New World. He would write three copious volumes, encompassing the first three decades, before he died in 1566. The Dominican friar wrote of eight reasons that made him undertake such a monumental work, foremost among which was his intention that the *Historia* would contribute to the greater glory of God. His second reason was more telling; he said he would write "because of the common, spiritual and temporal, utility that this work may give this infinite number of people, that is if they are not first completely annihilated before this story is fully written."[5] Already an old man when he undertook the task, Las Casas thought it possible that he might outlive the native populations on whose behalf he was to write.

This was a terrifying thought to Las Casas, not just because of the horrible human catastrophe it would amount to, but also because once the people were gone his project of universal conversion would also be destroyed. In other words, as the native populations of the Caribbean were decimated by war, slavery, disease, self-obliteration, and exile, Las Casas came to fear the ultimate failure of his enterprise. He could really see the same disaster happening on a continental scale, as indeed, it almost did.[6]

This fear of Las Casas was further strengthened by what at one point he had come to propose as a short-term way to address the lack of laborers in the islands: the importation of thousands of African slaves. He had first argued for the enslavement of Africans in his *Apología,* where he had set forth six instances when the Church could dispose of infidels at will. The first instance was when Muslims occupied lands that had once been under Christian rule. Africa was one of these because, according to Las Casas, "At one time, all of her (peoples) worshipped Christ."[7] Thus Las Casas reasoned that the enslavement of Africans would be an act of Christian piety. Enslavement, it seemed, was a small price to pay for salvation. During the course of his life he would come to change his mind, not on account of the need to reclaim Africans for the Catholic religion but because of the perceived threat that the Africans posed to the stability of early colonial societies in the Indies. In the final days of his life this problem would come to deprive the Dominican friar of a clear conscience.

In a most intriguing moment, toward the end of his *Historia de las Indias* Las Casas organized his view of the New World around the image of a pest, an infestation, a plague of ants that had come to devour most of the crops on the islands of Hispaniola and San Juan (Puerto Rico). What Las Casas wrote about in chapters 125 through 130 of book 3 was the foundational moment of mulatto America. Antonio Benítez Rojo has already masterfully identified and explained this moment in terms of the history of the plantation.[8] He has also related this passage in Las Casas to a similar one in the work of the nineteenth-century Cuban historian José Antonio Saco and to certain discursive positions in creole nationalist thought. What I propose here is to do a close reading of that passage and of Benítez Rojo's reading of it, to include in the coupled origins of the Plantation and of creole discourse the politics of *mulataje* and the germ of the antinational that the formative moment seems to have carried from its inception.

The five chapters cited above are an important "intercalation"[9] in the last book of the *Historia.* The passages studied by Benítez Rojo belong to chapters 128 and 129 and were, in turn, inserted into the intercalation. Lewis Hanke refers to those two chapters—the ones that tell of the plague of ants that ravaged plantings in the islands of San Juan and Hispaniola—as part of the "abundant general information that has nothing to do with the Indians."[10] Indeed this passage conforms to the "disorder" that Hanke attributes to Las Casas's prose.[11] But it is also an important digression in a text that is at times nothing but a concatenation of the digressive. Indeed, the *Historia,* as the foundational text of Caribbean historiography, is also a foundational text of Caribbean thought, a treatise that moves through space in the manner of the metaphorical subject, changing place, time, context, and action with the shifting winds that blow between the islands and across the Ocean sea.

There was, however, a method to the madness of Las Casas. The chapters I will focus on hereafter—the insertion within the intercalation—are part of a larger narrative that, in turn, was intercalated into a brief moment in time. The account that comes to an end in chapter 129 begins in chapter 106, where Las Casas tells us of his dealings in Spain with Cardinal Cisneros and in the court of Charles V between the years of 1517 and 1518. In other words, the entire discussion in chapters 106 to 129—which deals with the events in the Indies, from the execution of Vasco Nuñez de Balboa in 1517 to the extermination of the Indians in Hispaniola and the introduction of African slaves—was inserted within Las Casas's account of his project to settle the Indies with European farmers, a project that was to fail utterly in Las Casas's time and that, to be precise, would have to wait for its implementation until the seventeenth century, when the English would begin the conquest and settlement of what would later come to be New England.

At the beginning of chapter 106, moving through the disorder that other critics see in his thought, Las Casas tells his readers that he is going to pause for a moment to *enhilar,* or "thread through," the history of the Indies in the year 1518, "while the king arrives and we wait for the Court to come together in Barcelona."[12] It cannot be overemphasized that here, for the first time, we have a narrator attempting to make sense of a story that is unfolding on two sides of the Atlantic, two narratives whose connections to each other and to other stories are complex beyond anything conceivable to that day. In this sense Las Casas represents the insertion of a certain perspective into the origins of modern thought that is truly transatlantic, where places at hand are in a constant play of superimpositions and events unfold as a complicated disgorging of concatenations. In a sense, Las Casas was the first one to discover the pleasures of the retrospective causality Lezama called the *sorpresa de los enlaces* (pleasure of the unsuspected connections), and his *revelment* in it is what may give the text the sense of chaos and disorder that has sometimes been ascribed to it.

In the time that it took Charles V to get to Barcelona Las Casas began to tell the story of the conquest of Mexico and related what amounted to the beginning of the end of the West Indies. The last part of the final sentence of chapter 124 and the first phrases of chapter 125 effectively make that vertiginous transition:

> ...and all in all we never saw in Cortés any intention to give restitution or to make amends, but rather he always triumphed by the blood and the toil of others.
>
> Chapter 125
>
> By this time important things were happening on the island of Hispaniola, one of them being that while the Indians were becoming extinct their Spanish masters kept working them in the same tortuous manner.....[13]

For las Casas, the end of the West Indies and the beginning of colonial Mexico were unhappily connected events revolving around the figure of Cortés. In turn, that fateful imago was a revisitation of the moment that had led to the destruction of the Arawak peoples who had inhabited the islands of San Juan (Borikén), Hispaniola (Haiti), Fernandina (Cuba), and Santiago (Jamaica). Cortés was not just the conqueror but also the *encomendero*.[14] As such, he was the one who triumphed on account of somebody else's blood and toil, and was thus the opposite of the farmer, who was the model of colonization that Las Casas favored. Ultimately Las Casas was predicting that the peoples of Mexico would suffer the same fate as had befallen the peoples of Hispaniola.

The subsequent chapters of Las Casas's *Historia* tell of the continuous reduction of all possibilities for peaceful coexistence between Europeans and Indians, describing in detail the last stand of the natives of Hispaniola. While trying to make sense of the consequences resulting from the introduction of African slaves, they also predict the imminent destruction of the project of Christianization in the islands. Making sense of this tumultuous world was not easy. Las Casas's attempt was based on his keen power of observation as a participant in most of the events narrated, aided by his prolific imagination and by his use of references to the Biblical plagues of Egypt as the organizing structure of his narration. He had witnessed and was able to relate the destruction of the native inhabitants with the end of the mining economy and the subsequent introduction of agriculture as the main economic activity.

He worried that this was not to be a farmer's colony but an economy based once again on slave labor. The aging friar reasoned that the introduction of African slaves that had followed the almost complete decimation of the Indian population in the islands would eventually result in the total destruction of the Indies as a site of Spanish colonization and of the project for the universal triumph of Christianity. As usual he was thinking on a large scale. The danger for Las Casas was the real possibility that, on account of the claim to the land of the obstinate and virulent *morenos,* the New World would never be morally whole or become the empire of faith he had once envisioned.

Guarocuya/Enriquillo/Don Enrique

Las Casas tells the story of Enriquillo, the last of the main caciques of the island of Hispaniola. He was probably known to his people by the name of Guarocuya and was the heir to the country of Baoruco, where his father, Magicatex, had ruled before being killed in the terrible massacre of 1503 perpetrated by Nicolás de Ovando and his army of seventy knights and three hundred foot soldiers. Guarocuya, then five years old, had been there and had been one of the few survivors on the day when Magicatex was burnt at the stake together with seventy-nine other caciques. The child was taken by the Franciscan friars, who, according to the *Historia,* raised him to be "well indoctrinated" in the Christian ways.[15] The Franciscans baptized the young Arawak noble as Enrique, but called him Enriquillo, or "little Henry." Like a Renaissance prince he was taught how to read and write, instructed in the art of horsemanship and fencing, and made to memorize all major prayers in Latin. In 1515, in the palace of the viceroy in Santo Domingo, he was married in a Christian ceremony to a mestizo woman by the name of Mencía who was one of the ladies in the service of María de Toledo, the daughter of the powerful Duke of Alba and wife to Diego Columbus. Mencía was Enriquillo's second cousin, the child of Don Hernando de Guevara and Princess Higuemota, the daughter of Queen Anacaona, who had been murdered by Ovando together with her nephew Magicatex and the other caciques.

By virtue of his Christian upbringing Enriquillo was a ladino Indian who had been thoroughly acculturated to the ways of the conquerors.[16] Esteban Mira Caballos states that Enriquillo's thinking process was conducted entirely in Spanish.[17] Throughout his life Enriquillo showed every sign of his intentions to model himself in accordance with the ideal of the virtuous gentleman and the pious man. Like his wife, Mencía, who had also been well indoctrinated, his aspirations were to live the life of the Spanish courtier and to be treated as a prince in the European sense. This was easy at first. Because of his noble origins Enriquillo enjoyed a privileged position in colonial society: he was in charge of providing the Indian laborers for a man by the name of Francisco de Valenzuela, whose *encomienda* was located in San Juan de la Maguana. By all accounts he did the job very well, treating the Indians in his gang with "force and severity."[18]

Enriquillo's troubles started with the death of his master and his passing to the ownership of his son, Andrés de Valenzuela. According to Las Casas, Andrés took from Enriquillo a breeding mare that was the Indian's most precious possession. At the time, in Hispaniola a mare was worth as much as about thirty Indians. Shortly thereafter, Valenzuela raped Mencía. Enriquillo was indignant and appealed to the authorities with much faith but to no avail. After being dismissed and then jailed for three days by Pedro de Badillo, then lieutenant governor of San Juan de la Maguana, he went to Santo Domingo and was given a document by the Audiencia that, as Las Casas admits, instead of protecting his interests caused him to receive the worst kind of abuse on the part of his master when he returned to the *encomienda*. Following this mistreatment and left without any recourse to appeal, Enriquillo rebelled and took to the mountains, where he was chased by Valenzuela. Soon the *encomendero* was captured by Enriquillo's men and set free by order of the cacique, who advised him not to return to the mountains and to be thankful for having been given his life back.

Thereafter Enriquillo's fame grew and the ranks of what came to be the first alternative community to the national imperial project swelled with volunteers, mostly runaway Indians and Africans from throughout the island, whom Enriquillo commanded using tactics learned from the Spaniards and wielding a sword of Toledan steel. This was the first guerrilla outfit in the New World, and it struck great fear among the Spaniards. Official reports to the king said, "They carry out many bad things, killing men and stealing from the properties of the Spaniards . . . and [the Spanish population of] the island is so frightened of them that they no longer venture out of the towns . . . because the Indians know so well the land and the mountains . . . and they can live for many days eating roots and other wild things they find around while the Spaniards must carry on their backs all of the food they will need for the duration of the campaign and they can never do any harm to them [the Indians]."[19]

Enriquillo set up a complicated system of farms and encampments. He posted lookouts in the fields and maintained spies in the colonial settlements. In order to avoid discovery he forbade his people to make smoke and ordered the cutting of the tongue of every domesticated rooster kept in his domain. Although the Crown declared war on Enriquillo on 19 October 1523, the pacification of what Joaquín Priego called the small republic of Bahoruco would not take place until 1534.[20]

What had happened? Clearly Las Casas narrated the last stand of the Indians of Hispaniola as an episode that need not have happened. He showed that Enriquillo was willing to submit and even when at war had refused to kill Christians unnecessarily or to stake any territorial claims beyond the inhospitable and rugged lands of the Bahoruco, limiting his actions to the most immediate defense of his sovereignty. In the Lascasian story, all Enriquillo wanted was to live as a good Christian. But the institution of the *encomienda* had turned the good work of the Franciscans around. To the friar, therefore, it seemed that the *encomenderos* were doing the work of the devil. Las Casas argued that Enriquillo, who was defending his natural rights,[21] was comparable to Pelayo, the legendary Visigoth king who resisted the initial Muslim invasion of the Iberian peninsula back in the eighth century. By default, in Las Casas's mind the *encomenderos* were betraying the work of evangelization. This is an important moment in the *Historia*—and in the history of coloniality; Las Casas proposes to his reader that in the Indies the Spaniards had symbolically turned into their worst enemy: the Moor who had come to take the land away from its rightful owners. It was as if somehow Saint James the Moor-slayer had fallen from his horse and were lying on his back, his arms outstretched like those of Caravaggio's Paul, blinded this time not by a divine light but by the tenebrous workings of humans. The history of Spain in the New World, as Las Casas saw it, had become fixed in a dangerous and awkward moment where the Spaniard saw himself as occupying the place of the infidel he had once pursued and vanquished, putting the entire work of evangelization in jeopardy. It now seemed as if the well-indoctrinated Indian was riding the apostle's horse, whereas the Moor-slayer had come to occupy the place of the Moor himself.

Las Casas believed that every Spaniard in Hispaniola was guilty and guilt-ridden. The *Historia* tells of how Ciguayo and Tamayo, two Indians who had separately risen up against the Spaniards following the example of Enriquillo but with only a handful of men each, had caused the greatest of fear in the three or four thousand Spaniards who lived on the island. Something must have definitely gone wrong for this to have happened to such valorous people as the Spaniards thought themselves to be. That thirty Indians could instill fear in three thousand Spaniards was seen by Las Casas as a sign from God, "who was giving us a signal of how he disapproved of our deeds and of how we shall suffer in the next life for having committed such great sins against God and against our fellow men, that is if our penitence in this world does not suffice."[22] The Spaniards in Hispaniola were reduced to hopelessness as Enriquillo's uprising continued. The world had been turned upside down, and it seemed that only divine intervention could set it straight again. To be sure, God intervened in the next episode of the story, sending two successive plagues to the island.

The First Plague: From Indians to *Indianos*

The first plague reportedly came from Castile. It was an epidemic of smallpox that, between 1518 and 1519, decimated the remainder of the Arawak populations in the *encomiendas*. Las Casas reasoned that this one was both God's way of liberating the Indians from their arduous and tortuous life and his way of punishing the Spanish oppressors so that they would realize their need for the Indians and also for him. Let us remember that Las Casas was condemning the *encomendero* for having ruined the possibility of the perfect *adoctrinamiento*, or indoctrination, of the Arawaks, such as that performed by the Franciscans in claiming the soul of Enriquillo for the greater glory of Christ. It is to be noted that Las Casas's Enriquillo takes to the mountains with rosary in hand, and there is never mention that he may have returned to the ancient gods of his people. Supposedly there was a church amid the runaway settlements of Enriquillo's Bahoruco, where even some of the *bohíos*, or native huts, were adorned with crosses. This is a strange moment; here Las Casas was trying to present to his Spanish reader, in the face of the Spanish turned moro, an image of the Indian turned into a sort of "defender of the faith." The good old Spanish monk, as Irving would have called him, was turning the tables, especially when he returned to the mythical moment in the construction of Spanish nationality by comparing Enriquillo to Pelayo. Undoubtedly, as if carrying the Zaharenian curse, this is a discourse of imperial decadence whereby the spirit that had once led the Spaniards to triumph over the Moors has passed to the victims of Spanish atrocities and threatened to undo all that had once been accomplished in the name of the faith, from Pelayo's Covadonga to the conquest of Granada and beyond.

The end was coming, but for whom? At this point Las Casas's project reaches a reductive moment of terror. In a way, he was making sense of the senseless destruction of an entire people. He was still a Spaniard, and a good Christian at that: the plague was good punishment for the sinner and a liberation for his victim. The corpses of the Arawaks were there just to teach the Spaniards a lesson.

More significant, with the Indians gone, the right of the king of Spain to rule over the Indies had been confirmed by default. This is an important moment in Las Casas; here the most ardent defense of native rights coincides in an uneasy relationship with the knowledge that the natives have been defeated, reduced, and effectively eradicated. In the passage where he revisited the origins of the Reconquest and plaits together the image of Pelayo and the figure of Enriquillo, he made a masterful defense of the natives' natural right to rule over the land. But the contradiction in the discourse of the Procurador de los Indios is a simple one: his is not a discourse of the absolute but rather a digression in the preterit. Although he seems to be most directly questioning Spain's right to rule the Indies, he is also arguing on behalf of the natural right of the Indians to rule themselves and their lands, a right that had implicitly been extinguished with them: "People who ignore the facts and the rights say that the king of Castile was the prince of this island and that to him they shall go to demand justice, and this opinion is false and mistaken; the reason being that the natural kings and lords of this island never recognized the king of Castile as being superior."[23]

The rulers of Haiti (Hispaniola) might very well never have recognized Spanish jurisdiction. It was simply imposed upon them by the oldest law in the books: the right of the strong over the weak. We will soon find out why Las Casas had the need to present such a double-edged argument on behalf of the Indians. But I should mention in passing that this moment in Las Casas has been confirmed and revisited time and again by later creole ideologues as they have come to face the Indian question, and as their own right to rule over the lands has been challenged. The Dominican Manuel de Jesús Galván's novel *Enriquillo,* which was published in 1882, is a case in point. In it Galván makes a passionate defense of the creole's right to rule, elevating Enriquillo to the status of national hero as a well-indoctrinated subject.[24] Galván, a creole who had defended the annexation of the Dominican Republic to Spain in 1861, was drawn to the figure of Enriquillo because, like the old ladino Indian, he too wanted to be accepted as an equal by the Europeans. In general, creole propagandists and thinkers in the Caribbean (and in Usonia) have taken the side of the Indian—against the black—once the Indian was no longer perceived as a threat. It was Las Casas who opened up the possibilities of this ambiguous and uneasy position toward the native in matters of hegemony and legitimacy. It could not have been otherwise, for if the king of Spain had no right to rule over the Indians, he had no right to appoint a Procurador de los Indios to speak on their behalf.

The first plague put an end to mining and to the economy of the exploitation of natural resources based on Indian slave labor. The colonists who remained in Hispaniola and San Juan were forced (by God, in Las Casas's view) to become farmers. But these were not the farmers that Las Casas had thought of bringing to Cumaná. These were the people who had abandoned their Christian ways, the people whose hands were stained with the blood of thousands of Indians. However, in the absence of other viable examples—remember that Las Casas was writing about all this long after his failed attempt to colonize the coast of Venezuela—these farmers would have to do. Las Casas tells of how the settlers began to plant *cassia fistula* (golden-shower tree)[25] with quite a lot of initial success. As Benítez Rojo points out, *cassia fistula* was "an interesting product for export."[26] It was used during these times in Europe as a purgative. Were the Christians-gone-astray of Hispaniola and San Juan purifying their souls as they were providing *cassia fistula* for Europeans to purge their bodies? After all, in Hispaniola *cassia fistula* was being planted in the fertile plains of the Vega Real, the same lands that had been the site of the Arawak holocaust.

According to Las Casas, the business of purgation was going very well. It was as if the islands where such unspeakable tragedies had occurred were being turned into a Purgatory on Earth, where the people were at work doing planting and farming, fending for themselves and not living by the sweat and blood of others. As we have seen, this was for Las Casas the only way that colonization could proceed on good

Christian terms. *Cassia fistula* was not only the crop that replaced mining and, as such, became the new model of economic enterprise, but also provided an image that speaks of contrition and repentance, and ultimately of salvation. The colonists were planting hope.[27]

In Las Casas's account an important change has occurred. In passing, and rather unceremoniously, Las Casas refers to the "people of this island, Spaniards, because one can no longer speak of Indians."[28] It is a remark as important for its brevity as for its colossal implications. Las Casas was of course aware of the importance of this moment, but—and this is curious—he seems not to have wanted his readers to linger on the point. But why? What happened to the Procurador de los Indios that made him give up with such haste and nonchalance the people he had vowed to defend? Why can we not speak of Indians anymore? One answer may be that if we linger in this interregnum between plagues for a while longer we will be moving through the story at a different speed than the one Las Casas wanted us to adopt. If we do, we will soon realize that there was more going on in this pivotal moment than what the monk wanted us to know. As I have noted, this moment announced the end of the West Indies as the center of Spanish operations and the beginning of Mexico as the seat of the future Viceroyalty of New Spain. Concurrently, agriculture replaced mining as the main economic activity in the islands. Furthermore, it was the moment when sovereignty was transferred from the Indians—those we have been told shall never again be spoken of—to the Europeans. With the Indians gone, the Spaniards had to fend for themselves. This was precisely the moment Las Casas celebrated, the moment when the Spaniard finally adapted to the geography and climate of the colony, when the soldier gave way to the farmer and the European gave way to the creole—that is, to the European from the Indies, or the *indiano*, properly speaking.[29] In that brief interval between plagues Las Casas set up a new order in his narration; he staged a masterful coup in the *Historia* through which the old friar came to place his hopes in the reconstitution of his once broken utopian dream. This was the moment when the defender of the Indians took the side of the *indianos*.

But Enriquillo and his people were still holding onto their "reconquered" lands in rampant contestation of Spanish authority. Las Casas himself told us repeatedly in the previous chapters that, God willing, he would concern himself with the remainder of Enriquillo's story in his next book. But this was a book he died before beginning to write. If the Indians were still around, why was Las Casas in such a hurry to dismiss them from all historical protagonism? Could it be that, just as in the Iberian case, the people who fought to "reconquer" the lands were not the same ones who lost them? I think that Las Casas saw Enriquillo for what he was, that is, for a well-indoctrinated Christian. The record indicates that he was no longer an Indian in the sense that he laid claim not to the land but rather to an ideal of Renaissance humanism he wished to emulate. It could be argued that Enriquillo saw the writing on the wall and that he decided to make peace with a formidably superior enemy instead of facing complete annihilation. But he was too fast to make a deal and too willing to submit. Enriquillo sustained his uprising until 1534, when he secured the first paper treaty between Indians and Europeans in the New World in the form of a letter written to him by Charles V that he is said to have eagerly placed over his head as a sign of submission. Representationally speaking, once Enriquillo put Charles's letter over his head and accepted the superiority of the king of Castile, there were no more Indians left in Haiti.[30] When Enriquillo became Don Enrique, exchanging his kingdom for the lesser title of Spanish nobility that the *Don* conferred, he abdicated in favor of the Habsburg king. In fact, Don Enrique became the first native of the Indies to write back to the Spanish monarch in perfectly good Castilian penmanship confirming the terms of his surrender. He did so while being hosted in Santo Domingo during a celebration in his honor that lasted for twenty days. He was then treated not as an Indian king but as a Renaissance prince, and as such he was only too happy to write back thanking Charles for his generosity, thus recognizing the Christian king's authority and happily accepting vassalage in exchange for what he had always wanted, that is, the possibility of being accepted as a Spaniard by the Spaniards. In this sense, this Indian was already an *indiano* and an early precursor of creole subjectivity.

The treaty conferred certain privileges on Don Enrique and his people. In exchange for peace they would be given land whereon to build a settlement that, according to Dieve, was located near the town of Azua.[31] This would be a *pueblo de indios,* a village where the natives of the Indies would willingly come to enjoy the urban utopian dream of the well-indoctrinated ladino. But just like the first European settlement in the Indies, the fortress of La Navidad, Don Enrique's pueblo would meet a terrible end. In the treaty Enriquillo had agreed to become the official slave-catcher for Charles V in Hispaniola. His men would take up the task of pursuing all runaway Indians and blacks through the forests of the island, including some of their former comrades, returning them to the Spanish in exchange for four cotton shirts a head. The people of Enriquillo, like the Spanish roosters they kept, had gotten their tongues cut off. Through his actions in pursuit of the European ideal, Don Enrique showed that he would always remain the well-indoctrinated "little Henry," who confessed to Las Casas that during the long years of runaway life he had never eaten meat on the Sabbath and had always dutifully continued to pray the rosary in honor of the Immaculate Virgin.[32] In this sense Enriquillo came to occupy a site in opposition to that of Guerrero on the continuum of cultural *mestizaje.* If Guerrero would not return to the Spanish side, and the mulattoes of Esmeraldas would later prove to be able to make the most out of the political possibilities of metaphorical movement, Enriquillo was proving to be the prodigal son of the European ideal, the *ladino* enforcer of the coloniality of power. Far from being the leader of a small republic and a sort of Renaissance prince in the Indies, he was the first Indian leader who gladly accepted the enslavement of his people in exchange for being the recipient of the emperor's most gracious gaze. The Franciscans had done an excellent job.

Enriquillo would not live to see the ultimate fate of his people. He died a year after his "return" and was given a Christian burial in the church of Azua. A decade later, in 1547, his pueblo was ransacked and so thoroughly destroyed by a band of runaway slaves that today there is no trace that it ever existed. Apparently there were only about a dozen survivors, and they, in turn, were swallowed up by the forest as they went to hunt down the *morenos.* Just as the European gave way to the *indiano* with the disappearance of the Indian and the Indian claim to the land, the vanquishment of the Indian *(ladino)cimarrón* would now leave the *moreno* as the torchbearer of the tradition of resistance to imperial hegemony. The island was ready for a second plague.

The Second Plague—This One from Africa

The second plague spread quickly through the islands of Hispaniola and San Juan during the year 1521. Just as the penitent Spaniards of the New World "began to sow the fruits of their labor and their hopes started to be realized,"[33] a terrible infestation of black ants set the stage for what Benítez Rojo calls "Las Casas' chaotic fable."[34] From the beginning of his account of it, Las Casas makes it clear that he is still speaking of matters concerning the settlement and future population of the islands. Just as the smallpox epidemic resulted in the impossibility of speaking about Indians as such anymore, this second plague could have left the islands uninhabited altogether: "God sent a plague, mainly to this island [Hispaniola] and to the island of San Juan, that could have been feared to have left them completely uninhabited were it to have really grown."[35] He was alluding to the possibility of a second depopulation of the islands. The victims this time would be the Spaniards.

The next thing Las Casas tells us is that the bite of the ants was more painful than a bee sting and that it was practically impossible to sleep at night unless the legs of one's bed could be set in four jars of water so that the terrible pests could not climb up them. In this seemingly "chaotic fable," Las Casas is masterfully setting the stage for what is to come. Terribly deprived of sleep, the *indiano* is restless in what is perhaps a symptom of the recovery of consciousness—in the Christian sense of the guilty conscience—that must have accompanied the act of repentance Las Casas has described before in relation to the Spaniards' reaction to the decimation of the Indian population. At the same time, the combination of sleep deprivation and remorse puts the *indiano* into a trance that will ultimately yield an apocalyptic vision of the New World.

What was this vision about? The first thing that must be said is that these were not regular ants. Las Casas tells us that the ants in Hispaniola attacked the roots of plants, turning the trees black and drying them until they were dead. In that way they killed all the orange and pomegranate trees as well as all the *cassia fistula*. But ants do not eat the roots of trees, and the only antlike insects that eat wood are termites, or white ants, and even these eat only dead wood, and they are not black like the ants in Las Casas's vision. What, then, could Las Casas have been alluding to in this image of devastation? I will argue that it refers to the African and to the imminent threat, spiritual and material, that Las Casas foresaw in the practice of slavery and in what I call *mulataje*. Las Casas interpreted this plague as an omen of things to come. In fact, in his *Historia* there is a triumvirate of plagues, all of which can be seen as references to the same preoccupation. My initial suppositions are readily confirmed when, at the end of the story of the second plague, Las Casas tries to give his reader an idea of what might have caused the plague: "The cause that gave rise to this infestation of ants, according to what some said and believed, was the introduction and planting of plantains."[36] Benítez Rojo has convincingly argued that this is a direct and clear reference to the introduction of African slaves to the Caribbean islands.[37] In addition to the direct textual references to the African threat, it should also be noted that two years before the plague of ants, during the Christmas season of 1521, the first major slave uprising in the Indies had taken place, resulting in a revolt that gathered strength as the self-emancipated blacks passed from one sugar mill to the next freeing slaves, looting and burning all properties along the way and killing Spaniards.

Now that we know the principal referents of these pests, can we not relate Las Casas's black ants to the termites that Cervantes mentioned in relation to the *moriscos*' detrimental influence on Spain? The connection is there, as the Africans had come to displace the Indians as the major threat to *indiano* and European interests in the New World. The overlap of these two images is no coincidence. Initial proof of the connection between the African slave and the moro or *morisco* is the fact that, as Las Casas relates, the ants attacked the orange groves and the pomegranate trees. This is yet another *sorpresa de los enlaces:* orange trees were invariably planted in the atriums of the Alandalusi mosques, and the pomegranate's fruit is none other than the one that in Spanish is called *granada* and that was then, as it is still, the symbol in Christian heraldic iconography of the city crowned by the Alhambra.

There is one more reason to think that the plague of ants should be seen as a manifestation in the New World of a common trope in the mechanics of nation building. In the middle of the terrible destruction the Franciscan friars of Concepción de la Vega came up with a solution in the form of a *piedra solimán,* a solid chunk of mercuric chloride weighing a few pounds by Las Casas's estimate. Mercuric chloride is a highly toxic poison, very irritating to the eyes and nose, and the sale of it to blacks and Indians in Hispaniola at the time was strictly forbidden.[38] But its Spanish name indicates a venom of a different sort. Solimán (Suleiman), also know as the Magnificent, was the Ottoman Sultan who ruled the areas of the eastern and southern Mediterranean from 1520 to 1566. He was the greatest enemy of Charles V of the Habsburgs and of Christianity during Las Casas's life, and he ruled precisely during the time that Las Casas was writing his *Historia* (1527–66), dying the same year as the Procurador de los Indios. The references are indirect, but it is undeniable that in presenting this second plague as the most virulent threat to the European during this second phase of colonization of the New World, Las Casas used allusions that pointed in the direction of the traditional enemy of Christianity.

In the previous chapter we saw how during this time the principal threats to the Christian state, and to Spanishness, came to be perceived as coming from an external or foreign agent, and hence how the Turk came to replace the moro as the antithesis of all things Spanish. The importation of African slaves represents the analogical revisitation of the foundational moment of Spanish nationality in the context of the Indies: as the Turk had become the principal threat to Spanish hegemony in the Mediterranean, the African came to replace the Indian in the principal contestatorial site to European subjectivity in America. The mulatto, as I will show, would later come to embody the internalization of this threat. Anyhow, could it have been a coincidence that the *piedra solimán* was placed by the Franciscans in Concepción de La Vega, the same settlement where the first sugar mills were established with African slave labor and, quite possibly, with *morisco* know-how as well?

The *piedra solimán* worked as a magnet once it was placed on the roof of a building in the monastery, an act that in itself was symbolic enough. Let us not forget that Concepción de la Vega was the principal settlement in the Cibao Valley, where Columbus's *entrada* of 1494 had led to the holocaust of Arawak civilization. In fact, the Franciscan monastery was raised over the graves of thousands of people, some of which have been opened in recent years by archeologists. Set on the side of a hill overlooking the Vega Real and a half-hour walk from the settlement of Concepción, this was in fact the first utopian community in the New World. The Gothic basilica and its adjoining cloister were made of good quarry stone, and in the first years of the colony, before the construction of the Cathedral of Santo Domingo, it was the most prominent symbol of Christian civilization in the Indies. The *piedra solimán* was thus placed at the symbolic heart of the religious enterprise, set aside from the fort of Concepción, the military settlement and site of the former gold-smelting operations. Placed atop the roof of the monastery, the *piedra solimán* was symbolically closer to Heaven than anything—or anyone— else Spanish in that land. Certainly, in an architectural sense it was the manmade point of reference farthest removed from the vast mortuary that lay just below the surface of the monastery grounds and the entire vast plain of the Cibao.

The black ants, Las Casas writes, came from as far away as half a league, climbing on the roof to taste the poison and die. In the end, "the top of the roof was as black as if it had been covered with charcoal dust."[39] Later Las Casas writes: "As soon as the religious men realized that the only thing the *solimán* was useful for was to bring garbage into the house, they agreed to take it down."[40] These two images are revealing. First, the black ants came into the monastery attracted by this strange substance that, as Benítez Rojo argues and I have shown, has the status of a major character in the story.[41] Soon they had infested the monastery, turning everything black. Second and more important is the domestic metaphor. The ants had come into the house and were littering the place with their presence. What Las Casas illustrates in this seemingly chaotic passage is a classic case of the cure's being worse than the disease. The *piedra solimán* worked as it was supposed to; it effectively killed the ants. But it also attracted them to the monastery, and although they had come to die in the place, they polluted, contaminated, and soiled the house, unacceptably invading and threatening the domestic space of the religious friars. Could this have been an allusion to the way in which African slavery led the to corruption of the European ideal through the process of *mulataje?*

Forgetting about the original need for the poison, the Spanish friars unanimously agreed to remove the stone and throw it away. Then:

> They [the friars] marveled at two things, and they were worthy of praise; one was the natural instinct and the strength given to sensible and insensible creatures such as these ants that felt, if it could be said in those terms, or at least that were guided by their instinct to the solimán from such a great distance; the other was that although the solimán, before it is milled, is as hard as alum, and perhaps harder, and almost like a stone, such a small and tiny little animal (like these ants that were so tiny), could bite into the solimán with such strength and end up diminishing it and reducing it to nothing.[42]

What attracted the ants to the *solimán,* and how could something so small have the capacity to consume such a strong entity? Behind these questions lie other preoccupations of Las Casas and a clear sense of vulnerability. We might never extricate the meaning of the *solimán* as a concrete, unified, or consistent image from among its many allusions.

But mechanically there are here two concerns that should be noted. The first is the uncontrollable attraction that brings the plague into the house from such considerable distances. The second is the paradox that such a small agent might consume a seemingly indestructible thing. Between the two images there is a sense of inevitable doom and a movement of corruption that leads to obliteration. The (African) ants had come to soil the house in this powerful metaphor of contamination. They had come from afar, attracted by a poison (slavery?), which for the time being seemed to be keeping them from causing the *(indiano)* depopulation of the island. But as more of them came, the poison was increasingly reduced. The solution would not hold for long. This would be the fear of the *indiano* on the plantation, the recurrent nightmare that the Cuban creole ideologue José Antonio Saco would conjure up three centuries later by arguing that the West Indies were dangerously on the verge of becoming black-ruled nations in the New World.[43] This was a critique of slavery based on fear and not on principle. More important, hidden in this obscure passage is a foundational moment of modern racial discursiveness. The friars may have wondered about two things that instilled fear in them, but they were already establishing the basis of the most devastating discourse of terror by pondering whether these ants were moved by sense or by instinct, a distinction that would first be used to justify slavery and later to judge the right of blacks and mulattoes to assume any degree of participation in the public sphere.

As in the case of the previous plague, only divine intervention could set things right, both in the context of the story and in its mechanical entanglement. The people of Santo Domingo decided to call upon Saint Saturnine, and through his intercession the plague was reduced and eventually eliminated. Here Saint Saturnine is a curious figure. In fact, this might be a reference not to the Christian saint but rather to the Roman god Saturn, who, after being expelled from the heavens by Jupiter, went to the Latium to teach men how to farm and work the soil, ushering in a period of peace and prosperity. Chances are that Bishop Geraldini, who in a letter to the pope called himself "a man from the Latium,"[44] had a hand in the selection of the saint/god. In any case, both names proceeded from the same Latin root, *sator,* meaning sower or planter, and reinforce the moral of the Lascasian story, that only farming by European settlers and evangelization can ultimately succeed in claiming the lands of the New World in the name of God and for the king of Spain.

In fact, the choice of saint might have been related to the *Saturna regna,* a symbol of hope and regeneration for the ancient Romans. In the *Eclogae* Vergil, whom Las Casas quoted throughout his text, announces the return of the Golden Age in the expression "redeunt Saturnia regna."[45] The worship of the god of planting would usher in, in any case, a Golden Age for Europe. But in the New World the image of Saint Saturnine was a bad omen, as it conjured up the terror of the Plantation.

The Golden Age would never come to the West Indies. Soon the islands would slip into the background of the Spanish enterprise in the New World as the center of colonial power in the Caribbean shifted from Santo Domingo to Mexico. In turn, a population of farmers and merchants would develop along the northern shores of Hispaniola. In time this economy was to be eradicated with fury and particular vengeance by the Spanish authorities.

Once the ants were gone, so was the *cassia fistula.* A new crop had to be found. It was then that the colonial government decided to subsidize the construction of sugar mills. The plantation had been set in motion. At this point in his story, Las Casas becomes one of its principal characters. He tells how, before the sugar factories were invented, he had acted on behalf of some *encomenderos* and already obtained permission from the king to introduce African slaves into the islands on the condition that upon their arrival the Indian slaves would be set free. Following his advice, the king decreed that four thousand slaves be imported into the islands. At this point Las Casas confesses his guilt and adds that he soon experienced remorse at the realization that he had caused the beginning of an enterprise that was to prove as detrimental to the Africans as it had to the Indians, and that the latter would never be freed or be able to live any better than before the slave trade had begun. Other permits were subsequently granted after the license he had secured, so he could report that more than thirty thousand slaves had been brought to Hispaniola and upward of one hundred thousand to the Indies altogether. Curiously, a few lines down Las Casas tells how the King of Spain built himself two palaces, one in Toledo and the other in Madrid, financed with the taxes levied on the slave trade. Thus the slaves taken to the Indies performed a similar role in the production of the imperial persona and of the proto-national symbols of the state as had the *moriscos,* who were taxed before being expelled from Spain so that Charles could build himself a palace in the Alhambra.

But the situation in the Indies differed greatly from the peninsular one. Las Casas tells us how before they were placed in the sugar factories Africans were thought to be strong and very healthy people: "In this island we thought that, unless they were hanged, blacks would not die since we never saw one of them die of disease."[46] Now things were different, Las Casas argued. On account of the conditions and treatment in the sugar mills, many of them died every day. Consequently, "In order to free themselves from captivity, whenever the opportunity presents itself, they escape to form bands and they rise up to kill and inflict cruelties upon the Spaniards, and for this reason the small towns of this island cannot feel safe, as this is another plague that has come upon her."[47] Here we have it: the Africans are yet another plague. Remember that the Indians were perceived as a diminishing threat, so much so that Las Casas felt free to discard the Indian element before telling the end of the story, that is, before telling how and when Enriquillo's rebellion came to an end. But let us also remember that even when he was in open contestation of Spanish rule, Enriquillo had been raised inside the Franciscan monastery. He was thus a known quantity: he understood and was understood by the Spaniard; he killed only in self-defense and was, more than anything, a conciliator, a good Christian in Las Casas's book. Not so the Africans: they were the plague that threatened the house of God, and also the villages of the island. They were an unknown quantity, and their need for revenge was absolute. Theirs was an imminent and mounting threat. The sense of desperation in Las Casas is clearly perceivable as he confirms that the small Spanish settlements were helpless against the bands of runaway slaves.

Far from Eden

The future of the West Indies could not have been bleaker. First threatened by the smallpox epidemic that killed the Indians, then by the ants that destroyed the crops and by the Africans that threatened to do away with the Spaniards, the island colonies were for Las Casas the setting of an American apocalypse. In his *Historia,* as soon as he concludes that the Africans are yet another plague Las Casas remembers to speak of the wild dogs that roam the countryside. At one point the image of the *perro cimarrón* becomes indistinguishable from that of the runaway slave: "And we cannot neglect to mention the other [plague] that came on top of the ones previously described, and it was the great number of dogs, so many that cannot be counted nor estimated, and the great damage they do and have done."[48]

There is a direct correlation between the Africans and the dogs, who in Las Casas's account share the forests and frontier lands of the West Indies. To begin with they are both *cimarrones,* or runaways. They are also connected by the fact that they represent the two principal solutions to the Indian problem, at the two ends of the question. During the conquest phase, the dogs were brought in to hunt down the Indians. Following the decimation of the Indians, the Africans were brought in to take their place as slaves on the plantations. Furthermore, the dogs and the Africans are connected on account of the fact that both quickly became acclimated to the country, and thrived by reducing its resources. Las Casas continues: "There were very many pigs in this island . . . and the woods were full of them so that every league there were marvelous, beautiful and plentiful herds, all of which have been destroyed by the dogs and, not satisfied with the pigs, they have also gone after the calves, mainly when these are newborn and cannot defend themselves; the damage they have done and continue to do is immense, and this is what we can expect from them in the future."[49]

I have said before that the pig was the food of the Christian. In this Lascasian fable we can go even further and state that the pig stands for the Christian. That is, if the African could be thought of as the wild dog, the European could be said to be the wild pig, whose great and thriving herds were threatened by the canine invasion. Once before Las Casas had assigned human attributes to animals. When he described the second plague, he wrote that the friars marveled that from such a far distance the ants "felt, if it could be said in those terms, or at least that their instinct would guide them to the solimán."[50] This time, in considering the havoc wreaked by the dogs on the populations of wild pigs, he ascribes human sentiment to them: "Not satisfied with the pigs, they have also gone after the calves."[51] In this coincidence between runaway dog and runaway slave was born the terrible image of the baby-killer who attacks the newborn calves like a strange sort of West Indian hyena. It would be revisited often in the history of the coloniality of power, most notably during the Haitian Revolution.

There is no question that Las Casas had a terrible feeling about the African presence in the Indies. He thought that, like the dogs, they were there to consume the resources that the *indianos,* following the deactivation of the Indian claim to the land, had come to think of as their own. There had been a moment of hope and redemption in the brief interregnum between the first and second plagues. As for the herds of wild pigs, it was a marvelous, happy and productive time for the Europeans turned *indianos*. But they had not found the way back to the Garden of Eden. Far from it. A terrible thing had happened there, resulting in the eradication of the original dwellers of the forest. The moment of hope had been turned into another curse. And so the *indianos* were, in Las Casas's view, stuck in the Indies, facing the memory of the genocide they had caused and suffering the curse placed on their descendants, condemned as they were from now on to share the land with the Africans who would forever hold a competing claim. Las Casas's final words are visionary, as they express the basic position the *indiano* occupied in his time and the creole still occupies to this day. They are both a warning and a call to arms: "It should be our duty to remember that we found this island very much full of people whom we killed and plucked from the face of the Earth and we have filled it with dogs and beasts, and by divine judgment, forcibly by force, these shall be harmful and troublesome to us."[52]

The *indiano* in Las Casas laments having killed the natives and having replaced them with "dogs and beasts." The Christian in him knew the price to be paid was eternal penitence. For the rest of time, "forcibly by force," the *indianos* would remain exposed to the "harmful and troublesome" realities they had brought upon themselves. Forcibly by force, too, they would need to rule if they were to prevail over the *morenos*.

Setting the Example

As the maroon communities grew the situation in the colonial enclaves became increasingly untenable. More than in the time of Enriquillo, settlers grew wary of venturing into the countryside unless accompanied by a military escort. The *negros cimarrones* were everywhere, and they were numbered in the thousands. Finally Las Casas's prophetic view of creole power came true, as Alonso de Cerrato, governor and president of the Real Audiencia of Santo Domingo, was ordered to eliminate the threat posed by the runaways. Cerrato was able to capture the principal leaders and to defeat most bands, but not without a great deal of torture and killing that terrorized the maroon communities. When he was done in 1546, Hispaniola had been pacified for the first time in half a century of Spanish rule. By then the geopolitics in the New World had changed significantly.

In 1543 the flota system was established. This was a system of armadas or armed naval convoys that was intended to fix and secure all trade routes between Spain and her overseas empire. In 1561 the precise routes were sanctioned and regulated by the king, and Santo Domingo—as well as all of the cities in the Antilles with the exception of Havana— was left out of the main circuits, its inhabitants officially left abandoned to their own resources as the interest of the imperial authorities shifted to the far wealthier lands of Mexico and Peru. In the Padrón general, the secret world map that confirmed the Habsburg claim to universal rulership, the West Indies lost all economic significance, retaining in a lopsided imbalance the strategic geopolitical importance that would shape the mental and physical structures of coloniality in this part of the world for centuries to come. The Antilles became the islands of the Mexican Archipelago, the first line of defense against the enemies of Spain, the guardians of the empire, and, as the city of Havana came to be known, the key to the Indies.

As a consequence sugar cultivation, which relied on heavy capital investments and guaranteed access to transatlantic transportation and markets, declined in favor of informal cattle raising. Left orphaned by the keepers of the Sevillian monopoly, the peoples of Hispaniola came to depend for their subsistence and profit on the practice of the *rescate*, or contraband economy, a dangerous but necessary means of livelihood that involved trading with the enemies of Spain, mainly the French, English, Portuguese, and, most important, Dutch merchants who came to the coast of the island evading Spanish patrols. In exchange for rawhide, the commodity that during the early modern age held the importance that today we might assign to plastics, the peoples of Hispaniola obtained European articles ranging from soap and tools to wine and weapons, as well as slaves and Bibles. Imagine the proportions of such an economy on an island that had some eighty-five harbors or good anchoring sites and that had been forced by the House of Trade in Seville to negotiate its livelihood exclusively and most impossibly only through the port of Santo Domingo.

By far the best harbors were on the northern coast, or *banda norte*, in the towns of Puerto Real—later to be resettled and renamed Bayahá— as well as Montecristi and Puerto Plata. Together with the settlements along the western coast, of which the most prominent was La Yaguana, these became the principal nuclei of most of the activity associated with the *rescate*. It was no coincidence that these were also the regions that were farthest away from the city of Santo Domingo. The same occurred on the other three islands of the Greater Antilles. In fact, it was during this period that the contraband economy began to create a common culture that linked together the peoples of the eastern regions of Cuba, the *banda norte* of Hispaniola, the western parts of Puerto Rico, and the northern coast of Jamaica, as these were the areas farthest away from Havana, Santo Domingo, San Juan, and Santiago de la Vega (present-day Spanish Town), respectively. This contraband economy established the geographic and cultural foundations of the mulatto world of the Caribbean.

The communities of farmers and cattlemen that grew up along the coastline of this extraofficial world began to reproduce socioracial spaces that established what Benítez Rojo calls a "marginal creole" society constituted around the hybrid types of the mestizo and the mulatto.[53] By all accounts it was a society that flourished as an alternative to the official imperial order of commercial and religious exclusivity, inhabiting a precarious geography that was wedged between a world of pirates at sea and maroons in the mountains. Contacts between the townspeople on the *banda norte* and these floating communities that surrounded them on land and sea were producing profound transformations. In a land that, as Fernández de Oviedo pointed out, came to be "the very image of Ethiopia,"[54] the relaxation of commercial and ideological controls also led to a parallel relaxation of socioracial mores, even though slavery was still practiced in the *banda norte,* where it was nevertheless not as intense as on the plantations in the hinterland of Santo Domingo.

From an official vantage point there were several reasons for alarm. First of all, most men involved in the cattle business were armed with butchering knives, machetes, and sometimes even firearms. Since 1533, for fear of a black uprising, it had been strictly forbidden "for any said blacks to carry offensive arms made of iron, wood, or of any other kind."[55] A second reason for alarm was that complaints were repeatedly being voiced in Santo Domingo that children born in the towns of the *banda norte* were being given Lutheran godparents on the day of their baptism. In the eyes of Spanish officials and clergy, the penetration and acceptance of Protestant beliefs was nothing short of treason.[56] A third reason was that business on the *banda norte* not only rivaled the official colonial economy of Santo Domingo and its vicinity but went against the intent of all repressive codes set up during the sixteenth century, as they were ever more clearly intended to keep the rising numbers of *morenos* politically disenfranchised and otherwise condemned to poverty. The Ordenanzas of 1544, especially the ones passed on 29 April, are clear on this point, as they were intended to relegate free blacks and mulattoes to a life of total privation of freedom and enterprise. Article 2 decrees:

> That no free blacks enter into business or contract, buy or sell, or take into their house other black men or women, under any circumstances. Neither should they feed or sell food to anyone, be it in their house or in any other place, and they shall not sell beverages or have taverns for selling wine. They shall not have in their home or [on their] person any offensive or defensive weapons. They are not allowed to set up shop or to enter into any other business or contract beyond the selling of firewood, water, and herbage, and they shall remain inside their huts under penalty of whippings and exile from this Island.[57]

All in all, the peoples of the *banda norte* seemed to have set up a loosely organized set of communities that were ethnically diverse, multilingual and multireligious, marginal and yet increasingly prosperous and disdainful of officialdom. In contrast to the unitary and encapsulated essence of the European ideal, these communities evolved following the aesthetics of the marvelously entangled and undifferentiated forms that I have identified in what I call the West Indian Gothic.

The wealth that could be created by exploiting with little effort the incredible number of beasts, or *monterías,* that had over the decades thrived and roamed wild through the dense forests of the island meant that for the first time in decades there was plenty for almost everyone to eat and most could make a living. Everyone, that is, except the residents and merchants of Santo Domingo, who came to see their profits wane and their meat supplies significantly reduced as the economic activity shifted away from the city and the sugar mills that surrounded it. The situation there worsened, especially after the attack by Francis Drake in 1586, when the English privateer burned down the city and many of the sugar mills.

Everywhere else people must have been reasonably optimistic, because the foreign traders seemed to have been willing to do business with just about anyone who was able to supply them with rawhide. Large cattle interests led by increasingly powerful *indianos* shared in the trade with communities of runaways. Compared to the famine and the plagues, to the terrible cruelty of the *encomienda* and the plantation, the economy of the *rescate* must have made sense to many. Even the Church found out that the work of God was more rewarding if carried out in the *banda norte*. The Dominicans alone had a church-monastery complex in the town of Puerto Plata that was founded by Las Casas and built partly of good quarry stone. In addition they had six very profitable plantations in the immediate vicinity of the town that had been bequeathed to them. The wealth produced through the contraband economy, together with the guilt produced by knowing that said riches came from an association of mutual convenience with Lutherans and heretics, resulted in sizable contributions to the Church. On the banda norte, soon people were able to bribe their way all the way into Heaven—or so they believed.

In more than one sense, the people of the *banda norte* were playing with fire. Throughout the last decades of the sixteenth century Seville and Santo Domingo sent judges to impose fines on the smugglers and their collaborators. Punitive expeditions were also prepared, and more than once the bishop of Santo Domingo threatened entire populations with eternal damnation. In 1573 the relocation of the northern coastal settlements was proposed for the first time as a way of stamping out the practice of the *rescate*. Six years later the town of Puerto Real and other smaller settlements were relocated to the new town of Bayahá in the hope of curtailing the illegal trade. The effort was made in vain. Fifteen years later, in 1594, at a major trial in Santo Domingo five prominent citizens of the *banda norte* were condemned to exile, two of them in perpetuity.[58]

Of course, the business of the *rescate* was in itself dangerous. For the most part traders were accountable to no one, and the difference between merchants and pirates was often purely cosmetic and dependent on the satisfaction of the visiting merchant. Coastal populations lived under the constant threat of pirate attacks, such as the one in 1600 that resulted in the almost complete destruction of Puerto Plata. Life in towns was not much safer. These were places where things and people tended to disappear rather easily. Such was the case with a silver trophy that Gaspar Gil, a resident of Perú, sent to his father in Seville. The old man never received it, and in 1544 he levied a formal claim before the House of Trade alleging that the captain of the ship that had been carrying his present and some other of his son's belongings had come ashore in La Yaguana, where he had died and, subsequently, all of his precious cargo had been seized.[59] There was also the story of the *San Gregorio,* a ship that was captured by pirates in the same locality. After looting the San Gregorio the pirates decided to "sell it back" to the captain.[60]

Notwithstanding the perils of doing business beyond the limits of imperial jurisdiction, the greatest fortunes amassed in Hispaniola during the sixteenth century were made on the *banda norte.* Major ranchers had between fifteen hundred and twenty-five hundred head of cattle to their name, whereas minor cattle herders had between one hundred and eight hundred. By the start of the seventeenth century Hernando Guerra, a cattle rancher from La Yaguana, complained of having lost part of his possessions to government reprisals, listing them as follows: one frigate, thirty-three hundred head of cattle, fifteen hundred pigs, six carts and thirty-two oxen, over two hundred horses, thirty chairs, four beds, eleven wooden chests, and two slaves.[61] Guerra was one of the many victims of what came to be known as the *devastaciones,* or devastation, a most drastic and systematic destruction of the towns and villages associated with the contraband economy.

In 1603 Philip III, who six years later was to order the final expulsion of the *moriscos* from Spain, signed a decree directing the president of the Audiencia of Santo Domingo, Governor and Captain General Antonio de Osorio, to destroy La Yaguana, Bayahá, and Puerto Plata and to relocate the population in the hinterland of Santo Domingo. In his zeal, and true to the spirit of the times, Osorio set out at the head of 150 soldiers from the Puerto Rico garrison and conducted a campaign of terror that resulted in the burning of the three towns, plus San Juan de la Maguana and Montecristi and other secondary settlements near Niebla, Santiago, and Azua.[62] By the time Osorio was done executing his orders in 1606, over twelve hundred people had been arrested and hundreds hanged, mostly blacks.[63] The *devastaciones* marked the first time in modern colonial experience that the possibility of profound and sustained economic development away from the plantation economy and mercantile exclusivism was squelched by the imperial authorities.

Those who resisted the imperial crackdown were organized, militant, and able to demonstrate a certain programmatic cohesion. As soon as the royal orders were made public, the most influential inhabitants of the affected towns came up with contingency plans. Those of Monte-cristi proposed to Osorio, among other things, that they be moved to a good place and given enough time to move their cattle and belongings; that the Crown pay for the building of a new church, all official buildings, and houses for the poor; that the people of the town be given back the right to elect their own mayors; that they be granted lands and tax exemptions; and that they be given five hundred slaves, to be paid for in eight years.[64] The demands of the cattle ranchers were completely ignored by the governor. Armed resistance followed. The people of the Guava Valley rose up against the Crown under the leadership of a mulatto by the name of Hernando Monitor, who was one of the principal cattle ranchers of Bayahá. He was captured and butchered by Osorio.

The immediate aftermath of the *devastaciones* was a succession of bubonic plague epidemics, which lasted until 1608 and drastically reduced the slave population. A century after the Christian invasion, the colonial experiments in Hispaniola had decimated the population of the island several times and forced the remainder of the inhabitants to retreat into a life of poverty in the towns or into a life of subsistence farming and official anonymity, of pure *cimarronaje*, in the mountains. Officially, there were only about six hundred people on the entire island by 1630, down from four hundred thousand in 1492 and seventeen thousand in the middle of the sixteenth century. The colonial experiment had consumed itself.

The Body and the City

With the destruction of Santo Domingo—hardly another term could be more appropriate to describe the first century of colonial enterprise in the island—the imperial presence in the Antilles was reduced to a handful of fortified enclaves. These became floating citadels of sorts, and they were more closely connected to each other as appendages to the flota than they were to the lands to which they were "moored." These poor and otherwise neglected little enclaves were sustained more in principle than in actuality by the Mexican treasury through an annual subsidy called the *situado*, and they came to be ruled by military governors under whose aegis the architecture of humanist utopia came to clash with the realities of humanist terror.

Nowhere was this movement better embodied than in the relationship between the settlement of San Cristóbal de La Habana and one of the forts that was built to defend it. The map of a young Havana in 1567 (Figure 15) depicts the harbor as a sort of natural womb. The portrayal of the trees, the hills, and the grasslands around the water's edge as a sort of soft biological tissue is reminiscent of similar techniques employed at the time by artist-dissectors to describe the insides of the human body and its anatomy.[65] In contrast to this tender landscape, the mouth of the bay is cordoned off with a thick chain, a sort of chastity belt that runs from the castle of La Punta to the Morro castle across a narrow channel that was the passageway into the womblike world of the inner harbor. Facing the Atlantic, the port was thus safely guarded against the attacks of the heretical Dutch, English, or French pirates. On the other side of the chain can be seen a small town developing rather randomly under the weight of a menacing structure. That structure was the castle of the Real Fuerza, the first major military construction built in the New World by the Spaniards. Its plan was based on the perfect geometries preferred by Renaissance military architects: the circle and the square that a few decades earlier had been placed at the service of the empire and the Ideal by Charles V in the design and construction of his imperial palace in Granada. The Real Fuerza was designed and built as a simple square building, with walls ten meters high and six meters thick, defended by a massive triangular bulwark on each of its four corners. The castle, in turn, was surrounded by a moat that, at least as depicted on the map, seems to have softened the imposition of such perfect—and thorny— geometries upon the landscape.

Clearly the building's design was an exercise in the application of proportion, regularity, and order. Its function might have been military, but its movement toward perfection and beyond utility is analogous to that of the Ideal Body and of the Ideal City and not altogether distant from the well-known projects of theorists like Filarete, whose fifteenth-century plan for the city of Sforzinda was also an architectural utopia based on Vitruvian models. These were the mechanics of humanism, seemingly benign and perfect but ultimately always imposing a regime of analogical conformity that attempted to make the body and the city surrender to the perfect geometry of the Ideal. As in the case of the palace of Charles V in Granada, the representational embodiment of the European Ideal in Havana was to be built by the victims of that

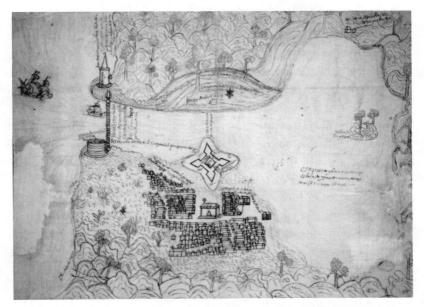

Figure 15. *Havana in 1567* (artist unknown). Courtesy of the Archivo General de Indias, Seville.

utopia and of that claim to universal rule that sustains the practices of humanist terror. All the blacks and mulattoes of Havana, irrespective of whether they were freemen or slaves, were requisitioned to work in the erection of the Real Fuerza.

Of course in the colonial settings the practice of utopia was relegated to the construction of the ideal fortification and not of the ideal society. The latter would be the project of the plantation as the "perfect" economy. On account of its location, Havana had become the port where all the galleons of the flota rendezvoused before departing for Europe carrying the treasures of Mexico, Peru, and the Orient. More than anything, the castle of the Real Fuerza, seat of the royal government and the main military structure in the islands, was the symbol of the flota, or perhaps even an image of the permanently anchored galleon floating inside its own moat. It was there to protect the galleon trade, the empire, and the European Ideal more than the city, a condition that is rather evident on the map, where the main public space of the town is submitted to the competing claims of the military and the Church. There is no ideal *civitas* (self-governing city) here; there is only a town ruled by violence and fear.

The structure of the Real Fuerza, which was depicted on the map as a sort of foreign object attached to the wall of this womblike bay, was in a tense relationship to the main public and ceremonial space of Havana, its western bulwark thrusting into the open end of the Plaza de Armas (Government Yard) opposite the church. The relationship between the city and its fort is an image of the irreconcilable tension between order and disorder. This structure of perfect Renaissance design, albeit modest in scale, dominated the city in an uneasy equilibrium between its claim to universality and the particular conditions of the settlement, which the map depicts as growing around it in a careful yet haphazard way. Like the European Ideal, the Real Fuerza was self-contained as if frozen in its perfection. By contrast, the town was bound to expand around it, a process that is ongoing to this day, as the Real Fuerza, the embodiment of utopia and of the European Ideal, remains an inassimilable accident around which this great cosmopolis of the mulatto world has grown. Strangely, the "umbilical" Vitruvian geometries of the castle are in sharp contrast to its "contraceptive" symbolism. The map of 1567 depicts Havana and its harbor as a representation of chastity, impenetrability, and captivity. But it also describes a difficult moment, perhaps of the permanently unborn and perhaps also of that which grows against all odds.

Related to this idea, and perhaps most important, is the fact that the dichotomy depicted in the sixteenth-century map also presents a corporeal image of the city wherein the castle of the Real Fuerza figures as the head of a body whose uncontrollable growth is described by the representation of the urban fabric in all its unchecked potential for contingent development. The buildings, packed tightly around the Plaza de Armas, were distributed along streets that were somewhat timidly organized in an orthogonal arrangement. But on the northeast side of town, the poorest neighborhood in the city is depicted as a loose cluster of small huts growing diagonally away from the orthogonal imperatives of the main plaza and already responding to the geometry of the Real Fuerza by running parallel to the northwest wall of the castle. There, between the castle and the sea, this peripheral neighborhood had adopted a more accommodating relationship to the Real Fuerza than the one described by the "thorn-in-the-side" arrangement between bulwark and plaza. This neighborhood may be seen as a buffer zone of sorts between the castle and the town. But I think it is more important to see it as a third element that was already negotiating its own relationship to both.

This peripheral space, which grew up around the castle while keeping a safe distance from it, was the originating site of the mulatto world in an urban colonial context. This was the sector of town where the marginal population lived. The inscription on the map reads: "These are [the] huts of the blacks."[66] It was there that the troops stationed in the city and the thousands of men who came once a year with the flota mingled with the local women and where the mulatto margin experienced its largest expansion. Indeed, this marginal mulatto sector can be seen to have been moving away from the church and from the plaza—the very center of the representative order of *indiano*-creole society—traveling toward the building that was the representational embodiment of the European Ideal. Curiously, this movement also implied an undoing of the analogical principle and of the ideal of the well-formed European body, because it was in that neighborhood that the Europeans became mulattoes, not just in the common and limiting senses of the coloniality of power, but in the very real spatial sense of folding—or being folded— into a movement of metaphorical subjectivity that was already leaving its imprint on the growing city.

Thus, if the institutional tension between the city and the castle was exemplified by the contest for dominance of the main plaza, the corporeal ambiguity and disconnection between head and body, between order and disorder in the colonial enclave, was both breached and exacerbated by the mulatto, a problematic social organism that had already come to represent and internalize all of the contradictions of colonial society, much in the same way that the people pictured in the *Mulatos de Esmeraldas* were able to adorn their bodies with as many accoutrements as they could bear. Here the constitutive elements of mulatto society are seen to have been present in the embryonic stage of what was always a city of two tales, a city where the Ideal was ideally victimized by the uncontrollable social outgrowth that was invariably submitted to the terror of humanist utopia.

CHAPTER FOUR

The Creole in His Labyrinth

The Disquieting Order of the Being Unbecoming

> To say it crudely for once, the Baroque spirit does not know what it
> wants.
>
> —Eugenio d'Ors y Rovira, *Lo barroco*

The colony of Hispaniola never recovered from the history of destruction and terror that culminated in the *devastaciones*. One hundred years after the start of colonization, practically everyone involved in the process had either died or fled the surviving settlements. Both the native and the slave populations were officially extinct, and the people who remained in Santo Domingo were for the most part indigent. It is said that when Governor Osorio's replacement arrived in the city in 1608, very few of its residents went to greet him because most people could not afford to dress up for the occasion. From then on, for the next two centuries, the colony would be subjected to a regime of official abandonment that came to characterize the general state of affairs throughout the Spanish Main, perhaps with the exception of the city of Havana.[1] This was the inconsolable scenario that Moreau de Saint-Méry was to encounter even when he visited Santo Domingo in the 1780s: "A capital city that is itself the picture of decadence, other very minor settlements here and there, some colonial operations that cannot be honored by referring to them as factories, large estates called *hatos*, where animals are raised without any care; that is all that can be found in this colony where Nature offers her bounty to men who are completely oblivious to her calling."[2]

The changing times soon brought about a change in the geopolitical nomenclature. In the seventeenth century the Antilles became known as the islands of the Mexican Archipelago, reflecting their dependence on the treasury of the Viceroyalty of New Spain and their role in the defense of the empire. For the next two hundred years Spain would lay claim to these islands solely on account of their strategic importance, dispatching forces as needed to defend the fortified citadels that secured the routes of the galleon fleets against the mounting threat posed by Dutch, French, and English marauders. The abandonment of the islands as sites of major colonial enterprise and their reduction in geopolitical terms to the strategic significance of small military enclaves was so dramatic in some cases that the islands of Hispaniola and San Juan came to be known by the names of their principal fortified citadels, that is, as Santo Domingo and Puerto Rico, respectively. In the process these outposts became veritable floating fortresses, better linked to each other as accouterments of the flota than to the islands to which they were moored. Residents of these military enclaves were reduced to a meager life punctuated by the invariant visits of the king's ship bringing the yearly subsidy, or *situado,* that sustained the colony. This generalized indigence was aggravated by the ever-present threat of enemy attacks. By the time the geopolitical changes noted earlier were recorded on P. Vincenzo Coronelli's map entitled *Archipelague du Mexique,* which was printed in Paris in 1688,[3] all of the Antilles with the exception of Cuba, Santo Domingo, Puerto Rico, and Trinidad had been captured by Spain's rivals, and only Saint Vincent remained in the possession of the Caribs. As a result, royal officials and clergy in the Spanish colonies hardly ever ventured beyond the outskirts of the towns that circumscribed their jurisdictions.

Beyond the colonial enclaves a frontier geography opened up to the enterprising ventures of Spain's rivals. More important, official neglect helped realize the common dream of the survivors of the first colonial enterprise of modern times. Having effectively been "left alone by the authorities,"[4] an economy based on subsistence agriculture, cattle raising, and contraband came to guarantee the livelihood of what Quintero Rivera calls a runaway peasantry that in the margins of empire created a culture of ethnic heterogeneity and amalgam.[5]

However, the virtual official abandonment of the islands did not put an end to the history of the colonial experiments that had led to their devastation. In more than one sense Mexico was to inherit not only the primacy of being the center of all imperial enterprise in North America but also the same "harmful and troublesome"[6] types of social agents that had first been seen in Hispaniola during the early formative years of coloniality in the sixteenth century. Over the next two centuries the curse that Las Casas saw descending on the *indianos* of Hispaniola would come to haunt the Mexican creoles who, in an attempt to control the production of socioracial difference, would establish a fluid and complicated hierarchy of differentiation called the *castas* system. By the middle of the eighteenth century, when the system reached its full level of development, there were sixteen possible categories for what R. Douglas Cope calls "the products of miscegenation,"[7] that is, for the offspring of any of the possible pairings of the "pure" types—Spanish, Indian, and black—and of their descendants as they, in turn, produced offspring that would become members of other *castas,* or socioracial castes.

In 1692 the *castas* rioted in Mexico City. It was an event that shook the very foundations of viceregal society, culminating in the burning down of the royal palace. A first-hand description of the events was written by a prominent member of Mexican creole society by the name of Carlos de Sigüenza y Góngora, an astronomer who, among other titles, was royal cosmographer to King Charles II and professor of mathematics at the Academia Mexicana. His account is a revisitation of Las Casas's fable of chaos, complete with a flood of the city, a solar eclipse, and a plague that destroyed the wheat crop.[8] "May God open our eyes!" Sigüenza wrote after having arrived at the realization that "we are to blame for the terrible carelessness with which we live among these many plebeians while at the same time pretending to be so formidable."[9] A few lines before he had described the character and composition of the commoners, mentioning together with the Indians, blacks, and poor Spaniards six of the so-called *castas* and describing this plebs as "being plebeian to such an extreme that it was reputably the most infamous of all plebs on account of being composed of Indians, native blacks, and *bozales* of different nations, *chinos* (mixtures of *lobo* and black or Indian), mulattos, *moriscos* (mixtures of Spanish and mulatto), mestizos, *zambaigos* (mixtures of *chino* and Indian), *lobos* (mixtures of black and Indian), and also Spaniards who, declaring themselves to be *zaramullos* (which is to say knavish, mischievous and thieves) and forsaking all their obligations, are the worst among such vile rabble."[10]

Sigüenza, whom Lezama called the "*señor barroco,*"[11] or the very personification of the Baroque spirit, was the first creole writer who as a modern (colonial) individual arrived at the realization, to use Maravall's description of the period, that "things were not going well."[12] Creole society in New Spain was facing formidable internal pressures from blacks, mulattoes, and Indians. Regrettably, Sigüenza recognized, "there no longer was a Cortés who could put them in their proper place."[13] Indeed, there was a sense among Sigüenza's creole contemporaries that Spain could no longer guarantee social peace and stability in her dominions and that, moreover, as was evident in the Antilles, she was increasingly unable to stop the pillaging of her empire by her European competitors. Sensing this vulnerability, Sigüenza chose the Lascasian path of asserting creole hegemony "forcibly by force," as is evident in the rage and contempt expressed in the passages quoted above.

More important, however, Carlos de Sigüenza y Góngora was the first American ideologue to take a step beyond the Lascasian legacy by attempting to endow the creole subject with an image of universal validity that would outshine the prevalent notion of the creole as inept and inferior to the European. Irving Leonard has synthesized what for the peninsular Spaniard came to be the principal claim to superiority over the creole subject: "This discrimination was, in part, a calculated policy of the Spanish crown which feared separatist tendencies in the overseas realms. . . . It rationalized this injustice by embracing the popular belief that the climate and environment of the New World had an enervating effect on children born of European parents there. These offspring, it was assumed, matured early in a sort of 'rotten ripe' fashion, and quickly entered upon physical and mental decline which, of course, clearly disqualified them for the heavy responsibilities of high office."[14] Sigüenza's attempt to undermine this image was, however, wholly unsuccessful, producing instead a sort of colonial morality tale that fell far short of the epic of a great and confident civilization. The work in question was published in Mexico City in 1690, two years before the riot. It is entitled *Infortunios de Alonso Ramírez*,[15] and it is a brief descriptive account of a young man's circumnavigation of the globe.

During the last quarter of the seventeenth century Alonso Ramírez, a boy from San Juan de Puerto Rico, traveled the world, going first from his native city to Mexico, continuing on to the Philippines, rounding the Cape of Good Hope, and, after reaching the coast of Brazil, making his way back to New Spain, where, fifteen years after his departure, he was shipwrecked on the coast of Yucatán. Eventually he made it back to Mexico City, telling such an interesting and sorrowful story that he got an audience with the viceroy himself. It was the viceroy who, sometime in the spring of 1690, arranged for Ramírez to meet Sigüenza, thinking that his story might contain some interesting information worth recording. Sigüenza was so fascinated by the account that he took down the entire testimony and published it, with some embellishments and commentaries, before the year was over.

Circumnavigation narratives had begun to appear after Magellan's voyage in the late 1520s and were by this time rather common. This one, however, was different in that Alonso Ramírez was not the typical protagonist of such heroic journeys, a point immediately apparent to the keen eye of the author-astronomer. Alonso Ramírez was a "Spaniard" from the Indies, and as such not so much a Spaniard as a creole.

By recording Ramírez's story Sigüenza gave us the first narrative to make a colonial subject from the New World the main character of what until then had been the exclusive epic genre of the "European global or planetary subject." I am here using Mary Louise Pratt's terminology, especially as she relates this global or planetary subject to the two "totalizing or planetary projects" of the Age of Navigation, that is, to the circumnavigation of the world and to the mapping of the world's coastlines.[16] At a time when the European Ideal was being promoted through literary means into an ideal of a totalizing subjectivity, increasingly relying on narrative protagonism over the earlier techniques of spatial representation, Sigüenza gave the world a new kind of narrative antihero. Taking the place of the European in the saga of circumnavigation—and in the ideological scaffolding of the coloniality of power—was taking a role that would prove disastrous for Alonso Ramírez. Instead of being a voyage of heroic proportions, a test of perseverance and of eventual triumph over Nature and adversity, Alonso Ramírez's voyage in the *Infortunios* was a long concatenation of misfortunes, a story that conspired against its own protagonist, frustrating all his attempts to secure happiness.[17] Perhaps this was the price to be paid for hijacking the role; perhaps the narrative structure of the epic of circumnavigation functioned exclusively in the service of a European subject. In the space that separated Magellan from Ramírez a new society had emerged from the Ocean sea, a society that in the trials of this young man from San Juan was going to experience the birth pains of its self-awareness.

In this sense, Ramírez's story was in contrapuntal tandem with that of William Dampier, an English hydrographer and pirate who circumnavigated the globe in a voyage from 1679 to 1691, paralleling and quite possibly also intersecting Ramírez's odyssey of 1675 to 1690. In contrast to Sigüenza's narrative, which is to this day practically still unknown to those outside the field of Mexican colonial literature, the account of Dampier's adventures received wide acclaim when it was first published under the title *A New Voyage Round the World* in 1697. Back then, the book served as a major source of inspiration for Jonathan Swift's *Gulliver's Travels* and Daniel Defoe's *Robinson Crusoe,* and today it is still touted by the English as one of the foremost "tales of maritime adventure and exploration produced by this country over the centuries."[18] Indeed, the importance of this work within the context of a national English literature is surpassed only by the role the work played in the construction of the English national imperial imaginary and in how the life of this self-professed buccaneer came to stand for and reveal the true nature and origins of modern empires. As Giles Milton has pointed out, "Clearly, Dampier's own mission was very much at one with that of his country," and "It is rare, in the modern explorer, to see so deep a conjunction between public and private aspirations."[19] This was a story that seemed to be seamless and transparent, as was the match between the perfect geometries and the well-formed human body in Vitruvius. "I write for my Countrymen,"[20] Dampier wrote in the preface, and we may add that his country and his countrymen were also written in him. Dampier came to be the very symbol of the English global and planetary subject.

A Question of Authority, a Problem of Legitimacy

Seen from an English perspective, Dampier's narrative can be described as a "charming book" of national epic proportions.[21] Critical observers beyond the English shores may conclude otherwise if they take into account that, in the tradition of Drake, Dampier's story may very well be the symbol of a national empire born of piracy. Either way, the truth is that *A New Voyage Round the World* is a hopscotch of a text described by Dampier himself as a "Mixed Relation of Places and Actions."[22] In addition, the credit for authorship does not rest solely in the buccaneer's hands, for he had the work "revised and corrected by friends."[23] Regardless, the nature and legitimacy of the work seems to be beyond question or reproach: the work is part of a national literary canon. The case is precisely opposite that of the *Infortunios,* a text that has hardly been read for its useful insights into the "spirit of the age" and that critics have preferred to discuss almost exclusively by questioning its discursive modality and authorial legitimacy. Sadly, while critics seem to have given Dampier a letter of marque to sail the seas freely in search of Englishness, they seem to be determined to keep Ramírez held up in customs indefinitely. Such is the misfortune suffered by the *Infortunios.*

The question that worries most of those who have previously studied the *Infortunios* is whether this text is a testimony of historical facticity or a novel written following the tradition of the Spanish *picaresca.*[24] To be sure, the *Infortunios* has elements of both while conforming to neither. It is thus more appropriate to see in this text an interplay between the *concierto* and the *desconcierto,* the order (hierarchical) and disorder (difference/excrescence/chaos) that were the two favorite ideological modalities of the Novohispanic Baroque. Conforming to Baroque aesthetics, this is also a text where act and form conquer and defeat each other endlessly,[25] and where metaphor is elevated to the category of the real.[26]

Such is the world that is confined to the cavernous interior of the Chapel of the Rosary in the Church of Santo Domingo in Puebla de los Ángeles (Figure 16), where the profusion of detail seems to attack every remnant of structural form to envelop it with its excrescence.[27] But the interior of the chapel is also a radiant and majestic moment of light, as the intricate *yesería* details are covered with gold and shine with the light that enters the chapel through some thirty windows. The Chapel of the Rosary is a luminous cave, a cavern where light itself comes to seek refuge. The symbolic and numerological possibilities of the rosary posed fascinating challenges for New World Baroque designers as they tried to produce an image of a hierarchical order that could govern the production of difference.[28] As I have pointed out before, the image of Mary was the favorite icon used during this period to promote social cohesion and racial peace.

One enters the chapel under a barrel vault that is divided by two transverse arches into three sections symbolizing the three theological virtues, by which one progresses toward God: Faith, Hope, and Charity. At the end of this progression we reach the transept. The dome above bears a representation of the Holy Spirit enshrined inside a golden sun. This is a mestizo combination of Christian and pre-Columbian symbols. Around the chapel the mysteries of the rosary and the life of Jesus and Mary are illustrated with countless figures and references to the scrip-

Figure 16. Chapel of the Rosary, Church of Santo Domingo, Puebla de los Ángeles. Photograph by the author.

tures. In the thick *yesería* skin that covers the walls everything seems to be in its proper place, but no single moment appears stable. The sense of gravity is overridden by the illusion of flow to such an extent that the body itself is forced to comply and to follow the movement through the walls and rise to the light in an experience that induces in the participant a certain sense of vertigo and decentering not unlike the one promoted in the Sala de las Dos Hermanas and the Sala de los Abencerrajes in the Alhambra.[29] This is architecture as a practice of space that seduces the body into surrendering to the rhythms of corporeal obsolescence, a principle that no doubt acquired added significance—as it acquired such exquisite architectural manifestation—in the world of the *castas*. If the sense of vertigo and decentering that one can experience in this architectural jewel is the most vivid testimony to the spirit of the age, the *Infortunios* is its most pronounced narrative exposition.

Sigüenza states in the dedication of his book to Don Gaspar de Sandoval Cerda y Mendoza, count of Galve and viceroy of New Spain, that the *Infortunios* is his account of Alonso Ramírez's "pitiful pilgrimage."[30] To this he acknowledges having added his own hydrographic and geographic observations.[31] Understood in this way, the *Infortunios* is an attempt to record the voyage of (self-)discovery that took Alonso Ramírez around the world, and as such it marks a curious appropriation on the part of the *indiano* subject of the descriptive modality of the age. Sigüenza, through Ramírez, also set out to map the world. But this was not a claim of imperial proportions so much as a careful exploration of colonial space. In the *Infortunios* Carlos de Sigüenza y Góngora takes us on a path of innumerable possible and impossible deviations within the core and beyond the limits of coloniality, painting a critical picture of the world of the Viceroyalty of New Spain, and of the *flota*, in the final years of the seventeenth century. In the process Sigüenza's vision proves as problematic as Ramírez's experience. His position is seldom fixed as he tries to keep the creole house—and Ramírez's ship—in order while moving through a seafaring world of shifting winds and treacherous currents, a world of pirates and of that most favorite Baroque trope, the *naufragio*, or shipwreck. In terms of memory and imagination the *Infortunios* is a fascinating pilgrimage, from the gest of the conquest against which the creole in Sigüenza measures himself to a world Sigüenza finds difficult to comprehend and control, a world that comes to be increasingly dominated by the exploits of the English pirates who seem to rule the seas in the name of a mercantile venture turned nation-state.

Jorge Fornet finds it difficult to place the *Infortunios* in a clear ideological category.[32] Perhaps the reason for this unreason, this *razón de la sinrazón,* lies in the fact that this work is a tentative and somewhat *desconcertado* attempt to address an entire catalogue of the "harmful and troublesome" realities that Las Casas had predicted would befall the *indiano.* It is a clear enunciation of the most fundamental characteristic of creole discourse: insecurity. In Sigüenza this discourse found an early spokesman, as he tried to speak on behalf of all other subjects of the empire, bringing order to the colonial cacophony. As the riot of 1692 would confirm, the reason for the lack of confidence in creole discursiveness was a fundamental crisis of legitimacy that besieged creoles from above (peninsular Spaniards) and below *(castas).*

Sigüenza knew this problem very well. His father, Carlos de Sigüenza y Benito, had come from Madrid in 1640 with the new viceroy, the Marquis of Villena. Carlos's mother was Dionisia Suárez de Figueroa y Góngora, a descendent of a well-known Sevillian family related to the famous poet Luis de Góngora. In fact, young Carlos decided to keep the poet's name in order to advertise his prestigious peninsular relations. Of course Sigüenza was a Mexican-born Spaniard and therefore always less than a "real" or ideal Spaniard. He also had experienced rejection when, as a young novice in Puebla, he had been expelled from the Jesuit seminary for having escaped one afternoon to spend a night in town. The incident occurred in 1667. After that his whole life was an exercise in repentance characterized by a desire, bordering on the pathological, to prove himself worthy of being readmitted to the order. To be sure, he became a highly regarded member of viceregal society, befriending the viceroy himself. But he was never truly recognized as he thought he deserved. Toward the end of the narrative, referring to the moment when he had met Ramírez, Sigüenza lists his names and titles, adding that "these are well sounding titles of little value, which are employed less for convenience than reputation."[33] As we can see, Sigüenza himself was a typical creole, spending his entire life in search of recognition, honor, and legitimacy at all costs.

In the testimony of Alonso Ramírez, Sigüenza thus found a most unique opportunity. Even the censors thought so when they approved the manuscript for publication on account of its unique nature, stating that "an unprecedented case is worth being recorded for posterity."[34] For a creole man of letters whose insatiable intellectual curiosity had to compensate for his lack of travel, the incredible account of an illiterate man who had sailed through the empire and beyond confirmed many suspicions. It could be argued that in many ways Ramírez helped open Sigüenza's eyes to the problems he addressed in the publication by pointing out Spain's inability to protect the periphery of her empire, repudiating the corruption that plagued the sphere of civil administration, and destroying the myth of the New World as a paradise or a land of opportunity, especially for, in Sigüenza's view, its most talented and deserving creole inhabitants.

The fact that in his unfortunate voyage Ramírez had fallen prey to the English, the archenemies of Spain, made the need to publicize the story all the more compelling. In other words, the story of Alonso Ramírez's pitiful pilgrimage gave Sigüenza an opportunity to sound the alarm by manifesting the disquieting apprehensions of the creoles vis-à-vis what they had begun to perceive as the internal and external threats to their socioracial status and their political position. Accordingly, in Sigüenza's text Ramírez encounters wealth and power, dignity, knowledge, and a civilization worth admiring only in Mexico City, the seat of the viceregal court and home to Sigüenza. Elsewhere this is seen as an empire where poverty and starvation seem to predominate, a collection of distant lands divided by vast bodies of water that more often than not seem controlled by pirates bearing the worst intentions toward the Spanish and their subjects. Furthermore, the peoples of New Spain are portrayed as a varied collection of types, including mongrels, whose interactions with the creole subject represented by Ramírez are problematic when not dysfunctional. At the same time, and because we are dealing with a set of preliminary and veiled complaints that are not yet demands of a mature political project, Sigüenza left no doubt as to the nobility of the viceroy and the sanctity of the Church: his work—and his life—would not have been possible otherwise. Moreover, in an act of unyielding loyalty, Sigüenza would go to great lengths to defend Spanish civilization against the Black Legend, condemning the English heretics as the most vile and inhuman people. Such was the position assumed by this colonial creole as he placed himself in medias res, between a will to power and the veneration of authority.

There is no uncertainty, however, when it came to taking command of the narrative authority. Indeed, in the *Infortunios* Sigüenza laid claims "forcibly by force" to the position of the subject whose testimony he recorded.[35] In the first sentence of this first-person narration, Sigüenza places himself as the narrative "I," thus eliminating both Ramírez's "interference" as the source of the story as well as his own inference as the chronicler of events: "I wish for the curious, who might read this for a few hours, to be entertained by the stories of the deadly trials I suffered for years."[36] Offering Ramírez's misfortunes to the reader as a comforting type of entertainment, Sigüenza simultaneously disposes of Ramírez's body while extending a veiled warning to those who might suspect foul play. Curiosity killed the cat—and almost killed Alonso Ramírez: enjoy the reading and learn the lesson. But in the face of such blatant exercise of narrative discretion and authority, Sigüenza will have a difficult time trying to make sense of many incidents in Ramírez's journey, which is, in part, why Aníbal González places the *Infortunios* "in a tradition of 'unspeakable' [*indecibles*] texts, of texts where the frequent claims to authorship and truth are placed in check by the writing itself."[37] Like the thief who sneaks in and carries off the loot in the dark of night, Sigüenza hardly knows what he has just placed inside his bag.

The game of complicity in this first sentence is as terrible as Alonso Ramírez's experience at the hands of English pirates. In one quick move the written story has hidden itself behind the verbal account, the author behind the narrator, and the narrator himself behind the main character. In political terms, the *señor criollo* has chosen to speak for the entire colony even when inconspicuously shielding himself from opinion and censorship by using poor Alonso Ramírez as a scapegoat. At the same time—and this is a foundational moment in creole discourse—the violent passion with which Sigüenza moved against Alonso Ramírez makes us suspect that, coupled with the desire to speak on behalf of the colonial populations, there was also a strong and urgent need on the part of this creole to occupy, if only by proxy, the place of the European in the saga of circumnavigation. Even when Alonso Ramírez's journey was to prove disastrous and self-defeating, an unbridled colonial instinct compelled Sigüenza to approach the European Ideal by taking charge and commandeering this eventual shipwreck "forcibly by force."

The manipulations do not end there. Let us remember that Sigüenza lived under the vigilant watch of the Inquisition and that among the literary modalities that were prohibited by the Holy Office in the New World were stories of fantastic proportions and, in general, most narrative accounts, particularly those in the form of novels. The ease with which the book was cleared for publication is a story unto itself. The censor, Francisco de Ayerra Santa María, was not only a very close friend of Sigüenza but also, like Ramírez, a native of San Juan.[38] Not surprisingly, as soon as Ayerra read the story he fell into the trap (or participated in the entrapment). Granting his approval for publication, the censor confessed: "In blind obedience of Your Lordship's decree ordering me to censure the story of the *Infortunios de Alonso Ramírez,* my compatriot, described by Don Carlos de Sigüenza y Góngora . . . and because of the delicious novelty of such a promising argument, I put myself to the task of reading the work and, if at first I went at it by obligation and curiosity, in time, because of its variety, order and structure, I came to regard my arduous task as a grace beyond estimation."[39]

In a curious turn, a narrative of certain inventiveness had managed to slip through the fingers of the censor by presenting itself as a simple *relación,* or account of the facts, surrounding Ramírez's tour around the world. The facts of utility concerning maritime and land routes through the empire, coupled with the story about a fellow *Sanjuanero,* or citizen of San Juan, that to Ayerra had a redeeming moral, compelled the censor to grant his approval. But there was more to it. This was not just an entertaining story, a *picaresca.* Further along in his declaration of approval Ayerra wrote, praising Sigüenza: ". . . and he was crowned with applause as he found the golden thread to that labyrinth of entanglement and subterfuge."[40] Sigüenza had not just accidentally found a way to avoid censorship. He had indeed circumvented the censors by showing them a world of which they had never dreamed, by presenting in this story of circumnavigation a comprehensive picture of the world that an American subject could understand and relate to as his own.

Here was a vision of empire from within the colony, a vision that with all its blind spots still managed to tie together the feelings and anxieties of the reading public in the world of the viceroyalty. Whereas for the previous two centuries, as Laura Benítez Grobet has pointed out, the aim of scholars had been to showcase América to Europe,[41] the *Infortunios* marked the first instance in which an American public generally accustomed to reading religious texts was being shown the world that lay beyond the colonial labyrinth. For Ayerra, the choice was easy. In a poetic exercise of political ventriloquism he pronounced a variation on the famous dictum that encapsulated the modus operandi of the colonial authorities: "acato pero no cumplo" (I obey but I do not enforce the law). Under this motto Spanish functionaries accepted their mandate, pledging obedience to the sovereign while choosing to disregard at will the implementation of laws and policies sent to them from Spain.

In fairness to the text, all we might be able to say about its character and category is that, as Lucrecio Pérez Blanco indicates, the *Infortunios* "navigates between eulogy and vituperation."[42] Alonso Ramírez's pitiful pilgrimage was a roundabout journey through a space of ever-shifting boundaries and uncontrollable destinies. Ultimately he failed to escape the condition he was born into. That is, even when he had traveled the world full circle, Ramírez was unable to forego the duties he was assigned at birth as a creole from San Juan, which, as I will show, entailed the unquestionable disposition to sacrifice himself for the preservation of the empire.

Of the *Patria,* or Fatherland

The story of Ramírez's journey begins in the city of San Juan de Puerto Rico. San Juan is mentioned in the account as Ramírez's *patria,* or fatherland, and the island of Puerto Rico as the marker of the boundary that divides the Gulf of Mexico from the Atlantic.[43] The origin of this epic voyage is thus a heavily fortified citadel or presidio, one of the most important defensive positions that were set up to defend Mexico, the Caribbean, and the flota itself from English, Dutch, and French pirates and privateers.[44] The map of San Juan in 1678 (Figure 17), by Luis Venegas Osorio, describes the settlement solely as a function of its military relevance. Except for its windward side, which is protected by a cliff and by the two massive castles of San Cristóbal and San Felipe del Morro, the entire precinct is surrounded by a heavy wall punctuated by massive bulwarks. There are a few ships, all hoisting Spanish colors, drawn as being safely anchored in the harbor. Inside the walls a blank space describes the area where the actual village is supposed to be. The only houses shown are the barracks locked within the Morro castle. It is as if the settlement itself had been swallowed up by the land, and there is an eerie presence of absence in this colonial outpost that, as Sigüenza describes it, floats at the edge of the Atlantic. The fact that the people of

Figure 17. Luis Venegas Osorio, *San Juan in 1678*. Courtesy of the Archivo General de Indias, Seville.

San Juan have been made irrelevant to the point of being erased from the picture can only mean that the walls and bulwarks of this citadel are not there to protect her inhabitants but rather to safeguard the routes of imperial commercial monopoly.[45]

There could be no doubt that the protection and defense of the imperial frontier was Ramírez's birthright, his burdensome duty as a child of the flota and as a native of the place we might call, to use a term from the *tagarino* world, *San Juan de la Frontera* (San Juan of the Border).[46] Thus the starting point of the story is both the colonial city and the frontier, a particular type of boundary that "separates the limits"[47] of two worlds and that must be defended, for it itself protects the entire armature of the colonial enterprise. Nothing could be further from the genesis of the standard epic. Alonso Ramírez was a native of a place that was the end not just of one world, but of two. He was, as we say in Spanish, caught *entre dos aguas*, trapped in the ebbs and flows of two bodies of water and of two complementary conditions: the impossibility to increase and the sentence to decrease.

Curiously, Puerto Rico was not just a marker between two bodies of water. Back then it was also an important source of water, an island oasis that figured as the first stop of the flota upon arriving in the New

World. Because of this, the image of the natural spring became one of the iconographic symbols of the city in a complicated interplay of overlapping imagery anchored around the figure of Saint John the Baptist and of the Agnus Dei, or the Lamb of God. In 1792, almost exactly a century after the publication of the *Infortunios,* this iconographic tradition would be masterfully expressed in a painting of Saint John the Baptist (Figure 18) by José Campeche y Jordán, a mulatto artist from San Juan. The painting was commissioned for the Regimiento Fijo, the main military detachment that manned the guns of the city's imposing fortifications. Thus the painting of Saint John is a symbolic tour de force intended to represent the city of San Juan and its inhabitants. Indeed Campeche's canvas could be considered the first flag of Puerto Rico. Of course it is a colonial standard, which explains why the purported character of the city's inhabitants is thus representatively embodied in the figure of the Baptist and in the Lamb of God, who is at once the personification of docility and submission and of the sacrificial victim.[48] But for now I am more interested in the representation of the island per se, in the miniature image of the lamb atop a rock that is framed under the crown of the escutcheon in the lower center section of the painting (Fgure 19).

There it is, San Juan de la Aguada (San Juan of the Watering Station), the rock from which a spring emanates to pour fresh water into the ocean. The source of the spring marks the spot where the city of San Juan would be located if this image were a representation of the island's northern coast. It is my contention that such is indeed the case. As the cartographic history of Puerto Rico demonstrates (look again at Figure 17), the European sailor always approached the island from the Atlantic side, that is, directly facing the northern windward coast, on which lies the capital city. According to this interpretation the fresh water falls on the European side of the boundary, on the Atlantic and not on the Mexican side of the waters separated by the "rock." Here, in this spring that does not irrigate the land from which it emanates, is the symbol of the perfect colony, of the land from which all wealth is extracted without any residual shortfalls. This is a moment that fits perfectly with the symbolic figure of the Baptist as the one who had to decrease so that Christ could increase.[49] San Juan de la Aguada is seen as guarding a font that, like the wound in Jesus' side at the moment of his sacrifice—when Jesus was fulfilling his role as the Agnus Dei—gives of itself so that others may drink and be saved.

Figure 18. José Campeche y Jordán, *Saint John the Baptist*, 1792. Courtesy of Museo de América, Madrid.

Figure 19. José Campeche y Jordán, detail from *Saint John the Baptist*, 1792.
Courtesy of Museo de América, Madrid.

Adding yet another layer to this representational armature, San Juan de la Frontera and San Juan de la Aguada is also San Juan del Cordero Alzado, that is, the city of the standing lamb. This image of Puerto Rico is rather unique as a moment in which the docile lamb stands up, that is, the moment when, paradoxically, docility rules. The standard representation of the Agnus Dei is as the lamb holding the flag of Saint John while lying on the book of the seven seals of the Apocalypse.[50] But the lamb of Campeche's miniature contradicts standard depictions and stands in complementary contrast to the main image of the work. Here, under the image of docility depicted above in the homoerotic figure of the puerile saint with the submissive lamb resting its head on his thigh and over his groin, San Juan del Cordero Alzado is an image of rampant disposition and heroism. This is the rock of militant docility, a scar on the surface of the seas on top of which the colonial subject stands ready to defend the imperial frontier.

This is the space Ramírez would have needed to occupy or face dire consequences, a place that, as in the iconography of the Baptist—and in the map of 1678—is described by a movement of decrease of the colonial subject in favor of the imperial master. As in the counterpointing between the principal image in Campeche's painting and the miniature in the escutcheon, this decrease is inversely proportional to the other's rise and, in the context of the rise of the European global or planetary subject, it could perhaps be described as a "being unbecoming" of the colonial. Could it be an accident that this escutcheon is also a bastard shield where the lamb is facing the sinister flank? As we will see, in his voyage around the world, which was also a terrible rite of passage from boyhood to manhood, Alonso Ramírez attempted to escape from the sentence to decrease and strove to promote himself beyond the circumstances of his birth, only to come back, after much disgrace, to the place he was originally meant to occupy, the place of his sacrifice to empire.

From the outset, young Alonso's fate was sealed. He should have known better: as a native of San Juan he should never have abandoned his post.[51] But this land of bounty and life for the foreigner was one of danger and wretchedness for its inhabitants. In a passage that reminds us of Las Casas, Sigüenza wrote that the gold that had originally given the island its name (Puerto Rico, or rich port)[52] could no longer be exploited for lack of sufficient Indian workers and that, previous to Ramírez's departure, a hurricane had destroyed the cacao plantations that were then the major source of wealth for the island's inhabitants. In essence, San Juan was living in the aftermath of the Lascasian plagues. In addition, it was also subjected to pirate attacks that made life in the fortified citadel one of almost unbearable duress. Against such threats this important boundary had to be protected. Sigüenza already spoke of the castle of San Felipe del Morro at the entrance to San Juan's harbor as the most prominent marker of the island's geography. Perched atop a hill, the castle rose above the city and stood apart from it.[53] No doubt an ominous sight to pirates and a beacon to Spaniards, to the people of San Juan the Morro signified both protection and containment and was the symbol of their difficult vocation to decrease. All in all, the walls of San Juan offered a sense of secure incarceration. This was the same miserable security that one of her inhabitants was soon going to exchange for a life of tormented freedom on the open seas.

In the Name of the Father and of the Fatherless

Ramírez was the son of an Andalusian ship carpenter, Lucas de Villanueva, and of a woman born in San Juan by the name of Ana Ramírez. As was customary then, Alonso learned the trade of marine woodworking from his father. In this the figure of Alonso was emblematic of all young men in the poor colonial outpost of San Juan. In 1670, five years before Alonso's departure from the island and twenty years before the publication of Sigüenza's account, a royal decree ordered that henceforth all young males in San Juan who did not have an occupation were to learn the trade of ship carpenter so as to better serve the needs of the flota.

Beyond his training as a carpenter, Alonso's emblematic figure underscores a larger preoccupation. Why did he inherit a trade and not a last name from his father? Why was he not called Alonso de Villanueva? This is never explained in the narrative. But, assuming that such a person did exist, the reason could have been that, like most able-bodied men of the time, Lucas had been in San Juan for just a short time while on his way to Mexico or Peru.[54] In fact, in 1626 a man by the name of Lucas Villanueva was authorized to return to Peru as the servant of Cristóbal Mejía de Osa.[55] If this was the same man who on a later voyage might have spent some time in San Juan, he would have been at least fifty years old at the time his son was born.

At any rate, the text of *Infortunios* insinuates that Alonso Ramírez did not really know his progenitor. His father was overheard stating that he was from Andalusia, but Alonso's character never says he actually heard his father speak: "Even though I do not know where he was born, I know for a fact that he was Andalusian because he was heard stating the same many times."[56] Perhaps Lucas de Villanueva abandoned the family when Alonso was an infant. If this was the case, Alonso's figure was twice emblematic, because at that time most children in San Juan were "fatherless." It follows, then, that Sigüenza might have knowingly participated in covering up Alonso's fatherlessness as an attempt to avoid mentioning the condition of illegitimacy that is the stigma imposed on all colonial subjects and that, back then, was manifest in the division between the native-born European and the rest of the population.

Identifying Villanueva as an Andalusian makes the character even more representative of what we know was the principal origin of peninsulars who came to the Caribbean. At the same time, it also makes us suspicious of the religious and ethnic background of the Villanuevas. In fact, theirs was the sort of last name that was commonly adopted by converts to Christianity. In 1545 one Francisco de Villanueva, a resident of Moguer, was denied a license to go to the Indies as a merchant under suspicion that he had lied to the authorities, trying to hide the fact that he was the son of a man who had been accused of heresy and burned at the stake by the Inquisition.[57]

It is also important to consider that the name of Alonso's father could have been Sigüenza's invention. As we will see when we hear of a character named Juan del Corcho, the writer also liked to come up with appropriate descriptive names for the subjects of his story. In this respect the name Lucas de Villanueva is revealing. In Spanish, *Lucas* is not just the name Luke, but also the word for *naipes,* or playing cards, and as such it is at least somewhat related to the telling of fortunes and to the taking of chances, or *albur.* The name Villanueva is also quite appropriate to this story of New World origins: it can be translated literally to mean New-town, or Newton. In addition, Villanueva was a typical name of what in medieval France were called *bastides,* or fortified royal towns, which were also planned and implemented by decree in Castile during the war against Islam, such as Villanueva del Duque or Villanueva del Rey, both in Cordoba. It is a thin thread, but in the name of Lucas de Villanueva we find an allusion to one who seeks fortunes in new lands and an augury of the fortunes and misfortunes that this boy of the "Villanueva de San Juan" was to encounter on his journey.

Whether his father was made up or not, the uncertainty about his paternity made Alonso Ramírez a bastard. And if Lucas was real, Alonso was possibly the bastard child of an Andalusian servant who could even have been of *morisco* origins.[58] In any event, the protagonist of the *Infortunios* is a most emblematic figure of a marginal creole living at the very edge of the colonial world. As such, young Alonso did what most boys in San Juan did as soon as they could manage. Having no name, and because the business of ship building was a difficult trade in this military outpost in the middle of the western Atlantic, he decided to emigrate: "Recognizing that there was no steady work or way to make a living, and even though I was just a boy, I decided to steal my body from my country and to go find better opportunities in foreign lands."[59] Ramírez decided to abandon his fatherland, or *patria,* in a moment that from the beginning was paradoxical. But what fatherland did he abandon if he did not have a father? In fact, was he not indeed launching himself after his father? It seems plausible to propose that the *patria* of

Alonso and of thousands like him during that time was not San Juan, Mexico, or Spain, but the flota itself. If anything, what they had was a motherland, or a *matria*.[60]

But let us not lose sight of the importance of this moment. The value of the *Infortunios* as a colonial critique lies precisely in the gap opened up by Alonso's act of stealing his body away from his fatherland. After all, Alonso abandoned his post. A viceregal reading of this text would confirm that all the trials he was to suffer were the fair consequence of having deserted his proper role and the duty to which he was born, which was to stay in San Juan and to guard that rock against the Dutch, the English, and the French. To be sure, this book was written neither as an act of direct contestation nor as an attempt at subverting the colonial paradigm. Yet at every point it shakes the foundations of the imperial armature by merely visiting and moving through its contradictions and by revealing its weak points. Even when Ramírez returns in the end to the "*patria*," his actions will have a critical value beyond his simple notions or even beyond Sigüenza's own intentions. His return was to prove less a reinstatement or an act of contrition than a sort of conditional certification of empire. Ramírez had seen too much, more than he could confess. His attempt to escape his colonial origins might have failed, but his actions—running through Sigüenza's filter—forever destabilized and deauthorized colonial rule in the Americas.

Escape

Alonso Ramírez's fate had been cast. He left San Juan at the age of twelve aboard a ship bound for San Juan de Ulúa (Veracruz) via Havana. The ship's captain went by the name of Juan del Corcho. Because *corcho* means cork, Sigüenza was in picaresque fashion trying to let us know from the beginning what this voyage was going to be about: "I must confess that, perhaps as an omen of things to come, I had my doubts as to whether anything good could come of this being that I set out in search of fortune [floating] on a cork."[61] As the representative embodiment of colonial subjectivity, Alonso Ramírez would be taking "our creole nation,"[62] as Sigüenza would call it, for a ride in the most unheroic and uncontrollable of ways. Like a cork, he would never sink, but he would always be at the mercy of currents and circumstances he could not control. In a way, he not only stole his body from his fatherland but took with him the colonial city of San Juan in his travels around the world. The sentinel had abandoned his post, but his post had not abandoned him. In his attempt to escape his unfortunate origins and in his search for riches and titles, he would always be claimed by his birthright, a curious reversal of sorts that could happen only in a narrative that, like the *Infortunios,* was an epic turned opera buffa.

Upon reaching San Juan de Ulúa, Alonso quickly abandoned his captain and walked all the way to Puebla, where he found employment as the assistant to a carpenter in a city that originally fascinated him just on account of its considerable size. But a bad job in a big city was not the opportunity he was looking for: "In the six months I lost there, I suffered more hunger than in Puerto Rico."[63] He therefore decided to go on to Mexico City, a place whose magnificence overwhelmed him. He spent a year there making a good living by working under an *alarife* of renown. Mexico was then an island in the middle of a lake. How fitting that the most important city in the world of the flota was also a floating city. But unlike San Juan, this was an island of greatness and opportunities, where "everything needed to spend a life without having to work for a living is in abundance."[64]

Alonso had found his dream of prosperity in Mexico City, a dream he had fashioned after the life of the hidalgo, the Spanish gentleman of lesser nobility who wore gloves for a living, thereby forsaking all manual labor. Realizing this dream was more easily said than done, and soon Alonso began to suspect that the cards might have been stacked against him: "I blame my dark star for having had to exercise my trade in order to make a living."[65] But he was determined to step from under the shadow of his dark star. Having heard that a relative of his mother was *regidor,* or alderman, of Oaxaca, he decided to abandon Mexico City in a rush.[66] Unfortunately, eighty leagues down the road Alonso Ramírez found out that this relative, Don Luis Ramírez wanted nothing to do with him and recognized no such relation. His father had not given him his surname, and now he had come to understand that not even on his mother's side of the family could he make a claim to Spanishness and to the benefits of a good and legitimate provenance.

Ramírez was now on the verge of joining the ranks of the *zaramullos,* the poor Spaniards whom Sigüenza would later describe as knavish, mischievous, and thieves on account of their close relations with the *castas.*

But that would have been the end of the story, at least insofar as Sigüenza was concerned. Having forsaken Mexico City with such confidence a few days before, he found himself unable to go back to it if he was to preserve his honor. Alonso, who had come to Oaxaca in the hope of not having to work ever again, was forced to employ himself with a trader who ventured through mountains and jungles to barter with the Indians. In contrast to the relatives that would not recognize him, Alonso found in his new employer, Juan López, a sort of father figure. He followed López with devotion until the trader's untimely death, whereupon Alonso realized that this type of relation was no relation at all. The heirs to López's fortune dismissed any claim he could have levied and treated him poorly, leaving him no other option but to return to Mexico City, broke and with wounded pride.

Once Ramírez was in Mexico, his luck seemed to turn around. He found stability and opportunity for social advancement by marrying the niece of the dean of Mexico City's cathedral. Almost immediately, however, all of his good fortune vanished when his wife died giving birth to their first child. It was as if a curse had been placed upon him. Confused, he left for Puebla as if retracing the steps that had brought him to New Spain. But once in Puebla his instincts were overridden by his memories of home, and he decided not to retreat farther. Ramírez took drastic measures: "I was desperate to be somebody, and finding myself both accused and convinced of my guilt of ineptitude in the court of my own conscience, I decided to condemn myself for such a crime, accepting the punishment given in Mexico to delinquents, which is to send them into exile in the Philippines."[67]

Begrudgingly, he had worked as a carpenter. He had tried the fast way of getting to the top by going to see an important relative. To no avail he had also tried his hand at commerce and had searched for the father he apparently never had by being loyal to a good man who ended up dying on him. He had married well, and just as he thought he had it made, all his hopes were dissolved with the death of his wife and child. Alonso Ramírez was convinced that there was something wrong with him and that somehow everything was his fault. He was a desperate man and was willing to do anything to change his fate. He must have thought that things could not get worse when he condemned himself to oblivion.

Freedom and Power in the South Seas

What had Ramírez just done? Had he not in fact accepted his condition of colonial servitude by judging himself a typical creole, guilty of ineptitude? Why did he perceive that the problem was in himself and not elsewhere? Had he really been born only to be a sentinel in San Juan? No, he could not go back the way he had come. But he hated himself, and because of this he would attempt to flee his condition through the most drastic manner, accelerating as fast as he could and heading as far as it was then possible to travel in an attempt to get out from under his dark star. Through this action, Ramírez was revisiting a movement that described the geography of the world of the flota. He shipped himself off to *el carajo*.

The Spanish *irse al carajo* is akin to the English expression *to go to Hell*. According to Camilo José Cela, the *carajo* is "a place far away, remote and obscure—and without a doubt undesirable—that the troublesome, the annoying, or the impertinent is sent to or thrown into."[68] To the men of the flota, to be sent off to the *carajo* was to be removed from the rest of the crew, cast aside from a world of outcasts, which the sailing communities of the day were.[69] The *carajo* was—and still is—a place of temporal punishment, not of eternal damnation. This makes sense, because it could be argued that the colonial subject, like Ramírez, was already damned by birth and thus could only be condemned or punished by being sent off to the ends of the Earth, where hunger, solitude, and certain death would be the only companions of the twice or thrice exiled, for the men of the sea who were then the veritable outcasts of nations. The expression *irse al carajo* is perhaps the most important souvenir of the world of the flota in the Spanish and Portuguese languages. To this day, its use links together the most varied lands and peoples throughout the globe, from Seville west to Manila.[70] In the Spanish-speaking Caribbean, *irse al carajo* is a complementary modality of escape to *irse al monte*, which is, as I have pointed out before, following Quintero Rivera, the constitutive movement of runaway tradition and culture. *Irse al monte* always carries the positive connotation of being a proactive choice, whereas *irse al carajo* tends to have a pejorative meaning insofar as it tends to be tied to an act of punishment or condemnation. In both cases, however, the action results in the disappearance of the subject from the world of officialdom, so it is a liberation of sorts.

Alonso Ramírez thus sent himself on his way to the *carajo*, throwing his body into the deepest of exiles in a last attempt to flee from his fate. He thought that perhaps in the farthest reaches of the empire he could turn his luck around. Certainly in that land of exiles and outcasts he would have a chance to become a Spaniard and to live the promise of empire. As it turned out, he was seriously mistaken, for the more he tried to escape, the more he would sink into the morass of his originary clay. In contrast, the project of European pirates was much simpler, as Dampier unaffectedly confessed: "Our Business was to pillage."[71]

In the Pacific there is an island world that mirrors the Caribbean and that has been tied to it ever since the galleon fleets were established. To this day, the history of the Philippines and Guam finds a parallel in the fortunes and misfortunes of the peoples of Cuba and Puerto Rico, their first cousins in the album of colonial relations. Alonso Ramírez was the first official colonial discoverer of that point where the East Indies meet the West Indies. In terms of colonial history, this was perhaps the most important moment of his journey. Ramírez crossed the Pacific from Acapulco to the Philippines to find the marker that to the sailors of the times signaled their arrival in the East Indies. Like San Juan de Puerto Rico, San Juan de Guam was a rock that occupied a boundary, the one that divided the Pacific Ocean from the Philippine Sea, and it marked the entrance to the East Indies from the Mexican side.

For Alonso Ramírez, his arrival in Guam and in the Philippines must have been a terrible experience of déjà vu. He loved it, though, on account of a new attitude he had decided to assume: "Disillusioned by the course of my voyage and seeing that I should never break outside my sphere when I knew others less deserving than myself had done so, I decided to put all perplexing thoughts out of my imagination for a few years."[72] Ramírez had suffered a *desengaño*, that typical existential modality of the Spanish Baroque that was a sort of fatalistic disillusionment and that, in this particular sense, must have been a rite of passage for all creoles, who at some point in their lives came to realize that they were not really Spaniards and that others less deserving rose above them simply on account of having been born in Europe. It just was not fair, Alonso lamented, that he was still caught up inside his sphere. It was a hopeless situation, and apparently his belief system had been thrown overboard somewhere in the middle of the Pacific, so that upon his arrival in Manila he was set to suspend all judgment for a few years. Having exiled his body to the Philippines, he was now also ready to cast away his mind. It worked. Manila was perfect for Ramírez. Somehow it must have seemed to him like a prosperous San Juan. He decided to stay and settle in Cavite, a small enclave in Manila's harbor that, like San Juan, was also a presidio located on an inlet and surrounded by walls.

How could Alonso have traveled to the opposite extreme of the globe, only to find himself at home? It was as if in his voyage from one border condition to another he was traveling in accordance with the whims of that most Baroque of forms, moving from the curve to the counter-curve, from one volute to another through that indescribable moment where the direction of a spiral movement is somehow reversed without affecting its integrity.[73]

There, on that other continent of islands halfway around the world, Alonso Ramírez managed to do well for himself for about five years. In this world of the other side—and of the countercurve—where the land and the sea had the same colors and smells as the landscape he had once known in his native Caribbean, Alonso Ramírez's fate enjoyed a happy reversal. Little did he know that it was there, in that other bound-ary land, that he would lay down his body as payment for having origi-nally dared to steal it away from his native land. For the time being, however, he was terribly contented: "I managed in this way not only to trade in a lucrative and promising business but also to see various cities and ports of India on my different trips."[74] He found profit, promise, and mobility, which were exactly the things his birth had denied him. Ramírez traveled the seas as a merchant and a sort of explorer of the colonial condition, visiting the entrepôts of all major European nations in the East Indies. He went from the Philippines to Madras (English since 1639) and from Macao (Portuguese since 1557) to Batavia (Djakarta), the capital of the Dutch East Indian empire and a city that impressed him more than any other:

> I was in Batavia, the most famous city they [the Dutch] have in Java and
> where the governor and captain general of the Dutch East Indies resides.
> Her walls, bulwarks and fortresses are admirable. There are countless
> numbers of ships of Malays, Celebesians, Siamese, Boogies, Chinese,

Armenians, French, English, Danish, Portuguese and Castilians. There
is in this emporium every single European artifact and every single
one that Asia sends to Europe in return. For those interested in their
purchase, excellent weapons are manufactured there. I really say it all
when I say that everything in the universe is there.[75]

Alonso Ramírez was at the height of his short-lived success. He had
abandoned his land, exiled his body, and cast off his mind. In return he
had acquired the life of the modern individual, a life of freedom, progress, and happiness. He might not have been concerned anymore with
titles and positions. He might not have been necessarily interested in
living without having to work—as long, that is, as work implied an adventure of certain financial interest. Batavia seduced him. The emporium was for him the perfect city: strong, bustling, thriving, and open
to the world. If Mexico City was the capital of colonial monopoly, Batavia
was the center of the mercantile universe. I cannot help but think that
this was also Sigüenza's opinion. The creole scholar was certainly levy-
ing a most pronounced critique against the closed system of trade and
wealth extraction that Spain had instituted in her colonies. As a creole,
Sigüenza was dangerously moving away from the august precedent of
the conquistador—the creole always looked back at that figure with devotion—and leaning dangerously toward the example of the mercantile
entrepreneur and the heretical privateer. This was the movement that
had caused the *devastaciones* just over half a century before. Now poor
Alonso Ramírez would have to pay the price for having such a sacrilegious vision.

Following the radiant description of Batavia there is an awkward
transition where Ramírez—and Sigüenza—tries to save face before the
censors: "More out of convenience than because it was what I chose, I
came to this line of work, but there were plenty of occasions when,
obeying those who could command me, I did the right thing; and it was
precisely one such occasion that caused the disgraces I suffer and which
began thus."[76]

After Ramírez has given us such a brilliant picture of Batavia we cannot think that he worked as a merchant out of convenience and that he
did not really like it. We can sense his irony when he states, through
Sigüenza—or is it vice versa?—that he ended up doing the right thing
by being always willing to recognize the authority of his Spanish supe-

riors. The definitive proof that Ramírez is not entirely sorry for having leaned toward the heretical Dutch and the alternative way represented by them is that he blames his misfortunes on having obeyed precisely such an order from his superiors in Cavite. In a curious reversal of creole politics, the narrator is saying, "Cumplo pero no acato," I enforce the law but I do not respect it. Alonso Ramírez would have to pay twice, once for his vision and once for his insubordination.

It turns out that, finally, after he was apparently well on his way to deserting the world of the flota altogether, Ramírez was appointed captain of a frigate that was sent in search of provisions for the presidio of Cavite. He was given seven firearms and two handfuls of shot, hardly enough munitions to defend the frigate and the twenty-five men who had been placed under his command and who, we are told, were all men of the sea.[77] Once they had supplied the ship in Ilocos and were on their way back to the presidio, Alonso Ramírez's frigate was fast outgunned, boarded, and easily captured by fifty well-armed English pirates on Tuesday, 4 March 1687. Ramírez not only had few munitions with which to defend his frigate, but he also mistook the pirate ships for two Spanish ones that were known to have been sailing the waters between Pangasinan and Cavite carrying "rice and other supplies"[78] for Manila. Thinking that those were the ships commanded by Captains Juan Bautista and Juan Carballo, Alonso Ramírez allowed them to sail in close proximity to his own "without any misgivings."[79] As it turned out, he should have been more careful, and he should have known that Spanish hegemony, even in waters so close to Manila, was but a memory of times past. In fact, Captains Bautista and Carballo had been captured eleven days before in the same waters by a group of English pirates on their way to Manila. Dampier was among them. In his book the English pirate wrote about that day with excitement and anticipation of the riches to be had in their next port of call: "The Master of this Prize was Boatswain of the Acapulco Ship which escaped us at Guam, and was now at Manila."[80]

Curiously, the Sanjuanero who had fled the disastrous condition of his fatherland—in part a result of the city's being subject to continuous attacks by pirates—had traveled halfway around the world to find himself captured by the same people who three times before had attacked his native San Juan. But more than an unfortunate coincidence, this was yet another episode that allowed Sigüenza to present the complaints of the creole elites of New Spain. To them it was becoming evident that Spain could not safeguard the sea routes and protect the periphery of the empire. As José Juan Arrom has pointed out, Ramírez's ill-equipped frigate was a symbol of the weak defenses of the entire Spanish empire and of the perils that much of its dominions suffered under the threat of being raided if not actually taken over by pirates and the mercantile companies of the nascent European nations.[81] Indeed Ramírez had arrived in the East Indies precisely at the time that scholars now identify as the era of piracy that followed the end of Spanish expansion and control of the East, a period between 1671 and 1720 when the most dangerous occupation in the South China Sea or the Bay of Bengal was to sail a merchant ship under Spanish colors.[82]

Ramírez's English captors laughed at him and his crew for being such easy prey. If for Sigüenza this was a way of implying the inability of Spain to protect her colonies, for Ramírez the fact that he had not been given sufficient arms or ammunition to defend his ship must have driven home the idea that his fate was of the utmost insignificance to the Crown. Ironically, just when he might have given up on the idea of being a Spaniard, to his English captors he became not just a Spaniard but the very embodiment of Spain as the captain of His Most Catholic Majesty's ship. Sadly for him, the only ones willing to recognize him as a Spaniard were the enemies of Spain, a people who, precisely because they were not Spanish, were in no position to confer on him the rights of Spanishness. In a most perverse way, Alonso Ramírez got what he asked for and, as a colonial antihero, perhaps also what he deserved. Finally, he was to be treated as a Spaniard, not through the conferral of titles and preferential treatment but through enslavement, abuse, and the most extreme degradation of his person. Ramírez and his crew were now slaves to 150 Englishmen under the command of Captain Bel (Bell?) and Captain Donkin (Duncan?).

The European Cannibal

From this point Sigüenza attempted to rescue the Spanish reputation from the Black Legend propagated as the first major coup of modern propaganda by the Dutch, the English, and the Jews of the Low Countries and northern Europe. He did do so by throwing the legend back upon the English, who are presented as truly inhuman. He gave us a hint of what was to come when, immediately upon boarding Donkin's ship, Alonso Ramírez described the vessel, pointing out that a foul odor came from the kitchen, where there were "pots filled with various ingredients of the most foul odors."[83]

Early in Ramírez's ordeal the pirates came upon the island of Con Son, off the coast of what is today Vietnam. There Ramírez was horrified at "the most shameless and infamous conduct I ever saw. Mothers brought their daughters and husbands took their wives, and they gave them to the English as things of beauty in exchange for a simple blanket or similar trinket."[84] The island of Con Son, or Puli Condore, was then a haven for English pirates, who came to this strategically located outcropping in the middle of the major shipping routes of the East Indies to careen their ships and indulge their bodies. The best-known visitor to Con Son was Dampier, who arrived there for the first time a week or so before Ramírez. He would later recall that the inhabitants of the island "are so free of their Women, that they would bring them aboard and offer them to us, and many of our Men hired them for a small Matter."[85]

As it turned out, Ramírez's captors spent four months in Con Son raping and stealing because, as Ramírez's character recalls, "they could not live without stealing."[86] Assuming that it took his captors the same number of days to sail from Manila to Con Son as it took Dampier— that time of the year the prevailing winds are northwesterly and thus favorable for sailing that route—Ramírez would have arrived in the pirate haven around 20 February 1687. This means that the two men were on the island from the end of March to the end of June. During this period Dampier was there twice, from 14 March to 21 April and from 24 May to 4 June. Thus the stays of Ramírez and Dampier in Con Son coincided for a total of forty-five days, give or take a day or two. Yet it is strange that neither text makes reference of this. This may not be surprising in the case of Alonso Ramírez's testimony, because he was a captive and as such confined to the boat. But Dampier had time to thoroughly explore the island. His book is filled with detailed descriptions of its flora and fauna, and he even drew a detailed map of the entire place. Added to this, there is only one safe anchoring point on the island, so if these men were there at the same time, as they must have been, their vessels were certainly anchored within view of each other.

Why would Dampier neglect to mention the presence of his fellow Englishmen at such a happy destination? His silence was eloquent. After describing the place in detail and telling of his experience with the

natives, Dampier ended the fourteenth chapter of his book with a statement aimed at putting all suspicions to rest: "There was nothing else of
Moment that happened while we stayed here."[87] Alonso Ramírez's testimony leads us to conclude otherwise, and, in that sense it is a most welcome critical contestation of the romantic myth that bombastically posits
the institutions of European nation-states as rising above obscurantism
and despotism and nurtures the image of the modern man of action as
a figure that acquires global or planetary relevance through the application of scientific principles and the exercise of reason.

Before leaving, Ramírez's English captors decided to set fire to the
native village and to kill everyone they could get their hands on. Sigüenza
makes a point of stressing that they were murdering their own unborn
children together with the rest of the inhabitants of the village. Here his
chastising of the English hides behind a denunciation of major proportions. In a sense he is saying that the English—like Irving's Columbus a
century and a half later—would have nothing to do with the castas and
the racial hybrids. In this case they preferred to commit genocide rather
than accepting responsibility for what they would deem the production
of mongrels.

Returning to the ship from the mayhem, the English pirates brought
with them a human arm that had been burnt in the fire: "Every one of
them cut a small piece for themselves, and praising the taste of such
good meat, they cheered as they ate. I was scandalized and saddened by
such bestiality, when one of them came up to me with a morsel and told
me rather forcefully to eat it. When I refused he told me that since I was
a Spaniard and therefore a coward, I would do well in having some and
not being so finicky, thereby being as brave as they were."[88] Though the
term cannibal was not used by Sigüenza, he nevertheless accused the
English of eating other human beings. As Peter Hulme has argued, cannibal has the same origin as Carib, and it is related to the idea of the native who resists European domination. Hulme has shown this in both
Spanish and English texts dating back to Columbus's diaries.[89] In the
Infortunios, however, the image was used in an implicit performative
way to describe a particular type of European. In a sense, in Sigüenza
the Englishman had come to displace the Carib—the unyielding native—as the major threat to Spanish rule in the Indies. Like the Carib of
yesteryear, the Englishman had come to roam the seas and to pillage
colonial settlements. Their war of colonial and mercantile expansion

was nothing short of barbaric. In this sense the *Infortunios* confirms what Hulme argues, mainly that cannibalism was a European invention and, in the case of Ramírez's testimony, also a European—and more particularly an English—practice and pastime.

Of course, even supposing that Ramírez or Sigüenza came up with this tale to add color to their story—or to get revenge against the English enemy, who had over the years put together equally detrimental propaganda with regard to Spain's destruction of the Indies—the fact is that the whole tale provides confirmation of the idea that cannibalism is the operative modality of empire, both as a justification for European intervention and as a model for colonial relations. In this case cannibalism was both real and analogical in its movement, for the English had also come to cannibalize the Spanish empire, coming aboard Alonso Ramírez's frigate and taking him and his men for a "walk on the wild side." How ironic that Ramírez, who as a creole wanted nothing more than to be treated as a true Spaniard, finally got his wish at such a trying moment. If the Spanish were Spanish precisely in refusing people like him all claims to Spanishness—his "relative" in Oaxaca had been a case in point—and thus condemning the colonials to a condition of "being unbecoming," of decreasing so that the Spaniards could increase, Alonso Ramírez was to find in the readiness of the English to consider him a Spaniard the desire to reduce him not just to the level of the subhuman but to an object of consumption, a movement that could potentially reduce him absolutely. At this moment in his story the English were eating Consonese; could he be next? Soon he would find out that the "protocols of consumption" among Christians were different.

When the pirates offered Ramírez a morsel of human flesh to eat, he refused to oblige them by acknowledging that he was a Spaniard and thus, according to the Englishmen's definition, too much of a coward to participate in such an exercise. Sigüenza gives us a "Spaniard" who prefers to call himself a coward rather than ceasing to be honorable. Of course in true picaresque fashion he still manages to call the Spaniards cowards, quite an affront on his part, because especially in the colonial context the image of the Spaniard was traditionally and unquestionably that of the brave and heroic conquistador. Let us remember that it took the riot of 1692 for Sigüenza to sound the alarm questioning the image of formidability that the Spaniards had created of themselves and regretting the fact that there no longer was a Cortés who could put the Indians and the plebs in their proper place.

But there is more hidden in this brief moment in the text. Keep in mind that Ramírez eventually ended up in Spanish territory, where he was forced to explain how he had managed to survive for so many years aboard an English ship. In other words, the story that got him an audience with the viceroy had to be above all a story of heroic resistance against the English and an uplifting account in favor of the Spanish Catholic cause. And so it was. At a time of economic downfall and social instability, the Spanish subject had remained loyal to the Crown. He had resisted all temptations. But had he? The insistence of the narrator on proving Ramírez's refusal to join the pirate society makes us suspicious. There was another moment when the pirates exhorted Ramírez to join them. Again he refused, arguing that because he was a Spaniard and a coward, and a man who was afraid of bullets, he was not worthy of being their comrade: "They proposed to me, as they had done before on other occasions, that if I swore to join up and be forever loyal they would give me weapons. I thanked them for the invitation, explaining to them what my obligations were by birth and respectfully telling them that I would much rather be their servant than have to fight, being as I was much afraid of bullets, and that on account of being a Spaniard and a chicken I was not worthy of their company."[90]

Once again Ramírez's character managed to deactivate the insults to which all things Spanish had been submitted by the English. He did so by assuming the adjectives that had accompanied his captors' prejudices and commanding them in a way that redeemed what he believed was the quintessential idea of an honorable man. Was the creole in Sigüenza doing with English prejudice the same thing he was accustomed to do when faced with Spanish peninsular deprecation of his social persona? Was he not *entre dos aguas* when he seemed to be staking his claim to Spanishness by defending Spain at all cost while at the same time finding himself unable to resist the opportunity to belittle the peninsular standard? In this game of reversals and subterfuge Sigüenza revealed in Ramírez the full spectrum of creole insecurity concerning issues of identity and loyalty. On the one hand, Ramírez defended the name of his father, that is, of the Spaniard whose name he does not carry. On the other, it might be argued, Ramírez's character eluded his peninsular captors through an act of symbolic mockery. In any event, the exquisite manipulations and the difficult ambiguities in Sigüenza's text—and in Ramírez's initial account to him—must be far from the truth. As a creole man of letters Sigüenza might not have wanted anything more than to be accepted as a Spaniard and to be granted the same rights and entitlements as the peninsulars enjoyed. His proximity to the Ideal made it all the more desirable. Yet Ramírez was a poor bastard from a desolate colonial outpost in the geography of the *rescate*. Could we not think that the true measure of his possibilities—and, deep down, his ultimate desire—might have been to leave the colony for a life of freedom and power as a buccaneer?

We will never know what really happened to Alonso Ramírez aboard that ship. But could we not suspect that he might have actually joined the English? After all, his skills as a ship carpenter must not have gone unnoticed, a circumstance that might help explain why Ramírez came out of the entire ordeal relatively unscathed. How else do we reconcile the fact that his captors eventually set him free under conditions that are never explained in the text, giving him a frigate loaded with a modest treasure and all the men who wanted to accompany him? If this was indeed the case, Ramírez could have been deluding the Spaniards themselves and fooling the viceroy, the censors, and even Sigüenza. Perhaps somewhere in this game of reversals Ramírez really escaped, even if only momentarily. Álvaro Félix Bolaños goes as far as suggesting that Ramírez was unavoidably attracted to the life of the English pirate and to Protestantism, but that upon his return to New Spain he had to defend himself against the possibility of being accused of treason and thus had to paint a terrible image of the English.[91] This contrasts with the view expressed by Concha Meléndez, who refers to Sigüenza's character as "Alonso Ramírez the Good,"[92] thus paying tribute to what she understands as a virtuous model of loyalty and fidelity to the Crown, thereby validating Ramírez's services rendered in defense of the colonial institutions and making his figure the perfect example of the docile Puerto Rican. But was there not also an Alonso Ramírez the Bad?

The next months at sea were characterized by more of the same sorts of episodes. The English looted villages, boarded ships, committed treason against their own, and, as Sigüenza points out, kept on stealing even when fleeing from the Dutch and the Portuguese. They got as far as New Holland, today Australia. After a few other acts of piracy they decided to set sail back to Europe, rounding the Cape of Good Hope and heading for the coast of Brazil and then north to the Amazon River delta, where Ramírez and his crew were finally let go and given a captured frigate in which to return to the Spanish dominions.

When they were set free, only eight of the original twenty-five men were left. One was Juan de Casas, a Spaniard born in Puebla and thus as much of a Spaniard as Ramírez. It is important to point out that because of his last name (*casas* means houses) Juan may be the symbolic representation of the civilizing principles around which Spanish colonization was organized: the casa, the *pueblo de indios*, and the city as a mechanism for conquest and conversion. There were also two Philippine Indians, Juan Pinto and Marcos de la Cruz. Antonio González was Chinese and Francisco de la Cruz, we are told, a mestizo Chinese. Juan Díaz was from Malabar, and Pedro, Ramírez's slave and the only one not to have a last name, was from Mozambique. These were all men without a country because they, like Ramírez, were in a permanent condition of exile as men of the sea who lacked a viable or desirable launching place to which to return rich and triumphant. Their stories serve not as metaphors for the national epic, but more as words of caution to those who, coming from the "wrong" place, might be looking for the right time to turn their misfortunes around by looking to the European Ideal for the "resolution other peoples have achieved."[93] Thus Alonso Ramírez was captain of a motley crew that was representative of the vast geography of the flota. His ship was manned by men whom Washington Irving, like Sigüenza, would have seen as a collection of mongrels and vile rabble. But before telling what happened to this crew once it was reassembled and set free, it is necessary to discuss, as Ramírez's character does once the pirates have, so to say, moved on in the narration, what the English did to them while holding them in captivity. As it turned out, the English had a way of relating to such mongrelity in more exquisite ways than in the simple genocide allegedly witnessed by Ramírez in Con Son. Ramírez recalled two such institutions.

Perhaps the most telling of all was a ritual to which Ramírez's men were subjected at the start of every week. "Monday was the day we feared the most," Ramírez tells us.[94] On such occasions all of his men were taken up to the deck and forced to undress. They were then placed in a circle around the mizzenmast with their left hands tied to a rope. While the pirate crew cheered, the captured servants were made to whip each other in the back at knifepoint. Then, Ramírez's character recalls, "Our humiliation and pain was equal to the cheerfulness and applause with which they celebrated."[95] Of course in the language of the time this image of male bondage was probably a metaphor for the continuous sexual exploitation to which the captured seamen were subjected as harlots of their pirate masters. Nevertheless, for Alonso Ramírez and Carlos de Sigüenza to have come up with such an image required them to search deep in their respective colonial psyche. If the self-fulfilling prophecy of the European is embodied in the cannibal, the one that best describes the colonial subject is the one where all the less-than-European peoples of the colonies are tied in a circle, stripped of their differences, and forced to flog each other in solidary complicity. Ramírez, aspiring albeit marginal creole that he was, must have been horrified. He was the captain of a crew he could not trust to help him escape from the English "because there was no other Spaniard among them than Juan de Casas."[96] And now, irrespective of status or socioracial origin, Indian, Chinese, African, and creole, free and slave, were all breaking their bodies for the amusement of the Europeans who had inherited the sea and the empire from the Spanish.

There is at that moment a horrible projection of things to come. In a sense, there is a ship within another ship, two visions of empire, one within the other. On the one hand, there is the Spanish ship with its crew of colonial misfits engaged in a strange Baroque opera of tormented souls and bleeding bodies. On the other, the English ship on the deck of which the Spanish ship performs is a spectacle of torture based on the reduction of mongrelity and its separation from a new European standard symbolized by the English as cannibals. For the English, who preferred eliminating any trace of their paternity when it came to hybrid types as they did in Con Son, perhaps there was nothing more amusing than sodomizing the mongrels of empire at knifepoint. After all, it was the only safe way to engage in the carnal pleasures of empire building without leaving a trace or, as Sigüenza would have surely preferred, without having to deal with the vile rabble of the *castas*.

In line with the humiliation, exploitation, and consumption rituals already outlined is a final moment where master and servant, pirate and captive, English and non-English seem to come together. At one point Juan de Casas, the other "Spaniard," was apparently too weak to work. According to Ramírez, Captain Bel, chief of the English pirates, decided to force his own excrement down Juan's throat, but not before properly diluting it in water. This was the ultimate humiliation. Yet it was a normal and straightforward consequence of what I am calling European cannibalism. Indeed, if in the end Captain Bel's relationship to his captive included the possibility of ultimately devouring him, then to make the captive eat his master's excrement was to propose the consummation of all potentiality in colonial captivity through the utmost act of destruction, self-consumption. In essence, by drinking his master's excrement Juan de Casas was eating himself. This, after all, might be the ultimate form of decreasing, the absolute value of the "being unbecoming," and it might also have been the inversely proportional movement to the complementary symbolism that coupled the image of the excrement-eating prisoner and the master who sodomized him, which, in turn, made Juan de Casas's body the less than ideal receptacle of everything the European Ideal could offer in the theater of creole coloniality.

Shipwrecked

Upon being set free, Ramírez sailed with his crew on a north-northwest course, passing through Trinidad, east of Barbados, and close to Guadeloupe, where the captain proposed to make a landing for fresh provisions. Because Guadeloupe was a French island, he told them, they would certainly find good Catholics to help them out. His men refused to go ashore, arguing "that because of their color and on account of not being Spaniards they would surely be made slaves and that they would think it more sensible for me to throw them into the sea with my own hands rather than placing them in the hands of foreigners who would treat them with harshness."[97] Ramírez had himself experienced the same kind of panic once before, when on their way back from the South Seas the pirates had tried to leave him and his men in Mozambique, the land where Pedro, his slave, had been born. The creole slave owner had then implored his captors to spare him the terrible fate that would surely follow: "Considering the barbarous state of the black moros that inhabited the area, I got on my knees and kissed their feet profusely, and after proving to them how well I had served them and offering myself as their slave for the rest of the trip, I got them to agree to take me with them."[98] In this earlier episode, Alonso Ramírez had been willing to become a complete slave to the English before being left behind in Mozambique. He was reflecting the worst fear of the Spaniard and of the creole: the fear of

166 The Creole in His Labyrinth

being turned over to the black moro, that blend formed by the figures who had historically been their civilizational nemesis. Similarly, his men would rather have died than gone ashore in Guadeloupe. Somehow it was as if these men of the sea, these pariahs of nations, were safe only in the world of the flota, to which they apparently wished to return as they set sail hoping to come across a Spanish ship or hit the coast of New Spain.

Throughout their voyage, in the Atlantic and in the Caribbean Sea, Ramírez and his men saw signs of the English, including a major squadron. The Spanish were nowhere to be seen. Once again, Sigüenza was pointing out the weakness of Spain's defenses and her inability to protect the periphery of her empire. Still, in a moment that reflects colonial subjectivity—and the benefits of what Derek Walcott calls "a sound colonial education"[99]—in pristine form, Ramírez was lost in his own backyard and was only able to assume that he was somewhere in the West Indies. Just a few islands away from his native San Juan, Ramírez was incapable of recognizing his position: "Whoever reads this should not be surprised to note the ignorance we had with respect to those islands, because since I left my fatherland at such a young age, I never knew (and never cared to learn thereafter) which were the neighboring islands and their names."[100] Ramírez was finally free. But he was lost in his freedom, sailing through a sea that he had "never cared to learn" and that seemed to be controlled by the English. In this way he sailed north and then west, past Antigua and Puerto Rico, Hispaniola, Jamaica, and the Cayman Islands, where once again they saw signs of the English.

The story of Alonso Ramírez as a creole reached a climax at this point; the frigate crashed against the reefs of a flat and broad coast. The shipwreck, as a literary trope, was a metaphor that allowed Sigüenza to present his readers with an alternative vision where the established order had been upset. For a brief moment in the story Sigüenza took the liberty of proposing what could only be termed a partial yet forceful alternative creole order. The situation was critical. The seas were high, and with every wave the crew feared the ship would split in half. It was then that Ramírez decided to take action: "Knowing that time was of the essence, making fervent acts of contrition, and wishing to be worthy of God's mercy by sacrificing my life for that of those poor people, I threw myself into the water tied to a thin rope that the men were to let go slowly."[101]

The creole was to sacrifice himself for the poor bastards of empire who made up his crew—and was confident that they would hold onto the other end of the rope. Or did he simply want to save himself before the ship broke in half? In any case, Ramírez succeeded in getting ashore, and he brought the rest of the crew in by means of the rope. The next day he swam to the shipwreck twice, first to get an ax and then a barrel of water. The day after he returned with Juan de Casas, the other "Spaniard," to get some more things, including weapons and ammunitions. Juan also accompanied Ramírez on a reconnaissance mission a day later, when they killed two wild pigs and took them back to the men, who were growing sick on account of the foul water they had been drinking from nearby ponds. The creoles were on the move, saving and sustaining the lives of the other crew members. Thirty days they waited there hoping for signs of other people while their lives and energies withered away. Finally they decided to move on. After considerable pains they found a stream with fresh although reddish water. Ramírez decided to go on from there with Juan de Casas, because the rest of the men—the "non-Spaniards"—were all fatigued and very ill. In Bartolomé de las Casas's account of Hispaniola there had been only an indirect reference to the fact that the Spaniards had become *indianos,* but here in Sigüenza we have definite, if rather forced, testimony of it. The creole was at home in the Indies and in command of their inhospitable geography. The problem, however, was that they seemed to have landed in the *carajo.* The Chinese, Filipinos, and African were all feverish and bloated. They were in fact dying, which is why they asked Ramírez not to leave them behind. They made Ramírez cry: "Holding onto me, very full of love and tenderness they asked me that I please not abandon them and, since even the strongest of them would hardly live more than four days, and since that was such a short time, that I consider remaining by their side to give them my blessing on their last breath as the father I was to all of them, thereafter continuing with Godspeed in search of what their unhappiness and misfortunes in such an extreme climate denied them."[102]

This episode is an important example of creole self-fashioning, one in which Sigüenza's heavy-handedness in appropriating the figure of Ramírez to promote certain creole political aspirations shows through with particular transparency. Ramírez had saved his men, and as they lay dying they called out his name with love, asking him, as their father, to remain by their side while they died. In the extreme climate, or *climas extraños,* in which they found themselves, perhaps the most extreme condition was that the creole "Spaniard" had fully assumed the paternal role formerly reserved for the peninsular Spaniard in the album of socioracial power relations. The creole in Sigüenza was taking command "forcibly by force" if only under the cover of an accident of destiny. Six days later, seeing that none of them had died, Ramírez decided to get his people moving ever so slowly. Then, in a scene like a Mexican Pietà, Francisco de la Cruz, one of the Chinese men, died in Ramírez's arms. The other Chinese, Antonio González, died next to Ramírez while he slept. After a few more days, the other men seemed to have regained their health, while Ramírez's was deteriorating. It was a heroic moment, one in which the creole had almost sacrificed himself for the good of all.

Alonso Ramírez was now feverish (confirming creole insecurity concerning the capacity to handle the affairs of state?), and he was left in the care of his slave Pedro while the others went hunting. Right then he had the worst nightmares. He thought for sure that they were in Florida, where the natives were known to be "extremely cruel."[103] Ramírez was having a historical vision. He was, in a way, expecting to die the heroic death of the conquistador as had the colonizer and first governor of his *patria,* Juan Ponce de León, waiting for the attack of the cruel Indians with his loyal slave at his side. Just then, his "boy"[104] woke him up, pointing out that there were people walking up the beach. Forgetting his fears of the Florida natives, Ramírez ran to them in a desperate attempt to find out where he was and how to find his way back. They were two Indians. Both were naked and unarmed. As soon as Ramírez heard them speak in Spanish, he hugged them. They were in Yucatán, he was told, not far from the village of Tihosuco. The lands in which they had been marooned were quite remote and could be escaped only through navigation. Had the Indians seen the strangers first they could have run into the woods and hidden from them, and Ramírez and his men, with no boat, would have eventually perished in complete abandonment.

Soon after being rescued, Ramírez and his men went with Juan González, the *encomendero* for whom the Indians had been collecting amber on the beach. They were taken by González and his Indian servants to a small island where, next to the ruins of a Mayan temple, they extracted pure, fresh water from hand-dug wells. The references to the *encomienda* and the ruins of the Mayan temple cannot be overlooked, as they were a throwback to the days of conquest and to the first generation of conquistadors from whom the creoles claimed to have descended. It was as if here, at the edge of the world, lost in time, Ramírez and his men were saved by ghosts from the past. Once on the open sea, they came upon a small sailboat manned by Indian traders, which they decided to board in order to procure sufficient food for their voyage back home. Apparently piracy was seen as a hostile act only among Europeans, as there was no hesitation on the part of the narrator to characterize this act of boarding an Indian vessel as nothing other than a ritual of survival. In this story written following the originary movement of the Columbian legacy, the Indians rescued Ramírez from imminent failure. They confirmed his location, gave him directions, supplied his men, and sent him on his way. This was the way the Indies had been conquered, and this was precisely the tradition that Sigüenza pointed to as the mythological origin of the creole nation. In a way, Sigüenza was claiming the Spanishness of the creole by going back to a time when the Spaniards were really Spaniards, so to speak, a past of heroic proportions that only the creole, as the supposed descendant of the conquistadors, could claim.

After landing on the coast of Mexico, the party proceeded to cross a mountain range. At some point Ramírez misfired his gun and lost consciousness. The shipwreck and the intervening episode of creole domination had come to an end. The hero of the story was back to being Alonso Ramírez the Good as they reentered the viceregal world, a process that would take him step by step from the periphery of the colony all the way to the palace in Mexico City. Ramírez and his men came to the town of Tila, where the Mayans received them with much excitement. They were fed and given horses. From Tila they moved to Tihosuco, where they were received by the priest, Cristóbal de Muros,[105] and taken to church to give thanks and praise God for having delivered them from the English. To Ramírez it must have seemed that they indeed had been saved. The priest hosted Ramírez and De Casas, the two "Spaniards," for eight days.

From there they went to Valladolid, where they met the two mayors and *encomenderos*, Francisco de Zelerún and Ceferino de Castro.[106] Things did not go well in Valladolid. News of their shipwreck had preceded them, and soon many opportunists tried to take advantage of Ramírez's "booty," including Ceferino de Castro, who forbade Ramírez to go back to the shore to rescue his treasures. Ramírez demanded that justice be done, at which point he was taken to Mérida, where he was made to recount his tales many times while being poorly treated and hardly fed. It seemed that the higher he went up the hierarchy of Spanish officials and the closer he got to the historical present—coming back as he was from the myth of the conquistadors—the more closely he came to be followed by his dark star. Having experienced such horrible trials for the past fifteen years—it was now December of 1689—Ramírez was a victim of his own experience. But he was not the most victimized. Starving and in need of clothes, for three hundred pesos he sold Pedro, his slave during their years in the Philippines and his companion during their captive years aboard the pirate ship. Indeed, it can be said that Alonso Ramírez consumed Pedro.

Their stay in Mérida was quite problematic, because they were at the mercy of corrupt officials who attempted to keep for themselves the cargo of Alonso Ramírez's wrecked frigate. At one point Ceferino de Castro suggested that a road be cut between the town of Tihosuco and the beach, as mules could carry the cargo faster and more efficiently than Indians. But Cristóbal de Muros opposed the idea, arguing that such a plan would open the country to pirate raids on the interior. Here the prevailing contradiction that pitted creole against peninsular was being played out between the *encomendero* and the priest. The first, albeit for reasons contrary to Ramírez's best interests, wanted to open the country up. The second thought that keeping it closed would allow them to hold onto the land and the Indians. What a coincidence that the priest's last name was Muros, which in Spanish means walls. Right around this time the closed world of Mérida must have seemed to Ramírez a long way from Batavia.

Just when things were once again taking a turn for the worse, Ramírez's life seems to have turned around. In May 1690 he was granted an audience with the Count of Galve, viceroy of New Spain, who at that time was Sigüenza's personal friend and patron. The viceroy took an interest in his story—and, as did everyone else, in his loot—and intervened on his behalf, defending him from the corrupt officials who were trying to steal his precious cargo. After listening to his account, the viceroy sent Ramírez to Sigüenza, who at the time was ill, in the hope that the story of the lost adventurer would be of therapeutic value to him. Sigüenza was fascinated and saw in the story an opportunity, a sign open to interpretation that no good astronomer could let pass without measuring it and leaving an appropriate record. As he would write a year later upon observing the solar eclipse of the 23 August: "I stood with my quadrant and telescope viewing the sun, extremely happy and repeatedly thanking God for granting that I might behold what so rarely happens in a given place and about which so few observations are recorded."[107]

Like the eclipse, having stumbled across the story of Alonso Ramírez presented a once-in-a-lifetime opportunity. And as in the case of the eclipse, if it had not been for Sigüenza there would be no record of it. In fact, just like the eclipse, Alonso Ramírez was soon gone. All we know is that, according to Sigüenza, he was commissioned as a captain of musketeers in the Royal Fleet of the Windward Islands in the Archipelago of Mexico, of which islands Puerto Rico is the one in the center of the arc. We are thus led to believe that Alonso Ramírez eventually returned whence he had come. Ironically, fifteen years earlier he had abandoned his post as an inhabitant of San Juan. Now, having survived his escape, he had come back to guard the empire as a captain of the flota. Essentially, he had gotten nowhere. He was still a child of the flota, a native of San Juan, the land of the "being unbecoming," the boundary from which he had attempted to steal his body but that now he was going to be protecting with his life.

By offering this interpretative possibility to the reader, Sigüenza wished to prove through Ramírez's misfortunes that the colonial subject had to stay put. Gone were the days when America had been the land of bounty for those who aspired to the rank of hidalgo and to a life without work. The memory of the conquistador could be invoked, but his feats were already history. In a way, as Fornet explains, giving a brief summary of the economic realities of New Spain, Ramírez's world was one of movement, while the economic realities of the day presupposed that one had to remain fixed, tied to the land or to a position in order to prosper.[108] This idea is not altogether foreign to us. There is a certain resemblance between Las Casas and Sigüenza, as they both proposed that the world of the *indiano* should be based on the idea that the New World held no promise without hard work and commitment to the land.

Yet, unlike Las Casas, Sigüenza proposed no program of action. At no point is there a more serious proposition than that the creole be substituted for the Spaniard at the helm of the viceregal ship. Quite the contrary; the position of the creole remains fundamentally unfixed and unstable. Sigüenza at once praises the viceroy and pledges his loyalty to Spain while demonstrating a strong desire to occupy the space of the

European. We have seen him unwilling to abandon the Spanish standard by attacking the Black Legend, and at the same time calling the Spaniard a coward. The creole in the *Infortunios* both denounces Spain's inability to protect the periphery of empire and admires the world that exists just beyond the monopoly of the flota. What is more, in his desire to speak on behalf of the peoples of empire, we find a strange moment of incoherence and complicity. His crew disappears and resurfaces at his convenience. They are there to confirm his authority and to provide him with an opportunity for martyrdom and sacrifice. They are there to call him by the name of father, to die in his arms—to decrease for his symbolic edification—when he enters into a secret compact with the climate and the geography he feels he can legitimately claim.

In the end, of course, the viceregal order was restored. The movement of destabilization described in the *Infortunios* was still rather timidly staking a claim to a world that was dangerously drifting as a cork between order and disorder, *concierto y desconcierto,* hierarchy and difference. Perhaps the creole spirit in Sigüenza is best described by Eugenio d'Ors y Rovira's definition of the Baroque essence: "To say it crudely for once, the Baroque spirit does not know what it wants. It wants the pro and the con at the same time. . . . It wants—I remember a certain fat angel, on a certain gate, in a certain chapel of a certain church in Salamanca—to raise his arm and lower his hand at the same time."[109] Contrary to the pretensions of the censor Ayerra y Santa María, Sigüenza did not find his way out of the creole labyrinth of entanglement and subterfuge.

Disquieting Relations in the *Cuadros de Castas*

It would take the creoles of New Spain half a century more to develop a less precarious and timid political discourse. Even then, this would not be a claim levied against the Crown, but rather the result of a continuous attempt, clearly already under way during Sigüenza's time, to build and protect what R. Douglas Cope calls the creole "sense of exclusivity"[110] against the rising menace posed by those whom Sigüenza called the vile rabble of plebeian society. "Forcibly by force" they would attempt to submit the peoples of the viceregal world to a *sistema de castas,* a hierarchical order that, when fully developed during the middle of the eighteenth century, would recognize sixteen possible *castas* resulting from the sexual and moral interaction between European, Indian, and

African subjects. On the verge of independence these were societies that would attempt to build nations from within and not from without by protecting the exclusivity of the European Ideal—unitary, stable, and self-contained as it had been thought to be since the Renaissance—against the growing numbers of commoners who could never measure up to it and who were its aesthetic counterpoint as the ever-unstable subjects of racial fractionization and contamination. Cope has estimated that by the start of the seventeenth century plebeian society already comprised 85 percent of the population of Mexico City.[111]

As in the Alhambra, the European Ideal would be imposed on a practice of life that conformed to a different geometry. In principle, this was an impossible project destined for failure. Classifying the production of difference that resulted from the sexual interaction between the three "races" of the Atlantic world was the social equivalent of attempting to reduce to a number the prismatic explosion in the fractional geometries of the honeycomb domes in the Halls of the Two Sisters and the Abencerrajes. Using such a plastic metaphor underscores the fact that the method to the madness of the *castas* system was a fluid and three-dimensional pyramidal model of prismatic forms that exploded exponentially with every new generation in a vertiginous geometric progression. The creole system would be the most *desconcertado concierto,* or disquieting order, upon which only a fragile political project could be built.

There is no more poignant testimony to the hazards faced by such a project than the *cuadros de castas* (paintings of castes), a particular modality of secular painting developed in the viceroyalties of New Spain and Peru—the Mexican and the Andean Schools, respectively—to record in a pictorial catalogue all the official human types in American colonial society.[112] Invariably, each of the paintings depicts a couple and the child who was the result of the mutation in the orders of miscegenation. The setting is either public or domestic and is always indicative of the niche the *casta* was supposed to occupy in the socioracial almanac of the viceregal world.

One of the best-known series is attributed to the Mexican painter José Joaquín Magón.[113] It is introduced by a legend that is a clear enunciation of the creole conundrum: "In America peoples of different color, customs, temperaments *(genios)* and languages are born."[114] This series identifies the *castas* by adding to each of the images a brief text that speaks to the "moral" character of the type. Thus the mestizo is said to be "naturally humble, peaceful and simple."[115] Holding a sheet of paper up to his Spanish father, the mestizo child proudly shows him how his mother, an Indian woman of seemingly noble birth, has taught him to write. The paper is itself a sign or marker of identity. It simply reads: *parco,* or parsimonious. Other types were thought to be inclined to gamble, to be restless or lazy or good and benign, according to their relationship to and distance from the European Ideal. It is important to note that, unlike the biracial Usonian system of the "one-drop rule," whereby anyone suspected of having a single black ancestor is considered black, the *castas* system was based on the assumption that mixing "hybrids" with Spaniards—or members of the other two "pure" types—for two to three successive generations would render the offspring of the hybrids "pure." This was of course a frivolous promise in a world where few but the wealthiest could present proof of ancestry and where in any event, as it now appears, *casta* status seemed to have been assigned more by phenotype than by lineage.[116] Invariably, the mixing of the so-called "races" was an uncontrollable process, regardless of whether it was rationalized as arguably "reversible," as in the Mexican model, or whether it was designed to contain "hybrids" and condemn them to eternal ostracism, as in the Usonian one.

Under the assumptions of the *castas* system the albino (offspring of a Spaniard and a *morisco*[117]), for example, one generation away from "returning" to the Spanish standard, was described as benign. But the process of going back took its toll. The albino, we are also told, was weak and delicate and would have a short life. In contrast, the lobo, or wolf, a mix between black and Indian, would be a natural purse-snatcher. It is worth noting, as Isidoro Moreno has pointed out, that most of the categorical descriptors used in the *castas* system were derived from the zoological vocabulary and that, save for the mulatto, these names were reserved for the mixes that did not involve the "well-formed body" of a Spaniard.[118]

Precise moral attributes were not easily bestowed on the more complex combinations where the offspring had ancestors of all three "pure" types. The twelfth category in Magón's series was the *no te entiendo,* literally meaning "I do not understand you." Such an individual was the result of a union between an Indian and a *cambuja* (originally a dark-colored or reddish mare), the latter of which was the offspring of any of nine possible combinations, none of which included a European progenitor. The *tente en el aire,* or "hold yourself up in the air," was Magón's last category. We are told that this individual was a "bad graft" between the *torna atrás,* or "comes back" (the offspring of any of three possible mixes), and the *albarazado* (from the Arabic *al-baras,* or white leprosy, the child of any of eleven possible combinations). In essence, the categories that pertained to the higher degrees of mixture, the lowest of the *castas,* had passed the point of no return. For them there was no redemption; they drifted away into the unspeakable. In this sense, the *tente en el aire* was literally and symbolically the furthest removed from the gravitas of the Ideal Body and of the European Ideal in the context of the coloniality of power.

At first glance the observer would tend to see these *cuadros de castas* as some sort of scientific attempt to document the human types of the New World. Indeed, they would seem to respond to a sort of Linnaean categorization of human types, being not so much art as science, not so much a capricious manifestation of the creole spirit as a creole project of the Enlightenment.[119] But this is not the case. The *cuadros de castas* responded to a Baroque order of representative embodiment and to an equally Baroque movement of hierarchical imperatives. More than a protoscientific attempt to determine the states and stages of the human "fauna" in America, this was a project that aimed to legitimize and sustain the socioracial scaffolding of the old regime by presenting its Baroque spheres of order camouflaged as a discourse of reason. In this sense the *cuadros de castas* may be more closely related to the practice of racial classification in the French colony of Saint-Domingue, a mathematical exercise that broke down the mulatto subjects into nine possible categories of racial mixture between black and white (going back eight generations and assuming that people have 128 "units" of inheritance), than to the work of the anthropologist J. F. Blumenbach, who is credited with developing the first "scientific" classification of human variety according to the concept of race. In truth, however, all of these systems are related insofar as all methods of racial classification are invariably models that justify, facilitate, and support racial oppression. To say it crudely for once, race is a political construct with no scientific or moral validity: it can be legislated and practiced in the coloniality of power, but it can never ultimately be justified.

The need to make sense of and control this world where "peoples of different color, customs, temperament and language are born" was as strong as the resistance of the society to conform to clear definitions and demarcations. The *cuadros de castas* are revealing in both senses, as they express both the dreams and the nightmares of the creole imaginary. At one end of this continuum was the dream of the nation. At the other, in true Lascasian fashion, was the *moreno* threat.

One of the earliest known *casta* paintings (Figure 20) is by Luis de Mena and dates from the mid–eighteenth century. It is of great relevance, as it combines all the major iconographic moments and representational tricks of colonial creole discourse. Most dominant of all is the figure of the Virgin Mary, in this case as Our Lady of Guadalupe. We already know that, as in the case of the Virgen de los Reyes, images of Mary had become the preferred symbolic instruments for the promotion of social peace and racial unity throughout the Spanish empire. In this painting she is flanked by two important images of public life representing the major division of viceregal society between the *república de indios,* or Indian nation, and the *república de los españoles,* or Spanish society. To the left a group of Matachine Indians offers a dance to the Virgin in front of the church in Tepeyac, near Mexico City, which was built in her honor during the early years of the eighteenth century. To the right is a view of the Paseo de Jamaica. The *paseo* was then the most cherished public ritual of the *vecinos,* that is, of Spanish and creole citizens.[120] Thus, flanked by an image of Indian docility and worship and by a view of the most important ceremony of the Spanish public sphere, Our Lady of Guadalupe becomes a protonational symbol of creole society, a standard of sorts, representing the aspirations of those who wished to be placed in the center as an "intermediary species," claiming the land from the Indians and the moral and political legitimacy enjoyed by the Spaniard while at the same time, like the Virgin of Guadalupe herself, floating on a cloud above the *castas.*[121]

In the middle section of the canvas eight *cuadros de castas* are depicted. Of these, the two *castas* closest to the Spanish standard are also closest to the Virgin. The *castizo* (a mix of Spanish and mestizo) and the *español* (a mix of *castizo* and Spanish) are at her feet. In an almost miraculous way, the original mestizo (far left, next to the *castizo*) has been cleansed of his Indian blood to become once again a Spaniard.

The role of women in this painting is also quite significant, as the "Spanish lady" comes to play a prominent and uncharacteristic role in a representative modality where the Spanish element was seldom de-

Figure 20. Luis de Mena, *Scenes of Mestizaje,* mid-eighteenth century. Courtesy of Museo de América, Madrid.

picted as female. Out of the eight total representations, she is portrayed in three of the four to the right of the Virgin, beginning at the far left with the original act of miscegenation where, dressed in the most elegant of fashions, she appears next to a naked Indian with whom she has had a child. In all other known representations the mestizo is the child of a Spanish father and an Indian mother, both usually of high birth. Of course according to heraldic codes the three Spanish women occupy the legitimate side of this Mexican coat of arms, a condition that appears to be reinforced by the fact that two of the women on the left side, a Spaniard and a *morisca* (offspring of a Spaniard and a mulatto), are looking up to the Virgin, who now seems to be an apparition existing in the same spatial-temporal moment as the other figures. Are they offering their children to her or asking her forgiveness for having borne them? Her holy gaze seems to be a benediction on miscegenation itself. But is it not strange that a saintly virgin should preside over a catalogue depicting the products of the carnal passions of those whom Sigüenza called the vile rabble?

Giving weight to the painting, in its lower section is a *bodegón*, or still life, depicting a table bearing the fruits of New Spain. It is an image of plenty, representing a natural geography that is bountiful and inexhaustible. Like the *castas*, the fruits too are labeled and numbered, responding to a will to order that is also a will to power. In other words, the naming and categorization of the American cornucopia expressed the desire to possess the fruits and the peoples of the land. As if mimicking nature, the flora serves to support the fauna in this still life of life standing still, where the vertiginous movement of hybridity has been frozen, its complex profusion of bodies and mischief cleanly disentangled, labeled and exhibited for public display. But as in the *castas* system, not all the fruits in the basket are native to the country. The first one to be labeled and numbered is none other than "Plátano guineo," the plantain from Guinea, which we understand as a clear allusion to Africa and the Africans.

Other representations clearly emphasize this movement of creole self-fashioning, most notably the ones that depict the "Spaniard" as the *encomendero*, or the master of the plantation. I am particularly thinking of an anonymous painting of the mestizo from the latter part of the eighteenth century that depicts a creole landowner with his Indian wife, probably a princess judging from her clothes, and their son.[122] It is a bucolic scene of natural bounty, the utopian dream of the landed class. In this creole paradise, which comes complete with happy-looking laborers and white doves flying above, the master stands raising his right hand in the air, confident in his possession of the land and firmly in command of the people who work for him. Before him a worker bends over a pile of fruits that have just been picked. Directly under him and closest to the foreground, two bundles of plantains, arranged as an inverted pyramid standing on one point, seem to be keeping the entire pile in place. It is as if the African element were the one upon which rested the delicate balance of the American cornucopia.

In their will to power and in the exercise of their imaginary, the creole elites of Novohispanic society were no bourgeois vanguard, but they certainly were representative of their time and, more important, of the age of high empire to come. As the *cuadros de castas* demonstrate, this was a project not of freedom, equality, and mercantile expansion but of racial oppression, institutional stability, and home rule. One of the most eloquent images in all of the collections of the *castas* paintings is an anonymous one depicting the mix between the Spaniard and the albino, resulting in the *negro torna atrás,* or "the black comes back."[123] It belongs to the latter part of the eighteenth century. The family trio occupies the foreground, while a careful depiction of Mexico City's famous Alameda occupies most of the pictorial space. The family is standing atop the Guardiola Palace, and the creole man looks through a small telescope at the world below in the Alameda, which is not just a representation of the city but also of the entire viceregal society, from the soldier who guards the central fountain to the "castaways" who inhabit the streets beyond the fenced precinct. Here is, to borrow from Mary Louise Pratt, the creole "monarch-of-all-I-survey."[124] He is the master of all that he can see, a position that is promoted by his albino wife as she kneels before him in admiration. Behind her, their black son places his right hand on her shoulder as a sign of respect and obedience. But in contrast to the standard representative modality of taking possession of lands and peoples in the Victorian Age of empire, this eighteenth-century surveyor is looking in and not out, into a world over which he claims paternal authority. Yet it is a world to be discovered, observed, and analyzed, a social space that still needs to be brought under control. Like Alonso Ramírez sailing through the Caribbean, this creole seems to be lost in a geography about which he had heretofore never cared to learn.

One of the mottoes of the creole of this period might have been "When in doubt, resort to violence." Terrible scenes in the *cuadros de castas* describe the problems that were part of the uneasy relationship between the creole and the world to which he laid claim. One of the most carefully thought out and best rendered representations in all of the collections is an anonymous depiction of the mulatto.[125] In a kitchen—the preferred setting for the black woman in these *castas* paintings—a Spanish man feeds a small parrot in what is a classical image of bondage: I feed you; now you must sing for me. The idea is reinforced by the figure of the mulatto child, who is holding a cup between his hands as if begging for food. The complex politics of servitude are enunciated in a more profound way if we consider the references to consumption and sexual exploitation. The Spaniard is approaching the black woman from behind, and, although he is feeding the parrot, his eyes are fixed on the turkey the woman is eviscerating. The woman's handling of the carcass, her hand halfway into the cut in the turkey's underside, is an image of vaginal penetration or female masturbation. This image is further confirmed by the phalluslike neck of the bird, which in turn is pointing in the direction of yet another turkey that has been cut open and resembles another vagina. Even the sausage hanging on the wall resembles an anus. The apparent peacefulness of the scene hides a terrible discourse of violence that speaks of the creole's desire to possess the human geography of the country "forcibly by force."

For all the frankness of this unique representation, there is one yet more direct. It is the "standard" depiction of the mulatto that recurred in at least four other series dating to the last quarter of the century. These are the series that can be said to best embody the condition that Las Casas had prescribed two centuries before when he identified the element in colonial society that was to be forever "harmful and troublesome" to the *indiano*. In one of these depictions, part of an anonymous series from the Mexican School (Figure 21), again set in a kitchen, a black woman wields a mallet and has succeeded in hitting her Spanish master at least once in the forehead. He is bleeding and trying to hold the woman, who is at the same time pulling his hair. Two pots are boiling over the fire on the stove, and the mulatto girl pulls her mother by the skirt and seems to be saying: "Please, mother, don't hurt my father." In this image of violence and insubordination the will to power of the creole is checked by the representative *negra,* the embodiment of the ants and of the wild dogs that clouded every vision of the future in the Lascasian imagination. Here is the black who confronts the *indiano* "forcibly by force" in a movement of engagement and repulsion where the two forces seem to be inversely proportional. This curve-countercurve movement, which could be thought of as a plastic metaphor of the very

Figure 21. Anonymous, *4. De Español y Negra: Mulata*. From *Series of Sixteen Scenes of Mestizaje*, Viceroyalty of New Spain, second half of eighteenth century. Courtesy of Museo de América, Madrid.

"being unbecoming" at the level of the creole body politic, appears to be frozen in a tense moment of irresolution. The mulatto child is the only agent that can upset this disturbing equilibrium. Which way will the mulatto go?

In a similar painting (Figure 22), by Andrés de Islas, the child is literally in the middle. She is the *tertium quid,* an unstable subject of infinitely divided allegiances who is, in this sense, the opposite of the "naturally humble, peaceful and simple" character ascribed to the mestizo. As Las Casas foresaw, the *indiano* and the black have come to fight over the land. The mulatto, as the offspring of this unhappy and unfortunate union, will carry the weight of this moment, at times following the movement of the *concierto* by upholding the European Ideal, at other times describing the movement of the *desconcierto* by inhabiting the most metaphorical of conditions through a movement of camouflage and subterfuge that is the very nemesis of the coloniality of power.

As if wanting to place this representation in its full context, Andrés de Islas included a still life of the American cornucopia. Could it be that he put it there as the reward of the victor, or did he intend it as a

Figure 22. Andrés de Islas, *N° 4. De Español y Negra: Nace Mulata,* eighteenth century. Courtesy of Museo de América, Madrid.

reminder of what was at stake in that terrible contest? In the immediate foreground, behind the woman, the first "fruit of the land" to be labeled is sugarcane, the crop of the plantation: four stalks bundled together like a fasces stand as a solitary symbol of unity in a world that seems to be falling apart.

CHAPTER FIVE

Undoing the Ideal

The Life and Passion of the Mulatto

> The mulattoes [of Saint-Domingue], as with us, were the children of
> the slaveholders.
> — Ramón Emeterio Betances (after Wendell Phillips)

Judging from the *cuadros de castas* it is evident that by the middle of the
eighteenth century the body of the mulatto had become the most prominent site where the tensions and contradictions, the divergences and
overlaps of the relationship between master and slave, colonizer and
colonized, white and nonwhite, Christian and non-Christian acted upon
each other both to give cohesion and to destabilize the foundations of
the coloniality of power in Mexican creole society and in the global
geography of the flota. We have seen how some of these tensions had
begun to build in the pre-1492 world of the Iberian frontier and how
they were coherently though in a somewhat veiled manner enunciated
by Las Casas at the foundational moment of American society. Furthermore, we can now compare two separate and very distinct moments of
representational duress where the mulatto has been symbolically captured and precariously fixed or "stabilized." I am referring to the
princely triumvirate of the *Mulatos de Esmeraldas* and to the indefinite
tertium quid of the *castas* paintings, works that act as bookends to the
standard timeline of the classic colonial period and that are, without a
doubt, among the most powerful and eloquent testimonies to the mysteries, paradoxes, and contradictions around which American societies
have been organized. The first were the embodiment of social camouflage

and the second the most potentially dangerous agent provocateur of social instability. The paintings that depicted them were conceived as representational entrapments designed to catch that strange kind of social organism whose essence was the production and reproduction of difference ad infinitum, that subject in medias res that in the Manichaean world of Christianity and of the plantation was from the very beginning hard to place, impossible to figure out, and dangerously unpredictable. Of course this was the most utopian project in the history of the plantation and of coloniality, because the official sanctioning of "racial" difference, that is, of the mechanisms for measuring the degree of variance of a person's *figura* from the Ideal Body and the deviation of a person's *genio* from the European Ideal, always ran against a practice of everyday life that resisted enforcement and thrived precisely in variance and deviation from all such ideals. It is for these reasons that I choose to refer to the movement of *mulataje* as both the symbolic counterpoint to and the most powerful practice of contestation and undoing of the coloniality of power.

The mulatto came to be the *tagarino* of the great Atlantic contact zone. In fact, it could be said that the expansion of the mulatto margin engendered a process of reverse colonization—not that different from what Lezama called the practice of the counterconquest—through which the subjects of the mulatto world of the Caribbean appropriated the very accoutrements of the European Ideal, manipulating and reconstructing them in unsuspected ways. This process occurred with particular intensity on the island of Hispaniola, coming into clear focus during the 1780s and developing unstoppable momentum during the course of the nineteenth century. There, in the former French colony of Saint-Domingue, the contestation of the Ideal would lead to the undoing and unmasking of the European as the subject of historical protagonism. Later the poems of the Cuban known as Plácido would reveal the great potentiality of a movement of being that was irreducible to bipolar constructs and to the simple movement of analogical concatenation that has always informed the practices of humanist terror. Ultimately even the reduction implied in the process of building a nation "island by island" became a contranatural and even an undesirable process for important sectors of the mulatto peoples of the Caribbean. All in all, these were the most volatile years in the history of the seemingly uncontrollable mulatto versatility.

Codifying the Difference

In an attempt to control the subject's perceived volatility, colonial iconography depicted the mulatto as the master of the in-between and as a
gatekeeper of sorts. The mulatto was a translator between the Spanish
and the Indian in the Esmeraldas and a mediator between master and
slave on the plantation. In a paradoxical moment similar to the one we
have already seen in the San Juan portrayed by Campeche as the symbol
of the place where docility ruled, the mulatto would be made to preside
over a terrible contradiction as the enforcer of a process that ultimately
implied his own self-effacement and disappearance.

In 1784, seven years before the start of the Haitian Revolution, Colonel
Joaquín García y Moreno, who was then second in command of the military forces *(teniente de rey)* and would soon be governor of Santo
Domingo (1788–1801), wrote to the Audiencia expressing the urgent need
to rein in "the mulattoes of all species," whom he characterized as the
"termites of the State," conjuring an expression that we know had been
used by Cervantes against the *moriscos* and later by Las Casas in an indirect allusion to the *morenos,* an expression that in all cases was a reference to those subjects whose reduction was necessary for the success of
the "great national" imperial project. García, who had already lived on
the island for two decades, made it clear from the language of his report
that the happiness or detriment of the colony would be a function of
the state's own ability to control and police the boundary occupied by
the mulattoes. He said he was writing

> concerning the different types of blacks and their descendants, being of
> transcendental importance to the happiness or detriment of this state
> the relation, connection, leanings, communication and protection
> from either side, between the slaves, the new freedmen as well as those
> manumitted long ago, and the mulattoes of all species, who thinking and
> acting in a similar irrational, lazy and barbarous way, are by themselves
> incapable of aspiring to any other happiness but that begotten from the
> satisfaction of their most immediate urges or appetites and who, conse-
> quently, are (without the regulation in question) the termites of the
> State, instead of being useful to society and to themselves.[1]

García's remarks were part of a larger debate concerning what came
to be known as the Código Negro Carolino, or Spanish Negro Code, a
set of recommendations that was put forth by the planters of Santo

Domingo at the request of the Crown and that, even though never en-
acted into law, was part of the Bourbon Reforms implemented by King
Charles III (1759–88).[2] On the eve of revolution and after almost two
centuries of official abandonment, Santo Domingo had once again become the object of the Crown's attention for two major reasons. First
was the unprecedented boom of the plantation economy in the neighboring French colony of Saint-Domingue, then the most profitable colony
in the world. Second, escaped slaves from Saint-Domingue were seeking
asylum and crossing over to the Spanish side in ever-increasing numbers,
forming new runaway communities in the mountains of Bahoruco that
Enriquillo had once claimed. A map of the period (Figure 23) describes
and highlights the perceived threat posed by these new maroons. In it
the Bahoruco region is depicted as an impregnable peninsular geography
in the south central area of the island, a chevronlike chain of mountains
wedged onto the leeward side of Hispaniola as a dark foreign object
that appears to weigh the island down. The summary and introduction
to the Código Negro explains that its mission was "to repair and
improve" what it describes as the "two hundred–year decadence of the
Island of Hispaniola and of its agriculture." The decadence of the island
had both a reason and a culprit. The first was "the old abuses committed when it [the colony] was established." The second was the "idleness,
independence and pride of the blacks and slaves" who had come to inhabit the land.[3]

In numerical terms the population of the Spanish colony had barely
recovered from the *devastaciones.* Although it had experienced significant
growth during the second part of the seventeenth century, the island
had fewer than seventy thousand inhabitants in the 1780s.[4] This was less
than one-fifth of the population of the neighboring French colony of
Saint-Domingue, which occupied one-third of the island. Culturally,
however, the situation was different. By all accounts, the world that the
devastaciones had been meant to reduce had managed to take root and
prosper, in large part thanks to the official neglect the colony had "suffered" for two centuries, which allowed those whose aim was to be left
alone by the authorities to go about their business raising cattle and dealing in contraband without much fear of prosecution. This prolonged
relaxation of controls meant that by the end of the seventeenth century,
just as in the rest of the Spanish Caribbean, most of the inhabitants
of Santo Domingo were mulattoes.[5] By all accounts the entire Spanish

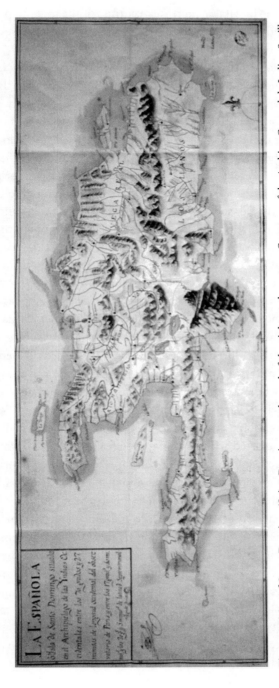

Figure 23. Map of Santo Domingo/Saint-Domingue at the end of the eighteenth century. Courtesy of the Archivo General de Indias, Seville.

Caribbean had reached the point of "saturation" and leveling-off that results from the inevitable increase over time of the mulatto presence in plantation and counterplantation society, rising from modest levels to numerical predominance.

The situation in the English, Dutch, and French colonies in the Caribbean, while less developed, was not that different. Even in the English colonies in North America, where slavery was more jealously instituted around a two-tier racial distinction and the mulattoes were not recognized as a distinct racial category, the existence of a "mixed" or "colored" population composed of both blacks and mulattoes was significant from the earliest times. Donald R. Horowitz has related the larger degree of recognition of the "colored" (read mulatto) populations in the Caribbean context to the higher social class of the whites who fathered children there with black or mulatto women. In the Caribbean, he argues, the scarcity of white women was a constant and continuous factor that contributed to miscegenation. In contrast to the English North American colonies, where the phenomenon allegedly occurred much more frequently between white servants and black slaves, in the Caribbean it was common practice for planters and persons of wealth and higher status to live in concubinage with their slaves. By virtue of their provenance, we are to believe that the children of these unions were placed above the other slaves and, if not in legal terms, at least in racial ones, also above the free blacks.[6] Unfortunately this opinion seems to be a throwback to old prejudices, implying that English gentlemen—the Founding Fathers included—were morally superior to the decadent Spanish caballeros, who could not be trusted with guarding the ideal of the well-formed European body because they had a difficult time keeping their trousers properly fastened at the waist. But what about men like Thomas Jefferson, whose concubinage with female slaves made them founding fathers in more than one sense? Was it not the "natural tendency" of all creole planters to exercise the power of their superior office by having their way with their slaves? Who will argue that rape was not the ultimate exercise of power in the plantation economy? Or are we supposed to think that here again, as in the case of Irving's Columbus, and despite plantation colonies named Maryland and Virginia, Usonian civilization was the result of immaculate conception?

In any case, the growth in the mulatto population seems to have been closely related to the development of the plantation economy and to the degree of its impact, permanence, and intensification in any given area.[7] As a rule, in the Spanish Caribbean the introduction of Berber, *moreno*, and African slaves during the early colonial period and the subsequent relaxation of controls that followed the almost complete collapse, destruction, and virtual official abandonment of Hispaniola resulted in a parallel relaxation of racial boundaries and divisions. In the English, French, and Dutch colonies the rise and sustained growth of the plantation economy tended to reinforce, at least officially, the principle of racial separation upon which the system was predicated. A look at the colonial populations in the English colonies, for example, readily confirms this. In 1830, 81.2 percent of the total colonial population in the English Caribbean was composed of slaves, 12.2 percent of freedmen, and 6.6 percent of whites.[8] Keep in mind that as a general rule freedmen tended to be predominantly mulattoes,[9] as were many of those labeled as slaves. The regional scenario instilled the greatest fear in creoles like the Cuban reformer José Antonio Saco, who warned his contemporaries of the very real possibilities that the Caribbean could be ruled by the majority of its inhabitants, thus becoming a black or mulatto sea. In 1845, after reporting the number of blacks and mulattoes on the Caribbean islands, excepting Cuba and Puerto Rico, Saco added the following apocalyptic vision:

> If we add to this formidable number of 1,862,306 the great population of colored peoples who inhabit the shores of Colombia and the one hundred and seventy thousand blacks of the English, French and Dutch Guyanas, and the Gulf of Honduras, the situation of Cuba becomes all the more alarming. And as if this were not enough, the North American republic offers us, among its institutions of freedom, the painful abnormality of having almost three million blacks of whom two and a half are enslaved and who are all congregated in its southern regions, so to speak, at the doorstep of Cuba.
>
> Who does not then tremble at the thought that there are more than five million people of African origin closing around Cuba?[10]

It is obvious that in a pan-Caribbean context there have been important differences in terms of the development of the mulatto populations if we observe the phenomenon historically, empire by empire, island by island, plantation by plantation. Nevertheless, in this Galapagos of the plantation the mulatto phenomenon is ubiquitous and must be considered important, if not central, to any discourse on the nature of those Atlantic American societies whose peoples can be said to be "children of the slaveholders." This is even true in the United States, where Eugene Genovese has estimated that today three-quarters of those considered blacks are actually mulattoes.[11] What is even more interesting about Genovese's assertion is the fact that in the 1860s the highest percentage of mulattoes anywhere in the United States seems not to have exceeded 20 percent. Consequently, it would appear that the phenomenon of "mulattoization" deepens with every successive generation.[12] This is a consideration of the utmost importance insofar as mulattoization appears to be the dominant trend and the final station that every former plantation colony can aspire to.

This much was already evident to the planters of Santo Domingo at the end of the eighteenth century, as they complained in the Código Negro that the "white and civilized"[13] were without occupation and were dismayed at the realization "that the intermediate population of blacks and mulattoes has acquired together with their freedom the right to live in idleness and free from all yoke."[14] Judging from this description, the majority of the population of Santo Domingo had freed itself from all yoke before the idea of Equality had fueled revolution and the cause of Liberty had filled the sails that would later help to propel the movement of independence. The challenge to be met by the Código Negro was to find a way, through education, to inspire the blacks and mulattoes— who were thought to be naturally inclined to sedition and seduced by a geography "that invites them to the inaccessible mountains"[15]—with "the ideas of loyalty to the Sovereign, love for the Spanish nation, submission to their masters, subordination to the whites . . . and the rest of the social virtues."[16] This, of course, would be a binding relationship, as the masters, inspired by "those principles and rules compatible with slavery as dictated by humanity," were obligated to treat their servants "as good patres familias treat their children."[17]

Behind all this apparent benevolence there was a bottom line. The planters of Santo Domingo as well as the Crown were envious of the prosperity of the neighboring French colony. Their plans hide visions of rivaling and surpassing the production of sugar in Saint-Domingue through the controlled dramatic increase of the population of the colony, an imperative that could not be met without the massive importation of more slaves.[18] According to Antonio Sánchez Valverde, a Dominican whose book *Idea del valor de la Isla Española* was coeval with the Código Negro, the reason for the discrepancy between the wealth of the French colony and the poverty of the Spanish was not the superior genius of the French and the indolence of the Spaniards—as was commonly argued, primarily by the French, who at the time thought of themselves as the standard-bearers of the European Ideal—but rather the fact that the Spaniards lacked "the key to open and to take advantage" of the resources of the land. "Are the Spanish or creole colonists by chance ignorant of what that key may be?" Sánchez Valverde rhetorically asked his readers, only to respond: "Of course not: they know very well that it is, primarily, the hands of the blacks."[19]

There was only one obstacle standing in the way of all expectations regarding the reestablishment and invigoration of the plantation economy in Santo Domingo: the mulattoes, who formed the largest section of the population and were by definition neither black nor white. In an attempt to rein in this intermediate population the proposed Código Negro created four "spheres" between black and white, whereas the French had identified nine categories for the offspring of relations between black and white. They are contained in the section entitled "On the Police" and are arranged in a generational sequence of six spheres (the four spheres created by the Código Negro in addition to the spheres of black and white), in a movement of *blanqueamiento* (whitening) that proceeds from the black—the sphere of lowest "quality"—to the "principal sphere" of the white.[20] In this scheme the four intermediate generations describe the different spheres of mulatto offspring, all of whom have a white parent. The divisions are labeled as follows:

1. *Negro* (black)
2. *Pardo* (brown), or first-generation mulatto *(mulato primerizo)*
3. *Tercerón* (terceroon, or third in descent from a black)
4. *Cuarterón* (quadroon, or fourth in descent from a black)
5. Mestizo (fifth in descent from a black)
6. White[21]

Note again that spheres 2 through 6 were the result of mixtures of whites and mulattoes, encompassing five generations of moving away from the black and toward the white, a clear enunciation of what in the Spanish-speaking Caribbean is know as *mejorar la raza,* or improving the race through repeated injections of "white blood" over subsequent generations of interracial relations.[22]

Of course this system was as impracticable as that of the Mexican *castas* and as impossibly reductive as the French system. Nowhere in the entire Código Negro is there provision for a record-keeping office or a set of guidelines for determining the "quality of the person" who failed to provide evidence of ancestry. We know that in the Mexican case custody of each family's "pure blood" quantum was the most pressing concern of the creole elites, who were the most preoccupied with maintaining their delicate position between the European Spaniards and the *castas*. In the Caribbean, however, the creole claim to racial purity was a moot point. Code or no code, racial difference in Santo Domingo was determined through opinion and observation, and as such was precariously tied to social standing and circumstance, as well as to the counterpointing of the *genio* and the *figura*. In 1762 Luis Joseph Peguero divided the peoples of Hispaniola according to phenotype, only to confess a certain apprehension at the introduction of the wigs that came to "hide the natural hair that attests to the quality of a person's provenance."[23] From this we are to believe that there were only blacks and whites in Santo Domingo, the latter category including all of those who could afford to buy wigs and some powder to avoid, in Peguero's own words, being "genealogically reduced by the common people."[24] Thus the wig became the symbol of the will to rein in and reduce the mulatto spheres, a movement that responded to the economic plan to reinstate the plantation and to the creole desire to approach the European Ideal at all costs, even if at the price of self-obliteration. As I will show, nobody came to embody this movement better than Sánchez Valverde.

Getting Rid of the Mulatto

Not surprisingly, in this economy of phenotype the Código Negro would also make it possible to purchase whiteness. Accordingly, the code provided that a cotton, tobacco, or coffee planter, whose enterprise was deemed to be of great utility to the colony, "even when he might be black or *pardo*, may ascend from the fourth generation of his stock to the hierarchy of the whites."[25] These planters would be allowed to have up to a maximum number of four slaves each.[26] In the happy marriage between the creole landed interests and the Crown's reformist spirit, the Código Negro was intended to grant secure access to whiteness to a planter class and a creole aristocracy whose claim to racial purity otherwise might not have been that clear. Back in that day, Moreau de Saint-Méry had observed that, wig or no wig, "it is strictly true that the great majority of the Spanish colonists [creoles] are mestizos who still have more than one African trait that betrays them."[27]

But as in any "happy marriage" in the plantation world, terror lurked behind the official and selective relaxation of standards. With its codification of a continuum of generational "cleansing," the Código Negro was demonstrative of the master's will to consume the slave. Regardless of whether the slave owner was European or creole, white or mulatto, male or female, the Código Negro described a movement of sexual violation to which, at least in principle, the black and mulatto slave was submitted. If the master's forcing his excrement down the throat of the captive in the *Infortunios* had signaled the ultimate in decreasing—in the being unbecoming of the creole—the rape of the slave woman was the basis for the production of a society that, forcibly by force, would be made to reproduce against its will in the most devastating practice of physical exploitation. In the pursuit of the Ideal this creational moment in which the master played God to a world he willed into existence through his testicles—*por sus cojones,* in Spanish—and not his divine breath, would in turn be religiously revisited as a pilgrimage site by all members of that world, regardless of whether the intercourse was forced or recreational and irrespective of whether it involved a lighter man and a darker woman or vice versa, or whether it took place among homosexuals of different racial stations. In the mulatto world there is no greater pleasure than difference and no greater violence than the one implied in the possibility of bridging it in the direction of the European Ideal.

In the twists and turns of the mulatto world the Código Negro also described an expiatory movement that was to further legitimate and strengthen the plantation system. The child of the mestizo and the white was to be more than just the last step in the process of depuration in the movement toward improving the race. Responding to a sort of Lascasian morality, he or she would also be tangible proof that the original sins of the white man, who had raped the black woman and enslaved his own mulatto child, had been redeemed. In the Código Negro the mulatto described a movement toward the white through which the master was to be reborn and reinvigorated, legitimized through the six generations of sacrifice to the white gods, resulting in the psychosocial category I label the *amo torna atrás,* or the "master comes back." Ideologically speaking, however, this *amo torna atrás* could be seen not as "white" but, more properly speaking, as a mulatto who thought himself as no longer in medias res, but as a legitimate subject who had been racially "stabilized and morally redeemed." This mulatto, who would think of himself as having achieved the very ideal of whiteness, if not necessarily of Spanishness, could be thought of as having become a creole. Keep in mind that, like all sociracial categories in the mulatto world, *creole* and *mulatto* are not mutually exclusive terms racially or otherwise.

Just as in the case of the exception made for blacks and *pardo* planters, the Código Negro tacitly recognized that the mulatto was a member not of a race in between but a nonrace, part of a movement that would, it was hoped, have a felicitous outcome. The forgers of the code were correct regarding the mechanics but not the outcome of that movement. Describing the mulatto in this way helps us consider the possibility—which was never proposed by the creoles—that black and white are not races either. Indeed, as Verena Martínez-Alier explains, the mulatto, especially the freedmen among them, "put in doubt the consistency and the continuity of the system [of racial categorization],"[28] which is precisely why, I would argue, the system retaliated by placing into question the mulatto's own consistency as a subject and by dismissing the possibility of the continuation of mulattoes as a legitimate group in the racialized society. From the vantage point of the mulatto, who moved toward the ideal (of whiteness), black and white were exclusively ideological positions to be assumed or to be eschewed. Indeed, when trying to describe the ideological complexities of *mulataje,* the external signs of such a condition—what in Spanish is called *mulatez*—are almost irrelevant. What mattered was not so much the shade of brown, the kind of hair, the economic power, or the particular ancestry used to place a person in the fastidiously differentiated sociracial categories of creole plantation society, but rather how that internal dialectic between the notions of the well- (or fully) formed and the less than ideal played out in every subject of the mulatto world regardless of the individuals' skin "color." Little has changed. In the end, just as was the case ipso facto in Santo Domingo at the end of the eighteenth century, in the mulatto world there are no blacks and whites, only mulattoes who might or might not be thinking of themselves as being on their way back to the ideal categories of racial "purity" represented by the white and the black.

Let me emphasize that the mestizo, or almost-white, is not exclusively a moment reserved for the mulatto elites. In fact, some of the lighter-skinned peoples in the Spanish-speaking Caribbean are found among the peasantry. In rural western Cuba or high in the central mountain range of Puerto Rico, for example, the *guajiros* or *jíbaros* developed as a people historically and geographically distant from the people of the plantation world. They are the "white" peasants of the Caribbean, the descendants of the marginal creole communities that I mentioned in the third chapter, as they were "whitened" during the eighteenth century by officially sanctioned emigration from the Canary Islands, a phenomenon that was also generalized throughout the Spanish-Caribbean from Mexico to Venezuela. In fact, *jíbaro* means wild, as in the wild dogs that roamed the mountains in Las Casas's fables. The major difference that sets this "white" peasant apart from the black and mulatto is that, because of his lighter skin, the law allowed the *jíbaro* to carry a machete. It is also interesting to consider that the name *jíbaro* was assigned to one of the Mexican *castas,* generally to a third- or fourth-generation hybrid. In one of the series of *cuadros de castas* attributed to Magón, the *jíbaro* is presented as the offspring of an Indian and a *calpamulato* (an offspring of a mulatto and an Indian). He was said to be "naturally restless and always arrogant."[29] More often the *jíbaro* was presented as the offspring of a *calpamulato* and an *albarazado.* The *albarazado,* whose name, as I pointed out before, comes from the Arabic *al-baras,* or white leprosy, was in turn the offspring of any of twelve other possible unions. He was the one who was "stained with white."[30] In turn, we might say that in the context of the plantation the jíbaro and the *guajiro* were irrevocably unstable, as was the mulatto, and according to the dictates of protocol in the socioracial annals of the viceroyalty, they were white only to the degree that they were spotted with "white stains." Once again, in the great Lascasian purgatory of the plantation and the world of the counterplantation everyone was, in one way or another, the "children of the slaveholders," and as such, everyone could have been said to be stained with white.

As the colonial authorities attempted to appropriate and control the mulatto movement of difference and instability, the Código Negro came to describe the ideal condition of the plantation body politic, or what Benítez Rojo calls the Plantation (the society dominated by the plantation economy).[31] Under the ideal conditions, blacks should be the majority of the population, and "[the mulattoes] will be the intermediate [class], the one which in a certain kind of way will constitute the fair balance and just equilibrium between the black and the white populations."[32] These were the complicated mechanics that the Código Negro would promote by stipulating, among other things, that according to their degree of racial impurity the six spheres of the plantation society were to be divided down the middle in terms of access to education and the right to aspire to whiteness. Chapter 3, law 6 of the code denies public elementary education to all black and *pardo* freemen. This was in response to "the sinister impressions of equality and familiarity" [33] that extending public education to all free peoples, irrespective of their race, was creating between whites and the mulattoes of all kinds. Therefore, all free blacks and *pardos* were to work exclusively in agriculture, and only terceroons, quadroons, and mestizos would be entitled to education, to the practice of arts and trades, and to the pursuit of the European Ideal. In fact, the latter were to be taught in separate rooms from the white pupils but by white instructors who would instill "in their hearts, from the start, the feeling of respect and the inclination toward the white with whom someday they would be able to compare themselves."[34] Of course, that someday would never come. If the creole planters proposed to raise the black and *pardo* growers of cotton, tobacco, and coffee to the category of the quadroon or mestizo, it was because that movement would affect their own status, propelling them, in turn, and in the best of cases—those in which wigs were required to hide the quality of a person's provenance—from the category of quadroon or mestizo to that of white.

In any event, under the cloak of order and assured prosperity that the Código Negro Carolino described, there was a hidden movement toward reduction that was nothing short of genocide. If by inhabiting and populating the boundary condition the mulatto was the wrench in the works of the Plantation, the system would retaliate by expelling him from that space and reinstating the original and ideal separation between the races by running the line of demarcation right through the body (politic) of the culprit, that is, between the *pardo* and the terceroon. This precise operation could be graphically described by a body that has been cut in half through the waist. Instead of anchoring the point of the compass at the navel to give the well-formed European man universal validity, the mulatto was being deactivated as a subject in the most dramatic way. As in all such Negro codes, the fine print of this one was in the penal laws. The division in the body politic of the mulatto world would be made clearest in the punishment set forth for taking up arms against a white or a Spaniard. A black or *pardo* convicted of such an offense would receive a hundred lashes, then would get his hand nailed to a board, and if this were a second offense, the hand would subsequently be cut off. In comparison, for an equal offense a terceroon or his descendant would be condemned to six years in prison, a significantly less severe and arguably much less painful punishment than losing a hand to the executioner's blade.[35] While the Código Negro praised the merits of the Spanish model, which had produced the mulatto as a buffer zone of sorts, and looked down on the models of the plantation colonies of other European countries, where the creoles claimed "having never mixed with the blacks (whom they look upon with hate and aversion),"[36] the fact is that the entire document, as I have hinted, was nothing but an attempt to legislate the Spanish colony into an improved replica of the French model. The question was not whether the mulatto population could be reduced, but rather how long it would take. If the Código Negro had been enforced, the *devastaciones* of 1606 would have paled by comparison.

As in Francisco de Goya's *Saturn*, the plantation had come to devour her own children.[37] It was as if the master had succeeded in overpowering the black female slave in the *cuadro de casta*, capturing the mulatto child and throwing her in the fire as the defective offspring of a new Spartan plantation. But in the terrible complicity of the mulatto world this was also a movement of self-effacement. In his book Sánchez Valverde made an ardent defense of the creoles of Hispaniola and of the Spanish nation against the "insolence" of foreigners "who out of contempt have dared open our veins and stain the blood of both the West Indian-Hispanics [creoles], as well as that of their European ancestors."[38] This was a direct rebuttal of Weuves (le jeune), whose book *Reflexions historiques et politiques sur le commerce de France avec ses colonies de l'Amérique* Sánchez Valverde quotes: "In one part he says of the first [the creoles]: 'If the inhabitants of the Indies can be called Spaniards, their blood being so much mixed with that of the Caribs and Negroes that it is rare to find a single man whose blood does not contain such mixture.' In another part: 'There is no Spanish or Portuguese colony where Mulattoes are not seen holding the highest offices. It is for this reason that perhaps these two nations have no single drop of pure blood, whether they mixed with the Negroes or with the old Moors.'"[39]

Sánchez Valverde's repudiation of Weuves would prove to be passionately ambiguous, a fact that can be understood only in the context of his own life and work. Antonio Sánchez Valverde, born and raised in Hispaniola, was a Jesuit-educated priest who also studied law under the Dominicans. In 1763, at the age of thirty-four, he traveled to Spain, where two years later he became a lawyer and was able to secure a position as prebendary in the Cathedral of Santo Domingo.[40] Upon his return home he suffered what could only be described as the "curse of Alonso Ramírez." All doors were closed to him, and he was repeatedly denied promotion within the Church. The first time this happened, in 1766, the governor and president of the Audiencia noted that Sánchez Valverde "has a very lively character *[genio]* and expresses himself with much freedom, even when he takes to the pulpit."[41] As Alonso Ramírez had done a century before, Antonio Sánchez decided to "steal his body from his country," setting off for Caracas in search of better fortune. Things did not go well there, so he decided to depart for Santiago de Cuba, whereupon, failing to get an appointment, he became desperate enough to take extreme measures: Sánchez Valverde fled to Spain without a license and went directly to promote his case before the king. Like Enriquillo, Sánchez Valverde had been well indoctrinated, and like the old prince, he also suffered a great disappointment when he realized that the law that applied to the Spaniards did not apply to him in the same ways. He was thrown not only out of court but out of Spain altogether. The king had looked down on his subject with some impatience and set forth in a royal decree of 4 December 1778 that Antonio Sánchez Valverde had twenty-four days to get to Cádiz and to find a ship that would take him back to Santo Domingo.

Once there, the unfortunate Sánchez Valverde got entangled in a legal case where his loyalties were questioned partly because of his Jesuit upbringing: the pope had disbanded the Jesuits in 1773, and their sympathizers were being fiercely persecuted in the Spanish Dominions. His license to practice law was revoked for two years. Soon thereafter, in 1781, the president of the Audiencia accused him of having stepped out of line while preaching from the pulpit of the cathedral, insulting the Spanish officials and setting a bad example before the commoners. Sánchez Valverde fled once again. He was captured ten days later in the French colony. Eventually he would be sent into exile to Mexico, where he died. But before that he would leave a most valuable testimony of his thought and opinions in the records of his defense and in his *Idea del Valor,* which was published in Madrid in 1875.

Denouncing his arrest as an illegal act, Sánchez Valverde wrote to the president of the Audiencia in the strongest of terms, accusing him of overstepping his authority in "the sacrilegious attempt (pardon me Your Lordship for the propriety of the expression) to violate my immunity."[42] He also accused the president and governor of being wrong and naïve, passionate and violent, and he went as far as to suggest that the president had lost his religion, which was no minor accusation at the time. At the same time he pledged allegiance to the authorities and was careful to point out that his escape had been conceived of a need to satisfy his honor and not with the intention of denouncing the inadequate administration of the colony before the king. In a tour de force that showed what Utrera has described as Sánchez Valverde's ability "to persuade to the contrary of that which his words seem to be meaning to persuade,"[43] the old Jesuit priest nevertheless denounced the affairs of the colony by stating that he did not intend to go to the king "to speak of the government, of the sale and supply of goods, of the elections, of private interests, etc. etc.," adding that he would "enjoy the good with pleasure and endure the bad with patience, like everybody else, without promoting discontent or wishing to cause trouble."[44] The president of the Audiencia must have thought himself lucky indeed to have captured Sánchez Valverde before he embarked for Spain.

There is no doubt that Sánchez Valverde was a formidable opponent, a man of education and a pundit well known for having a strong character and for never backing away from a good argument. Why, then, did he offer what can only be considered a timid and precarious rebuttal of the accusations of racial impurity that Weuves had levied against the Spaniards of Santo Domingo and their creole descendants? In the end, after much ado, he resigned himself to pointing out that all (European) nations had been unable to keep their blood pure through "the revolutions they have all suffered," simply adding that the *americanos*—as the Spanish creoles were beginning to call themselves at the time—had done their best to preserve Spanish blood, "which is as pure as that found in any other Kingdom," and that, in any event, the Spaniards had been more successful at it than the French, "whose counts and marquises marry rich mulatto women in the colonies of Santo Domingo."[45] Considering that in his entire book he had worked up to this point, the argument can hardly be thought of as a good counterattack. For the first time in his life, Sánchez Valverde could not offer a strong rebuttal. All he could say on behalf of his people was that the Spanish creoles had done the best they could to uphold the European Ideal.

The reason for Sánchez Valverde's trepidation on this point is revealed in the order given for his arrest in 1781. In it he is described as a "moreno" who "regularly goes in disguise."[46] As it turns out, Antonio Sánchez Valverde was what the Código Negro would label a terceroon or a quadroon. His grandfather had arrived in Hispaniola from southern Spain as a foot soldier in 1692. There he had married Bernarda Martínez, who was the daughter of a man unknown to history but not to María Cuello, who was her mother and who, presumably, was either black or mulatto. They were all from the town of Bayaguana, which had been founded following the *devastaciones* by bringing together the survivors of Bayahá and La Yaguana.

Were it not for the arrest warrant, we would have never known of the "quality" of Sánchez Valverde. His racial condition is never mentioned in the work. If a century before Alonso Ramírez had suffered the worst fate on account of his desire to escape his unpromising birthplace, Antonio Sánchez's own *infortunios* could be explained only as a function of his attempt to conceal the condition of his birth. There is no reason to doubt that, as he argues, Sánchez Valverde was never interested in anything but the salving of his wounded honor, an honor that, as is evident in his life story, became increasingly wounded the more he strove for satisfaction. A popular *décima,* or ten-line stanza, of the times illustrates the existential conundrum that puzzled a large part of the population of Santo Domingo, and perhaps most particularly those mulattoes of higher social standing who, like Sánchez Valverde, were anxious to arrive at that "someday" when they would be able to compare themselves with the whites. This *décima* is reproduced in Peguero's book and placed at the very end as if it were the moral of the (hi)story:

> Quite a funny thing it is,
> Conjuring pleasure and blithe,
> Those who pretend to be white
> Without a white wig and chemise:
> White as precious silver is,

Its pursuit may be no sin,
But the whiteness of the skin
Is no satisfying meal
And no reason to conceal
Juanelo's madness of kin.

May this poem be the tie
That gives my discourse an end,
And so help us comprehend
All the truths about this life.
Everything alas shall die,
White and black in all dominions,
And I am of the opinion
That in matters of ability
Some are born into nobility,
While true knights rise from oblivion.[47]

Sánchez Valverde may not have suffered the madness of the "Juanelo" (Johnny) of whom the poem speaks because he had the resources and the ability to disguise himself. After all, he was the proprietor of two small plantations and quite possibly a slave owner. But he was still a mulatto, and realizing that his body had never been a *quantum sufficit*, he strove to remedy the situation by engaging that movement whereby the slave tries to disappear into the master, the colonized into the colonizer, the victim into the victimizer. No doubt he was definitely among those mulattoes who relentlessly pursued the European Ideal and was decidedly bent on overcoming the circumstances of his birth. Here was a man who, even when repeatedly denied the opportunity to be considered and treated as a Spaniard, never took a step back in his quest. His racial quality was unmentionable. Could it have been otherwise? Peguero tells us that people were then judged on account of three main attributes: beauty, quality, and understanding. Accordingly he argued that just as no one ever judged himself ugly or ignorant, "we have never heard anyone say... I am mulatto."[48] Seen from this perspective, the Código Negro came to confirm what already was a prevalent practice in colonial society, mainly regarding the reduction of *mulataje* as the constitutive movement of mulatto subjectivity, especially among those mulattoes of higher social standing, who were, perhaps more than anybody else, "stained with white." Simply put, nobody ever aspires to an intermediate condition in a closed social system that is organized around an ideal of the perfect and well-formed as the absolute standard from which all power and all rights derive. Accordingly, the mulatto in Sánchez Valverde's world denied that he was a mulatto and would recognize that condition only in others below his position.

Here the self-repudiation of *mulataje* is closely related to the constant movement of negation that has characterized creole societies to date, where the practice of racial oppression is accompanied at every point by a discourse that aims to dismiss and disavow the very existence of racism. Generally this is a face-saving measure intended to keep the often prepotent enunciator from being singled out as a carrier of a less than ideal racial condition.[49] The first thing Sánchez Valverde complained about to the governor was the treatment he had received from the feared *maréchausée,* or slave-catching regiments of the French colony.[50] His captors had had him "tied by the arms to a mulatto."[51] He was indignant at their audacity. Was he not a Spaniard? Should he, then, have been treated in such a way? Apparently he did not consider that to the authorities he was as much of a mulatto as the man to whom he had been tied. In fact, at that moment the colonial authorities had seen him as nothing but a runaway slave.

Here was the terrible unresolved and seemingly unsolvable contradiction to which the mulatto was reduced in the world envisioned by the Negro codes. Placed in medias res between the no longer whole and the not yet white, the mulatto subject was to remain suspended, always fleeing from his constitutive moment and aiming toward a promise of resolution, anxiously awaiting for a someday that was never to arrive. Yet the mulatto would find a way out, following a movement that is best described by the curve-countercurve. It is no coincidence that Sánchez Valverde's most noted attribute was his skill to persuade to the contrary of that which his words seemed to be meaning to persuade. Sánchez Valverde might not have been a Spaniard, but in his dexterity in shifting allegiances according to the circumstances and in negotiating his immediate survival in a world where stringent laws had come to be devised against his kind, the Dominican mulatto was the direct ideological descendent of the peninsular *tagarino.* Was it not fitting that his pulpit had as a backdrop the horseshoe window of the Cathedral of Santo Domingo?

As for the negation of his own *mulataje,* Sánchez Valverde is not alone in the annals of American history. To this day we still find it hard to account for a third term in a system originally built to accommodate only two. As Arnold Sio argues concerning the literature on the mulatto, the discourse has tended to propose that "the people of colour were marginal to Caribbean slave society: neither black nor white, neither African nor European, and neither slave nor free."[52] But the mulatto could be considered marginal if only because historically he has been systematically marginalized. Perhaps the resistance to exploring the complexities of such a difficult subject is a testimony to our own *mulataje*.

It should not surprise us, then, that in the historiography of New World societies the mulatto seems to be a *postergué*, more of a thorn in the side of American history and politics than a subject worthy of historical and political protagonism. As a whole, the subject of mulatto history and identity has been neglected and poorly studied. When it has been dealt with, scholars have often unknowingly reproduced some of the precepts of the Negro codes. Almost invariably a certain aversion to "racial mixture" is reflected in attempts to reinforce the lines that separate white and black, free and slave, "good" and "evil," no matter what the ideological position of the author might be. There are, of course, notable exceptions to this tendency as in the work of Quintero Rivera.[53] Orlando Patterson, however, characterizes the relationship between white masters and free coloreds as a type of partnership for slavery and frames it within a pathos of cruelty: "The racially mixed 'free Coloreds' were seen as a vital buffer between the masters and the mass of black slaves. The freedman class strongly identified with the master class and exploited its buffer status to good effect. Notoriously, freemen were among the cruelest masters."[54] In this sense, the role Patterson assigns to the mulatto does not deviate from the role conferred upon the mulatto in traditional "white" historiography. Early in the last century and in the context of the United States, Everett V. Stonequist wrote that the "buffer role of the mulatto was a natural one given the slave system and the lowly condition of the slave, the jealousy and hatred of the poor white, and the caste attitudes of the planters. The free mulatto had little choice. . . . His white blood and his superior culture and education turned him away from the black man and toward the white. This attitude, in fact, has lasted for a considerable period after slavery."[55]

Patterson's position can be contrasted with the voice of Esteban Montejo, a former slave and Cuban patriot who, when interviewed in 1963 at the age of 104, recalled the life of the slaves as one filled with, among other disgraces, great animosities and conflicts between slaves of different

African origins and between the blacks and the creoles of "all colors." Montejo remembered with respect the elders of African origin and spoke with disdain of the black "dandies" or "smart Negroes" who were favored by the masters. Speaking of his own kind as a plantation-born slave, he said that they "were born thieving little rascals" and "learned to steal like monkeys."[56] As for the rest, in Montejo's view the black-skinned Congolese, of which he said "there were many of mixed blood with yellowish skins and light hair," were vengeful people who solved problems but "were cowardly as a rule"; the Lucumis were the most rebellious and could tell the future; the reddish-skinned Mandingas "were a bunch of crooks"; the "Gangas were nice people, short and freckled"; and the "Carabalís were like the Musungo Congolese, uncivilized brutes."[57] The fact is that in slave societies, both on and off the plantation, there was about as much solidarity between the utterly dispossessed as there was treason and complicity.

If there is a recurring and fundamental stereotype of the modern slave, it is what came to be labeled in the Usonian Antebellum South as the *sambo* syndrome. The English term comes from one of the *castas* of colonial Spanish America. The *zambo* (from the Latin *strambus,* or bow-legged) was the offspring of a black (or mulatto) and an Indian, and thus the originary mixture of the non-European pure races.[58] The image of the *zambo* is that of the incongruent body of "he who has knock-knees and the legs sticking out."[59] The *zambo* was the mulatto at his most unbecoming, a distant relative, at best, of the Vitruvian man. His body was the site of tension and unresolved conflict, as his crooked legs were locked at the knees in the very image of contradiction. This was a feud that resulted in a certain decentering or shift in the body's generative point away from the navel. The *zambo* in this sense was a degenerate subject whose body was unsuited as a site in which to harbor the analogic principle that sustains the Ideal.

Patterson argues not only that the *sambo* stereotype was the prevalent view of the slave in North American societies but that "sambo ideology" was also well established in the Caribbean and that indeed the stereotype was "an ideological imperative of all systems of slavery, from the most primitive to the most advanced."[60] Stanley M. Elkins, whom Patterson quotes, described the *sambo* syndrome as follows: "Sambo, the typical plantation slave, was docile but irresponsible, loyal but lazy, humble but chronically given to lying and stealing; his behavior was full of infantile silliness and his talk inflated with childish exaggeration. His relationship with his master was one of utter dependence and child-like attachment: it was indeed this childlike quality that was the very key to his being."[61] This definition is more verbose but as reductive as the ones that accompanied the *casta* paintings by Magón. Unfortunately, this is the "unreconstructed" view of the mulatto that tends to predom-inate, especially among scholars of the non-Hispanic island societies, no doubt partly reinforced by the work of C. L. R. James, who inaugu-rated the tendency to depict mulattoes as a counterrevolutionary class.

The French Mulatto

In *The Black Jacobins: Toussaint L'Ouverture and the San Domingo Revo-lution*, C. L .R. James establishes a contrast between André Rigaud, the mixed-blooded politician leader of the mulattoes whose first name in-terestingly enough James never mentions, and Toussaint L'Ouverture, the black general whose life and deeds are exalted in the book. In con-trast to the mulatto Rigaud, James invariably refers to L'Ouverture by his first name, as if writing about a comrade-in-arms. Although it is one of the most important books ever written about what is perhaps to this day the most significant episode in the history of the Plantation, *The Black Jacobins* is a carefully prepared ambush on the part of James, as he closes rank with the blacks against the mulattoes. Yet although it cannot be argued that L'Ouverture was a mulatto "by blood," James's argument leaves room to ponder the possibility that L'Ouverture was indeed a mulatto "by vocation," both in terms of James's characteriza-tion of mulatto subjectivity and in terms of the traditional role of the mulatto in the Plantation.

In his portrayal James speaks of L'Ouverture as "a general, a Black, and ex-slave like themselves [the blacks]."[62] In this assertion James dis-misses the complicated allegiances that existed on the plantation as re-called by Esteban Montejo. The first question James failed to ask was What kind of a slave was L'Ouverture? The evidence presented suggests that L'Ouverture was not a slave like the other blacks. First, he seems to have had what James presents as a benevolent master in the Marquis de Noé, owner of the Bréda Habitation or Plantation, and in the person of Bayou de Libertas, the overseer of the same estate. Most important, we are told that upon recognizing that Toussaint was the son of a petty chief—a master in other lands—his owner gave him five slaves to help him cultivate a plot and that, later on, he placed him in a position that until then had been exclusively reserved for peoples of lighter color; he was made steward of all the livestock on the Bréda estate. So Toussaint did indeed enjoy a certain privileged position on the plantation, a position he defended until it was no longer defensible, and a position, interestingly enough, that at least in terms of precedent was generally occupied by poor whites and, most significantly, more often than not by mulattoes. Let us remember that this was also a pre-plantation tradition in the Caribbean. We have seen how on the *encomienda* the well-indoctrinated Enriquillo, lord of Bahoruco, had a similar job description. In fact, the figures of Toussaint and Enriquillo overlap in more than one sense. James does not tell us, but Toussaint's father, Pierre Baptiste Simon, was raised from a very early age by Catholic priests. He might have been the heir to titles in other lands, but he was "well-indoctrinated."

But in a sense—and this is a connection to which James never alludes—Toussaint's loyalty to his benevolent master seems to have been transferred from the level of the concrete to that of the more abstract, as with the uprising he was forced to switch his allegiance from that owed his immediate master to a belief also worth dying for: his new-found loyalties to the forms of political representation that were being practiced in France during the revolutionary and counterrevolutionary periods that led to Bonaparte's dictatorship and to the development of the first "great nation" of modern Europe. This does not warrant our demotion of L'Ouverture; it only makes his position more complex. He was indeed a conciliator whose allegiances rested in a complicated and serpentine curve of tension and compression. He owed his authority both to his African father and to his European master and, like a plantation version of the well-indoctrinated Indian ladino prince turned runaway, he had to weigh and check the forces of both those loyalties all his life.

Like Enriquillo, L'Ouverture never did break with his past, an opinion that James pursues correctly although not to its more troubling implications. We are never presented with the idea, which must at least be considered, that L'Ouverture was, by vocation, a slave driver. We are told that "even Dessalines, the Tiger, was afraid of Toussaint, and this excessive reserve and aloofness."[63] Neither are we encouraged to consider, even with all the evidence that is openly presented, that L'Ouverture always did see the French as the masters, especially Governor Laveaux, who, like his former owner, supposedly was "kind-hearted"[64] and who, we are told, was Toussaint's only friend. To him at one point L'Ouverture wrote: "How happy I am to have so good a father who loves me as much as you do."[65] Like Alonso Ramírez, Toussaint spent his life in a futile search for a suitable father figure.

Consequently, as a general Toussaint "never troubled to explain over-much to subordinates. Their business was to obey."[66] Indeed, as had been the case on the Bréda estate, the explanations were reserved for the French. He was an intermediary between whites and blacks, a bellicose master to the slaves and a gullible slave to the masters. On an island with a population that was two-thirds African-born and where the Europeans had been violently displaced by the insurgents, L'Ouverture's role as liaison between Europeans and Africans suddenly acquired an unrivaled primacy. For him the French were always the patres familias, whereas he is quoted by James as telling his (in)subordinates: "O you Africans, my Brothers! How long will I have the mortification of seeing my misled children fly the counsels of a father who idolizes them!"[67] Thus we can see the unresolved contradiction in L'Ouverture as he assumes the position of the prodigal son vis-à-vis the French governor and that of messiah vis-à-vis the Africans. He was a conciliator and translator, liberator and enforcer, father, brother, and son. Could anyone but the mulatto, in all his subjective disposition to metaphoricity, wear so many disguises?

L'Ouverture, the slave of Bréda, opened with his mighty will a path along which loyalties were divided between Europe and Africa, between the runaway communities and the *maréchaussée*, between the Revolution and the Plantation. Sometimes he was a servant, sometimes a master; sometimes a father, others a child. Most of the time he was attempting to redirect his training as enforcer of the Negro Code in the direction of lawgiver to a society of self-emancipated slaves. He would always be, as he signed his proclamations, the "very humble and very obedient servant"[68] of much-divided loyalties and affections. Here Toussaint can even be seen to have fit the description Orlando Patterson gives of the mulatto. In fact, L'Ouverture's legendary ability to break through any resistance—hence his *nom de guerre,* which means The Opening—on the battlefield might have had a counterpart in his ability to be all things to all people, a condition he shared with the Virgen de los Reyes (Magos) of the old Sevillian *morenos.*

Sometimes the course of human events can propel its participants to new states of consciousness, and indeed of being. In the case of L'Ouverture, the man remembered by James as well as the one who died so far away from America—L'Ouverture perished at the hands of Napoleon in the prison of Joux in 1803—it would be possible to argue that because of the particular circumstances and the structure of the society he both defended and helped to destroy, this Caribbean victim of European nationalist revolutions experienced a truly transcendental change. He was one generation away from becoming a mulatto. But history could not wait that long: at least politically, this black was already a mulatto. Ramón Emeterio Betances, a Puerto Rican mulatto who was a champion of abolition and Antillean independence, wrote a memoir in 1870 in which he described the Saint-Domingue leader dying in his cell at Joux: "They say that in his last days, the black prisoner heard only the voice of consolation of the mulatto Rigaud, who cried close to him at the cell next door. A historical lesson that we should reflect upon."[69] So far away from home, this was a Caribbean Pietà, with the black leader of the self-emancipated slaves of Saint-Domingue figuratively dying in the arms of a mulatto. Indeed a moment to reflect upon, as Toussaint, the son of the Plantation and the father of Revolution, was always the embodiment of mulatto subjectivity.

As we have seen in the writings of Sánchez Valverde, the mulatto faced the possibilities of his own *mulataje* by engaging in a ritual of self-effacement. Could it be that James understood this movement as also a process of self-mutilation? In his own aversion to *mulataje* as a generalized malaise, James accuses Rigaud of having been "undoubtedly narrow-minded. He wore always a brown wig with straight hair to give him an appearance as close to that of a white man as possible."[70] Why did this upset James so? Did he not know to expect that a mulatto who frantically desired to erase some of the signs of *mulatez* within the span of his own lifetime—that is, without having to wait for generations of consistent "blood cleansings" to do the trick—would decide to hide his hair? After all, given the mulatto desire to belong to and be accepted into the household of the master—and in some cases the real possibility of doing so—we find even more terrible examples of mutilation and dismemberment. Such was the case in L'Ouverture's relationship to Laveaux. At some moments the desire of the former slave to find in the French governor a figure of paternal comfort and support expressed itself in images of literal dismemberment, expressions that might seem romantically inoffensive in any other context but not in the theater of the Plantation: "Yes General, Toussaint is your son. You are dear to him.... His arm and his head are always at your disposal, and if ever it should happen to him to fall, he will carry with him the sweet consolation of having defended his Father."[71] Once again we see that L'Ouverture embodied the full potential and the terrible contradictions of the mulatto subject. He was no doubt a revolutionary. Yet, unavoidably, he carried in his body the virus of what was a generalized pathology in the plantation colonies among those who were exposed to both the perceived instability of the mulatto and the insecurity of the creole, which manifests itself in a willingness to sacrifice body (arm) and mind (head), *genio* and *figura*, in pursuit of the European Ideal.

James's repulsion at the sight of the wig-wearing mulattoes reminds me of a passage in the writings of Jamaica Kincaid where she reproaches her father for wearing all his life a hat that did not fit his head: "Felt was not the proper material from which a hat that was expected to provide shade from the hot sun should be made, but my father must have seen and admired a picture of an Englishman wearing such a hat in England, and this picture that he saw must have been so compelling that it caused him to wear the wrong hat for a hot climate most of his long life. And this hat—a brown felt hat—became so central to his character that it was the first thing he put on in the morning as he stepped out of bed and the last thing he took off before he stepped back into bed at night."[72]

The idea, however, is not to condemn "mulatto vacillation"[73] or mulatto "treachery,"[74] but to understand it and explore the origins and nature of the otherwise versatile social persona of the mulatto. We may choose to denounce the apparent headlessness of the person who wore the wrong hat all his life. But we may also choose to see in this practice of social camouflage the most feared weapon of a social actor who, as was evident to the plantation owners of Santo Domingo—or to the judges in the Audiencia of Quito back in the days of the *Mulatos de Emeraldas*—was capable of undermining, through sinister impressions of familiarity, the fundamental assumptions that sustained the European Ideal. The mulatto's negation of *mulataje* and his apparent lack of a

critical position against racism might not be altogether unrelated to the
movement of rejection of race as a valid instrument of social organization. The movement of camouflage through which the mulatto adopted
the exterior adornments of the well-formed European body was also a
practice that undermined the Ideal while sustaining, as Quintero Rivera
would remind us, the values of spontaneity and freedom.[75] If the hat
fits, why not wear it?

The End of Europe

I have spoken thus far of the movement toward the white, which defined mulatto space, seeing it advance in its desire for self-obliteration.
Could it be possible, however, that there were other moments through
which mulatto subjectivity circulated? After all, we have seen that the
presence of the mulatto was inherently destabilizing to the plantation
system. So was there a mulatto practice that contraindicated what some
see as the *sambo* syndrome?

During the first months of 1802, the French troops under Captain
General Victor-Emmanuel Leclerc laid siege to the fortress of Crête-à-
Pierrot, located in the Cahos region in the interior of Saint-Domingue
near Petite-Rivière and defended by a contingent of blacks and mulattoes under the command of Jean Jacques Dessalines. The troops of First
Consul Napoleon were to suffer upward of two thousand casualties in
the assault. But the real victim of the ensuing mayhem was going to be
the Ideal Body and the European Ideal, as they were to be broken and
undone under the creole battle cry of "Kupé tete, brulé kaye" (Cut off
the heads, burn down the houses). The siege of Crête-à-Pierrot was part
of a larger offensive intended to pursue L'Ouverture's army to its last redoubt. The French, according to the memoirs of General Pamphile de
Lacroix, were anxious to obtain a definitive victory against an enemy
"that fought back in a rather irregular way"[76]: L'Ouverture's men, following in the tradition of Enriquillo, disappeared into the mountains
when being pursued, only to regroup and ambush the French on some
other occasion. What is more, the blacks and mulattoes of Saint-
Domingue seemed to be fearless when they faced the army that had
conquered Egypt. On their way to Crête-à-Pierrot a French division encountered some resistance. They positioned their cannons and fired
against the insurgents: "The first volleys did not frighten the Blacks:
they started to sing and to dance; they charged their bayonets while shout-

ing: *Come on! Shoot your canons at us.* A battalion of the Fifty-sixth Regiment took them at their word and placed them under such heavy fire that in an instant those who were not dead or wounded were scattered and disorganized."[77]

The accounts of the bravery and fearlessness of the blacks and mulattoes are accompanied in Lacroix's memoirs by poignant tales of savagery attributed to Dessalines and underlaid by a terrible sense of impending doom and outright fear on the part of the French. On 9 March 1802 the French General Boudet entered the village of Verrettes to find only the charred remains of buildings and people:

> The piled-up corpses still held the expressions of their last moment: we could see them on their knees, with their hands outstretched as if asking for mercy; the stiffness of the dead bodies had not erased their gestures: their features revealed as much supplication as anguish.
>
> The girls, with their bosoms torn open, seemed to have been asking for their mothers to be spared; the mothers whose children's throats had been slashed, held them in their broken arms close to their breasts.[78]

It is interesting to compare these images of devastation and torment of the European body with that of Leclerc's wife. Marie-Paulette Leclerc was more commonly known as Pauline Bonaparte. While her husband fought the revolutionaries of Saint-Domingue, Napoleon's sister lived a life of luxury and excess among the ruins of Cap François, the capital of the colony, which the insurgents had set on fire before her arrival. She restored Government House, decorating her boudoir in blue and silver and her bedroom in white and gold. Every evening she held concerts and dances in her drawing room. Each member of the makeshift orchestra wore a pompous uniform she herself had designed: "a dragoon's coat, the seams heavily laced with gold; trousers of crimson cloth, Mameluke style; a helmet of white horsehair!"[79] While Leclerc's men were being decimated by the insurgent army and later by a terrible epidemic of yellow fever, Pauline was collecting specimens for a makeshift zoo she had built in the courtyard of the palace. She had trees uprooted and replanted in the courtyard so that they could be covered with sails to form a large birdcage. In Saint-Domingue Pauline reigned like the empress of the Plantation while twenty-five thousand of her husband's thirty-four thousand men were dying around her. One of the dead was Leclerc himself, whom Pauline had embalmed in Egyptian manner after his heart was removed and placed in an urn. Who would have thought that six years later the tragic Pauline was to remarry, wedding one of the richest men in the world, and that as Marie-Paulette Borghese her likeness was to be sculpted in the whitest marble by Antonio Canova when she posed for his *Venus* (1808), thus becoming the very representational embodiment of the Ideal Body of the European (woman) at the height of Romantic Neoclassicism? Who would have suspected that, through some strange process of metamorphosis, the woman who had played Cleopatra in the tropics while the bodies of the former slaves were being blown to pieces and the bosoms of the French women were being slashed would be representationally reborn to be crowned beauty queen of Europe?

As the French laid siege to Crête-à-Pierrot, they realized, "We do not inspire any moral terror, and that is the worst possible thing that could happen to an army."[80] Even though the blacks and mulattoes were trapped and it seemed would surely perish, the revolutionary vanguards of the Napoleonic Army had lost their moral high ground and confidence. The number of French casualties began to rise, and they became so many that the French did not have time to bury them but had to resort instead to burning their corpses. Lacroix noted that it all became a frantic attempt on their part to rid the atmosphere of the stench of death: "I had the unfortunate idea of believing that I could easily burn the source of the pestilence that infected everything around us."[81] The entire operation resulted in a debacle of putrefaction and disintegration of the European body. It was as if a Lascasian plague had come to revisit the island and was now consuming the French who had set out to reestablish slavery in Saint-Domingue in order to underwrite the pursuit of the national imperial project. Lacroix's vision was apocalyptic:

> Be it because we did not gather enough wood, or because the foul smells of the rotting bodies made us stop the collection and piling up of the corpses, our burning operations went all wrong. Then, an even more unbearable smell came to impregnate the atmosphere, and it was so penetrating that I was never able to disinfect the clothes I wore while presiding over that toilsome operation.
> I realized through that ordeal the way in which wool absorbs and keeps the smell of the contagious miasma that can saturate it.[82]

The situation was desperate. The French were not just incapable of defeating the insurgents; they could not even handle their own dead. It almost seemed as if the dead were outdoing the living, depriving them of rest and leaving them feeling uneasy and unable to shake off the stench of death that filled the miasmatic atmosphere. They were in Hell.

Crête-à-Pierrot was to be a Pyrrhic victory, the hard-won battle that would cost the French the war.[83] Napoleon's troops were hopelessly drifting into a situation that would lead not only to eventual defeat and to the loss of the colony but, more important, to the undoing of the European Ideal. This was going to be a moment of universal importance, as it would be there, lost in the Cahos, that the European subject was going to be displaced from the role of main historical protagonist. What Alonso Ramírez had unknowingly and very unsuccessfully tried to do, the blacks and mulattos of Crête-à-Pierrot were going to pull off by defiantly ("Come on! Shoot your cannons at us") defending their hard-won freedom. It is important to note that we are no longer dealing exclusively with an abstract representational order. This was the result of a thoroughly mulatto movement of metaphorical subjectivity that took place in real space and whose ultimate consequences, while still somewhat incalculable to this day, were already feared by Lacroix and his men as they began to suspect that something very strange was going on:

> While we were laying siege to the fort, we could hear the enemy singing patriotic verses to the glory of France.
>
> In spite of the indignation we felt at the atrocities committed by the Blacks, those songs troubled us. Our soldiers looked at us dumbstruck as if saying: "Could reason be on the side of our barbarous enemies? Are we no longer the soldiers of the Republic? Have we become the servile instruments of politics?"[84]

As master of the historical narrative, the European subject was, however, momentarily displaced from his role as the protagonist in his own story by the blacks and mulattoes of Saint-Domingue, who now sang the *Marseillaise* as if they had written the lyrics themselves. If becoming "white" was an impossibility for the *morenos* on the Plantation, overcoming the white was altogether possible in the revolution against it. Who were the real revolutionaries, and what had happened to the European Ideal once the blacks and mulattoes, simply by accelerating historical time, completed the movement implied by the "someday" promised in the Negro codes?

The precise moment that the blacks and mulattoes overcame the universalist claim of the European Body can be pinpointed with exactitude.

It happened as Dessalines was moving his troops toward Crête-à-Pierrot while being closely pursued by General Jean François Joseph Debelle and his men. Early one morning the French fell silently upon Dessaline's men, who were sleeping. Everyone set out toward the fort in a scramble. The blacks and mulattoes got there first. Upon reaching the fortress, the insurgents jumped into the dry moat and began firing back at the French, who were then in the open and terribly disoriented. Lacroix remembers: "From that moment we were unmasked, the redoubt fired back with all it had, and instantly everything about us was turned around."[85] The French, and the Ideal, were unmasked and turned around.

In the end, James was partially correct when he located the origins of modernity in the Caribbean between the first factory, the *ingenio,* and the first successful revolution against it: the events of Saint-Domingue. For James, the slave was the first proletarian. He had a clear reason to rebel against property, because he was property. But the Haitian Revolution was more than a structural operation. The actions of the defenders of Crête-à-Pierrot already were describing the potential of a new discursive practice that was to destabilize the very foundations of the Ideal of the European body/subject as it came to be redefined in the revolutionary project of the French masters. The blacks and mulattoes of Saint-Domingue had forced the French under Lacroix to undress in a frantic attempt to remove the stench of death from their woolen uniforms. Suddenly their world had been turned upside down. The elite troops of the French Republic had been unmasked: by singing the last line of the *Marseillaise* with more reason than the French, the former slaves had denounced the *sang impur* (impure blood) of Europe. Naked before the world, the French were thus representatively disembodied as the most heroic subjects of political and historical protagonism. Meanwhile Pauline was busy carrying on with her duties as empress of the Plantation, making uniforms for bodies that could no longer wear them.

The elite troops of the First Consul feared that they had become the instruments of policy. The former revolutionaries turned slave-catchers were justified in their uneasiness and apprehension. The revolution, too, had been unmasked, confirming the representative order that heralded the foundation of the "great nations" of modern times. Nine years before the siege of Crête-à-Pierrot, Jacques-Louis David had foreseen the same when he painted his monumental tribute to the revolutionary Jean-Paul Marat, one of the most radical Jacobin leaders of the French

Figure 24. Jacques-Louis David, *Marat assassiné* (The death of Marat), 1793.
Courtesy of Musées Royaux des Beaux-Arts de Belgique, Brussels.

Revolution (Figure 24). *Marat assassiné* (The death of Marat, 1793) is a
masterful pictorial accusation where all the clues to his assassination
are readily observable and point in unison to the murderer: Charlotte
Corday, the agent of the state. I see this work of art as the immediate
precedent to the detective novel. In contrast to what Habermas calls the
code of "noble" conduct of representative publicity that had sustained
the ancien régime,[86] *Marat assassiné* is a composition based not on a

rhetorical formula upheld by faith, but rather on the mechanics of discourse, the force of dictate, and the system of dialectics.[87] This is art as pure ideology. In this sense, the mechanics of the painting are essentially responding to a movement of disembodiment through which the actual representation of the victim's body is an act of deception. In this rationalization of the historical occurrence, Marat's corpse is just one more proof pointing in the direction of the guilty party. In other words, the only body in this picture is the body of evidence, and the flesh and bones depicted in the painting are important only insofar as they are a narrative component of a legal or political argument promoted through pictorial means. *Marat assassiné* marks the moment when art was put at the service of what Koselleck called "the automaton, the great machine" set up in the Enlightenment, whose function was "to make and maintain order."[88] At the time, that greatest of machines was, of course, the Napoleonic Army, whose elite troops were turned around in Saint-Domingue. Known as the Grande Armée (Great Army), this was the first "great machine" driven by ideology.

But unlike the siege of Crête-à-Pierrot, this painting was a discursive act of legitimization. Marat, the revolutionary, had fallen. He was forever immortalized by David as a *martyr de la Patrie,* performing for the state much the same role as the peasants who, as Marx rightly observed, were turned into heroes through their participation in the army at "the culminating point of the *idées napoléoniennes.*"[89] Those peasants turned heroes were the same ones who had once run naked through the rainforests of Haiti assuming the unheroic role of enforcers of the Negro Code. Marat, too, lay naked; he suffered from a terrible degenerative skin ailment that prevented him from wearing clothes or going out in public. The political man had become unpresentable and had been forced to retreat into the private realm. This moment ran opposite to the events in Saint-Domingue, where the slaves fled the private realm of the plantation to assume control over the public sphere.

Moving transversely through the analogical chain that links together David's painting and Canova's sculpture, one can consider these representations of two reclining naked bodies as a symbolic tandem of sorts. David was giving us the Ideal that exists beyond the material world— utopia, or the more romantic lost cause. Inversely, Canova presented us with the Body in its most idealized physicality. In the time that spanned the creation of both works, 1793–1808, Europe witnessed the rise of the first "great national" imperial project of the nineteenth century: the king of France went to the guillotine in 1793, and in 1808 Napoleon's empire reached the height of its power. Yet halfway between these two moments was Crête-à-Pierrot, where the blacks and mulattoes of Saint-Domingue came to unmask and turn around the same project while singing patriotic verses to the glory of France with more enthusiasm than the French ever could. In another tribute to Marat, David painted him "just as he was when he died."[90] The engraving, which is dedicated to Marat, "The Friend of the People,"[91] reads: "Failing to corrupt me, they have murdered me."[92] The epitaph to the European Ideal in Saint-Domingue might simply have read, "They murdered me for being corrupt."

A Mulatto Nation?

It was in Crête-à-Pierrot that Dessalines was the first to propose that the revolution against the plantation should result in independence. In the first years of the nineteenth century, the Haitians realized that they could not guarantee the permanence of their freedom and of their self-given rights without independence. Over the next several decades, in the Spanish Main, creole leaders would try to make nations out of plantations, recalling with fear the events in Saint-Domingue and carefully guarding themselves against the revolutionary—and counterrevolutionary—potential of the mulattoes and the blacks.

Simón Bolívar would be among the first creoles to realize that there could be no liberty without emancipation. But he did not arrive at this conclusion on his own. He was convinced of it in 1816 by the mulatto liberal Alexandre Pétion, president of the République d'Haïti who, as James remembers, "nursed back to health the sick and defeated Bolívar, gave him money, arms and a printing press to help in the campaign which ended in the freedom of the Five States."[93] After leaving Port-au-Prince, Bolívar wrote in the manifesto to the Venezuelan peoples of 8 May 1816: "I have not come to you as a law giver, but I implore you to listen to me: I recommend to you a united Government and absolute liberty so that we may not repeat the same absurdity and the same crime, for we cannot be both freedmen and slaves at the same time."[94] Although this was a document designed not to upset the planter class, it nevertheless clearly enunciated the problems that slavery posed to the project of independence and to the future nations. In his proclamation to the inhabitants of Río Caribe, Carúpano, and Cariaco, Bolívar was more emphatic: "Thus, there will be no slaves in Venezuela but those who wish to be slaves. All those who prefer freedom over tranquility will pick up arms to defend their sacred rights and will be considered citizens."[95] Bolívar kept his promise to Pétion. In the same way that the Haitians had realized there could be no freedom without total independence, the creole had come to accept that there could be no independence without total freedom.

But the originary movement toward independence in Saint-Domingue would not progress in a straight path toward nationhood. The blacks and mulattoes of Haiti who had so irrevocably triumphed over the French nationalists continued to be the offspring of the master in ideological terms: they would defeat the white but would be unable to tame the movement toward the white.

Two years after Crête-à-Pierrot, with L'Ouverture and Rigaud dead, Pétion was at the side of Dessalines when he proclaimed himself emperor of Haiti in 1804 after having ordered the execution of all the remaining whites of Saint-Domingue. Unlike L'Ouverture, Dessalines did not want to be French in the republican sense. His model was Napoleon. A year later his constitution would decree that henceforth all Haitians were to be known as blacks. Closing the door to the recognition of the mulatto led to a racial dictatorship that was not structurally different from the intentions of the Negro codes. Dessalines and his successors did not really rid themselves of the European or relinquish their claim to the Ideal. In a terrible movement of reversals, they turned themselves into black "Europeans," becoming the masters of their own creole plantations.

For his part, as the president of the mulatto Republic of Haiti in the south of Saint-Domingue, Pétion decreed that only people of Indian or African descent would be granted property rights. The mulatto, it seemed, tried to control his unstable condition by negating all European claims to the land. Pétion was looking in the wrong place, because the European claim to the land was easily contestable, whereas the same could not be said with regard to the influence exercised by the specter of the European Ideal over the *genio* and the *figura* of the mulatto: it was a matter of looking not behind the bush or beyond the sea, but rather under the wig. The revolution was on the verge of turning itself around.

Pétion's successor, Jean Pierre Boyer, who from 1818 to 1843 would rule over a reunified country—including the Spanish side of the island, which he seized in 1822—officially reinstituted the plantation in 1826. His rural code tied peasants to the land, restricted their freedom of movement and association, and announced severe penalties for those who did not conform to the will of the overseers and planters. The mulatto movement towards the white had become the law of the land. Among the peasants the idea of Haiti was clearer than the official discourse. For them Haiti was a country where "the rich Negro is a mulatto and the poor mulatto is a Negro."[96] The master had come back, from within the mulatto subject, to reinstate the Negro code in the name of the nation, which had become the next step toward the symbolic representation and pursuit of the Ideal.

There was one place during this period, however, where a radical experiment in emancipation led to a unique though ultimately unsuccessful revolution against both the colony and the socioracial legacies of the plantation. It was the Independent Republic of Cartagena, on the southern continental coast of the Caribbean, which was established in 1811 and lasted until 1816.[97] On 11 November 1811 the government of Cartagena fell into the hands of the blacks and mulattoes, who forced the creole elites to decree the absolute independence of the city. A terrified pro-Spanish observer had seen this moment coming when a few months before he had written to the viceroy decrying "the effrontery of the sambos, blacks and lazy mulattoes," who were a majority of the population of the city.[98] In 1812 the constitution of the Independent Republic of Cartagena became the first such document in the history of the coloniality of power to expressly proclaim the equality of all men, regardless of skin color. Cartagena was soon isolated; it was not only in open rebellion against the empire but also besieged by its neighbors, most notably from the city of Santa Fe de Bogotá, whose Andean creole elites held fiercely to their position of socioracial supremacy over the *castas* and who had always claimed Cartagena as a dependency. In desperation the government of Cartagena was forced to issue an open invitation to all Caribbean pirates who could be interested in coming to the defense of the city in exchange for a letter of marque and an "official" flag under which to sail.

The mulattoes of Cartagena held onto their independence as best they could, while their city became a pirate heaven. No doubt this was a radical experiment in freedom. But, as all sorts of refugees and outcasts of nations came to anchor in the well-defended harbor—including Bolívar, who took refuge in the city after the fall of Caracas to the Royalists in 1812—Cartagena became anything but a nation in the making. In reality, Cartagena was constituting itself more as a mulatto Caribbean city-state than as a creole Latin American nation-state, a significant difference that remains to be further studied and theorized. In the end, as Alfonso Múnera argues, Cartagena fell back under Spanish control because of the inability of her creole and mulatto inhabitants to come together, and also because she faced the Spanish forces on her own, without any support from the other provinces.[99] According to Múnera, the entire period was characterized by the "weakness and complete failure of the nascent national discourse."[100]

With the fall of Cartagena the road was cleared for the rise of creole national projects in the southern Caribbean. The subjugation of the city and its hinterland to the rising power of Bogotá and the Andean elites would be part of a tortuous process of national consolidation that, in the case of Colombia, has remained an unfulfilled project to this day.

The Color of Ambiguity

The exercise of power and hegemony seemed to undo the metaphorical movement of mulatto subjectivity. It was becoming increasingly clear that the constitutive currents of Caribbean subjectivity, the *irse al monte* and the *irse al carajo*—whether they were channeled in the direction of the European Ideal, constructing a nation-state "according to (the Negro) code" as in Haiti, or unable to survive the onslaught unleashed by the competing creole nationalist doctrine as in Cartagena—had merged to form a deadly alliance. The mulatto Caribbean, it seemed, was a world caught between two waters where the possibility of running away was always checked by the impossibility of getting away. And then there was Plácido, a Habanero poet who during the first half of the nineteenth century came to move in and out of the Plantation—and into and out of the postemancipation possibilities—in the most artful of ways.

Plácido was the natural son of a quadroon barber, Diego Ferrer Matoso, and of a Spanish dancer, Concepción Vázquez, who, weary of the stigma that would certainly befall her for having borne a child to a mulatto, placed the newborn in the rotating blind door of the Real Casa de Beneficiencia y Maternidad, the orphanage of Havana where unwanted children were abandoned. It was 5 April 1809, and the baby was barely eighteen days old. That same day he was baptized with the given names of Diego Gabriel de la Concepción, following the directions given in a note left by the mother with the baby. It seems that, facing the impossibility of giving the child family names, the mother had decided to cradle Gabriel between the first names of both parents, as is often done in the Islamic tradition. But the name was also a signature of sorts, as Gabriel de la Concepción can be taken to mean Gabriel, the son of Concepción. Even more intriguing is the fact that the name literally means Gabriel of the Conception, being thus a direct reference to the archangel who announced to the Virgin Mary the visitation of the Holy Spirit and the miracle of her conception of Jesus. So it would seem that this child was born to embody contradiction from the start, as the unwanted mulatto was named after the miracle that produced the Chosen One among the Chosen People: Iesus Nazarenus Rex Iudaeorum.

Diego Gabriel de la Concepción was given the last name of Valdés, as it was customary to baptize the children of the Real Casa in honor of Bishop Gerónimo Valdés, who had founded the orphanage in the first years of the eighteenth century. On his certificate of baptism Diego was described as a mulatto who was "almost white." Even when he was later rescued from the Real Casa by his paternal grandmother, he was never called Gabriel de la Concepción Ferrer Vázquez Matoso, the name he would have been entitled to use had he not been an illegitimate child. He was called Gabriel de la Concepción or Gabriel Matoso, names that alternatively referred to one of his parents but never to both at the same time, as is customary in the Spanish tradition. Thus he was born to suffer all his life the double stigma of being a mulatto and a bastard in a slave-owning society that was in every sense extremely conservative and where people like him were expected to assume their proper place, learning a trade but not necessarily learning to write, and certainly not good enough to call themselves poets.

Eventually Gabriel de la Concepción would be known simply by the pseudonym of Plácido (Placid). Like the parco mestizo described by Magón as "naturally humble, peaceful and simple,"[101] this placid mulatto was expected to be "docile and of a transparent tenderness."[102] Ironically, his gay, tumultuous, and complicated life was anything but placid. In 1843 he was accused of being one of the principal leaders of the Escalera Conspiracy, a bloody episode in Cuban history in which the Spanish authorities under Captain General Leopoldo O'Donnell courted and rallied in defense of the interests of the sugar plantocracy, accusing the nonwhites of conspiring, with the logistical support of the British consul and renowned abolitionist David Turnbull, to kill the whites in the city of Matanzas. The repression was severe. Blacks and mulattoes were rounded up together with white separatist partisans. Hundreds were imprisoned and tortured, murdered, or exiled. Plácido was tried and summarily executed by a firing squad in 1844. To this day, however, historians disagree as to his participation in the episode. Was Plácido a conspirator or a scapegoat?

The difficulties in explaining Plácido's death are only compounded by the cloud of mystery that surrounded his life and by the relative obscurity to which his work has been relegated in Cuban letters. To begin with, just as in the case of Sánchez Valverde, there is no contemporary image of Plácido, so although there is no doubt as to the excellence of his *genio,* there is no testament to his *figura.* It is as if he was physically unrepresentable in his day. Such is the sense we get from reading the words of the nineteenth-century Puerto Rican Eugenio María de Hostos, a liberal creole educator and abolitionist who described the mulatto poet in almost pathological terms: "Like the transition period in which he was born, Plácido was physiologically in transition. He was coming from the African race on his father's side and going toward the Caucasian represented by his mother. He was going from black to white.... He was ... of an irresolute color somewhere between white and mulatto."[103] Hostos thought that this mulatto poet was the embodiment of what the Negro codes had tried to control and reduce: forever unstable, ambiguous, and never a *quantum sufficit,* he was the very color of ambiguity.

Hostos, who was one generation younger than the Habanero poet, could not approve of Plácido's willingness to compromise, especially with the Spanish "side of the family." To be sure, Plácido wrote poems of a certain patriotic fervor or at least verses in which he condemned tyranny and called for Liberty. But he wrote many more poems in praise of the queen of Spain. Ultimately, Hostos tended to despise Plácido and to see his body and his life as symptomatic of what he saw as the terrible sickness of Cuba at the time: "While Plácido sang the praises of Isabel and Cristina, the people of Cuba were in the worst condition the enslaved could suffer: they were pleased with their master."[104] As a moralist Hostos could not tolerate the ambiguity and perceived inconsistencies of the mulatto. For Hostos, who was otherwise quite ambiguous himself when it came to measuring his person against the European Ideal, Plácido was immorality personified, and he was repelled by the way he saw him operating: "Adulating what instinctively he cursed, cursing what he had just adulated with adulatory verses, he was living proof of the detestable transition period he lived in, of the sick society that aborted him."[105]

These were strong words coming from a man who was pursued all his life by the tepid political visions he had put forth in his first book, *La peregrinación de Bayoán*. In it he visited the preferred creole trope of the noble Indian and proposed a rather cozy relationship between Spain and her Antillean colonies. Back then Betances, the mulatto leader of the Puerto Rican revolutionary movement, had written to remind him, "When one wants to make an omelet one must be prepared to break the eggs: omelets without broken eggshells and revolutions without revolting have never been seen."[106]

Why would Hostos, who was otherwise a liberal and an ardent champion of universal education, have such a difficult time with the mulatto poet? Why would the otherwise restrained Puerto Rican label Plácido a social miscarriage? What was it about Plácido that triggered such a visceral response from him? I am inclined to think that it was not so much what Hostos termed Plácido's "irresolute color," but rather the fact that to him, as to most of the creoles of the day, people like Plácido were the embodiment of a competing social agent whose growing access to the public sphere they resented and whose major claims to it they did not acknowledge unless it coincided with or buttressed their own political aspirations. It is for this reason that in Plácido's day as well as in that of Hostos the image of the Indian was a safe iconographic moment preferred by the creole elites in the construction of their anti-Spanish discourse.

The representative embodiment of this order was the statue of the *Noble Habana* (Figure 25), an allegory of the city of Havana—and of creole claims to the entire island of Cuba—sculpted of Carrara marble by Giuseppe Gaggini and commissioned in 1837 by Claudio Martínez de Pinillos, count of Villanueva. During Plácido's time Martínez de Pinillos was the most powerful representative of the planter class and of the creole elites of Havana in their quarrels with Captain General Miguel Tacón y Rosíque, quarrels that caused the competing interests to court the allegiances of the citizenry through the construction or rehabilitation of the built environment.[107] In this sense it is quite telling that the statue stands atop a fountain (the Fuente de la India) at the end of a vista on the southernmost point of the former Paseo de Extramuros (today the

Figure 25. Giuseppe Gaggini, *Noble Habana*, 1837, Havana. Photograph by the author.

Paseo del Prado or Paseo de Martí) and that on the other end of this prominent urban element once stood the municipal prison, better known in its day as Carcel de Tacón, or Tacón's Jail. The allegorical work depicts an enthroned woman sculpted in the classical Greek style and dressed in palm fronds and a crown of feathers. The image is supposed to be that of the Indian queen who greeted the first conquistadors and after whom the city was named. Guarded by four ferocious Greek-style dolphins, this noble savage is holding with her right hand the coat of arms of the city and in her left a cornucopia. As a representation of the creole planters' claims to power, this sculpture could not be better, as the woman seems to be proclaiming: I have the keys to the city and the secret to making this land productive.

In this monument the European Ideal has been dressed up in feathers: she is the Indian of the Indianos, a direct reference to the brave natives of whom, as Las Casas had reported four centuries earlier, one could no longer speak. No other image could have been further removed from the historical present of the time when it was sculpted. Unlike the black or the mulatto, the Indian was not an active social agent. And unlike Hostos's Plácido, the Indian did not have a Spanish mother who might have been liable to share the blame for "the sick society that aborted him." Quite the contrary: the Indian heralded as a protonational symbol by the creoles was a mythological abstraction intended to neutralize under the common banner of resistance to European despotism the permanent threat posed by the black and mulatto interests, as they represented, both historically and politically, the most consequent challenge to the hegemony of Spain and to the power of the creole plantocracy in the Caribbean. In contrast to the black and mulatto threat, made horrifically evident to the creoles of the day by the events in Haiti, this noble savage was the very image of the well–indoctrinated Indian, like Las Casas's Enriquillo.

Cuban critics have been more patient with Plácido, if only perhaps out of their desire to neutralize his inconsistencies and to promote him, despite his otherwise problematic image, to the level of a nonwhite hero of the nation.[108] He has also served as a very welcome token, a mulatto intellectual in a society where historically, from Manzano to Guillén, few nonwhites have ever been granted the distinction of being considered "thinkers."

Plácido's image was similar to that presented in the early twentieth-century equivalent of the *Noble Habana*, the allegorical sculpture called the *Alma Mater* (Figure 26). In urban as well as historical terms, this sculpture is in an inseparable representational tandem with Gaggini's statue. At the main ceremonial entrance to the University of Havana, atop its monumental staircase completed in 1927, this allegory in bronze

Figure 26. Mario Korbel, *Alma Mater*, 1919, Havana. Photograph by Alfonso Díaz Concepción and the author.

is a symbol of what Ángel Rama called the lettered city.[109] The sculpture was modeled by the Czech Mario Korbel in 1919 and cast by Roma Bronze Works in New York City. Atop the hill where the university is located, the *Alma Mater* was placed so as to preside over the city, just as a century before the *Noble Habana* had been placed so as to dominate the most symbolic axis of the city. There she receives with open arms all those who proceed up the staircase that leads to the rectorate and the main courtyard of the university. The architectural setting is a veritable Cuban Propylaea. But this Cuban Athena looks frozen in an awkward moment of anatomical imbalance. There is an uneasy equilibrium in her body, whose bilateral symmetry is somehow disturbed by the uneven weight and proportions that, as in the map of the city of 1567, seem to set the head apart from the rest of the body. The reason for this is readily understandable: the head (and the neck) portray a creole girl of sixteen, Feliciana Villalón y Wilson, the daughter of Ramón Villalón, who was the minister of public works when the statue was commissioned. The body was based on the figure of an anonymous mulatto woman. Recent critics have confirmed the intent of the artist and the program of the commission, pointing to what can only be termed as a Frankensteinian manipulation of the human body. Their somewhat ironic description of the statue speaks to the historical prejudice of Cuban academia: "The young girl gave a sweet and innocent, young and beautiful face to the Alma Mater. The grown woman gave it strength, vigor and elegance."[110]

In light of the creole traditions that are symbolically so clearly represented in the *Noble Habana* and the *Alma Mater,* is it any surprise to find that Plácido's perceived ambiguity was as intolerable to and undecipherable by his contemporary critics as is his legacy, to this day, of an irresolute color within the Cuban canon? With all the intrigue that surrounded Plácido's death, we know and understand it much better than his life. Who was this reluctantly recruited patriot who wrote more poems to the queen of Spain than to Cuba?

In one of his fables, "El hombre y el canario" (The man and the canary), Plácido revisited a common trope in the critique of slavery: the master and his jailed mascot. This exchange of words between the man and the canary ventures into the realm of *sambo* iconography and begins to explain the reason for the apparent adulation that characterizes his work, which Hostos dismissed as pathological:

I sing what I am taught,
For with my beautiful trill
Even when crying occult,
Their orders I must fulfill
To keep from suffering so.

I adulate him in disguise,
For I am my owner's enchanter;
But in my conscience I surmise
I masterfully fool my master,
So I may preserve my life.[111]

For Plácido, who had been raised by his mulatto grandmother, her-self a former slave, subservience was a matter of survival and adulation always a question of keeping up appearances. But these are not the con-fessions of a slave who was happy with his lot. On a more profound level this poem is an unusual and direct contestation of slavery. In the fable the bird is the slave. The master is not the Spaniard, though: he is the Cuban creole. In fact—and this was an unspeakable moment in the discourse of Cuban nationalism—Plácido placed the cause of freedom over that of independence, reclaiming the revolutionary possibilities we observed in the siege of Crête-à-Pierrot and elevating the practice to the level of discourse. Subverting with his serious irony the divisions made in plantation society between the thinking and the nonthinking, Plácido introduced an uneasy moment of instability by beginning the poem like this:

When everywhere one could listen
to the irrational ones speak
and man's understanding glistened
(not strange, for once the sun has risen
even the animals speak), ... [112]

That day, Plácido tells us, even the animals could speak. But that is not all. Curiously, he divides the speaking subjects into a triumvirate: animal/irrational subject/man. This trilogy can also be understood as mascot/slave/master. In the poetic fable, there is a strange movement between these three moments. On one level the canary speaks to the slave. On another level it is the slave who speaks to the master. This is no doubt the poetry of *mulataje,* the poesis of a fluid subjectivity that navigates through triangulation instead of oscillating between extremes, always resisting and escaping reduction, as when feigning adulation by promoting what Aldo Rossi would call "the richness implicit in the error."[113] Here, perhaps, we find a most graceful movement of metaphorical subjectivity. In this triad we have the option of reading the poem in the mascot-slave modality, which may seem a throwback to the romantic sensibilities of the epoch and to the figure of the tragic slave. But we can also read it in terms of the slave-master relationship. That way it becomes more intriguing, as it combines the idea of emancipation with a critique of independence:

> And ... as for being a slave ...
> Don't be shocked, I understand;
> Pardon me, a simple knave,
> For asking thus if I may,
> The same question of you, *man:*
> I have fallen, so you see,
> Into your trap, and all my will
> Cannot help me to be free,
> For you as my captor still
> Remain superior to me.
>
> But even when you profess
> Obedience only to God,
> To a man you must confess,
> Superior though he is not,
> You submit under duress ... !
>
> What sort of unstable client
> Would try such a trick on me?
> Or is it not rather deviant
> To want to find in a pygmy
> Greater strength than in a giant?[114]

There is no doubt that Plácido was talking to the creole as the (white) man. This was putting the pygmy before the giant, the mulatto before the Ideal, questioning with sarcasm the legitimacy of the nationalist discourse just as the defenders of Crête-à-Pierrot through their actions unmasked and undid the French and their slogans. Let me tell you about being a slave, he seemed to have been saying to the would-be patriots. Feigning adulation, like the canary, the slave tells the master what the master wants to hear. He cannot escape his bondage on account of his master's superiority. Then comes the vengeance of the irrationals. The slave questions the master and asks why he lets himself be enslaved by another man: the Spaniard. Here mulatto discourse unmasks the creole.

How can one be a slave to another slave? What kind of masters are these who let themselves be ruled by others? As a true master of metaphorical movement Plácido has redefined the entire triad, which now reads mulatto/creole/European, all the while labeling the creole subject with the very title of unstable. The coup de grâce arrives in the last verse. It is as if Plácido were saying to the creole not to count on him for his project of "white emancipation." If as a man he is a giant, he can get himself out of being ruled by the Spaniards.

The feud between the creoles and the mulattoes had been organized around the dichotomies of nation/plantation, independence/freedom. The national would be forged and undone according to two fundamental movements. On the one hand, like Plácido, the mulatto would curse what he seemed to adulate: the Ideal, or what Plácido called man. On the other hand, the creole would attempt to keep those whom Plácido sarcastically described as irrationals from enjoying the rights of nationality and the privileges of power. It would be in this permanent trial of wills, and not in the moment of transition that Hostos perceived in Plácido, that the possibilities of Caribbean emancipation would be at stake.

In the "sociopoetic" continuum of early nineteenth-century Cuba, Jose María de Heredia y Campuzano (1803–39) occupied the obverse side of the coin to Plácido. As Manuel Moreno Fraginals points out, he was "an idol to the white creole youths of the times."[115] As a creole nationalist forced into exile by the Spaniards, Heredia y Campuzano has always been regarded as a more clear example of *cubanía*—or that which is considered truly Cuban by creole nationalist standards—even though Heredia, whose parents were Dominican, was born in Cuba almost by accident and lived there for less than five years of his adult life.[116] Similarly, critics have overwhelmingly held that Heredia was a more accomplished poet than Plácido. After all, as Horrego Estuch was quick to point out with such hurriedness that he might have missed the point: "At the age when Plácido was beginning to acquire a taste for education, Heredia was translating Horace and was getting ready to publish various poems under the title of *Poetic Essays*."[117] Furthermore, Heredia has always been regarded as a more moral man than Plácido, who, as we know, has been accused of being too complacent and indecisive. Besides, some will argue, Heredia had to suffer a long separation from his native soil as he dreamt of the liberation of his fatherland. All the while

Plácido remained in Cuba, resigned to a life of internal banishment and seemingly singing, like the canary, happy birthday songs to the queen.

But Plácido had no choice other than to remain in Cuba and to keep a safe distance from a project that was all but inclusive. Seven years before the execution of Plácido, the Cuban creole José Antonio Saco was defending the rights of the planters before the Spanish Cortes. Although he was an antiannexionist, Saco nevertheless admired the United States, a country that, as he observed, managed very carefully to "promote the full development of liberal principles while at the same time restricting political rights exclusively to the white race in some states."[118] Not surprisingly, he was appealing to the Spaniards on behalf of those he called Cubans and dismissing the rights of slaves and *morenos* because, as he said, "those men can have nothing to do with the politics of nations as they are unable to appreciate the degrees of freedom that in smaller or larger measure may be granted to the Cubans."[119] Just as the good old Franciscan friars of Concepción de la Vega had done, Saco was arguing that, like the ants attracted to the *solimán,* "those men" were moved by instinct and not by sense.

Here lie the origins of the creole project of Cuban independence, origins that are always irrevocably tied to the defense of creole rights against those of blacks and mulattoes or, in true Lascasian fashion, forcibly by force. And just as for Hostos Placidian aesthetics were nothing but inconsistency and subterfuge, for the creole patriarchs the mulatto world that Plácido personified was—and may still be—essentially antinational. But why such visceral responses on the part of the creoles? The fact that racism is a practice of everyday life that in the world of the Plantation could almost be equated to a social instinct can only just begin to explain such otherwise rational positions.

In a terrible foreboding of twentieth-century creole caudillismo[120] politics, Saco had claimed to understand perfectly the nature of colonial plantation society, saying, "Those [Europeans] who know that there is a heterogeneous population in those islands [Cuba and Puerto Rico] ... are ignorant as to the nature of their inhabitants, cannot decipher the intent of their inclinations, do not comprehend the forces behind *casta* sympathies and antipathies, and least of all, do not know what buttons to push in order to operate a machine that runs smoothly when one knows its parts but that is complicated when one does not understand its functioning."[121] We know that to the creoles the mulatto movement had always seemed inherently destabilizing. Could it be that its basic incompatibility with the creole nationalist project was its profoundly antireductive nature?

Plácido's most revealing poems are his last ones, composed during his trial and his final hours. Among these are two sonnets, "Fatalidad" (Fatality) and "Despedida a mi madre" (Farewell to my mother), both of which deal with the misfortunes he was born into on account of his *mulatez* and his sociopolitical illegitimacy. Here are the first two stanzas of "Fatalidad," the poem that Plácido allegedly recited before the firing squad:

> Black deity who without forbearance
> Surrounded me with thorns at birth,
> Like a clear spring whose banks are dressed
> With wild agave and prickly pears.
>
> Between the crib and the womb
> The iron gate of honor you placed;
> And up to the clouds you had me raised,
> Just to see me tumble from the moon.[122]

In line with the mulatto movement toward the white, it was a black deity—in the sense of an antideity—who condemned Plácido to a thorny life. A question of honor separated him from his parents at birth, and his *mulatez* banished him to a life in the clouds and to a sort of permanent free fall away from the white standard represented by the moon. Here again we find mulatto subjectivity being described in opposition to the gravitas of the European Ideal.

In "Despedida a mi madre," a poem supposedly written while awaiting execution, Plácido revisited two important moments in the memory and experience of the mulatto, the moro, and the peregrine of the Caribbean traveling culture, respectively. Note that, as in the previous poem, Plácido represented his mother as the Ideal. Here is the entire sonnet:

> If the fatal lot that I have coming
> And the tragic end of my bloody story,
> At the exit of this life, transitory,
> Leaves your heart mortally bleeding:

Cry no more; the soul in grieving
Reclaime its peace; the moor in glory
And my placid lyre for your story
Its last sound for the grave be leaving.

Soundings holy, melodious and sweet,
Glorious, spiritual, pure and divine,
Innocent, spontaneous, like the weep

I uttered at birth; now my neck inclined
Wrapped in the holy sheets . . .
Goodbye, my mother! Farewell. . . . *The peregrine*[123]

Did this poem mark the end of the journey of a man who saw himself as banished in his own land, and his farewell to a transitory life? Or was it a farewell to a life of transition and of perennial misplacement? Like Toussaint with regard to his "French father," Laveaux, this mulatto would carry the memory of his white mother to the grave. But even then the movement of transition and incongruity would not be over: Plácido, the peregrine, would go to glory to find himself misplaced as a Moor in a Christian Heaven. It is important to point out that in the context of the mulatto world of the Caribbean, Plácido's reference to the Moor came from a memory, though a distant one, and was not, as in the case of Washington Irving, the product of a capricious Orientalist imagination.

Plácido's memory would nevertheless remain a unique moment in the history of the Caribbean. To this day he continues to be formally and genuinely misunderstood; his enigmatic figure is timidly elevated to the status of a patriot only by those who have inherited the national discourse from the people who, back then, never forgave him for having learned to write so well.[124] In the old quarter of the city of Havana, at the corner of Bernaza and Teniente Rey streets, there is a modest monument to Plácido. It sits rather prophetically to the side of the Church of Santo Cristo del Buen Viaje, or Christ of the Good Voyage. Against the background of a light-colored marine limestone is a bronze bas relief with a dark patina in which some unsung artist tried to show how the face of the city's most famous bastard might have looked. The monument is invisible to passersby and residents, as it lies abandoned like a deserted island in a sea of humanity. Perhaps it will remain so, in true Placidian fashion, forsaken at birth and for the most part forever unclaimed.

Plácido himself, however, was clear as to who would be the inheritors of his legacy. In one of his last fables he wrote of a rich man who left his inheritance to a Mr. So-and-So on the condition that he not pay a single debt of those he had left behind. The premise was telling in the context of the life of this mulatto poet who had been born to pay for every broken glass in his master's kitchen. Furthermore, the name of the heir was a signature of sorts. In the name Don Fulano de Tal, or Mr. So-and-So (in Usonian, John Doe), there is both a recognition of title and the reality of anonymity. In addition, the name Fulano is a reference to the Fulani, a people of sub-Saharan Africa whose lands extend eastward to the Sudan from the coast of Senegal. The name Don Fulano de Tal demands the recognition of the otherwise faceless and nameless *moreno*. Plácido wrote:

> He said: "I leave as my sole heir,
> in my last will, to forestall
> from paying all debtors,
> one Mr. Fulano de Tal."
>
> The heir upon hearing this
> Swore, well convinced of it all,
> not to pay a single bill
> until the Heavens shall fall.[125]

The mulatto poet was a Moor in Heaven, and in Cuba a Don Fulano de Tal—a Mr. Nobody. There Plácido remains, always unknown to many but no longer to himself. For the first time a mulatto had named his *mulataje* in all its complexity. It was the creole's turn to respond. On the morning of 28 June 1844, a day after he had written his "Despedida a mi madre," Gabriel de la Concepción/Gabriel Matoso/Plácido was one of eleven men who, found guilty of conspiring against the whites, was shot to death by a firing squad in the San Carlos Cemetery in Matanzas. Plácido's epitaph could very well have read, borrowing from David's tribute to Marat: "Unable to comprehend me, they have assassinated me."

Between *Patria* and Freedom

Plácido's understanding concerning the need to differentiate between independence and freedom came to be enunciated, as a cohesive if only frail political project, a decade later in the revolutions of the peoples of the Cibao Valley in 1857 and 1863. Santo Domingo had gained its independence from the Republic of Haiti in 1844 after twenty-two years of occupation. Soon thereafter, control of the government of the new Dominican Republic fell into the hands of General Pedro Santana, a wealthy cattle rancher and landowner "of pure Spanish blood,"[126] who led the effort to repel repeated Haitian attacks aimed at reestablishing control over the entire island. In the process, Santana assumed full dictatorial powers, effectively becoming the first in what would be a long succession of Dominican caudillos.[127]

In 1848, suffering from depression, Santana retired to his estate, leaving the administration of the government in the hands of his cabinet until major public dissatisfaction finally forced him to resign. General Manuel Jiménez was named to replace him, but a subsequent Haitian attack under Faustine Soulouque, the emperor of Haiti, forced the government to call Santana back to active duty in 1849 as the only one who could successfully lead the army and save the country from foreign domination. Santana repelled the attack and then marched to Santo Domingo, where after a brief civil war Jiménez fled to exile in Curaçao. Before retiring to his estate once again, Santana left the government in the hands of Buenaventura Baez, another creole landowner and an exporter of mahogany. A skilled politician, Baez moved quickly to transfer power to his own hands, forcing Santana, who was heralded as "the Illustrious Liberator of the *Patria*,"[128] to maneuver so as to get himself elected president at the end of Baez's term in 1853. Like Jiménez, Baez ended up in Curaçao. But he did not give up. For the next two decades Baez and Santana would fight each other for control of the presidency.

Baez came back to power in 1856, this time forcing Santana into exile. Soon thereafter the tobacco planters of the Cibao region revolted. Baez had previously tried to monopolize their business in collusion with French interests. But this time around the president had practically stolen the entire year's tobacco crop by having a group of associates buy it using worthless paper money he had printed for the occasion.[129] In response to the economy of pillage promoted by the second creole caudillo, the peoples of the Cibao rose up and declared his government illegal. Meeting in Santiago de los Caballeros, the Provisional Government of the Cibao heralded the fourteenth anniversary of the *patria*'s statehood by naming 1857 the first year of freedom,[130] thus clearly distinguishing between the creole notion of national independence as Liberty and the understanding of freedom as emancipation.

The Cibao Valley of the old Vega Real was the richest land in the entire island and the center of a tobacco economy organized around small to medium-sized family landholdings. Occupying a little over one-third of the country, it was also home to 66,500 predominantly mulatto inhabitants who comprised about one-third of the population of the Dominican Republic.[131] The city of Santiago, in the heart of the Cibao region, had an important merchant and artisan class that supported regional interests and viewed the city of Santo Domingo as a rival in many ways.[132] This could in part be explained by the fact that, almost four centuries after the founding of both cities, there was no good road linking Santiago and Santo Domingo, making them, in effect, the capitals of two practically separate countries. Santiago's port was the northern town of Puerto Plata, which, due to the economic primacy of the Cibao region, was a more active harbor than Santo Domingo. In contrast to the tobacco of Santiago, Santo Domingo's principal exports were mahogany and other woods, as well as meat and hides, which meant that the economy of the southern and western regions of the island was controlled by an oligarchy of creole landowners for whom Baez and Santana were the principal spokesmen. In any event, as they had been doing since the *devastaciones,* the majority of the people of the island still lived a life of relative independence and self-reliance based on the practices of subsistence farming and contraband trading. The plantation economy—and the planter class, which, contrary to the spirit of the Bourbon Reforms, had never had time to redevelop due to the Haitian invasions of 1801 and 1805—had all but disappeared, leaving the entire economy of the island drifting at the margins of the main currents of Atlantic trade.

In 1857 the rebels of the Cibao went a long way toward correcting the evils of the past, proclaiming the first openly democratic constitution of the country and naming Santiago the capital of the republic. The mulatto revolution was under way. Unfortunately, partly out of desperation at facing an enemy who controlled most of the nation's resources, the leaders of the Cibao Revolution decreed a general political amnesty that expressly allowed General Santana to come back from exile. Heralded as "the Meritorious General Liberator,"[133] Santana was seen as the only one who could defeat Baez, whose army was otherwise securely stationed behind the formidable walls of Santo Domingo. Santana came back immediately and proceeded to reassemble his followers, who were mostly peons and family relations from the western lands of El Seibo, where his estates were located. By September 1858 he had taken Santo Domingo, abolished the liberal constitution, and reinstated himself as the supreme leader of the *patria*. The revolution was thus stillborn: the *patria* had been spared at the expense of freedom.

From then on the contest between creole nationalism and mulatto freedom would acquire clearer demarcations. On the one side would be those whose sense of order dictated that they defend the patria and the caudillo patriarchs at all costs. In the hierarchical scaffolding of kingship relations in this world, the caudillo was pathetically heralded as the embodiment of the European Ideal, or at least as the best the land had to offer in that regard. On the other side, there were people whose sense of freedom was both symbolic and immediate, as well as rooted in a tangible historical memory and evident in the practices of everyday life. For them independence was not only a liberation from imperial authorities, tributes, and supervision but also a casting off of the very notion of European/creole superiority and excellence.

A year before Baez had written to the Spanish governor of Puerto Rico asking for anywhere between two and three thousand rifles. Trying to make his point more pressingly, Baez played on Spanish fears that the United States was giving support to the insurgents following "the new system of conquest that has been in existence for some time now in the New World, known as filibusterism . . . which incites and promotes internal dissensions in all the weak states fashioned by the Latin race."[134] A decade after the U.S. invasion of Mexico and with the famous filibuster William Walker[135] still running loose in Central America, there was no denying the threat posed by the Usonian expansionists, especially to the island of Cuba, which the Venezuelan Narciso López had already tried to invade at the head of a motley crew of radical proslavery Usonian and European mercenaries whose aim was to incorporate Cuba as a slave-holding state of the Union. The price to be paid in the Dominican Republic was the peninsula and the bay of Samaná, which is the largest and safest harbor in the entire insular Caribbean and which, at least since the first years of Dominican independence had been coveted by France and the United States.[136] There is no denying that the espionage, intrigue, and sheer pressure exercised by North Atlantic powers seeking territorial concessions in the country, as well as by Haiti, were the major factors contributing to the repeated setbacks on the road to Dominican independence.[137] The North Atlantic powers really did come to cannibalize the new country, pitting one faction against the other and playing on fears of the Haitian threat. But the interesting thing about the president's remarks is his characterization of the governments "fashioned by the Latin race" as naturally and irreparably weak. Had Baez come to accept the constitutive deficiency of the creole national program in the mulatto world?

Only the threat of Haitian invasion was holding this young country together, and then only precariously, always under the shadow of the creole strongman Santana, whose economic mismanagement and political despotism knew no bounds. In this sense, the events surrounding the failure of the Santiago Revolution are comparable to the process that, half a century before, had led to the rise and fall of the Independent Republic of Cartagena. Like the city of Cartagena de Indias, Santiago was the main city of a region whose economy was in conflict with the interests of the official capital. And like Cartagena, the Dominican Republic had had an early history that was characterized by the repeated collapse of short-lived instances of consensus between the creole elites and the mulattoes.[138] Thus the short-lived Revolution of the Cibao inevitably collapsed under the weight of caudillismo politics, which were, in turn, powerfully reinforced by more threats from the outside.

In 1859 there was proof that the Haitians were once again preparing to invade and suspicions that the United States might take over Samaná by force. These fears were later corroborated in October 1860, when a group of Usonian filibusters took the inlet of Alta Vela, off the southwestern coast directly south of the Bahoruco region, with the intention of exploiting its rich guano deposits. They planted the Stars and Stripes and declared the island part of the United States.

With the economy in a downward spiral, the Illustrious Liberator of the Patria did the unthinkable. Santana negotiated secretly with the Spanish, and, taking advantage of the temporary suspension of the Usonian expansionist agenda caused by the start of the War of Southern Secession, on 18 March 1861 he proclaimed the annexation of the Dominican Republic to the Kingdom of Spain, effectively abrogating all Dominican claims to national independence. On the same day Santana wrote to the captain general of Puerto Rico: "The flag of Castile waves above the fortresses of Santo Domingo thanks to the spontaneity and the impatience with which this heroic people wished to merge their destiny to that of the magnanimous nation that for more than three centuries ruled so happily over them."[139] Unlike Cartagena, this independent creole state had been unmade from within. As in the *Infortunios*, this creole shipwreck ended in the restoration of the ancien régime. The weak national project had completely failed, resulting in the instauration of a new colonial government that, both internally and externally, confirmed what had earlier been seen in Haiti, mainly that the master had come back to rule over the mulatto body politique. For its part, the Spanish government, acting in the same spirit that characterized Usonian expansionism in the hemisphere, commonly referred to as the Monroe Doctrine, justified the recolonization of Santo Domingo as a way "to keep the Dominican people from suffering the slightest reduction in the integrity of their territory and even the most minor attack upon their independence."[140] The Spanish victory was to be short-lived, however, as the Usonian claim to the Caribbean came to acquire unstoppable momentum during the last quarter of the century following the end of the U.S. Civil War.

The annexation of the Dominican Republic to Spain was not a happy process for anyone, including Santana, who immediately became a subaltern to the captain general of Cuba and saw his dictatorial powers significantly eroded. A year later he resigned and went back to his estate with the consolation of having been given a generous pension and the title of marquis. For years Santana had maintained the loyalty of his followers by liberally dispensing titles and honors among them. He had, in essence, paid his men in a currency of status, which after all proved to be the best way to secure allegiance in this unreconstructed mulatto society. Now the queen was bestowing upon him and his closest acolytes the Royal Cross of Isabella the Catholic in recognition of the services they had rendered on behalf of this new Spanish colonial Reconquista.[141] The politics of wiggery were alive and well in Santo Domingo at the time.

The new Spanish regime, however, placed the socioracial standard too high. Instead of making the incision between the *pardo* and the *terceroon* as in the old Código Negro, it placed the bar between the mestizo and the white. This was not a project to reestablish the plantation, requiring the reconstruction of the difference between black and white, slave and free. This was a project to reestablish colonial domination, and as such it was to become, at least in principle, a much simpler

operation to impose Spanish authority—and the European Ideal—
over the entire body politic of the mulatto world. As it turned out, Santana was not the only one being retired. The entire Dominican Army
was dismantled, its officers forbidden to wear the Spanish uniform. As
Moya Pons has stated, the Spanish soon discovered that they had come
to rule over a country where "the majority of the population were mulattos, and their customs varied enormously from Spanish tradition because of the centuries of isolation during the colonial period, and particularly after 22 years of Haitian domination and 17 years of national
independence."[142] Once again the mulatto population would be divided—and would divide itself—down the middle, between the
lighter and darker-skinned types. For its part, the Spanish government
came to this understanding: "In order to develop the great riches hidden in the island of Santo Domingo, it is foremost indispensable to procure the increase in its population," trusting that "fortunately the conditions of the country lead us to expect that the white race may fulfill this
first priority."[143] Here the Spaniards were continuing a policy of racial
stabilization that had been started by Santana in his Immigration Law
of 5 July 1847, while at the same time conjuring fears among blacks and
mulattoes that slavery was soon to be reinstated. Literally adding insult
to injury, the new measures radicalized the Dominican mulattoes.

By 1863 the War of Restoration had begun with a growing general
uprising in the Cibao. Santiago was liberated in September after it had
been completely burned to the ground by the Spanish Army. Immediately the republic was reinstated, with many of the former leaders of the
Cibao Revolution at its head. But this time around things would be
different. The second war for Dominican independence became a racial
war, waged predominantly by peasants who had previously been politically disengaged but who now feared that Spain would ultimately reinstate slavery. In the process the power of the creole class was significantly
eroded, both symbolically and in the field. The first act of the new government was to condemn Santana's treason and, by extension, that of
Baez and the entire class of the southern oligarchs. More important,
this war was fought by small guerrilla bands that elected their own leaders and that came together for large operations and disbanded at the
conclusion of the campaigns. This time around the fight for independence was first and foremost a fight for freedom waged by a peasant army
whose concept of what freedom meant was immediate, real, and rooted

in a long-standing historical tradition: they simply wanted to be left alone by the authorities. In the end they would defeat the Spaniards—and the European Ideal—only to retreat to their plots of land, as they seemed to be wholly uninterested in pursuing any sort of national agenda. As a group, the peoples of the Cibao, like the old *morenos* of Seville, seemed to claim no allegiance to the group but were fiercely loyal to the most radical practice of freedom. The Spanish were disconcerted at fighting against an invisible enemy, as when the Brigadier Fernando Primo de Rivera reported from Puerto Plata that his entire column was immediately forced to retreat into the town as soon as they set out for Santiago by an enemy that was "completely hidden and safe behind the underbrush."[144] These were the people of the *monte,* and the Spaniards, as in the time of Enriquillo, were once again defending themselves from an invisible enemy who controlled the mountains of Hispaniola. But these mulattoes were no ladinos; they were not interested in being accepted by the Spaniards. They were claiming the *monte* as their last redoubt. Clearly, that *tagarino* world was no nation. The *monte* was simply land and freedom.

Allied to the primitive rebels in the peasant armies,[145] however precariously, were the merchants and the liberal mulatto intelligentsia of the Cibao. Their program was clearly expressed in a letter written to the queen of Spain on 24 September 1863. The tone and character of the letter denotes the principal preoccupations and speaks to the historical memories of the mulatto populations who had been systematically denied all access to public representation during colonial days: "The forty years of civil and political liberties [since the invasion of the Spanish side by Toussaint L'Ouverture], the tolerance, in religious matters that the population enjoyed under the republican government, together with numerous other advantages among which it is fit to mention national representation and participation in public affairs, which is an indispensable right in a democracy, could not be reconciled with a monarchical system, and least of all with a colonial one."[146] Clearly, the mulattoes of the Cibao did not see the Haitians as the terrible menace that they had been made out to be by the creole caudillos. As this excerpt shows, the peoples of the Cibao had Toussaint to thank, and not the queen, for having brought the republican institutions to the old colony.

The letter to Queen Isabella is a unique and important document in which the revolutionaries of the Cibao, like the *Mulatoes de Esmeraldas,* can be seen to have approached the Spanish monarch—and the European Ideal—from a position of confidence and even with a certain degree of sarcasm. Referring to the deepening of the financial crisis that the annexation had brought about, the revolutionary leaders wrote: "Nevertheless, this disastrous arrangement, which in any other place in the world would have brought about a revolution, was borne here with the utmost resignation. The only signs of dissatisfaction on the part of the population were occasional supplications, lamentations and complaints, as if the population was hesitant to conclude that such grave faults could have been committed by the wise people of Europe whom, due to our modesty, we have considered our superiors with respect to intelligence."[147]

These revolutionaries might have been the inheritors of Sánchez Valverde's ability "to persuade to the contrary of that which his words seem to be meaning to persuade"[148] except for the fact that, unlike the old *moreno,* the revolutionaries of the Cibao had formed an image of themselves—and of the Europeans—that did not conform to the old dictates of the politics of wiggery. Cautious yet direct and self-assured, they had begun a movement that was best described by Plácido's verses. "The revolution that we are currently undergoing is imminently popular and spontaneous," they told the queen, warning her not to be informed to the contrary by people "who may hope that seeking the continuation of the war may lead to the betterment of their own social position!"[149] In essence they were asking her to take the oath of Don Fulano de Tal and not to fall into the trap of picking up the tab for a war that Spain could never possibly win.

As if wanting to teach Her Majesty a historical lesson, these revolutionaries reminded the queen of her namesake, Isabella I, and of how she had been kept in the dark by her advisors while the genocide of the native inhabitants of Hispaniola was being perpetrated back at the end of the fifteenth century. "We have been treated in exactly the same way,"[150] they stated, thereby assuming a position of historical protagonism that turned them into the self-proclaimed inheritors of a tradition of resistance to Spanish rule that, rhetorically speaking, could be traced back to the days of Queen Anacaona. Martínez-Fernández has written that "the Dominican War of Restoration was an anti-slavery, anti-European struggle."[151] I would argue that, although there is no doubt that it was indeed a war against the reestablishment of slavery, the position assumed by the mulattoes of the Cibao was evermore transcendental by virtue of being informed by an ancient aesthetic practice that allowed them to dance around the European Ideal with confidence. The letter in question demonstrates that, like a master of ceremonies who is well versed in the rituals of protocol, they were carefully telling the queen where to sit and when to stand up. Keep in mind that the statements contained in the letter were far removed from the professions of love and loyalty that Toussaint had once made to the French. Thus the mulattoes of the Cibao were neither moving against nor with the European, but attempting to undo the imperial legacy and to go beyond it through a movement of subjective transversality that was a veritable *plus ultra*.

On 3 March 1865 the queen annulled the annexation of Santo Domingo. The Spanish Army had been badly defeated, and what had at first seemed the project of a renewed and confident Spanish imperial enterprise had turned out to be a revisitation of the terrible defeat suffered by the French in Haiti half a century before. Such was the memory conjured up at the start of the Revolution of the Cibao by an article that appeared in the Madrid press: "The brief statements on the events of Puerto Plata provide the imagination of the most level-headed with a picture of horror that would leave anyone cold. Knowing that the insurgents are people of color, the memories evoked are those of the terrible scenes that took place at the end of the last century in the French part of the island of Santo Domingo."[152] Stating "What is occurring in our new colony is much more serious than it looks at first glance," the article made a direct reference to the Escalera Conspiracy that had taken place in Cuba in 1844, citing "the death of Plácido which caused so much consternation in Europe" and asking its readers to consider, in relation to "the movement of the colored people in Santo Domingo, could it be a symptom of a general conspiracy of the black race in our Antilles?"[153]

Even this early premonition could not have prepared the Spaniards for what was coming. The events of Santo Domingo were the start of the bloodiest war ever waged against a European empire in the New World. In a combined and monumental effort lasting thirty-five years, from 1863 to 1898, the peoples of Santo Domingo, Cuba and Puerto Rico would fight and continually conspire to expel Spain from the Caribbean. At the end of the bloody campaign Spain would lose her empire, but the mulatto offspring of the slave owners would get a new master, as Usonian hegemony was irrevocably imposed over the Antilles. Plácido's verses would resound then with deeper meanings:

> If the fatal lot that I have coming
> And the tragic end of my bloody story,
> At the exit of this life, transitory,
> Leaves your heart mortally bleeding:
>
> Cry no more; the soul in grieving
> Reclaims its peace; the moor in glory
> And my placid lyre for your story
> Its last sound for the grave be leaving.[154]

CHAPTER SIX

Moors in Heaven

A Second Columbus and the
Return of the Zaharenian Curse

The government that rules us . . . should begin to think seriously
about the destiny reserved by Providence for the Negroes and
mulattoes of America. From now on, this destiny is manifest, given
the present number of this race; and I believe the island of Santo
Domingo is called to be the nucleus, the model of its glorification
and individuality in this hemisphere.
— Homage to Gregorio Luperón, 1888

Spanish observers were not altogether wrong when they saw in the War
of Restoration the signs of a "general conspiracy of the black race in our
Antilles."[1] For a long time Santo Domingo had been a refuge for runaway slaves from Cuba and Puerto Rico.[2] Now the Dominicans were
also being supported by blacks and mulattoes of other islands, most
notably Jamaica and the Turks Islands. However, the waning influence
of the creole element in the first major revolution of the Hispanic Caribbean did not give way to the "Black nation" feared by Saco. Instead what
seemed to emerge was a movement of mulatto vindication that, faced
with the insurmountable problems of making (ideal) nations out of
competing regional interests and out of divergent political cultures that
responded to the legacies of plantation slavery and colonialism, as well
as to a culture of the counterplantation and *cimarronería,* would evolve
into a loose project for Antillean confederation. If what Buenaventura
Baez referred to as "the weak states fashioned by the Latin race"[3] tended
to sacrifice republican virtues in favor of caesarean figures and if any
project of liberation in the region was vulnerable to the mounting forces

of Usonian rapacity, the only way to protect the hard-won freedoms that the wars of liberation were to secure was through a project for the development of a supranational political and military association of the peoples of the Antilles. But on what would that project be based?

Unfortunately for those who wish to study the project for Antillean confederation, its major promoters were men and women of action who worked for the most part in clandestine ways and left few records of their ideas. To be sure, there had been trans-Antillean connections from the start of the movement for Dominican independence. A letter sent by the Spanish agent in Curaçao to the governor of Puerto Rico in 1844 tells that "a certain Ramon Levi" had gone from Haiti to Santo Domingo and was thought to be a Puerto Rican from the town of Hormigueros "or from somewhere between Mayagüez and Cabo Rojo." The document describes Levi as "a man who is close to the enemies of our colonies and who works to undermine their tranquility." He is also said to be of "mulatto quality."[4]

By the time the Spanish army was evacuated from Santo Domingo these trans-Antillean connections between revolutionaries had deepened considerably, as they came to revolve around the figure of another mulatto from Cabo Rojo: Ramón Emeterio Betances. The best description of Betances and of his Antillean thinking was given by Ángel Rama, who wrote of Betances, whose nom de guerre was *el Antillano* (the Antillean): "He engages Haiti thinking about the freedom of the Dominican Republic, fights for Cuba while thinking of the possibilities for a truly independent Haiti, and above all concerns himself with everything by always thinking of Puerto Rico."[5] In 1870, during a speech in the Great Masonic Lodge of Port-au-Prince, Betances uttered his battle cry: "The Antilles should belong to the offspring of the Antilles."[6] Twelve years later this man, of whom it was said that he looked more like an Arab than a Roman,[7] would meet with Lord Gladstone, prime minister of England, to advocate for the inclusion of Jamaica in the plans for the Antillean Confederation he was proposing. Saco must have been turning over in his grave.

The Republican Society of Cuba and Puerto Rico had been founded in New York City in December 1865, and on 8 January 1867 the Revolutionary Committee of Puerto Rico was constituted in Santo Domingo, composed of a number of Puerto Rican and Dominican patriots. Betances, who was present and instrumental in the constitution of both organizations, now had an important ally in the figure of the young Dominican general Gregorio Luperón. He was also a mulatto, and a merchant from Puerto Plata, who would rise to prominence as the leader of the Blue Party, representing the liberal interests of the Cibao against the conservative interests of the Santo Domingo oligarchies led once again by Baez, now under the banner of the Red Party.[8]

Expelled from Santo Domingo by Baez, Betances headed for Saint Thomas to pick up five hundred rifles that he had bought and that the Cuban Domingo Goicuría was to send to him. There he was to await Luperón's warship, the *Telégrafo,* which was to take his expeditionary force to Puerto Rico. But the Puerto Rican conspiracy was uncovered and quickly repressed by the Spaniards, and Betances was arrested in Saint Thomas. In the end, only a handful of revolutionaries rose up on 23 September 1868 in the town of Lares. They were soon captured. Nevertheless, news of the uprising helped boost the confidence of revolutionaries in Cuba, who on 10 October began what was to be the first war for Cuban independence. Known as the Ten Years War (1868–78), the revolution in Cuba was increasingly radicalized and racialized so that, in much the same way as in the Dominican Republic, creole influence diminished in favor of the so-called *mambises,* primarily black and mulatto—and Chinese—peasants from eastern Cuba who fought against slavery and peonage to guarantee their immediate freedom under the banner of Cuban independence. (In the entire war for the independence of Cuba, fought from 1868 to 1898, only one planter died in battle). By 1874 Cuban General Manuel de Quesada was writing from Saint Thomas exhorting Puerto Ricans to rise up against Spanish tyranny "so that we may then invite you to [form] one single society under the flag of Antillean unity."[9] When at the end of the war a group of seventy-two *mambises* were captured by the English off the coast of Guantanamo and brought to San Juan, the official newspaper of the Spanish loyalists in Puerto Rico described them as "all of color, more or less all of them black, which of course indicates the kind, character, and tendencies of the new rebellion."[10] Coming from a different vantage point, Betances had reached the same conclusion concerning his person and his family. Reminding his sister that no relative of theirs who possessed any degree of common sense had ever denied his or her African ancestry, Betances wrote: "It is perfectly understood that we are blackish, and that we do not deny it."[11] Could there have been any other way of approaching the project of Antillean confederacy, of eschewing the legacy of the Negro codes, and of keeping a safe distance from the European Ideal than parting from the acceptance of one's own *mulatez,* or from the assumption that, in one way or another, all in the Caribbean were the offspring of slave owners?

Among the most prominent leaders of the *mambises* were the Dominican general Máximo Gómez and a Cuban mulatto by the name of Antonio Maceo, who quickly rose to the rank of general. In 1878 as the creoles, fearful of black and mulatto victory, prepared to sign a peace treaty with the Spanish known as the Zanjón Pact, Maceo and five other leaders of the army of Cuba Libre, among them the Puerto Rican Juan Rius Rivera, issued what is known as the Protest of Baraguá, rejecting the peace accord between the creoles and the Spaniards and urging their followers to pursue the war of liberation to make Cuba "a new republic assimilated to our sisters of Santo Domingo and Haiti."[12] That same year Maceo, in exile in Jamaica and in collusion with Luperón and Betances, formed the Liga Antillana, or Antillean League, a secret organization committed to the complete independence and confederation of the Caribbean islands.[13] Almost nothing is known of the extent of the operations of the Liga Antillana or, for that matter, of what seems to have been its immediate predecessor, the Liga de las Antillas, founded by Betances in Paris four years before. What is clear is that the idea of an assimilated republic was eyed with much suspicion by creoles, who viewed it as incongruous with their national projects for the formation of insular states and, more specifically, as a proposal for black rule in the Caribbean.[14] The vision espoused by the Liga Antillana was for them a sort of nightmare à la Saco.

The Three-Winged Bird: Cuba, Puerto Rico, and the Dominican Republic

This creole suspicion was particularly strong in the case of Cuba, where creole opposition to Maceo's leadership during the final stages of the War of Independence (1895–98) probably caused Maceo's death at the hands of the Spaniards.[15] In October of 1895 Maceo had launched the invasion of western Cuba with seventeen hundred *mambises.* Three months later he had arrived in the westernmost province, Pinar del Río and established a stronghold in the Province of Havana from which his men raided settlements within a half hour of the capital. The war for the independence of Cuba was no longer a regional conflict but one of islandwide dimensions. Maceo gathered that with proper supplies and reinforcements the war could promptly be won. But the provisional government, composed exclusively of creoles and headed by the planter Salvador Cisneros Betancourt, marquis of Santa Lucía, refused to back Maceo, arguing, in the same vein as their grandparents in the days of Plácido, that Antonio Maceo and his brother José had a dictatorial plan to install a "black republic" in Cuba. The orders went out: all supplies to the Western Army were to be cut off. Maceo then wrote to Cisneros, telling him: "I believe that the sincere practice of democracy will produce healthy results when we become free."[16] The mulatto general was clear on the point that the war for freedom had to be won before the political apportionment of an independent Cuba could take place. For now he was worried: "I have not been informed of the suspension of my order asking for help."[17]

Stonewalled by Cisneros, Maceo asked the representatives of the Cuban government in the United States to send him thirty thousand rifles. They were never shipped. Seriously outnumbered by the Spaniards and fighting in open country, Maceo's men were running out of ammunition. The boldest and most decisive maneuver of the war—the one that had given it truly national proportions—was going to cause the war to be lost, not because of the lack of decisiveness on the part of the rank and file of the army, but on account of the fears aroused in the creole politicians by a military victory won by a nonwhite army under the command of a mulatto general. In November 1896 Máximo Gómez, then the highest military authority in the army of Cuba Libre, ordered Maceo to march against the western trench, a formidable system of fortifications built by the Spaniards to prevent the spread of the insurrection and to defend Havana. Maceo must have known he was walking into a trap. His death was to bring most Cubans together, if not in victory, at least in mourning. The consequences of this setback were disastrous: the army was seriously demoralized, and the provisional government was from then on irrevocably set on pursuing the direct intervention of the United States in the conflict as a way of strengthening creole claims to power through a strategic allegiance with the country that, as Saco had observed half a century before, had managed so well to "promote the full development of liberal principles while at the same time restricting political rights exclusively to the white race."[18]

Since 1868 the island of Puerto Rico had been far removed from the main focus of hostilities because, in the spirit of Antillean unity, the war for the independence of Puerto Rico—or at least its second campaign—came to be fought in Cuba by Puerto Ricans who responded to Quesada's call. According to official estimates, Puerto Rico was a country where the mulatto element had seemingly come to fill the role of buffer that had been the aim of the old Código Negro. In 1865 the Madrid government had called for a Junta Informativa, a special commission of inquiry that was to hear the demands of Cuban and Puerto Rican creole reformers. This move on the part of the Ministerio de Ultramar (Colonial Office) in Madrid was primarily in response to the outcome of the U.S. Civil War and its perceived consequences for Spain's last remaining colonies in America. On 10 April 1867, the liberal delegates from Puerto Rico presented a project for the abolition of slavery on the island. Their lengthy proposal, which to a large extent was also the first attempt by Puerto Rican creoles to write their own history, began very appropriately with a quote from Edouard Laboulaye's *Histoire politique des Etats Unis,* and it was an appeal to reason and a demand for reforms before there was a need for revolution or, more important, for outside intervention.[19] The Puerto Rican deputies Ruiz Belvis, Acosta, and Quiñones warned that if Spain did not abolish slavery in her possessions, "it would be also a good motive for foreign peoples to intervene in the life of the Antilles. This has become a greater danger since the last war in the United States.... It is important to mention this time and time again.... The United States, which has never ceased to think of itself as the head and thought of the Americas, and not for this as much as for the sense this makes with regards to their interests and their cause, will consecrate its forces to the cause of abolition throughout the New World."[20] Raising the alarm in the Spanish Cortes with the threat of direct Usonian military intervention in their last remaining American colonies, the creole abolitionists were now trying to coax the Spaniards to move in the direction of their program.

In the face of such an ominous external threat, all was quiet on the insular front. The three men presented an image of Puerto Rican docility that could be traced all the way back to the work of José Campeche a century before. The deputies from Puerto Rico assured the Cortes that the slaves on the island were law-abiding, happy, and submissive. Considering the possibility of slave uprisings and disturbances, they argued that "if such alterations of public order are improbable everywhere, in Puerto Rico they are impossible."[21] Puerto Rico, it would seem, was the perfect colony. According to Ruiz Belvis, Acosta, and Quiñones, what made Puerto Rico a country of peoples with such "sweet ways"[22] was the fact that the socioracial continuum was perfectly stable and balanced. If the continuous importation of slaves to Cuba required Saco's "Cubans" to constantly check and readjust the controls of their socioracial machinery, in Puerto Rico the machine ran almost by itself, without the need for much intervention or maintenance.

What made Puerto Rico such a perfect colony? The Puerto Rican delegates wrote at one point of the parallel and proportional growth of the slave and white populations and concluded with the happy observation that both groups "seem to constitute one single element and race that moves ahead and develops itself in a calm and constant progression."[23] In their eyes this movement was precisely sustained by a predominantly mulatto population whose members were anxious to consummate their movement toward the white. The authors argued that the mulatto population offered a buffer zone of sorts between slaves and masters, blacks and whites: "The free colored population that is so numerous in this island . . . is a shining and eternal ideal to the eyes of the African race."[24] Surely the freed slaves would join the rest of society in their eternal quest for the Ideal Body through the practice of *mejorar la raza*, or "improving the race." Of course, as the abolitionists argued in an exercise of "benevolent" paternalism, they would be entitled to a few days of rest before returning to work for their former masters.[25]

In the Dominican Republic, however, the situation was different. Since 1882 the reins of power in the country had been held by General Ulises Heureaux, a long-time aide and confidant to Luperón, who was now being heralded as the "Pacifier of the Patria." In reality the "pacification" of the Dominican Republic after decades of political anarchy was a high price to pay. Heureaux was to rule in the most ruthless of ways, eliminating all opposition and aggrandizing his image as the most accomplished of all nineteenth-century Caribbean caudillos. Betances, showing a keen understanding of the worst tendencies in mulatto society, described Heureaux as "this man, who hates foreigners because they are white, and hates blacks because he is black."[26] In 1888 Heureaux's old mentor, Luperón, ran for the presidency in a last attempt to prevent the rise of the new caudillo. Luperón was then heralded by the creoles as the mulatto who, following the rationale of the old Negro codes, seemed to be the only one that could keep the country together. The second part of the quote at the beginning of this chapter, about Luperón, reads: "And who better than you could begin to lay the groundwork, the foundation of this greatness? Who better than you could know how necessary the white race is to the achievement of this goal, but at the same time recognize the superiority of the combinations of this great race? And who better than you could melt, amalgamate and shape a homogeneous whole from the wisdom and ignorance of one and another family so that from today, we as a model of tolerance and restraint, may attract the benevolent gaze of the Universe and place ourselves, robust and free, in a highly enviable position?"[27]

The mulatto project for Antillean confederacy was quickly becoming a lost cause. In the Dominican Republic the mulatto revolution had degenerated into the worst dictatorship: Heureaux's pursuit of the Ideal had turned him into a "black" Napoleon. Meanwhile, Puerto Rico was living under the sign cast by creole reformers, who described her peoples with the same words used by Hostos to speak of Cuba in the Age of Plácido. Apparently, faced with the menace of Usonian intervention and with the failure to sustain a military campaign for independence after 1868, the Puerto Ricans had no choice but to be "pleased with their master."[28] By the end of the century creole autonomists had taken the initiative away from the old revolutionaries and were negotiating various measures for home rule with the same people who were denying every freedom to the Cubans. And in Cuba Maceo, "the Bronze Titan," had fallen victim to political conspiracy. Creole power was ascending.

Woe! Woe! Woe! To the Granada of the Indies!

The death of Maceo occurred under the reign of Captain General Weyler, known as "the Butcher" for his design and implementation of the first concentration camps of modern times. These were makeshift urban prisons where the rural population was resettled under the worst possible conditions in an effort to depopulate the rural areas and thus undermine the support for the insurgents and destroy their supply lines. Thousands were thus subjected to the worst possible conditions of disease and starvation. Back home Weyler's superior, Prime Minister Antonio Cánovas del Castillo, had sworn that Spain would fight for Cuba "to the last man and to the last peseta." During his early political career Cánovas had been a protégé of Leopoldo O'Donnell, under whose aegis the Escalera Conspiracy had been crushed and Plácido executed. Now the blood of Maceo—and of thousands of innocent children—was on his hands.

On 8 August 1897, Cánovas and his wife checked into the Cantabrian bathing resort of Santa Agueda. The prime minister was there to treat a urinary condition and to escape the difficulties of the Cuban situation and the related negotiations intended to keep the United States from intervening in the war. He had gone to mass that morning, and just before one o'clock in the afternoon, had left his room with his wife on the way to the dining room. Going down the stairs, she stopped to chat with a friend, and Cánovas went on and then waited for her, sitting on a bench at the bottom of the stairs. Just then Michele Angiolillo, a thirty-nine-year-old Italian anarchist, approached him and fired three shots at close range, hitting the prime minister in the head, chest, and back as his body rolled to the ground. Cánovas had come to pay with his life for a war that would cost Spain her empire and, three decades later, in the peninsular version of creole caudillismo under Francisco Franco, her very freedom.

Angiolillo had originally intended to assassinate the queen of Spain and her son Alfonso. But while in Paris he had paid a visit to Betances, who was then the representative of the Cuban Revolution in France. The old conspirator had convinced the Italian anarchist that killing a woman and a child would have little impact on the outcome of events and that it would certainly be detrimental to their interests. Then the name of Cánovas had come up. Wanting to avenge the death of Maceo and so many others, Betances gave Angiolillo all he had come to ask for: an inspired choice for a target and five hundred francs to pay for his passage to Spain. Following the events in question and the execution of the assassin, Betances was fond of welcoming visitors to his home just to have them sit on the same chair where Angiolillo had sat.[29]

Like Marat, Cánovas was also killed in the bath, but he was killed by the enemies of the state: the Italian anarchist and the mulatto revolutionary. Betances, of course, was a consummate revolutionary romantic for whom the murder of Cánovas was an act of desperation in response to the realization that the possibility of triumph in the struggle for which he had given his life was fast slipping away. Far from giving any impetus to the cause of Cuban independence, now in the hands of the creole elites, the assassination of Cánovas led to the deepening of the crisis in the areas under Spanish control in Cuba, adding fuel to the fire of the inevitable Usonian intervention. If anything, the assassination of Cánovas marked the moment when the cause of Antillean confederation was derailed and overcome by the infamous movement through which Spain and the United States came to negotiate, through a simple relay of colonial authority, the "Past and Present" of empire in the Caribbean and the Philippine seas (see again Figure 1).

The mulatto revolution also came to a grinding halt in a moment that came to be represented years later by a monument erected to Antonio Maceo along Havana's waterfront, or Malecón (Figure 27). The bronze representation of the "Bronze Titan," sculpted by the Italian Domenico Boni and unveiled in 1916, is part of a trilogy of heroic equestrian statues along the Malecón. It stands between the monuments to Máximo Gómez and Calixto García, the two other major military leaders of the wars for independence. However, Maceo's statue is in an interesting azimuthal counterpoint to the other two neighboring monuments. Gómez is riding his horse with the decorum of a Roman caesar, and García is portrayed as if charging against a Spanish column. The statues of these two creole generals are facing north toward the Florida Straits and the Atlantic, symbolically guarding the nation from foreign aggression. But Maceo's is not. His statue is facing south, firmly grasping the unsheathed machete in his right hand, and looking inland over the skyline of Havana and toward the Cuban countryside. His horse is standing on its hind legs—a symbol of his death in battle—as if ready to charge into the heart of Cuba one last time before continuing his ride to immortality. Turning his back on the Strait of Florida, Maceo has paused to contemplate the unfinished business of the war for freedom and against the Plantation, a war that was to have created a country both for the nations, and for the outcasts of nations, of the Antilles.

This idealization of the image of the mulatto general contrasts with the victimization his corpse suffered at the hands of the creole authorities during the early days of the Usonian military occupation of Cuba. In 1900 a commission of scientists was put to the task of unearthing Maceo's remains and conducting an anthropometrical study to verify what already had been decided would be the most socially responsible outcome of the investigation. The point of the exercise was to scientifically prove that although Maceo was clearly a mulatto, his body was

Figure 27. Domenico Boni, *Monument to General Antonio Maceo Grajales,* 1916, Havana. Photograph by Alfonso Díaz Concepción and the author.

closer to the Ideal Body of the European than to that of the black. His valor and his glory in the field of battle were unquestionable, but making room for his remains in the national pantheon was dependent on the results of such a test. They came back positive. As Aline Helg points out, summarizing the results of the study: "Although the proportions of his bones were characteristic of the 'black type,' he *approached* more the white race, he *matched* it, he even *surpassed* it in the general conformation of his head, the probable weight of his brain, [and] his skull capacity" (emphasis in the original text).[30] Apparently the creole sages determined that Maceo's body conformed to the perfect and umbilical geometries of the old Vitruvian model, a lesson to all who might think that the original foundations of the discourse of the Ideal Body were covered up by four centuries of ideological sedimentation as the European Ideal came to be subsumed under the notion of the "universal transcendence of the sublime."[31] Once again the standard that had sustained the coloniality of power came to be imposed, forcibly by force, over the harmful and troublesome elements that were perceived as standing in the way of the creole national project. But did the mulatto movement of freedom die with Maceo and with the Usonian military conquest of the mulatto world of the Caribbean?

The Hour of Desolation

By the time the U.S.S. *Maine* exploded in the Bay of Havana on 15 February 1898, the major leaders of the project for Antillean confederacy were all Moors in Heaven. Luperón had died in 1897, and José Martí, also a prominent defender of the cause, had been killed by the Spaniards in battle in 1895. Following the U.S. invasion of Puerto Rico, Betances himself was to fall victim to the realization that his beloved country was going to be a permanent colony. In the summer of 1898 he wrote: "If Puerto Rico does not react quickly it will be a U.S. colony forever."[32] Betances died in September, but his words could not have been more prophetic. To this day Puerto Rico remains a Usonian colony, officially referred to, in the terms devised by the U.S. Supreme Court in 1901, as a "non-incorporated territory" that "belongs to but is not part of" the United States.[33] Truth be told, the island was incorporated long ago. What remains, "belonging to but not part of" the United States, is her mulatto people, who were the recipients and are still the bearers of a promise unfulfilled.

Early in 1903 an almost full-page advertisement for Scott's Emulsion of Cod Liver Oil in the *San Juan News* proclaimed the arrival of "Una Nueva Raza" (A New Race) (Figure 28). In very suggestive language, it claimed that "due to the purity of its ingredients the legitimate Scott's Emulsion uproots all these ailments [the ones that cause malnutrition and infant mortality] and enriches the blood."[34] To make the point even clearer, the ad was accompanied by drawings of the cherubic white faces of a boy and a girl from Havana. The images and the wording—which was, by the way, different from that used in Scott's pitch to consumers in the United States[35]—could not have better targeted an audience that had been made keenly aware of its racial precariousness and sociopolitical illegitimacy by the new regime. Like a miracle drug, Scott's Emulsion was the milky liquid of legitimization, a movement toward purity that would strengthen the blood; like a sort of new *piedra solimán*, it had been concocted by the new master as the antidote that would uproot all the evils that beset the land. Within the context of the mulatto world this was a sort of racial purgative in a bottle, with the added convenience that the white infusion—or the infusion of whiteness—could now be readily bought in any drugstore. Leave it to the Usonians to bottle, package, and sell as a miracle cure the "someday" promised but never delivered by the old Negro codes.

A few years later, right at the corner of Cruz and San Francisco streets and presiding over San Juan's main ceremonial plaza, a larger-than-life-size sign carrying the trademark of Scott's Emulsion was hung between the second and third stories of the Farmacia de Guillermety, which was then the principal apothecary in the city. The image of a fisherman carrying a giant cod on his back successfully wrestled attention away from the city's coat of arms—the rampant lamb symbolizing the "rule of docility"—and from the Usonian flag waving above it, both of which crowned the façade of the town hall right next door to the pharmacy, as they do to this day, in a representational palimpsest of past and present imperial glories and as a symbol of the permanent though not exactly perfect colony. Scott's Emulsion and its transformative powers had become the emblem of the new age. Surely there could not have been a more descriptive visual metaphor for an island that had just been caught in the nets of Usonian imperialism.[36] But in this case, as the Usonians say, the proof was in the pudding: all those who tried the new imperial medicine could not help but notice that there was something rather fishy about it.

Now the directions to take a teaspoon of the emulsion a day were a renewed promise of a "someday" that, as in the old Negro codes, would be promised but never delivered. As in the story of the ship within a ship presented by Sigüenza in the *Infortunios,* a new colonial ritual designed for the reduction of mongrelity had been set in motion when Ramírez's native city finally fell into the hands of the English-speaking pirates. For the mulatto peoples of the Caribbean the adjustment would be difficult. But in the long run the consequences of this ongoing kidnapping

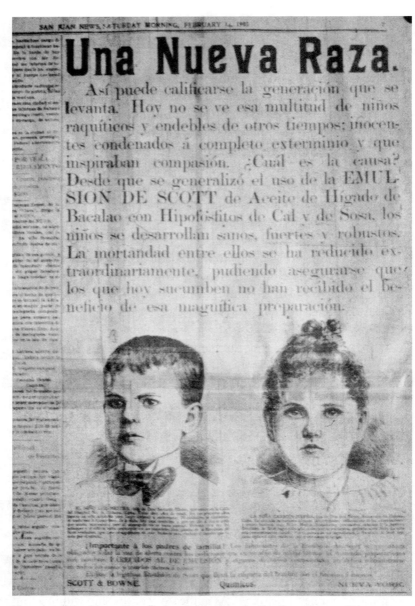

Figure 28. "Una Nueva Raza," advertisement in the *San Juan News*, 14 February 1903: 7.

may prove to be a bigger challenge to the ultimate creole nation-empire, to the nation that "has never ceased to think of itself as the head and thought of the Americas."

This much was already evident in the opinions expressed by Usonian politicians and ideologues following the end of the War of 1898, a well-assembled and broad panorama of which was published a year later by the well-known jingoist Murat Halstead at the end of his *Pictorial History of America's New Possessions*. Nobody expressed more doubts about the new course of Usonian expansion than McKinley's contender in the presidential elections of 1896, the "Great Commoner" William Jennings Bryan. He argued that "the colonial policy rests upon the doctrine of vicarious enjoyment."[37] For his part McKinley expressed the troubling opinion that has sustained Usonian expansion and interventionism ever since. He believed that Usonian belligerence obeyed "a higher moral obligation which rested on us and did not require anybody's consent." Speaking of the insular peoples who were now entrusted to Congress, he asked: "Did we need their consent to perform a great act of humanity?"[38] McKinley's thoughts were echoed by Henry Gibson, who took a broader view of the national imperial project by observing: "Where would the United States of America be to-day if the white men who landed on our coast had sailed away because the Indians objected to their coming?"[39]

With the advent of the Usonian empire, the great national project had finally been organized around an ideal of possibility that expressed, at the same time, the possibility of the Ideal in the very promise of empire for a creole nation born of Liberty. What is more, the advent of the national Usonian imperial era would be heralded through the adoption of the Irvian modality of creole discursiveness. "The dream of Columbus will soon be a realization," Murat Halstead announced at the conclusion of his book celebrating the new glories of what he called a "greater America."[40] The Usonian creoles had taken command of the most totalizing global project:

> The country which he [Columbus] discovered and added to the map of the world has now reached to the East Indies, and within a few days, or years at most, another Columbus, sailing westward from Spain to find the East Indies, will discover that greater America has already begun to provide a route by which a ship can sail westward to the East Indies through an isthmian canal. . . .

> And when this second Columbus shall sail he may stop with his
> vessel for supplies at the Island of Porto Rico, a possession of our
> country; he may pass through the Nicaragua Canal, under the control
> of our country; he can stop at the Hawaiian Islands, a part of our land;
> he can stop at the Ladrone Islands, belonging to us, and he can reach
> the Philippines and still be under the flag of the country which the first
> Columbus made known to the world.[41]

Clearly the acquisition of an insular empire stretching from Puerto
Rico to the Philippines went a long way toward helping dispel the "anomalous self-image" that had burdened the United States, as a less-than-
European country, during Washington Irving's times. But the new civilizing mission that made the United States a "great" nation in a movement
of legitimization whose mechanics could be illustrated by Ortega y Gasset's metaphor of the action through which "the bull's-eye pulls the arrow and draws the bow"[42] also revived the old Irvian anxieties concerning
the less-than-ideal character of Columbus's crew. These civilizational
insecurities now came to be directed against the peoples of the so-called
new possessions, a misnomer used to this day in an attempt to hide the
serious erosion of republican virtues caused by the happy acquisition of
colonial dependencies. Apparently, like Irving's Columbus, the United
States was now "doomed to command" a "dissolute rabble" of insular
misfits for "whom all law was tyranny, and order restraint."[43] Carl
Schurz, who as a senator back in 1870 had defeated maneuvers to annex
the Dominican Republic, worried about these matters "closer at heart."
He was truly concerned by the fact that the new colonies were "all situated in the tropics, where people of the northern races, such as Anglo-
Saxons, or generally speaking, people of Germanic blood, have never
migrated in mass to stay, and they are more or less densely populated,
parts of them as densely as Massachusetts—their populations consisting
almost exclusively of races to whom the tropical climate is congenial—
Spanish Creoles mixed with negroes in the West Indies and Malays,
Tagals, Filipinos, Chinese, Japanese, Nigritos and various more or less
barbarous tribes in the Philippines."[44]

Faced with the outright possession of the islands, Schurz cautioned
about promising much to their peoples: "If we have rescued those unfortunate daughters of Spain, the colonies, from the tyranny of their cruel
father, I deny that we are therefore in honor bound to marry any of the
girls or to take them all into our household, where they may disturb

and demoralize our whole family."[45] His view of colonial mongrelity was not that different from the one described three centuries before in the *Infortunios,* more specifically in the rituals of torment—and cannibalism—through which Captains Bel and Donkin practiced what William Jennings Bryan was now calling the doctrine of vicarious enjoyment.

More important, perhaps, Schurz's last words could have been taken right out of Las Casas's visions of the *piedra solimán.* Perhaps the acquisition of an empire was a solution to Usonian civilizational anxieties that made matters worse and that came "to bring garbage into the house."[46] Can we not see in Schurz's apprehension with regard to the new colonial types that "may disturb and demoralize our whole family" a preoccupation similar to the one expressed by Las Casas four centuries before at the foundation of American coloniality? Could it be that the same "harmful and troublesome"[47] elements that ultimately destroyed the Spanish empire were now to be passed along to the United States together with the trophies of war and conquest?

The quote at the beginning of this chapter is a good example of a movement that we first saw in the appropriation of all markings of identity by the Mulatos de Esmeraldas and in the unmasking and turning around of the European Ideal by the blacks and mulattoes of Haiti in the siege of Crête-à-Pierrot. In the age of the new system of conquest known as filibusterism that Baez had spoken about, the homage to Luperón was a symbolic act of piracy through which the author, in the name of the "Negroes and mulattoes of America," captured and carried with him the very spirit of the age under a variant notion of a civilizational (manifest) destiny that stood in sharp contrast to Usonian visions. The capture and turning around of the "spirit of the age" responded in this case to a long tradition of moving around and running through the Ideal. And even though the mulatto world of the Caribbean was now falling prey to the powerful designs of the filibuster venture turned national empire, it is important to remember that 1898 was the year when the neck of the Spanish imperial eagle finally came to be placed on the chopping block. As in the case of any beheading, the relevance of the moment was not so much mechanical as symbolic. Right at the moment of the sacrifice, during the very relay of colonial obligations between the Kingdom of Spain and the Usonian republic turned empire, a young Puerto Rican creole poet wrote the words for the obituary of the two-headed creature that had once proudly spread its wings at the

entrance to the cathedral of Santo Domingo. Virgilio Dávila's poem
"Redención" (Redemption, 1898) is a masterful denunciation of the
Spanish imperial legacy, and it focuses on an image of Columbus that
was in sharp contrast to the one heralded by Usonian ideologues as the
very symbol of the possibility of the Ideal:

> So be it, Patria, if it is written
> That your men should all be scorned;
> And your high banner be torn
> By the thorns of the road bitten.
> May the wrath of God thus risen
> Come to crush the tyrant's feat!
> And so the moment cursed be
> When the cunning sailor gazed
> On you, maid of the waves,
> In the midst of the Ocean sea![48]

Dávila's ire was directed at the four hundred–year history of Spanish
despotism. In good mulatto fashion, like a modern-day Plácido, he was
being more careful in his approach to the new master of men: in the
short book in which "Redención" first appeared, entitled *Patria* (1903),
there were three of what Hostos would have called "adulatory verses"
to the Usonian flag. Nevertheless, this creole poet—who, like James's
Toussaint, might be thought to have been already a mulatto—was unquestionably moving against the discourse of the European Ideal as
representationally embodied in Columbus. Only now, as the Ideal came
to be disguised in the figure of an Irvian Columbus and as this second
Columbus of sorts was planting the flag of the United States in a moment that marked the very fulfillment of the doctrine of Manifest Destiny, the creole republic turned empire was also acquiring, together with
caesarian laurels, the full force of the Zaharenian curse. Here again, the
swift victory accomplished by the United States military during the
course of the war with Spain would be checked by the heavy burden of
carrying off the loot in the dark without being at all certain what had
been placed inside the bag.

In his second poem, "To the American Flag," Dávila had already
warned of such a "strange metamorphosis" whereby, speaking of eagles,
"a feather turns into a scale."[49] In Dávila's work the movement of camouflage and subterfuge that is the very nemesis of the coloniality of power
greeted the new imperial eagle with a warning and a veiled curse. In a

terrible sort of Irvian déjà vu, the new colonial venture now ran the risk of being "constantly defeated by the dissolute rabble which he [the new Columbus] was doomed to command; with whom all law was tyranny, and order restraint."[50] In 1901 the future of this new Columbian crew—or of this Columbian crew twice over—was determined by the U.S. Supreme Court. The natives of Puerto Rico were to belong to but not be a part of the People of the United States. Deemed not to have quite the gravitas of the Ideal Body that stands on terra firma, and certainly not about to be set free on account of the island's strategic military importance, they would be abandoned at the shoreline like the two crew members and the Arawak woman in Randolph Rogers's representation of Irving's description of *Columbus's First Encounter with the Indians* (see again Figure 7). There they would remain permanently confined. Following the movement already prescribed in the representational coup performed in the *Columbus Doors* (see again Figure 5), Usonia, as the second coming of Columbus, would set itself apart from the new pariahs of nations—or the pariahs of nations twice over—of the West Indies. In the process the republic would be cleared of any wrongdoing, precariously holding onto a dubious assumption of civilizational immaculateness as if, like a second Columbus, it had not been the perpetrator of the rape of the Antilles. The *Columbus Doors* had been shut against the "unfortunate daughters of Spain" on whose defense the war of propaganda, in what was mostly a propaganda war, had supposedly been fought.

In the end, the map of the United states was considerably enlarged in 1898, and the "civilizational standing" of the creole nation rose considerably by the standards of the day. But so did the geography of the mulatto contestation of the Ideal and the specter of the "forcibly by force" that characterized creole responses to that movement and to all other sources of racial, national, and civilizational insecurities. In the end, too, the Usonian creole nation had captured an empire by militarily overwhelming a nearly extinct European imperial power but had failed, as it fails to this day, to conquer its own civilizational insecurities vis à vis the pursuit of the European Ideal in the midst of an ever-expanding mulatto world.

Like an uncanny vision of a newly vanquished Granada in the Indies, the mulatto revolution no longer had an army or an underground political network to propel its causes. But the metaphorical movement

264 Moors in Heaven

that had sustained the culture of *mulataje* would continue to check the advance of humanist terror and the claims of the national imperial project—the cause of Humanity as the Usonians would refer to it henceforth[51]—well into the future by reminding us all that the only subjects of the mulatto world are not the offspring of the "Spanish Creoles mixed with negroes" but of all those who, explicitly or not, always in complicity, have crossed through the real and imaginary geography of the greater Caribbean in search of freedom and escape or, alternatively, on their way to a "happier," more Ideal, and ultimately impossible, destination.

Notes

Introduction

1. José Martí, "Nuestra América," in *Nuestra América*, intro. Juan Marinello (Caracas: Ayacucho, 1977), 30–31. "Ni el libro europeo, ni el libro yanqui, daban la clave del enigma hispanoamericano."

2. Martí, "Nuestra América," 32. ". . . un pueblo emprendedor que la desconoce y la desdeña."

3. Martí, "Nuestra América," 26. "Es la hora del recuento, y de la marcha unida, y hemos de andar en cuadro apretado, como la plata en las raíces de los Andes."

4. Martí, "Nuestra América," 26. "Trincheras de ideas valen más que trincheras de piedra."

5. Martí, "Nuestra América," 32. "No hay odio de razas, porque no hay razas."

6. Ibid., "razas de librería."

7. Aníbal Quijano, "Coloniality of Power and Eurocentrism in Latin America," *International Sociology* 15.2 (2000): 218.

8. Ibid.

9. Louis A. Pérez, Jr., *Meditations on Martí: Keynote Address Presented at the Americas Conference, January 28, 1998, Tampa, Florida* (Tampa: University of South Florida, 2001), 3.

10. Pérez, *Meditations on Martí*, 4.

11. Quijano, "Coloniality of Power," 215.

12. Quijano, "Coloniality of Power," 221.

13. Ibid.

14. José Lezama Lima, "Mitos y cansancio clásico," in *La expresión americana*, ed. Irlemar Chiampi (Mexico: Fondo de Cultura Económica, 1993), 53.

15. The term *contrapunteo*, or counterpoint, refers to a modality of thought developed in Cuba by Lezama's generation and best expressed in the works of Fernando Ortíz. See Fernando Ortíz, *Contrapunteo cubano del tabaco y el azúcar* (Caracas: Biblioteca Ayacucho, 1978).

16. Ackbar Abbas, "Building on Disappearance: Hong Kong Architecture and the City," *Public Culture* 6.3 (1994): 443.

17. Lezama Lima, "Mitos y cansancio clásico," 54.

18. Lezama Lima, "Mitos y cansancio clásico," 56. "... una obligación casi de volver a vivir lo que ya no se puede precisar."

19. Guillermo Cabrera Infante, *El libro de las ciudades* (Madrid: Alfaguara, 1999), 15. "La arquitectura, a parte de unos pocos libros, es la única forma de historia posible."

20. Cabrera Infante, *El libro de las ciudades,* 15. "En algunos casos ni siquiera se conserva la literatura y queda la arquitectura sola como testigo mudo pero elocuente; un edificio vale más que mil palabras porque es una imágen dura que dura."

21. Aristotle, *Poetics,* 1457b. See *The Basic Works of Aristotle,* ed. Richard McKeon (New York: Random House, 1941), 1476.

22. Aristotle, *Poetics,* 1459a.

23. Lezama Lima, "Mitos y cansancio clásico," 59. "... una suerte de causalidad retrospectiva."

24. Edouard Glissant, *Caribbean Discourse: Selected Essays,* trans. and intro. J. Michael Dash (Charlottesville: University Press of Virginia, 1992), 21.

25. Glissant, *Caribbean Discourse,* 66.

26. Glissant, *Caribbean Discourse,* 67.

27. See Antonio Benítez Rojo, *The Repeating Island: The Caribbean and the Post-modern Perspective,* trans. James Maraniss (Durham, N.C.: Duke University Press, 1992), 12–16.

28. Arcado Díaz-Quiñones, "De cómo y cuándo bregar," in *El arte de bregar* (San Juan: Ediciones Callejón, 2000), 32. "Tiene la precisión de la imprecisión, y es notable la amplitud de imágenes segregadas por esa ambivalencia."

29. Aldo Rossi, *A Scientific Autobiography* (Cambridge: MIT Press, 1981), 81.

30. See again Aristotle, *Poetics,* 1459a.

31. In 1925 José Vasconcelos proposed the idea that out of the mestizo (mixed) cultures of Iberian America a fifth and superior race would rise possessing all the best attributes of the Indian, European, and African "races." See José Vasconcelos, *La raza cósmica: Misión de la raza iberoamericana* (Madrid: Aguilar, 1966).

32. For a critical look at the discourse of *mestizaje* as a homogenizing practice that does not escape the confines of racialism and of its counterpart, nationalism, see Juan E. De Castro, *Mestizo Nations: Culture, Race, and Conformity in Latin American Literature* (Tucson: University of Arizona Press, 2002).

33. Glissant, *Caribbean Discourse,* 23.

34. Because America extends from Alaska to Tierra del Fuego, I suppose no single people holds exclusive rights to the title of "American." For this reason I choose to refer to the citizens of the United States of America by the more proper term *Usonians,* avoiding derogatory and politically laden terms such as *gringo* or *Yankee.* I borrow the term from the architect Frank Lloyd Wright, who in the 1930s and 1940s developed his idea of a "Usonian House."

35. Lezama Lima, "Mitos y cansancio clásico," 80.

36. I use the term *creole* to describe a socioracial category of people of European descent born in the New World and belonging to the highest strata of colonial society.

37. See Lola Rodríguez de Tió, "A Cuba," in *Obras Completas* (San Juan: Instituto de Cultura Puertorriqueña, 1968), vol. 1: 319–21. "Cuba y Puerto Rico son/de un pájaro las dos alas/reciben flores y balas/sobre un mismo corazón."

38. See Ada Ferrer, *Insurgent Cuba: Race, Nation and Revolution, 1868–1898* (Chapel Hill: University of North Carolina Press, 1999), 1–12.

1. Tales of the Alhambra

1. Known to the Christians as Muley Hacén.

2. "Zahareño, ña," *Diccionario de la Lengua Española*, 1984 ed. Irving explains: "It had become so proverbial throughout Spain, that a woman of forbidding and inaccessible virtue was called a Zahareña." (Washington Irving, *A Chronicle of the Conquest of Granada by Fray Antonio Agapida*, ed. Miriam J. Shillingsburg, in *The Complete Works of Washington Irving* [Boston: Twayne Publishers, 1988], vol. 13: 11–12.) The name comes from *sahra*, which is Arabic for desert, and it was no doubt originally a topographic descriptor in this dry and rugged land. The town was founded in the eighth century following the Arab-Berber conquest of the Iberian Peninsula. It was captured in 1407 by the Christian prince Fernando de Antequera, remaining in Christian hands until its reconquest by the King of Granada 74 years later. Two years after that, in 1483, it was retaken by Rodrigo Ponce de León in a surprise attack that gained him the title of Duke of Cádiz.

3. In Irving's chronicle the story of Zahara is a revisitation of the initial invasion of the Iberian Peninsula by the Berber troops under Tariq in 711, a story Irving would later write under the title "Legends of the Conquest of Spain" and publish as part of *The Crayon Miscellany* in 1835. The surprise attack is thus representative of the Moorish threat and of the "sneakiness" through which, we are to believe, the Muslims held claims to lands in the Iberian Peninsula for more than seven hundred years. See Washington Irving, "Legends of the Conquest of Spain," in *The Crayon Miscellany*, ed. Dahlia Kirby Terrell, in *Complete Works*, vol. 22.

4. Irving, *Granada*, 22.

5. From an article by Irving in the *Quarterly Review* 43 (1830): 57–58, quoted in Irving, *Granada*, xxiv.

6. Irving, *Granada*, xxiii.

7. This was the sentence or "act of faith" pronounced by the tribunals of the Inquisition. The first auto-da-fé of the Spanish Inquisition was given in Seville in 1481, the same year that the final war against Granada got under way. The institution was not definitively abolished until 1834, three years after the end of Irving's first sojourn in Spain (1826–31).

8. Irving, *Granada*, 291.

9. Irving, *Granada*, 425.

10. See Jesús Mestre Campi and Flocel Sabaté, *Atlas de la "Reconquista": La frontera peninsular entre los siglos VIII y XV* (Barcelona: Ediciones Península, 1998), 4–7. For a thorough account of the Reconquest, as an ideology and praxis, see Derek W. Lomax, *The Reconquest of Spain* (New York: Longman, 1978).

11. John Adams, the second president of the United States, shared his views on the subject with Thomas Jefferson: "I have long been decided in opinion that a free government and the Roman Catholick religion can never exist together in any nation or Country, and consequently that all projects for reconciling them in old Spain or new are Eutopian, Platonick, and Chimerical. I have seen such a prostration and prostitution of Human Nature to the Priesthood in old Spain as settled my judgement long ago, and I understand that in new Spain it is worse, if that is possible." Adams to Jefferson, 3 February 1821, in *The Adams-Jefferson Letters: The Complete Correspondence between Thomas Jefferson and Abigail and John Adams*, ed. Lester J. Cappon (Chapel Hill: University of North Carolina Press, 1959), vol. 2: 571.

12. Terence Martin, "Rip, Ichabod, and the American Imagination," in *Washington Irving: The Critical Reaction,* ed. James W. Tuttleton (New York: AMS Press, 1993), 58.

13. Martin, "American Imagination," 56. Again, I am using the term *creole* to describe a socioracial category of people of European descent who were born in the New World and belonged to the highest strata of colonial society. In the United States the term has generally been used to refer to such elites—or to entire populations—of European descendants in the French, Portuguese, and Spanish colonies, whereas English creoles have been labeled as colonists or as Founding Fathers and their "American" descendants. In any case, the claim to European paternity on the part of the first generation of Usonians was at the time unquestionably clear, as the words of one of Irving's best friends readily confirm: "That divine gift [the gift of genius] has been as liberally imparted in the goodness of Providence to this nation [the United States] as to any other, that ever flourished on the face of the earth; and the English race, to which we belong, has always been preeminently distinguished in both the great branches, Saxon and Norman, that combine to form its mingled stock, by the favor of the Muses." (Alexander Everett, "Irving's Columbus," in *Prose Pieces and Correspondence,* ed. Elizabeth Evans [Saint Paul: John Colet Press, 1975], 52.) A creole nation would be a former European colony whose institutions after independence came to rest predominantly in the hands of such an elite.

14. He was a "man of moods, given to moments of self-criticism and depression." Claude G. Bowers, *The Spanish Adventures of Washington Irving* (Boston: Houghton Mifflin, 1940), 2. In fact, before going to Spain Irving had experienced a long period of insecurity and ennui during which he was trying to find a subject for his next work.

15. Francisco Pabón-Flores, intro. to Washington Irving, *Columbus, the Voyage of 1492* (Granada: La Gráfica, 1990), 9. The interconnectedness of all these events was embodied in figures like Columbus, but it was also the trademark of an entire generation of soldiers and sailors, religious and secular functionaries, and many others, such as captain Juan García de Sanabria, who participated in the siege of the town of Velez in Malaga during the War of Granada, served in the galleon fleets of the Indies, and participated in the conquest of Perú and in the pacification of the Chiriguane peoples. See Archivo General de Indias (Seville) (hereafter A.G.I.), *Patronato,* 132, N.1, R.8.

16. Washington Irving, *The Life and Voyages of Christopher Columbus,* ed. John Harmon McElroy, in *Complete Works,* vol. 11: 62. This moment is best exemplified in a letter from Ferdinand and Isabella that was sent to Columbus from Barcelona on 18 August 1493. There they urged him to depart as soon as possible and gave him instructions to follow on his second voyage. The letter also includes the monarchs' approval of the instructions given to Iñigo Arrieta and his fleet, which was charged with taking Grandada's King Abû'Abd Allâh to his exile in Africa. See A.G.I., *Patronato,* 295, N.19.

17. On 31 August 1826, six months into the work, he wrote to his English friend Thomas Storrow: "I am finishing Columbus; but it takes time to finish a work of the kind, where so many points are to be examined. I hope it may not be so dry as you apprehend. I have been much interested with the events of history, in writing them. If my work does not please I must say it will not be the fault of the subject." Wash-

ington Irving, *Letters, Volume 2, 1823–1838*, ed. Ralph M. Alderman, Herbert L. Klein-field, and Jennifer S. Banks, in *Complete Works*, vol. 23: 208.

18. In a letter to Everett, written in the port of Santa María near Cádiz on 12 October 1828, Irving told of "having been struck with the subject [of the conquest of Granada by Ferdinand and Isabella] while writing the *Life of Columbus*." Irving, *Letters*, 347.

19. Irving to Antoinette Bolviller 15 March 1828, in Irving, *Letters*, 283.

20. In the preface to *Legends of the Conquest of Spain* Irving wrote: "When the nation had recovered in some degree from the effects of this astounding blow, or rather, had become accustomed to the tremendous reverse which it produced; and sage men sought to enquire and write the particulars [of the Moslem conquest], it was too late to ascertain them in their exact verity. The gloom and melancholy that had overshadowed the land had given birth to a thousand superstitious fancies; the woes and terrors of the past were clothed with supernatural miracles and portents, and the actors in the fearful drama had already assumed the dubious characteristics of romance. Or if a writer from among the conquerors undertook to touch upon the theme, it was embellished with all the wild extravagancies of an Oriental imag-ination; which afterwards stole into the graver works of the monkish historians." Irving, *Conquest of Spain*, 241.

21. Irving, *Crayon*, 241. In the *Conquest of Granada* Irving had tried to create a new genre of writing that would combine romance with scientific history, a work that, as he said to his publisher, would be "more in my own way." (Irving to John Murray II, 21 December 1826, in *Letters*, 213.) Irving's idea was also to procure a broader audience by satisfying both history buffs and readers of novels. By all ac-counts, Irving as well as his critics to this day have agreed that "the trial proved brief and disappointing." (Earl N. Harbert, "*The Conquest of Granada*: A Spanish Experi-ment that Failed," in *Critical Reaction*, 155). Reasons for this apparent failure all point to Irving's inability to effectively bring his discourse under the control of what Partha Chatterjee would call an "ethics of rationality" that conformed to the scientific methods of treating historical materials practiced by all those who have found Irving's work problematic and unclassifiable. (See Partha Chatterjee, "Na-tionalism as a Problem in the History of Political Ideas," in *Nationalist Thought and the Colonial World: A Derivative Discourse* (Minneapolis: University of Minnesota Press, 1986), 16.) As we know, Irving had put aside the *Life of Columbus* to pursue his interests concerning Granada and the possibilities of such a project in terms of being accessible to the broadest possible audience. It was a direction that would test the historical and literary boundaries of his day. His English publisher, for one, did not agree to publish the *Conquest of Granada* under the name of Agapida as Irv-ing had instructed him to do.

22. The structure, designed by John Nash, was built between 1815 and 1823 for the future George IV. The building had Islamic domes and minarets, and its deco-rative elements were a catalogue of imperial conquests, its rooms ranging in style from Egyptian to Chinese.

23. Irving, *Letters*, 412. Irving's bewilderment with the myth and history of Spain would accompany him throughout life. The last major work he published be-fore his monumental *Life of Washington* was *Mahomet and His Successors* (1850), a work that he arguably would have never written had he not been captivated and

completely overwhelmed by Granada and the history of Islamic civilization in the Iberian Peninsula.

24. In a letter from Granada to his friend Antoinette Bolviller Irving tells of being in a place claimed, so to speak, by both the Reconquest and the Columbian stories. As if unable to make sense out of the coincidence, he sublimated both stories into his observations regarding the beauty of the landscape: "But Granada, bellissima Granada! think what must have been our delight, when, after passing the famous bridge of Pinos, the scene of many a bloody encounter between Moor and Christian, and remarkable for having been the place where Columbus was overtaken by the messenger of Isabella, when about to abandon Spain in despair, we turned a promontory of the arid mountains of Elvira, and Granada, with its towers, its Alhambra, and its snowy mountains, burst upon our sight." Irving, *Letters,* 282.

25. For a history of the use of the term miscegenation and its introduction into Usonian discourse in 1864 see Robert J. C. Young, *Colonial Desire: Hybridity in Theory, Culture and Race* (New York: Routledge, 1995), 142–47.

26. Although there is no direct proof that this was a conscious decision, least of all a policy directive, there are innumerable references in Irving's letters to the constant aid and supervision given by Everett, including Everett's obtainment of royal permission so that Irving could enter the Archive of the Indies, until then forbidden territory to foreigners. On 31 January 1826 Irving acknowledged Everett's paternity of the project, thanking him "for the literary undertaking you have suggested to me." (Irving, *Letters,* 168.) Two years later, on 23 April 1828, Irving wrote to Everett from Seville: "Happy to find you intend to review my work" and remembered that when the work was originally offered to him Everett had expressed surprise at the fact that "no complete history of Columbus was in existence." (Irving, *Letters,* 305.) In his critique of the work, which appeared in the *North American Review* in January of 1829, Everett referred to the *Life of Columbus* as a Usonian Iliad, a foundational text in what, thanks to Irving, could now be claimed to be a national tradition of "polite literature and poetry." (Everett, "Irving's Columbus," 51.) He even suggested that Irving's talent surpassed that of Sir Walter Scott, who was at the time England's most popular author. Behind the national vainglory there was also a celebration of his own role in being the matchmaker who had brought Columbus to Irving: "We cannot but think it a beautiful coincidence, that the task of duly celebrating the achievements of the discoverer of our continent, should have been reserved for one of its inhabitants; and that the earliest professed author of first-rate talent, who appeared among us, should have devoted one of his most important and finished works to this pious purpose." Everett, "Irving's Columbus," 79. That "beautiful coincidence" was no coincidence at all. Everett and the famous bibliophile Obadiah Rich (1777–1859), a Usonian expatriate who lived in Madrid at the time and whose valuable library served as Irving's main base of operations while in Spain, actively sponsored the work of young writers from the United States, including among others the historians William Prescott and George Ticknor. In a letter from Madrid to the latter, dated 20 April 1826, Everett wrote: "When I say *we* and *our* I mean to speak of Mr. Rich and myself—he being the person by whose aid I have been able to execute your commission as far as I have done it." (Everett, "Irving's Columbus," 208.) There is no doubt that both these men saw themselves as promoters of the young nation and of its need to produce a tradition of its own on a par with those of Europe. Proof of this can be found in Everett's own rather lengthy review of the *Life of Colum-*

bus, which is a veritable apologia on behalf of a Usonian intellectual tradition that he traces back to the pilgrims, then to the Founding Fathers, and finally to Irving, whom he stopped short of praising as the best writer of the day. The place assigned to Irving's project within Everett's enterprise becomes evident when we realize that only the last fourth of the article is dedicated to a discussion of the book.

27. I am making reference here to Todorov's assertion that "nomination is equivalent to taking possession." See Tzvetan Todorov, *The Conquest of America: The Question of the Other* (New York: Harper and Row, 1984), 27.

28. Peter Antelyes, *Tales of Adventurous Enterprise: Washington Irving and the Poetics of Western Expansion* (New York: Columbia University Press, 1990), 1. In a curious way, Washington Irving seems to have been predestined to occupy the preeminent place among those who first gave color to the national imaginary of the United States. It appears that one afternoon in 1789, when the six-year-old boy was walking with his nurse down Broadway Avenue in New York City, they came upon George Washington, who at the insistence of the nanny blessed his namesake. Thirty-six years later, in 1825, the last two major figures of the "Founding Fathers" generation died. With the departure of John Adams and Thomas Jefferson the first generation of "sons" was left in charge of upholding the institutions of the republic and of strengthening its nascent traditions. It was a time of anxiety for a people that could not easily match the ideals left behind by the first patriots with the realities of industrial and commercial expansion. As the son of John Adams, then-president John Quincy Adams might have provided the representative link between one generation and the other, but in matters of carrying on and sustaining national traditions and legends, Washington Irving was the anointed one. Irving would spend the last years of his life carrying on in his duties as the Usonian Homer with utmost devotion, conducting extensive research and writing his *Life of Washington.* When he finished the manuscript he literally collapsed, never to recover.

29. See, for example, Joseph P. Sanchez, *The Spanish Black Legend: Origins of Anti-Hispanic Stereotypes* (Albuquerque: University of New Mexico Press, 1990).

30. Irving, *Columbus,* 567.

31. Irving, *Columbus,* 83.

32. Irving, *Columbus,* 368.

33. Irving, *Columbus,* 367.

34. Irving, *Columbus,* 367–68.

35. Irving, *Columbus,* 567.

36. Martin, "American Imagination," 65.

37. See Roland Greene, *Unrequited Conquests: Love and Empire in the Colonial Americas* (Chicago: University of Chicago Press, 1999), 37.

38. A recent critic has said: "The elements of history and story-telling are present; yet they are combined in a puzzling mixture of fiction and fact that defies any simple labeling. For the few modern readers who have taken the time to consider Granada seriously, it has proved almost impossible to describe." Harbert, *Conquest of Granada,* 149.

39. José Ortega y Gasset, "How Castile Made Spain," in *Invertebrate Spain,* trans. Mildred Adams (New York: W.W. Norton, 1937), 29. The original Spanish version is entitled "Tanto monta," in *España invertebrada* (Madrid: Revista de Occidente, 1959), 43–48.

40. Ortega y Gasset, "How Castile Made Spain," 30.

41. Ibid. Of course imaginary futures are almost invariably dependent on an equally imagined past, as was the case of Irving's Columbus insofar as it was an image, as we have pointed out, of what Usonia wanted to be.

42. Ortega y Gasset, "How Castile Made Spain," 30.

43. In the case of Spain the process of constructing the nation would be difficult when not altogether abortive. In many ways, until very recently it was customary to refer to Spain in the plural, as in "Las Españas." At the same time, it could be argued that, accidental or not, the basis of the movement that led from the imperial dream to the national ideal was laid early on and that there has been a clear progression and development that can be traced from Ferdinand's dream of the "reconquest" of Jerusalem through Charles V's caesarian aspirations to unify the world of Christendom to Philip II's rule as Hispaniarum et Indianarum Rex and his administration of his vast empire from Madrid. Manuel Fernández Álvarez clearly stated that during the reign of Philip II Castile became aware of its own greatness. See Manuel Fernández Álvarez, *Felipe II y su tiempo* (Madrid: Espasa Calpe, 1998), 16.

44. See Malini Johar Schueller, *U.S. Orientalisms: Race, Nation and Gender in Literature, 1790–1890* (Ann Arbor: University of Michigan Press, 1998).

45. In a letter to his sister, Sarah Van Wart, dated 12 May 1829, Irving told of being "so pleasantly fixed" in "this old deserted palace, which looks like one of those enchanted palaces we read of in Arabian tales." Irving, *Letters*, 417.

46. Bowers, *Spanish Adventures of Irving*, 129.

47. See Pabón-Flores, intro. to Irving, *Columbus*, 10. Hemingway of course went on to Cuba, the jewel in the crown of the Spanish Empire in the nineteenth century and the quintessential object of desire in the Usonian imperial tradition. There he lived as a Crusoe look-alike, single-handedly patrolling the coasts of his island in search of German submarines and ruling uncontested as the philosopher king of Daiquiri paradise. In the end, Hemingway's estate on the outskirts of Havana might be stylistically distant from Irving's Alhambra—even though, like the old Nasrid palace, it sits amidst gardens atop a hill overlooking the city—but there is no question that villa "El Vigía" has a distinctly Irvian character. A walk through the premises—kept to this day as the master left them—quickly reveals that even though it is the house of an "American bohemian" and is, as such, full of souvenirs of foreign travels and properly stocked with consumer goods and collectibles from "back home," the interior spaces of the plain and open neoclassical shell, with the trophy heads of bulls hanging from the walls and other bullfighting souvenirs, have been arranged for the most part following the manner of the Spanish quinta or seigniorial country manor of the wealthy Andalusian cattleman or of a celebrated bullfighter. Like so many well-to-do Usonians of his time, Hemingway realized his Irvian dream in Cuba, that little country with so much Spanish flavor that it is like a tropical Granada but conveniently located only ninety miles south of Key West.

48. Antelyes, *Tales of Adventurous Enterprise*, 161.

49. Antelyes, *Tales of Adventurous Enterprise*, 167. Columbus's ultimate plan was to sail to the Indies to meet the Great Khan of China and, after securing his conversion to Christianity, procure an alliance with the Spanish monarchs to march against the Turks and liberate Jerusalem.

50. Antelyes, *Tales of Adventurous Enterprise*, 203. These are, of course, the origins of the nation imagined as a marketplace.

51. Prescott was a historian, part of a younger generation that followed and admired Irving. In fact, he had a bust of Irving in his study. Originally Irving had wanted to write a book on the conquest of Mexico, but he abandoned the idea after Prescott announced his intention to do the same.

52. Usonian accounts of the war of 1898 are many, and they all make use of such terminology and symbolism. See, for example, John J. Ingalls, *America's War for Humanity, Related in Story and Picture, Embracing a Complete History of Cuba's Struggle for Liberty and the Glorious Heroism of America's Soldiers and Sailors* (New York: N. D. Thompson, 1898).

53. William S. Bryan, ed., *Our Islands and Their Peoples, As Seen with Camera and Pencil* (Saint Louis: Thompson Publishing, 1899), vol. 1: 256.

54. The Rotunda frieze begins with the allegories of *America and History,* the *Landing of Columbus,* three panels of Spanish conquest, five of English settlement, and three of the Revolutionary War, with the *Declaration of Independence* framed between the *Battle of Lexington* and the *Surrender of Cornwallis.* It then depicts the *Death of Tecumseh* and two panels of the conquest and colonization of Mexico: the *American Army Entering the City of Mexico* and the *Discovery of Gold in California.* The last three panels celebrate the end of the Civil War, the victory in the Spanish-Cuban-American War, and the *Birth of Aviation.* Due to their symbolic character the first and last panels should be considered bookends. They are there to uphold and protect the alpha and the omega of an imperial tradition in the Americas through which the United States has commandeered the imperial history and the imperial leftovers of Spain, from Columbus to Manila.

Reflecting on the entire building as the representative embodiment of Usonian state ideology, Vivien Green Fryd has stated that "the subject and iconography of much of the art in the Capitol forms a remarkably coherent program of the early course of North American empire." See Vivien Green Fryd, *Art and Empire: The Politics of Ethnicity in the United States Capitol, 1815–1860* (New Haven, Conn.: Yale University Press, 1992), 1.

55. As Rosella Mamolizorzi has pointed out, the placing of Roger's doors in the Rotunda was the symbolic act through which Columbus was incorporated into the Pantheon of the Founding Fathers. See Rosella Mamolizorzi, "The Celebration of Columbus in Nineteenth Century American Art and Washington Irving's *Life of Columbus,*" in *The American Columbiad: "Discovering" America, Inventing the United States,* ed. Mario Materassi and Maria Irene Ramalho de Sousa Santos (Amsterdam: VU University Press, 1996), 64–65.

56. Since the end of the eighteenth century it had been common to believe that empires had been traveling westward from China, through Mesopotamia and into the Mediterranean. In postrevolutionary Usonia, as the United States began to set its sights on China, the view was held by many who thought of their own country as the last link in that chain. See Schueller, *U.S. Orientalisms,* 26–29.

It is important to note that the last three scenes of the frieze were painted only a few years after the United States emerged victorious and virile from the Second World War, having assumed a commanding position over the exhausted imperial powers of France and England, and only seven years after the dropping of the atomic bomb on Hiroshima, arguably the most forceful and devastating claim to universal hegemony ever made.

57. Irving and Vanderlyn were contemporaries, and they had met as young men in Paris, where in 1805 the artist sketched Irving's portrait. This portrait, by the way, was remarkably similar to Vanderlyn's own self-portrait of 1800, as the subjects of both are wearing almost exactly the same clothes and sporting long sideburns, with their hair combed forward. They were friends in Paris, and no doubt the plastic depiction of Irving's narrative was somewhat of a tribute to the old acquaintance, a circumstance that must have added to the desire to remain faithful to the text.

58. See Fryd, *Art and Empire*, 224.

59. Alonso de Ojeda was again at Columbus's side when he was captain of one of the vessels on the admiral's second voyage. But it was Ojeda's third voyage to the Indies, and the first expedition he commanded, that has brought him historical notoriety on account of having taken with him the famous mapmaker Juan de la Cosa and the explorer Amerigo Vespucci, after whose last name the New World came to be known.

60. Irving, *Columbus*, 72.

61. Irving, *Columbus*, 93.

62. Ibid.

63. Ibid.

64. Ibid.

65. Ibid.

66. See, for example, Lars Schoultz, *Beneath the United States: A History of U.S. Policy toward Latin America* (Cambridge: Harvard University Press, 1998).

67. Washington's troops had run from the redcoats and Hessians in New York City on 15 September 1776, at which point the Founding Father "whacked them with his cane, called them cowards, and tried to lead them back into the fight." (See Geoffrey Perret, *A Country Made by War: From the Revolution to Vietnam — The Story of America's Rise to Power* [New York: Random House, 1989], 32.) The general himself had exhibited a great deal of vacillation and pursued rather incoherent tactics and maneuvers, which gave him no other recourse than to retreat south to New Jersey under the close pursuit of the British. By the time he crossed the Delaware his army was practically in shambles, down to a force of four thousand and experiencing a combined rate of death and desertion of about one hundred men per day. See Perret, 29–39.

68. Fryd, *Art and Empire*, 136.

69. Adams to Jefferson, *The Adams-Jefferson Letters*, 571.

70. See, for example, S. F. Cook and W. Borah, "The Aboriginal Population of Hispaniola," in *Essays in Population History*, ed. S. F. Cook and W. Borah (Berkeley: University of California Press, 1971), vol. 1: 401–5.

71. See Karl Marx, "The Eighteenth Brumaire of Louis Bonaparte," in *Later Political Writings*, ed. Terrell Carver (Cambridge, U.K.: Cambridge University Press, 1996), 34.

72. There is a canvas of Columbus's arrival in Guanahani at the Museo del Hombre Dominicano, the museum of anthropology of the Dominican Republic, which is almost a carbon copy of Vanderlyn's. Interestingly enough, the figure of the admiral strikes a pose that also reminds us of the scene by Rogers showing Columbus's disapproval of his men's taking the native women. As in Vanderlyn's painting, Columbus holds a sword in his right hand while with his left he is commanding the natives to submit to his authority. The portrait of the admiral shows Columbus at

his most Washingtonian, his hair painted in imitation of the white wigs worn by gentlemen and nobles in the eighteenth century.

73. Ortega y Gasset, "How Castile Made Spain," 30.

74. The nineteenth-century historian Luis Viardot might have erred by not considering the larger panorama of world history, but he captured the essence of Al-Andalus when he wrote, "Never did a less compact, less homogeneous people occupy the same land under one and the same banner" (Jamás pueblo alguno reunido bajo un mismo cetro, y ocupando una misma comarca, fue menos compacto, menos homogéneo). Luis Viardot, *Historia de los árabes y de los moros de España* (Barcelona: Imprenta de Juan de Olivares, 1844), 199.

The tribal division between the *Qaysite* and *Kalbite* (or Yemenite) Arabs that bled the Caliphate in Damascus was imported into the Iberian Peninsula and aggravated by the fact that the bulk of the troops that were sent into the country were not Arabs but recent Berber converts from North Africa. In 713 the Arab governor Mûsà ibn Nusayr met in Talavera with the Berber conqueror Târiq ibn Ziyâd, who had come down from Toledo, the vanquished capital of Visigothic Spain. According to Muslim accounts, Mûsà, who was weary of Târiq's accomplishments in battle because they may have detracted from his own claim to glory, scolded Târiq and assaulted him with a whip. (See Abû Marwân 'Abd al-Malik ibn al-Kardabûs al-Tawzarî, *Historia de al-Andalus. Kitab al-Iktifa'*, trans. Felipe Maíllo Salgado [Madrid: Ediciones Akal, 1986], 67.) This episode attests to a foundational rivalry between an Arab ruling class and a Berber clientele, a division that from the beginning questioned Arab hegemony over the lands taken from the Visigoths and that would ultimately hamper the development of a stable Muslim state, because it was to be organized around a continuous dependence in the importation of mercenary troops from North Africa.

As they entered the peninsula, Muslims came to govern large populations of Christians who would come to be known as *musta'ribûn*, or would-be Arabs (Spanish mozárabes, English mozarabs), and also large populations of Jews. In turn the descendants of the Arabs would bestow upon themselves the title *baldiyyûn* (from *ahl al-balad*, Spanish baladíes) or natives of the country, and the descendants of the Christians who converted to Islam—the new Muslims who, at least in principle, were entitled to claim equal status with the *baldiyyûn*—would come to be known as *muwalladûn*, meaning adopted ones (Spanish muladíes, English muwallads).

75. I am borrowing the term *contact zones* from Mary Louise Pratt, who explains it as referring to "social spaces where disparate cultures meet, clash, and grapple with each other, often in highly asymmetrical relations of domination and subordination—like colonialism, slavery, or their aftermaths as they are lived out across the globe today." (Mary Louise Pratt, *Imperial Eyes: Travel Writing and Transculturation* [New York: Routledge, 1992], 4.) Subsequently she adds that the term describes "the space of colonial encounters, the space in which peoples geographically and historically separated come into contact with each other and establish ongoing relations, usually involving conditions of coercion, radical inequality, and intractable conflict.... 'Contact zone' is an attempt to invoke the spatial and temporal copresence of subjects previously separated by geographic and historical disjunctures, and whose trajectories now intersect." Pratt, 6–7.

76. Also known as the Marca Hispánica, or Spanish March, this was the southernmost dependency of the Frankish kingdoms, where in the eighth century the

Arab advance had been contained. It was therefore the frontier between Christian and Muslim Europe. Eventually under the control of the Counts of Barcelona by the ninth century, this was the cradle of the Catalan nation.

77. The Maghrib corresponds roughly to the area today occupied by Tunisia, Algeria, and Morocco, from Tripoli to Agadir.

78. In 1085 the old Visigothic capital of Toledo fell to the Christian king of Castile, Alfonso VI. In 1212 the Almohad armies suffered a catastrophic defeat in the battle of Las Navas de Tolosa, a mountain pass that leads from Castile to the valley of the Guadalquivir, the heartland of al-Andalus. Córdoba fell in 1236 and Seville in 1248. In 1263, under the leadership of the King of Granada, the conquered peoples made their last attempt at armed resistance. It failed. By the end of the century Granada, cornered and accepting to pay tribute to the Crown of Castile, was the last remnant of what once had been the most powerful state in the western Mediterranean. Nevertheless, the Granada of the Nasrids was a thriving cultural center and would remain to the last moment the wealthiest of all peninsular kingdoms.

79. The Kingdom of Aragon became one of the most important centers of Mudejar culture in the peninsula, and it was, after Granada, perhaps the saddest and most broken land following the expulsion of the *moriscos* from all the kingdoms of Spain in the seventeenth century. The traveler who has been in Aragon cannot avoid being impressed by the Mudejar brick towers that rise with authority above the oldest towns like minarets from which bells have been hung. In fact, in towns like Ateca near Calatayud, the belfries of the churches were built on top of the minarets just as in the famous Giralda tower in Seville. All of these are powerful physical testimonies to the complex coexistence of these peoples and of the difficult compromises that the so-called mudejars had to negotiate in order to remain in their country.

80. In essence they were sharecroppers.

81. Ibn al-Kardabûs, *Historia de al-Andalus*, 128.

82. See Ramón Menéndez-Pidal, *La España del Cid* (Buenos Aires: Espasa-Calpe Argentina, 1939).

83. See *Crónica anónima de los reyes de taifas*, ed. Felipe Maíllo Salgado (Madrid: Ediciones Akal, 1991), 51.

84. As Dozy and Engelman point out, the root of *tagri* is *tagr,* meaning frontier. At one point the name *tagarino* was given to the Andalusi peoples of Aragon, the land that was known in Arabic as *at-tagr al-a'la,* or the upper frontier *(la frontière supérieure).* Reinhardt Dozy and W. H. Engelmann, *Glossaire des mots espagnols et portugais dérivés de l'arabe* (Amsterdam: Oriental Press, 1869), 521.

85. Concerning the dealings of Cortés with Moctezuma, Todorov writes: "Cortés' behavior is often quite as contradictory in appearance, but his contradiction is calculated and has as its goal—and effect—to 'jam' its message, to leave its interlocutor in perplexity." Todorov, *Conquest of America,* 112.

86. Todorov writes: "Like Moctezuma, Columbus carefully gathered information concerning things, but failed in his communication with men." See Todorov, *Conquest of America,* 75.

87. Marco de Guadalajara y Xavier, *Memorable expvlsion ylvstrissimo destierro de los Morifcos de Efpaña* (Pamplona: Nicolas de Afsiyn, 1613), 77. "El eftado en que fe hallan las cofas de los Morifcos del Reyno de Valencia, es el mifmo que tienen las cofas que tienen los Morifcos de Aragon, y los de toda la Corona de Efpaña y afsi lo

que fe dixere de eftos, fe dize tambien de aquellos; porque el animo y obftinacion contra la Fè Catholica es vno en todos; y afsi mifmo el odio y aborrecimiento de su Rey natural, y el deffeo de verle debaxo el dominio del Turco, o de cualqueira otro tyrano, que les dexaffe viuir libremente en su Secta. Demanera, que lo que es fuftancia del negocio, ninguna diferencia fe puede dar, fi bien en lo que es accidente, como es andar vnos veftidos como Chriftianos, y otros a la vfança de los Moros; faber vnos hablar de ordinario Aljamia, otros no viuir vnos en lugares apartados, donde no ay mas que Morifcos, y otros mezclados entre los Chriftianos viejos: Pero todos eftos fabemos con euidencia moral, que fon Moros, y que viuen en la fecta de Mahoma, guardando y obferuando (en quanto les es pofsible) las ceremonias del Alcoran, y menofpreciando las leyes fantas de la Iglefia Catholica: Tanto que hablando con propiedad, deuemos llamarlos, no Morifcos, fino Moros."

88. "Ellos son su [España] hucha, su polilla, sus picazas y sus comadrejas; todo lo llegan, todo lo esconden y todo lo tragan." Miguel de Cervantes, "El coloquio de los perros," in *El licenciado Vidriera y El coloquio de los perros* (Zaragoza: Editorial Ebro, 1964), 112.

89. ". . . la provincia en España más fértil, y abundosa de todo lo que se puede dessear, por mar y tierra." (Sebastián de Covarrubias, *Tesoro de la lengua castellana o española, según la impresión de 1611, con las adiciones de Benigno Noydens publicadas en la de 1674*, ed. Martín de Riquer [Barcelona: Editorial Alta Fulla, 1993], 118). This is the same dictionary where the definition of *Moor* is summarized in the saying "A dead Moor means great aim" (A moro muerto gran lançada). See Covarrubias, 814.

90. J. H. Elliot, *Spain and Its World, 1500–1700* (New Haven, Conn.: Yale University Press, 1989), 224.

91. See Vitruvius, *Ten Books on Architecture*, trans. Ingrid D. Rowland, commentary and illustrations by Thomas Noble Howe (Cambridge, U.K.: Cambridge University Press, 1999), book 1, chap. 3. According to Vitruvius, together with utility and beauty, *firmitas*, or solidity, is one of the three interdependent principles to which architectural works must conform.

92. Alberto Pérez-Gómez locates the coming of age of this aesthetic movement in the new mechanics of the Galilean age: "At this historical juncture, geometry and number were able to become instruments for the technical control of practical operations and, eventually, for an effective technological dominance of the world. Through the new science of mechanics, man began to subject matter to his will." See Alberto Pérez-Gómez, *Architecture and the Crisis of Modern Science* (Cambridge: MIT Press, 1990), 10.

93. In his encyclopedic catalogue of world architecture, Sir Banister Fletcher was always able to pass precise judgment on every building except for the Alhambra. See Banister Fletcher, *A History of Architecture* (New York: Chas. Scribner's Sons, 1958), 948.

94. The Alhambra is today the most visited historic architectural masterpiece in the entire world. It is also one of the most thoroughly studied. At the same time, most of its history, functions, and aesthetic values remain a mystery. My reading of these spaces, while informed by knowledgeable sources and personal experience, is, like all other readings in this case, highly speculative.

95. The term *qamariyya* is, in turn, derived from *al-qamar*, Arabic for moon. See Marianne Barrucand and Achim Bednorz, *Moorish Architecture in Andalusia* (Cologne: Tachen, 1992), note 185, 227.

96. From the Spanish translation by D. Cabanelas and A. Fernández, in Jesús Bermúdez López and Pedro Galera Andreu, *Guía oficial de visita al Conjunto Monumental La Alhambra y el Generalife* (Granada: Editorial Comares, 1998), 118.

97. See Barrucand and Bednorz, 191.

98. See Vitruvius, *Ten Books on Architecture,* book 3, chap. 1.

99. See Vitruvius, *Ten Books on Architecture,* 189.

100. The design features a circular building of fifty thousand tons that is 231 feet in diameter and inscribed within a quadrangular precinct that is, in turn, marked by a peripheral wall eight feet high.

101. See Ramón Menéndez-Pidal, *Idea imperial de Carlos V* (Madrid: Espasa Calpe, 1955), 9–35.

102. See Leone Ebreo, *Dialoghi d'Amore,* trans. F. Friedeberg-Seeley and Jean H. Barnes as *The Philosophy of Love* (London: Soncino Press, 1937), 379. Hebreo's Jewish name was Judah Abrabanel. The work, originally written in 1502, was published fourteen years after Ebreo's death in 1535.

103. Ebreo, *The Philosophy of Love,* 381.

104. José Camón Aznar considered the building the purest work of Italian Renaissance design in Spain, but believed that because it was thrown rather violently on top of the traditions of Christian architectural practices it had very little influence on future architectural developments in the peninsula. See José Camón Aznar, *La arquitectura plateresca* (Madrid: S. Aguirre, 1945), 31, 113.

2. Contesting the Ideal

1. I am thinking here of James Clifford's observations on diasporic cultures. See James Clifford, *Routes: Travel and Translation in the Late Twentieth Century* (Cambridge, Mass.: Harvard University Press, 1997), 250–51.

2. By contrast, the Jewish presence in the New World has been studied, albeit insufficiently. See, for example, Paolo Bernardini and Norman Fiering, ed., *The Jews and the Expansion of Europe to the West, 1450 to 1800* (New York: Berghahn Books, 2001). In his introductory article Paolo Bernardini, like a modern-day Irving, suggests that Columbus was not only the first American but also very possibly a Jew. Similarly, this Jewish Columbiad is framed within an ethos of what Bernardini calls "a milder colonization." See Bernardini, "A Milder Colonization: Jewish Expansion to the New World, and the New World in the Jewish Consciousness of the Early Modern Era," in Bernardini and Fiering, 1–23.

3. Ángel G. Quintero Rivera, "Vueltita, con mantilla, al primer piso: Sociología de los santos," in *Virgenes, magos y escapularios: Imaginería, etnicidad y religiosidad popular en Puerto Rico,* ed. Ángel G. Quintero Rivera (San Juan: Centro de Investigaciones Sociales, 1998), 75.

4. See Clifford, *Routes,* 36.

5. The Spanish term *cimarrón,* as Quintero Rivera points out in citing José Juan Arrom, derives from the Arawak *símaran,* a word used by the native inhabitants of the Antilles to refer to an arrow that, once shot, was lost or never recovered. Thus the term must have evolved in the early years of the enslavement of the Arawaks as a self-descriptor of the fugitive native, eventually to be adopted by the Spaniards to refer both to Indian and later to African runaways. See Quintero Rivera, "Vueltita," 48. One of the earliest uses of the term was in a royal decree of 9 July 1532 that

speaks of "some Indians called *cimarrones* which is to say fugitives" (algunos yndios que llaman Cimarrones que son los fugitivos). A.G.I., *Indiferente, 737*, N.25. By the end of the sixteenth century the term was commonly used in referring to runaway blacks, as when the Audiencia of Panama informed the Crown of the *negros cimarrones* of Portobelo, Cerro de Cabra, Bayano, and Santa Cruz. A.G.I., *Patronato, 234*, R.6.

    6. Quintero Rivera, "Vueltita," 81.

    7. These are to a large extent the origins of Caribbean religious syncretism, an eclectic set of traditions that share a common modality of iconographic subterfuge. In every case, then and now, these syncretic religious practices have been based on the constant counterpointing of *genio* and *figura* according to the movement of the metaphorical subject. This movement is perhaps most clearly exemplified in the dressing and cross-dressing of religious symbols and images in a profusion of variable signs that are always accompanied by what is intended to be a credible profession of faith in the Christian images of devotion.

Here again see the excellent essay by Quintero Rivera, especially the discussion relating to the Virgen de los Reyes (the Virgin of the Kings) and the Biblical Magi. Quintero Rivera, "Vueltita," 56–85. For a classic example of this phenomenon see Antonio Benítez Rojo's description of the trilogy Atabey/Nuestra Señora/Oshun seen in the image and the cult of the Virgen de la Caridad del Cobre (Virgin of Charity of El Cobre). (Antonio Benítez Rojo, *The Repeating Island: The Caribbean and the Postmodern Perspective,* trans. James Maraniss [Durham, N.C.: Duke University Press, 1992], 12–16.) For a good testimony to the continuance and development of the same practices today, see the work of the Cuban artist María Magdalena Campos Pons, who literally dresses her body up in the colors of Eleguá in *Los Caminos* (1996), a Polaroid triptych, part of her series "When I'm not here. Estoy Allá..." (When I'm not here. I am over there...). In this work the body becomes the recipient of divinity as well as its sign. At the same time, the face becomes depersonalized—the opposite of the classical understanding of the face and of the building's façade as revealing the essential character of the person or of the building—and hidden behind its own material and symbolic excrescence.

    8. See again Vitruvius, *Ten Books on Architecture,* book 3, chap. 1.

    9. As J. H. Elliot has pointed out, "When plays were performed in the palace of the Alcázar in Madrid, the king was seated some ten or twelve feet from the back wall, at the exact point at which the perspective design of the stage set could be appreciated to the full. On either side of the room were standing rows of courtiers, with their eyes fixed on the king and queen as much as on the play. For in a sense the king and queen *were* the play." (See J. H. Elliot, *Spain and Its World, 1500–1700* [New Haven, Conn.: Yale University Press, 1989], 143–44.) This is precisely the representational system that Francisco de Velázquez would later subvert in *Las Meninas* (1656) by placing himself, as the artist, in the generating vortex of all perspectival and symbolic geometries and relegating the monarchs to the role of supporting his own opus of self-aggrandizement.

    10. Covarrubias defines *morena* as the color of a woman of a "color that is not quite black, like the Moors, from which the term was taken" (color, la que no es del todo negra, como la de los moros, de donde tomó nombre, o de mora). Sebastián de Covarrubias, *Tesoro de la lengua castellana o española, según la impresión de 1611, con las adiciones de Benigno Noydens publicadas en la de 1674,* ed. Martín de Riquer (Barcelona: Editorial Alta Fulla, 1993), 814.

11. "Moro," *Diccionario Crítico Etimológico Castellano e Hispánico,* 1981 ed.

12. Benzoni explains: "When the natives of this island [Española] began to be extirpated, the Spaniards provided themselves with blacks [Mori] from Guinea." See Girolamo Benzoni, *History of the New World* (New York: Burt Franklin, 1970), 93.

13. Andalusian emigration represented 32 percent of the total. See Peter Boyd-Bowman, *Índice geobiográfico de cuarenta mil pobladores españoles de América en el siglo XVI* (México: Editorial Jus, 1968), vol. 1: ix–xv.

14. Boyd-Bowman's work, which remains to this day the basis for all projections concerning Iberian emigration to the New World during the sixteenth century, is based on a representative group that accounts for about 20 percent of what he estimates must have been the approximate total number of migrants (some two hundred thousand before 1600).

15. Francisco Morales Padrón estimates that Seville had a total population of 55,000 to 60,000 in 1533. By 1565 the number of inhabitants had doubled to 109,015, reaching a peak in 1588, when the population was 129,430. (See Francisco Morales Padrón, *La Ciudad del Quinientos* [Seville: University of Seville, 1977], 65.) All other peninsular cities were dwarfed by Seville. Although cities like Burgos, in the heart of Old Castile, and Córdoba, the second-largest city in Andalusia, had seen their populations double during the same period, the first had only 20,000 inhabitants by 1561, while the latter had scarcely 11,600 by 1571.

16. Ruth Pike, *Aristocrats and Traders: Sevillian Society in the Sixteenth Century* (Ithaca, N.Y.: Cornell University Press, 1972), 17–18.

17. "Mucho más plebeya." Boyd-Bowman, *Índice,* vol. 2: xix.

18. See Pike, *Aristocrats and Traders,* 156–57.

19. One of the many connections between Triana and the cities of the Indies is the fact that in the old quarters of both Havana and San Juan there is a street named Sol, after one of the streets in Triana where the largest number of sailors of the Carrera de Indias resided.

20. See Pike, *Aristocrats and Traders,* 163–64.

21. Pablo E. Pérez-Mallaína, *Spain's Men of the Sea: Daily Life on the Indies Fleets in the Sixteenth Century,* trans. Carla Rahn Phillips (Baltimore: John Hopkins University Press, 1998), 23–63.

22. Pike, *Aristocrats and Traders,* 4.

23. See Morales Padrón, *La Ciudad del Quinientos,* 93–94.

24. See Pike, *Aristocrats and Traders,* 156.

25. Many scholars to this day have a hard time coming to terms with a phenomenon that contributed in large part to what Seville is today. José Luis Comellas is quick to point out that "the Moorish character of the city does not necessarily imply the existence of a Moorish mentality or of a Moorish environment" (El aspecto de ciudad moruna no implica necesariamente mentalidad moruna o ambiente moruno). José Luis Comellas, *Sevilla, Cádiz y América: El trasiego y el tráfico* (Málaga: Editorial Arguval, 1992), 113.

26. See Pike, *Aristocrats and Traders,* 166.

27. Juan de Ayala, *A Letter to Ferdinand and Isabella,* trans. Charles E. Nowell (Minneapolis: University of Minnesota Press, 1965), 45.

28. Carlos Esteban Dieve, "La cultura cristiano islámica medieval y su presencia en Santo Domingo," *Boletín del Museo del Hombre Dominicano* 18 (1981):156.

29. See Auke Pieter Jacobs, "Legal and Illegal Emigration from Seville, 1550–1650," in *"To Make America": European Emigration in the Early Modern Period,* ed. Ida Altman and James Horn (Berkeley: University of California Press, 1991), 59–84.

30. "... para que pregonen en las gradas de la catedral que todo el que quiera ir a la Española, hasta el número de 200 hombres, para hacer la guerra a Enriquejo y a otros indios que andan alzados, se les dará pasaje y matalotaje, comida durante la guerra amén de otras cosas." A.G.I., *Indiferente,* 1961, L.2, F.187v–188v. The steps, or *gradas,* of the cathedral were the preeminent place in Seville where all commerce, legal and illegal, took place.

31. In the end, the organizers of the punitive expedition against Enriquillo decided to take farmers instead of soldiers, thinking that the colonists in Hispaniola were already acclimatized and knowledgeable of the terrain and would, therefore, make for better soldiers. In any event, taking farmers from Seville, Carmona, and other Andalusian towns increased the likelihood that the expedition would be all the more *amoriscada.*

32. Kathleen Deagan, *Puerto Real: The Archaeology of a Sixteenth-Century Spanish Town in Hispaniola* (Miami: University Press of Florida, 1995), 90.

33. "... la región más andaluza del Nuevo Mundo." Boyd-Bowman, *Índice,* vol. 2: xxiii.

34. Comellas, *Sevilla, Cádiz y América,* 138.

35. Referenced from an article by María Ugarte in Eugenio Pérez Montás, *La ciudad del Ozama: 500 años de historia urbana* (Barcelona: Lunwerg Editores, 1999), 89.

36. According to Dieve, a decree of 1571 had forbidden black and mulatto women, whether slave or free, from wearing the light, long, all-covering *mantos de burato.* (See Dieve, "La cultura cristiano islámica medieval," 155.) A similar prohibition was passed in 1874 as part of the Spanish Negro Code to the effect "that black women, whether slave or free, as well as the mulatto ones, may not use veils" (que las Negras libres, o siervas, y las pardas, no puedan usar mantillas en lugar de paños). A.G.I., *Estado,* 7, N.3.

37. Flora Tristán, excerpt from *Peregrinations of a Pariah* (1838), in *Flora Tristán, Utopian Feminist: Her Travel Diaries and Personal Crusade,* trans. Doris and Paul Beik (Bloomington: Indiana University Press, 1993), 27–33.

38. Richard Halliburton, *New Worlds to Conquer* (Indianapolis: Bobbs-Merrill, 1929), 182.

39. Tristán, *Peregrinations,* 27.

40. Quintero Rivera, "Vueltita," 8–100.

41. Organized during the second part of the sixteenth century, the Fleet of New Spain and the Fleet of Tierra Firme carried the bulk of all commodities and the great majority of passengers that traveled between Spain and her empire in the East and in the West Indies. The New Spain fleet typically arrived in Puerto Rico once a year between June and August, stopping at the Aguada on the western side of the island, far away from San Juan, to replenish the supplies of the two most important items required to sustain life on board: drinking water and firewood for cooking.

42. Also expressed as *echar pal monte, cojer monte, huirse al monte, subirse al monte,* and *treparse al monte.*

43. Finisterre (Latin for "end of the Earth") is the westernmost cape in the northern part of the Iberian Peninsula. It was given the name by the Romans, who were the first to set up a lighthouse at this point where the land, and their world, came to an end.

44. See Cayetano Coll y Toste, *Leyendas y tradiciones puertorriqueñas* (Bilbao: Editorial Vasco Americana, 1968), 86–90.

45. "En los primeros tres siglos de formación de las sociedades del Caribe hispano, en la ruralía, frente a la plaza fuerte citadina que representaba la España del colonialismo, fueron gradualmente *encontrándose* y conviviendo personas cuyas culturas se encontraban amenazadas, y era precisamente frente a esa amenaza que se daba la huida que posibilitaba el *encuentro*." Quintero Rivera, "Vueltita," 45.

46. "Podría uno muy probablemente tener alguna ascendencia mora o judía (que, es importante recordar, no comían cerdo), pero uno desea que 'lo dejen quieto' las autoridades, no quiere ser perseguido. Ahora se es cristiano—español—y es importante demostrarlo." Quintero Rivera, "Vueltita," 75.

47. The terms *mestizaje* and mestizo derive from the Latin *misticius,* which in turn comes from *mixtus,* or mixed.

48. "Hermano Aguilar, yo soy casado, tengo tres hijos, y tiénenme por cacique y capitán cuando hay guerras; íos vos con Dios; que yo tengo labrada la cara e horadas las horejas; ¿qué dirán de mí desque me vean esos españoles ir desta manera?" Bernal Díaz del Castillo, *Historia verdadera de la Conquista de la Nueva España,* ed. Carmelo Saenz de Santa María (Madrid: Instituto Gonzalo Fernández de Oviedo, 1982), 50.

49. During the same period that Guerrero was lost in the Yucatán, in 1513 a judge of the Episcopal Tribunal of Concepción de la Vega in Hispaniola annulled the marriage of a Spaniard and an Indian woman on the grounds that she, as an Indian, was incapable of reasoning and understanding. The case was taken before the Inquisition in Spain, and the judge was made to confess his error and was, according to Las Casas, severely punished either by being sent to preach in a jail or by being shipped off to a monastery where he would have to live as if in jail. Bartolomé de las Casas, *Apología,* trans. Ángel Losada (Madrid: Editorial Nacional, 1975), 375.

50. "Como estaban casados con indias, e con sus vicios, e tenían hijos en ellas, apartados de la fe católica, vivían ya como indios, e no quisieron reducirse a la fe ni venir a la compañía de los españoles. Bien es de creer que los tales no podían ser sino de vil casta e viles heréticos." Gonzalo Fernández de Oviedo, *Historia general y natural de las Indias,* ed. Juan Pérez de Tudela (Madrid: Atlas, 1959), vol. 4: 9.

51. "Este mal aventurado, como se debiera desde su principio haber criado entre baja y vil gente, e no bien enseñado ni doctrinado en las cosas de nuestra sancta fe católica, e por ventura (como se debe sospechar) él sería de ruin casta e sospechosa a la mesma religión cristiana." Fernández de Oviedo, *Historia general,* vol. 3: 405.

52. This expression is synonymous in terms of content with the previously cited "genio y figura, hasta la sepultura," as they both refer to people whose old habits and beliefs cannot be changed.

53. "Y parece ser que aquel Gonzalo Guerrero era hombre de la mar, natural de Palos." Díaz del Castillo, *Historia verdadera,* 50.

54. "Aquel mal cristiano Gonzalo, marinero," or "aquel traidor y renegado marinero llamado Gonzalo." Fernández de Oviedo, *Historia general,* vol. 3: 405.

55. "E ya veis estos mis tres hijitos cuán bonicos son." Díaz del Castillo, *Historia verdadera*, 50.

56. Martín González, quoted in Claudio Esteva-Fabregat, *Mestizaje in Ibero-America*, trans. John Wheat (Tucson: University of Arizona Press, 1995), 34.

57. See Esteva-Fabregat, *Mestizaje*, 35.

58. Quoted in Edwin Walter Palm, *Los monumentos arquitectónicos de La Española, con una introducción a América* (Barcelona: Seix y Barral, 1955), vol. 1: 89.

59. In 1527 the royal official Diego Caballero was granted license to take his Spanish-speaking Berber slave *(esclavo ladino berberisco)* to Hispaniola. A.G.I., *Indiferente*, 421, L.12, F.154v.

60. A.G.I., *Indiferente*, 1961, L.2, F.115–115v. Following the letter of the law, in 1935 Juan de Alfaro asked to be allowed to take one white female slave to the Indies. A.G.I., *Indiferente*, 1961, L. 3, F.204r–204v.

61. A.G.I., *Indiferente*, 423, L.20, F.665r–665v.

62. A.G.I., *Indiferente*, 424, L.22, F.239v–241r. Successive prohibitions were passed as late as 1699. See A.G.I., *Indiferente*, 431, L.45, F.55v–57v.

63. "Esclavos y esclavas berberiscos que en esta ciudad se han hallado, una de cien piezas de ellos, sin los que había en la tierra de adentro... pasados con licencias expresas de V. M. y que están casados y con hijos y que los que son personas libres, a quien toca esto, son oficiales de albañiles y carpinteros y otros oficios muy provechosos para la población de la tierra." Quoted in Walter Palm, *Monumentos arquitectónicos*, 89.

64. The small fortress in Concepción de la Vega had two cylindrical towers at the end of a lengthwise diagonal bisecting the rectangular plan. It is a modest though interesting example of a Mudejar-style fortification related to much larger and contemporary peninsular examples, such as the castle of La Mota in Medina del Campo, built half a century before.

65. Alessandro Geraldini, *Itinerario por las regiones subequinocciales* (Santo Domingo: Editora del Caribe, 1977), 145.

66. The Audiencia of Santo Domingo had jurisdiction over Puerto Rico, Cuba, Florida, and the East Coast of northern South America, or what came to be known as Tierra Firme. In Castile at the time there were two such bodies: the Audiencia of Valladolid in the north and the Audiencia of Granada in the south of the peninsula.

67. Cortés had lived in Hispaniola from 1504 to 1511 as an *encomendero*, a planter who had been given Indian slaves and entrusted with the responsibility of teaching them the ways of Christianity.

68. See Frank Moya Pons, *The Dominican Republic: A National History* (Princeton, N.J.: Markus Weiner, 1998), 37–42.

69. "Suban airosas columnas/como oraciones al cielo;/y entrecrúcense los armos,/las bóvedas sosteniendo." (Geraldini, *Itinerario*, 171.) Geraldini is invariably seen as a Renaissance man. Yet, at least if this verse is an indication, he was also typical of the stylistic and ideological interregnum or overlap that characterized sixteenth-century Santo Domingo. The stanza has the energy of a confident humanism while relying on an aesthetic vision of forms that are clearly Gothic.

70. Walter Palm, *Monumentos arquitectónicos*, vol. 2: 42.

71. The Philippines had already been claimed by Magellan in the first voyage of circumnavigation of the globe in 1521, the same year in which the first stone of the

cathedral was put down. He had then called the archipelago the Islas del Poniente, or Islands of the Setting Sun.

72. Because this name was given to the island of Haiti by Columbus, it could also be claimed that the admiral not only "discovered" the New World but also renamed the Old, underscoring the important role the foreigner or outsider plays in describing the object and the contours of the national. Whereas Columbus died without knowing he had come upon a continent between Europe and Asia, he nevertheless named and, dare we say, discovered "Spanishness" by calling the center of his insular domains "La Española," a term that had not been used before to describe anyone or anything.

73. The horseshoe arch of the mihrab of the Great Mosque was also supported by the small attached colonettes that in Santo Domingo's cathedral frame the lower part of the window opening. An identical example among the few that have survived in Spain is the mihrab of the Aljafería Palace in Zaragoza.

74. Guillermo Cabrera Infante, *El libro de las ciudades* (Madrid: Alfaguara, 1999), 15.

75. Of these elements the Mudejar-style roof armatures, also called roofs of *par y nudillo* (rafter and joint), are perhaps the most substantive examples of the permanence in the New World of ancient Andalusi traditions that survived and in some cases even thrived in America long after they had come to be disused in Europe. A roof of *par y nudillo* is a complex assemblage of small pieces of wood that are cut on site according to complex angular geometries and then assembled following a very complicated numerology so as to form a sort of three-dimensional puzzle that locks into place without the need of nails or adhesives. The seventeenth-century Mudejar roof of the chapel of the Convent of Saint Clare of Assisi in Havana, for example, is a magnificent example of a large and complex work where Renaissance aesthetic preferences are given full reign in a structure that responds to the secret geometries so carefully guarded by the *alarifes*. It is always puzzling to ponder why in a place like Havana, which was then surrounded by dense tropical forest with large trees of precious woods, the *alarifes* went to the trouble of cutting the wood down to small pieces following the dictates of Arabian desert architecture.

The puzzle does not end there. Recent archaeological excavations have unearthed the lone remains of a man who was buried under the middle part of the nave. Cuban architectural historian Carlos Venegas Fornias speculates that the bones may belong to the *alarife* who built the roof above and who, according to documents of the time, donated his labor in exchange for such a prominent place of burial. The master builder, we know, was a mulatto, giving us further proof of the important connections between the Moors and the *morenos* in the Indies.

76. The town of Cholula, near Puebla, had been a very important destination of religious pilgrimage and one of the largest population centers of the pre-Columbian world. There the Franciscan friars built one of their first monasteries in Mexico during the second half of the sixteenth century. The complex is preceded by a vast atrium and composed of a fortified church, a cloister, and a *capilla real* or *capilla de indios* (Indian church). Stylistically, the buildings of the monastery are typically designed and decorated in eclectic fashion, combining Gothic, Mudejar, Plateresque, and native elements. But the *capilla real* is almost a carbon copy, to scale, of the Great Mosque of Córdoba, complete with minarets and a continuous band of merlons and crenellations crowning its exterior walls. Its design was in fact based on

that of the since-demolished Capilla de San José de los Naturales in Mexico City, which was the first Mexican copy of the Great Mosque and the model for all the *capillas de indios* built at the time. (See John McAndrew, *The Open-Air Churches of Sixteenth-Century Mexico: Atrios, Posas, Open Chapels and Other Studies* [Cambridge, Mass.: Harvard University Press, 1965], 340–411). The façade of the structure is almost a replica of the original design of the Great Mosque. In the sixteenth century its nine bays opened up to the atrium, which in Córdoba would have been the typical orange grove, or *patio de los naranjos,* which was a common feature of most peninsular mosques. The interior, which was topped with forty-nine vaults in the eighteenth century (the original nine brick barrel vaults had collapsed soon after construction in the sixteenth century) is a forest of capitals of the Tuscan order at a constant height.

To the visitor familiar with the unique execution of the mosque typology in the Cordovan example, the experience of this interior triggers a strange sense of déjà vu. Built of expandable arcades, this is a building that reproduces itself, and, as in the proven Andalusi model, it is an architecture of mass conversion. Of course, given the thousands of Indians who lived in Cholula, the design made sense. The *capilla* was in effect "nine churches in one," as her long bays were like nine naves placed in parallel arrangement next to each other. This alone explains why the Franciscan friars were building a magnificent mosque for the Indians of Cholula in which they might attend catechism classes at the same time that the persecution of the *moriscos* was in fashion back in Spain. At this time the mosque of Granada was being taken down, stone by stone, and the Great Mosque of Córdoba was being irreparably altered by the insertion of a cathedral church in its center. In any event, the *capilla real* in Cholula is a fascinating testimony to the degree of transculturation that had occurred in the peninsula and of the contradictions between idea and practice in the making of the Spanish nation and, most significant, of its empire. Even though the "mosque of Cholula" can be considered a purely practical structure, there are signs that point to the impossibility of ridding the empire of its Zaharenian curse. As Manuel Toussaint observes, a painting in the monastery depicts the Umbrian father of Saint Francis wearing a turban! Manuel Toussaint, *Arte mudéjar en América* (México: Porrúa, 1946), 12.

77. The degree of supervision and its competence are still open questions. We know, however, that the Sevillian Luis de Moya was in charge of the work in the cathedral for a time until he was replaced by Rodrigo de Liendo, who was from Santander.

78. As mentioned before, the Isabelino Gothic was an expression of a historicist architectural and aesthetic movement that was used to promote the image of a united and triumphant kingdom. Nowhere was this made clearer than in the late medieval church of San Juan de los Reyes in Toledo, founded in 1476 to commemorate the Castilian victory over the Portuguese in the battle of Toro and intended as the burial place of Ferdinand and Isabella in the years before they had taken Granada. There the coat of arms of the Catholic Monarchs, held between the claws of a fierce-looking eagle, is reproduced throughout the transept with the same obsessiveness with which the Nasrids of Granada had proclaimed the ultimate victory of Allah in the walls of the Alhambra. In this symbolic representation of a protonational spirit, the flock of eagles is there to emphatically proclaim unity through repetition, a theme that is emphasized in all iconographic details in a structure where,

contrary to what is seen in the Cathedral of Santo Domingo, there is no room for formal morphologic error or deviance. In the church of San Juan de los Reyes, Spain is Christian, and Christian means Gothic.

79. Esteva-Fabregat, *Mestizaje,* 33.

80. Dozy explains that *muwallad* means "adopted," in the sense that it was used to refer to "les Espagnols qui avaient embrassé la religion de Mahomet; c'étaient pour les Arabes *des adoptés*" (the Spaniards who had embraced the religion of Mohammed; to the Arabs they were *the adopted ones*). (Reinhardt Dozy and W. H. Engelmann, *Glossaire des mots espagnols et portugais dérivés de l'arabe* [Amsterdam: Oriental Press, 1869], 384.) In Arabic the term *muwallad* was originally used to refer to the hybrid animal, and then to the offspring of an Arab and a non-Arab. It was only in al-Andalus that it came to describe the Muslim neophyte or *muladí.* That is the connection that Engelmann uses to relate *mulatto* to *muwallad,* a conclusion that Dozy does not support. According to Engelmann, *mulatto* "designe celui qui est né d'un père arabe et d'une mére étranger. Il va de soi-même que ce mot n'a rien de commun avec *mule,* dont on a voulu le deriver" (describes the offspring of an Arab father and a foreigner mother. Accordingly, the term *[mulatto]* has nothing to do with *mule,* as has otherwise been supposed). Dozy and Engelmann, 384.

81. See "Moreno," *Diccionario de la lengua española,* 2000 ed. In the case of *loro* and *pardo,* each was a reference to a certain shade of brown that was difficult to point out precisely. The dictionary of the Spanish Royal Academy defines *pardo* in the most ambiguous of terms: "the color of earth, or of the skin of the common bear, intermediate between white and black, with a hue of yellowish red and darker than gray." (See *Diccionario de la lengua española.*) In every case the members of the Royal Academy seem to be referring to the infinite possibilities of the in-between.

In 1554 Gonzálo Gómez de la Cámara asked permission to take his wife, María de Alvarado, and his four children to the Indies. He also asked for permission to take his niece and his three servants, two of whom were "of mulatto color" (de color mulato). Their names were Juan de Alvarado and Elena Gómez de la Cámara, and they were both the offspring of an old Christian (white) male and a free black woman. A.G.I., *Pasajeros,* L.3, E.1977.

82. See Isidoro Moreno, *La Antigua Hermandad de los Negros de Sevilla: Etnicidad, poder y sociedad en 600 años de historia* (Sevilla: A. Pinelo, 1997).

83. Like Moreno, I prefer to add *Magos* in parentheses to differentiate this representation of Mary from its homonym, the other Sevillian-based Virgen de los Reyes, who is the patroness of the Spanish royal family and thus a wholly different symbol altogether.

84. Moreno, *La Antigua Hermandad,* 51.

85. Moreno, *La Antigua Hermandad,* 50–52.

86. In 1585 Francisca de Vega requested permission to take six personal slaves to Puerto Rico. Two of them, Gaspar and Baltasar, were named after the Wise Men of the Epiphany. A.G.I., *Indiferente,* 2062, N.10. In 1612 Juan Cano Moctezuma asked permission to take his family and servants to New Spain, including a mulatto by the name of Baltasar de los Reyes. A.G.I., *Contratación,* 5326, N.49.

87. Of a total population of 85,538 there were reportedly 6,327 slaves in Seville in 1565. See Pike, *Aristocrats and Traders,* 172.

88. Moreno, *La Antigua Hermandad,* 62.

89. José Luis Cortés López, *La esclavitud negra en la España peninsular del siglo XVI* (Salamanca: Universidad de Salamanca, 1989), 91–95.

90. Moreno, *La Antigua Hermandad*, 85.

91. "ni poseen poder económico o social alguno que pueda despertar temores o envidias, ya que en su mayoría son esclavos o de ínfimo nivel económico-social, ni poseen un fuerte nivel de idetidad étnica que pudiera generar una autofirmación frente a la sociedad dominante... porque, en realidad, los *negros* no existen como etnia." Moreno, *La Antigua Hermandad*, 40.

92. Juan Manuel de Cires Ordoñez, Pedro E. García Ballesteros, and Carlos A. Vílchez Vitienes, "Negros antes que esclavos," *Archivo Hispalense* 219 (1989): 38.

93. Cires Ordoñez, García Ballesteros, and Vílchez Vitienes, "Negros antes que esclavos," 31–37.

94. Cires Ordoñez, García Ballesteros, and Vílchez Vitienes, "Negros antes que esclavos," 38.

95. A.G.I., *Indiferente*, 425, L.24, F.13r.

96. In the parish of the Sagrario in Seville, out of a total of 1,267 slaves registered from 1565 to 1670, 49.8 percent were black, 8.9 percent mulatto, 4.2 percent Berber, and 2 percent *morisco*. There were small numbers of Turkish and Indian slaves as well as 35.6 percent whose ethnicity was not specified. See Cires Ordoñez, García Ballesteros, and Vílchez Vitienes, "Negros antes que esclavos," 36.

97. Alfonso Franco Silva, "La esclavitud en Sevilla a finales de la Edad Media y comienzos de la Edad Moderna," in Moreno, *La Antigua Hermandad*, 486.

98. Vicenta Cortés Alonso, "La población negra de Palos de la Frontera, 1568–1579," in *XXXVI Congreso Internacional de Americanistas, España, 1964: Actas y memorias*, ed. Alfredo Jimenez Nunez (Seville: ECESA, 1966), vol. 3: 609–18.

99. Cortés Alonso, "La población negra," 614.

100. Juan Manuel de Cires Ordónez and Pedro E. García Ballesteros, "El 'tablero de ajedrez' sevillano: Bautizos y matrimonios de esclavos," in Moreno, *La Antigua Hermandad*, 496.

101. Francisco de Orozco Villaseñor was the son of Juan de Villaseñor, a native of Vélez (any one of the three towns in Andalusia by the same name, located in Granada, in Málaga, or in Almería) who had come to Mexico with his brother, Francisco de Orozco, in 1524 and had been both a conquistador and an *encomendero* (early planter and owner of Indian slaves). See Boyd-Bowman, *Índice*, vol. 2: 390.

102. A.G.I., *Indiferente*, 425, L. 23, F.368 v.

103. Tierra Firme then occupied the continental areas that border the Caribbean Sea on its southern and western ends. After 1563 it was applied in more specificity to the Audiencia of Panama. A.G.I., *Pasajeros*, L.4, E.1078.

104. A.G.I., *Pasajeros*, L.6, E.1346.

105. There was Ana, an unwed mulatto from Huelva, the daughter of Cristóbal Beltrán and Catalina Peguera. She went to the New Granada in 1565 as the servant to Francisco Velázquez. (A.G.I., *Pasajeros*, L.4, E.4305.) In 1569 the president of the Audiencia of Quito, Lope Díez de Armendáriz, took with him to Peru one Isabel de Abrego, a mulatto from Huelva. (*Pasajeros*, L.5, E.1799.) In 1580 Inés de Campos was taken to Peru as the personal servant of Isabel López. She was from Seville. (A.G.I., *Pasajeros*, L.6, E.2772.) Catalina de los Ángeles went in 1598 as the maid of Ana de Argüello. (A.G.I., *Pasajeros*, L.7, E.5076.)

106. A.G.I., *Pasajeros*, L.7, E.5193.

107. A.G.I., *Pasajeros*, L.8, E.1107.

108. In 1562 Francisco Bravo was granted permission to take fifty black slaves to the Indies, a third of whom were female. A.G.I., *Indiferente*, 425, L.24, F.85v.

109. Quintero Rivera, "Vueltita," 57. "En un mundo marcado por la heterogeneidad y amalgama étnica era importante establecer que un negro podía ser cristiano y rey; y reyes y cristianos también personas de orígen difuso."

110. A.G.I., *Estado,* 7, N.3, Anexo 4. "Que a todos los Esclavos Negros, y Blancos, que se ausentaren al Monte huidos del servicio de sus Amos ō Señores, se les obligue vuelvan à dicho servicio dentro de quince dias, y si pasado este termino fuesen traidos contra su voluntad, les sean dados cien azotes, y les echen una Argolla de hierro, que pese veinte libras, y la lleven por tiempo de un año; por la segunda vez estando huidos veinte dias, les corten un pie; y por la tercera estando ausentes quince dias, que muera por ello, cuya pena no se execute en los que vuelvan voluntariamente."

111. A.G.I., *Estado,* 7, N.3, Anexo 4. "Que ningun Negro, ni Negra sea osado à desterrar, ni ayudar a ello, ni à soltar estando preso ningun Esclavo negro Berberisco, sopena de que le serà cortado el pie derecho; por el mismo caso si fuese Español, le seràn dados cien azotes, y pague el daño del esclavo al Señor."

112. "That the *bozal* slave will be the one who having arrived from Cape Verde or from Guinea had been on the Island (of Hispaniola) for less than a year, unless he were to have been considered already a ladino when he arrived, and that in every other instance, even when they may have difficulty speaking (in Spanish), they shall be considered ladinos if they have been in the Island for more than a year and as such they shall be dealt with in matters of punishment." (Que se pueda decir Esclavo Vozal, aquel que hubiere menos de un año, que pasò à la Ysla, de Cabo Verde, ō Guinea, salvo si fuese Ladino quando de alli viniese, y que en todos los demàs casos que fuesen cerrados en la habla, habiendo estado en la Ysla mas de un año, sean habidos por Ladinos, y como à tales se les impongan las penas.) A.G.I., *Estado,* 7, N.3, Anexo 4.

113. In article 25 of the Ordenanzas of 1528. See A.G.I., *Estado,* 7, N.3, Anexo 4.

114. "Mulatos y indios de guerra de la provincia de Las Esmeraldas." A.G.I., *Quito,* 209, L.1, F.155r–155v.

115. Writing to the Audiencia in Quito in 1601 four years after the land had been temporarily pacified, Phillip III ordered that "on account of the souls that have been taken and converted to our Holy Catholic Faith and of the great importance of continuing that discovery, pacification and settlement in what pertains to the security of that coast and the welcoming of my vassal's ships that may come upon them, and so that we may enjoy the bounty of the gold mines that exist in that land, and because it is important to open up roads between the settlements and the coast, because this could easily be done for the benefit of commerce and employment, and ports could also be built there so that it would be possible to go from there to that city [Quito], for all this reasons I wish for the pacification and settlement started by Doctor Juan del Barrio de Sepulveda to be completed" (por las almas que se avian reducido y convertido a nuestra santa Fe Católica y lo mucho que importava se continuase aquel descubrimiento, pacificación y población para la seguridad de aquella costa y acogida de los navíos de mis vasallos que alli arrivaren y para que se gose del fruto de las minas de oro que hay en aquella Tierra y que importa mucho abrir camino de aquellas poblaciones a la dicha costa que se podría hazer con facil-

idad y con que creceria el comercio y contratación y se Podrían Tomar allí puertos y desembarcar y yr por Tierra a essa ciudad y por que yo desseo que se acave aquella pacificación y población que començo el Doctor Juan del Barrio de Sepulveda). A.G.I., *Quito*, 209, L.1, F.155r–155v.

116. William B. Taylor and Thomas B. F. Cummins, "The Mulatto Gentlemen of Esmeraldas, Ecuador," in *Colonial Spanish America: A Documetary History*, ed. Kenneth Mills and William B. Taylor (Wilmington, Del.: Scholarly Resources Inc., 1998), 149.

3. Bartolomé de Las Casas at the End of Time

1. Las Casas, *Apología*, 370. "...la obstinada ceguera de los judíos y la impía truculencia de los sarracenos, los cuales, a conciencia, atacan al Evangelio de Cristo." The view that Las Casas enunciated with clarity in the middle of the sixteenth century divided Spain and her empire into three distinct camps: Christians, would-be Christians, and anti-Christians. Las Casas believed that Indians possessed a natural disposition to conversion. As for the Jews and the Muslims, the first were a contaminating factor on account of their being "related" to (or contained within) the Christian, and the second was the enemy that had to be pursued and reduced at every occasion as they were bent on destroying Christianity. Las Casas, *Apología*, 370–71.

2. Bartolomé de Las Casas, *Historia de las Indias*, ed. Agustín Millares Carlo, intro. Lewis Hanke (Mexico: Fondo de Cultura Económica, 1965), vol. 3: 98. "A tantas gentes inocentes hemos echado en los infiernos sin fe y sin Sacramentos...que todo cuanto hacemos y habemos hecho es contra la intención de Jesucristo y contra la forma que de la caridad en su Evangelio nos dejó tan encargada."

3. One of Las Casas's fiercest critics, Gonzalo Fernández de Oviedo, would relate in his chronicles: "What is of public knowledge and understood here and in other places is the following. I mean that he who is to be a captain should not go about guessing without knowing and being experienced in the affairs of war, and because he (Las Casas) knows nothing about these things, basing his decision on his good intentions, failed in the work he undertook; and thinking that he was going to convert the Indians, he gave them arms with which to kill the Christians, causing in turn many more damages that in the interest of being brief we shall not mention here. This and other things of the sort happen to those who undertake tasks of which they know nothing; because if he thought that by making the sign of the cross and setting a good example he was going to pacify the land, he should not have touched a single weapon, and should have left them securely stored in the custody of an able captain who would have been prepared to deal with whatever may have happened." (Pero lo que es público y notorio en estas y otras partes, aquesto es. Quiero decir que el que ha de ser capitán, no lo ha de adevinar sin ser ejercitado y tener experiencia en las cosas de la guerra, e por no saber él ninguna cosa desto, confiando en su buena intención, erró la obra que comenzó; y pensando convertir los indios, les dió armas con que matasen los cristianos; de lo cual resultaron otros daños que por evitar prolijidad se dejan de decir. Y aquesto mismo o su semejante acontescerá y suele acontescer a todos los que toman el oficio que no saben; porque si él pensaba santiguando y con su buen ejemplo pacificar la tierra, no había de

tomar las armas, sino tenerlas como en depósito en mano de un capitán diestro y cual conviniera para lo que subcediese.") Fernández de Oviedo, *Historia general,* vol. 2: 201.

4. Las Casas, *Apología,* 342. "No se debe utilizar la guerra como medio para preparar las almas de los infieles o para desarraigar la idolatría. . . . Los ejércitos armados son propios del pseudoprofeta Mahoma, quien decía que actuaba en el terror de la espada."

5. Las Casas, *Historia,* vol. 1: 19. ". . . por la utilidad común, espiritual y temporal, que podríra resultar para todas estas infinitas gentes, si quizá no son acabadas primero y antes que esta historia del todo se escriba."

6. According to the most commonly accepted figures, of the twenty-five million native people who in 1492 inhabited what came to be the Viceroyalty of New Spain, only a million were left in the very first years of the seventeenth century.

7. Las Casas, *Apología,* 193. "Toda ella en otro tiempo adoró a Cristo."

8. See Antonio Benítez Rojo, *The Repeating Island: The Caribbean and the Postmodern Perspective,* trans. James Maraniss (Durham: Duke University Press, 1992), 85–111.

9. I am here borrowing the terminology from Enrique Pupo-Walker as quoted by Benítez Rojo. See Benítez Rojo, *The Repeating Island,* 88–89.

10. Las Casas, *Historia,* vol. 1: lxxviii. ". . . abundante información general no relacionada con los indios."

11. "Sin embargo, en conjunto, la *Historia de las Indias* es una obra de difícil lectura a causa de su enorme extensión y del desorden con que está escrita." (Notwithstanding, as a whole, the *Historia de las Indias* is a difficult work to read because of its great length and of the disorderly way in which it is written.) Las Casas, *Historia,* vol. 1: lxxiii.

12. Las Casas, *Historia,* vol. 3: 194. ". . . entretanto que el rey llega y se aseinta la corte en Barcelona."

13. Las Casas, *Historia,* vol. 3: 259. ". . . y de todo ello nunca vimos en Cortés señal de restitución y satisfacción, sino siempre con la sangre y trabajos ajenos triunfar./ Capítulo CXXV/Por este tiempo cosas acaescieron notables en esta isla Española y una fué, que como los indios della se iban acabando y no cesasen por eso de los trabajar y angustiar los españoles que los tenían. . . ."

14. Cortés himself was given twenty-two Indian villages as his *encomienda.*

15. Las Casas, *Historia,* vol. 3: 259. In other words, he was well versed in the Christian faith, or "bien doctrinado."

16. As explained in the previous chapter, the term *ladino* also applied to Berber and African slaves. Among the latter, being a ladino was the opposite of being a *bozal.*

17. Esteban Mira Caballos, *El indio antillano: Repartimiento, encomienda y esclavitud (1492–1542)* (Sevilla: Muñoz Moya, 1997), 318.

18. Luis Joseph Peguero, *Historia de la conquista de la Isla Española de Santo Domingo, trasumptada del año de 1762,* ed. Pedro J. Santiago (Santo Domingo: Museo de las Casas Reales, 1975), vol. 1: 186. Although Peguero wrote his *Historia* during the middle of the eighteenth century, he based it on the *Historia general de los hechos de los castellanos en las Islas y Tierra Firme del Mar Océano* by Antonio de Herrera, a contemporary of Las Casas. I am interested, however, in the way that Peguero describes Enriquillo retrospectively, alluding to the language of the slave plantation

and the figure of the overseer. The passage reads: "... in the service of Valenzuela, Enriquillo showed force and severity when dealing with the Indians in his gang" (... mostrava Enriquillo gravedad y severidad con los indios de su cuadrilla con que servia a Valensuela).

19. A.G.I., *Indiferente*, 737, N.25. "Hazen muchos males de muertes de hombres y robos de haziendas en los españoles ... y esta aquella ysla puesta en tanto temor dellos que ya no osan salir de los pueblos ... como los yndios saben tan bien la tierra y la montaña en que andan ... se sostienen muchos días con Rayces y otras cosas silvestres que hallan y los españoles han de llevar a cuestas la comida para todo el tiempo que han de andar tras de ellos y no se les puede hacer daño...."

20. See Joaquín R. Priego, *Cultura taína: Compendio didáctico de la prehistoria de Quisqueya* (Santo Domingo: Secretaría de Estado, Educación, Bellas Artes y Cultos, 1967), 88. It took the Spaniards fourteen years, six campaigns using a total of more than a thousand soldiers, and over forty thousand ducats to put down an uprising that, by most estimates, never had more than 150 warriors behind it. In the year when Pizarro set out to conquer the mighty Inca Empire at the head of 138 men (1531) Enriquillo was celebrating a decade of invincibility, a fact that cannot be overemphasized when we consider that he was fighting against the people who had defeated the Aztecs in less than two years.

21. Las Casas, *Historia*, vol. 3: 262.

22. Las Casas, *Historia*, vol. 3: 267. "... que daba señal de la reprobación de tales obras y punición que en la otra vida hemos de padecer por tan grandes pecados contra Dios y contra los próximos cometidos, si penitencia en ésta no nos vale."

23. Las Casas, *Historia*, vol. 3: 262. "Algunos ignorantes del hecho y del derecho dicen, que el príncipe desta isla era el rey de Castilla, y que a él habían de acudir a pedir justicia, porque esto es falsa lisonja y disparate; la razón es, porque nunca los reyes y señores naturales desta isla reconocieron por superior al rey de Castilla."

24. For a critique of the novel see Pedro Enríquez Ureña, *La Utopía de América*, ed. Angel Rama and Rafael Gutiérrez Girardot (Caracas: Ayacucho, 1978), 260–62, and Pedro Mir, *Tres leyendas de colores: Ensayo de interpretación de las tres primeras revoluciones del Nuevo Mundo* (Santo Domingo: Editora Nacional, 1969), 195–204. For a more recent reinterpretation of the creole and hispanophilic legend of Enriquillo see Domingo Silie Gatón, *La causa de Enriquillo* (Santo Domingo: Editora Nivar, 1979).

25. The *cassia fistula*, a native of tropical Asia, is "very susceptible to attack by scale insects." See Elbert L. Little, Jr., and Frank H. Wadsworth, *Common Trees of Puerto Rico and the Virgin Islands* (Washington, D.C.: U.S. Department of Agriculture, 1964), 170.

26. Benítez Rojo, *The Repeating Island*, 90.

27. Las Casas writes that the people had placed their hopes in the plant and that it was to be believed that they would in turn give back to God: "poniéndo en la cañafístola toda su esperanza; y de creer es que desta esperanza darían a Dios alguna parte." (Las Casas, *Historia*, vol. 3: 271.) Benítez Rojo rightly observes this when he writes that "the interpolated text emerges from a void of Indians and precious metals that he tries to fill up with another void: hope." Benítez Rojo, *The Repeating Island*, 90.

28. Las Casas, *Historia*, vol. 3: 271. "... vecinos desta isla, españoles, porque de los Indios no hay ya que hablar."

29. The term *indiano* has two definitions. The first, which is the one I will at all times hold to, is synonymous with *creole* and describes the native "European" of the West Indies and, by extension, of the New World. The second was the name given in Spain to the Spaniard who, having made his fortune in the Americas, returned home a rich man.

30. The last Indian opposition to Spanish rule in Hispaniola was recorded in 1549. In any case, it was rather insignificant compared to the threat Enriquillo had posed.

31. Carlos Esteban Dieve, *La Española y la esclavitud del indio* (Santo Domingo: Fundación García Arevalo, 1995), 297. As with so much of the story and legend of Enriquillo, many things are not agreed upon. Some say he came to settle in Santa María de Boyá, and yet others say he settled in Sabana Buey, near the town of Baní.

32. See Peguero, *Historia de la conquista,* vol. 1: 210.

33. Las Casas, *Historia,* vol. 3: 271. ". . . comenzaban a gozar del fructo de sus trabajos y a cumplirse su esperanza."

34. Benítez Rojo, *The Repeating Island,* 90.

35. Las Casas, *Historia,* vol. 3: 271. "Envía Dios sobre toda esta isla y sobre la isla de Sant Juan principalmente, una plaga que se pudo temer, si mucho creciera, que totalmente se despoblaran."

36. Las Casas, *Historia,* vol. 3: 273. "La causa de donde se originó este hormiguero, creyeron y dijeron algunos, que fue de la traída y postura de los plátanos."

37. See Benítez Rojo, *The Repeating Island,* 95–6.

38. "Ordenanzas antiguas y modernas de la Isla de Santo Domingo," A.G.I., *Estado,* 7, N.3, Anejo 4.

39. Las Casas, *Historia,* vol. 3: 272. ". . . el suelo de la azotea estaba tan negro como si lo hobieran rociado con polvo de carbón."

40. Las Casas, *Historia,* vol. 3: 272. "Desde que vieron los religiosos que no aprovechaba nada el solimán, sino para traer basura a casa, acordaron de lo quitar."

41. See Benítez Rojo, *The Repeating Island,* 92.

42. Las Casas, *Historia,* vol. 3: 272. "De dos cosas se maravillaban, y eran dignas de admiración; la una, el instinto de naturaleza y la fuerza que aun a las criaturas sensibles y no sensibles da, como parece en estas hormigas, que de tanta distancia sintiesen, si así se puede decir, o el mismo instinto las guiase y trujese al solimán; la otra, que como el solimán en piedra, antes que lo muelan, es tan duro como una piedra de alumbre, si quizás no es más, y cuasi como un guijarro, que un animalito tan menudo y chiquitito (como estas hormigas que eran muy menudicas), tuviese tanta fuerza para morder del solimán, y, finalmente, para disminuíllo y acaballo."

43. José Antonio Saco, "La seguridad de Cuba clama urgentísimamente por la pronta abolición del tráfico de esclavos," *Colección de papeles científicos, históricos, políticos y de otros ramos sobre la Isla de Cuba* (Havana: Editorial Nacional de Cuba, 1960), vol. 2: 142.

44. Alessandro Geraldini, *Itinerario por las regiones subequinocciales* (Santo Domingo: Editora del Caribe, 1977), 185.

45. Publius Vergilius Maro, *Eclogae,* ed. H. E. Gould (Toronto: MacMillan, 1967), 10. "May the reign of Saturn return."

46. Las Casas, *Historia,* vol. 3: 275. "Teníamos por opinión en esta isla, que si al negro no acaecía ahorcalle, nunca moría, porque nunca habíamos visto negro de su enfermedad muerto."

47. Las Casas, *Historia,* vol. 3: 276. "Huyen cuando pueden a cuadrillas y se levantan y hacen muertes y crueldades en los españoles, por salir de su captiverio, cuantas la oportunidad poder les ofrece, y así no viven muy seguros los chicos pueblos de esta isla, que es otra plaga que vino sobre ella."

48. Las Casas, *Historia,* vol. 3: 276. "Y no es razón dejar de decir otra (plaga) que se añadió a las arribas puestas, y ésta es la multitud de los perros, que no se puede numerar y estimar los daños que hacen y han hecho."

49. Las Casas, *Historia,* vol. 3: 276. "Había en esta isla inmensidad de puercos (que como no se críen con grano, sino con raíces muy suaves y frutas delicadas, como son ovos y guaçimas, la carne dellos es muy sana y más delicada y sabrosa que muy delicado y sabroso carnero), y déstos estaban los montes llenos, por cuya causa a cada legua había maravillosas y alegres y provechosas monterías, todas las cuales han destruído los perros, y no contentos con los puercos, acometen a los becerros, mayormente cuando los paren las madres, que no pueden defenderse; es grandísimo el daño que han hecho y hacen, y bien se puede considerar los tiempos venideros dellos qué se espera."

50. Las Casas, *Historia,* vol. 3: 272.

51. Ibid. "No contentos con los puercos, acometen a los becerros." The term *contentos* can also be translated as happy. In any case, Las Casas's choice of words is interesting. As Roque Barcia explains, in Spanish "*contento* is a social joy, just as satisfaction is a pleasure of conscience" and "happiness is a joy of the soul." See Roque Barcia, *Sinónimos castellanos* (Madrid: Daniel Jorro, 1921), 130.

52. Las Casas, *Historia,* vol. 3: 276. "Debiéramos de pasar por la memoria que esta isla hallamos llenísima de gentes que matamos y extirpamos de la haz de la tierra y henchímosla de perros y bestias, y por juicio divino, por fuerza forzada, nos han de ser nocivos y molestosos."

53. See Benítez Rojo, *The Repeating Island,* 45–46. See also Kathleen Deagan, *Puerto Real: The Archaeology of a Sixteenth-Century Spanish Town in Hispaniola* (Miami: University Press of Florida, 1995), 101–4.

54. Fernández de Oviedo, *Historia general,* vol. 1: 125. "... que parece esta tierra una efigie o imagen de la misma Etiopía."

55. A.G.I., *Estado,* 7, N.3, Anejo 4. "Que ninguno de los dichos Negros traigan armas ofesivas de hierro, palo, ni de otra clase."

56. Even in Havana the bishop was forced to excommunicate many neighbors in the 1580's as the judicial and military authorities complained that nobody would give them any assistance in the capture of the "well know heretic" Gómez Rojas. A.G.I., *Escribanía,* 36 A.

57. A.G.I., *Estado,* 7, N. 3, Anejo 4. "Que ningún negro horro, trate ni contrate, compre ni venda, ni acojan en sus casas con otros Negros, ni Negras, con ningun pretexto, ni les den de comer en ellas, ni en ninguna parte, ni de beber, ni tengan taberna de vino, ni tenèr en casa, ni consigo armas ofensivas, ni defensivas, ni tengan tiendas, traten ni contraten, salvo vender leña, agua, hierva, y esten en sus bohios, sopena de cien azotes y desterrados de la Isla."

58. Deagan, *Puerto Real,* 466.

59. A.G.I., *Indiferente,* 1963, L.9, F.111.

60. A.G.I., *Indiferente,* 423, L.18, F.127r–128r.

61. Juana Gil-Bermejo García, *La Española: Anotaciones históricas (1600–1650)* (Seville: Escuela de Estudios Hispano-Americanos de Sevilla, 1983), 27–28.

62. Philip III had just recently been crowned in 1598 so that the spirit and intent of the *devastaciones* followed from the instructions left to him by his father, King Philip II, who had advised him to be as severe as he had been with those who opposed his royal designs stating that "punishing some is a lesson to all." From "Las instrucciones políticas de los Austrias mayores," quoted in Fernández Álvarez, *Felipe II*, 783.

63. At the time there were about five thousand freemen in the island, a thousand settlers and the rest soldiers, government officials, and clergy. Almost eleven thousand people were slaves, and there were a few thousand runaways who were not accounted for in official figures. Most slaves worked on the sugar and ginger plantations, a good number were domestic slaves, and a smaller number worked in the cattle industry.

64. Gil-Bermejo García, *La Española*, 17–18.

65. I am thinking here of the pen-and-ink drawings by Leonardo da Vinci, such as his "Embryo in the Womb."

66. "Estos son bohíos de los negros."

4. The Creole in His Labyrinth

1. The situation in Havana, however, was not that different. Only when the flota arrived did things significantly change, returning to the traditional air of abandonment as soon as the last galleons departed the harbor. Havana was a sleepy colonial enclave of pious God-fearing subjects of the Spanish Crown that once a year for a month or two became the busiest harbor—and prostitution depot—in the entire world. There are stories of an entire flock, priest and all, leaving church en masse halfway through a Sunday service and heading to the docks as the news of the first sails coming over the horizon spread through the streets. When the flota was in town, most of the gold and silver that fueled the European economy was safely guarded inside the harbor. The arrival of the flota turned the city on its head; customarily contracts were temporarily suspended, and servants and slaves were even "set free" so that they might profit at the expense of thousands of the king's soldiers and sailors who were looking for the best way to spend their salaries before again attempting the perilous Atlantic crossing. In 1585 a *moreno* by the name of Hernando Horro agreed to sell his services to Gaspar Pérez de Borroto for a year, contracting to serve him "in any manner that Pérez de Borroto may order, be it in the city or on the plantations, pig farm, etc." (en aquello que el dicho Gaspar Pérez de Borroto le mandare, ansí en esta villa como en estancias, corrales de puercos, etc.). A final clause in the contract stipulated that "as long as the flota remains in the harbor of this town, said Hernando Horro will be free from this obligation so that he may profit as best he might be able to manage" (quel tiempo que estuviese la flota en el puerto desta dicha villa, el dicho Hernando sea libre deste conçierto para que pueda ganar para sí lo que puediere). See *Índice de extractos del Archivo de Protocolos de La Habana, 1578–1585* (Havana: Úcar, García, y Cía., 1947), 309.

2. M. L. Moreau de Saint-Méry, *Descripción de la parte española de Santo Domingo*, trans. Armando Rodríguez (Santo Domingo: Editora Montalvo, 1944), 83. "Una capital que anuncia por sí misma la decadenicia, lugarejos distribuídos aquí y allá, algunos establecimientos coloniales a los cuales el nombre de manufac-

turas sería hacerles demasiado honor, haciendas inmensas llamadas *hatos,* donde se crían animales sin cuidados ningunos; he ahí todo lo que se encuentra en una colonia en que la naturaleza ofrece sus riquezas a hombres completamente sordos a su voz."

3. The map was printed by Jean Baptiste Nolin with the title *Archipelague du Mexique ou Sont les Isles de Cuba, Espagnole, l'Amaique, etc., avec les Isles Lucayes, et les Isles Caribes, connues sous le nom d'Antilles. Par le P. Coronelli, Cosmographe de la Republique de Venise* (Paris: Chez I. B. Nolin, 1688).

4. Quintero Rivera, "Vueltita," 75.

5. Quintero Rivera, "Vueltita," 57.

6. Las Casas, *Historia,* vol. 3: 276.

7. R. Douglas Cope, *The Limits of Racial Domination: Plebeian Society in Colonial Mexico City, 1660–1720* (Madison: University of Wisconsin Press, 1994), 4.

8. Left without bread, as after the smallpox epidemic in Hispaniola, the inhabitants of Mexico City came to realize their dependency on the Indian women, who were the only ones who knew how to make corn tortillas. The attack on the palace is a similar event to the ants' going after the *piedra solimán* on the roof of the San Francisco Monastery in La Vega. Finally, just as the plague of the ants ended following prayers to Saint Saturnine, this chaotic episode came to an end when the Virgen de los Remedios was implored. See Carlos de Sigüenza y Góngora, "Alboroto y motín de los indios de México," in *Don Carlos de Sigüenza y Góngora, un sabio mexicano del siglo XVII,* ed. Irving A. Leonard, trans. Juan José Utrilla (Mexico: Fondo de Cultura Económica, 1984), 224–70.

9. Sigüenza y Góngora, "Alboroto," 252. ". . . del culpabilísimo descuido con que vivimos entre tanta plebe, al mismo tiempo que presumimos de formidables."

10. Sigüenza y Góngora, "Alboroto," 245. ". . . siendo plebe tan en extremo plebe, que sólo ella lo puede ser de la que se reputare la más infame, y lo es de todas las plebes, por componerse de indios, de negros, criollos y bozales de diferentes naciones, de chinos, de mulatos, de moriscos, de mestizos, de zambaigos, de lobos y también de espanoles que, en declarándose zaramullos (que es lo mismo que pícaros, chulos y arrebatacapas) y degenerando de sus obligaciones, son los peores entre tan ruin canalla."

11. Lezama Lima, "La curiosidad barroca," 90. As Lezama's archetype of the Baroque in America, Sigüenza stood as the guardian and protector of "the two great syntheses that lie at the root of the American Baroque, the Hispano-Inca and the Afro-Hispanic." See Lezama Lima, 106. I differ from Lezama and would argue that Sigüenza was not so much the protector of those traditions as the enforcer of the creole tradition that systematically, since Las Casas, had claimed the land and its resources, moving "forcibly by force" against both Indians and blacks whenever possible and desirable.

12. "What is certain is that after the appearance of the type we have come to call the *modern individual,* there also began to develop in the individual the capacity to understand that things were not going well, principally in terms of the economy but in other branches of the collective life as well; more important, this modern individual began to wonder whether things could be better." José Antonio Maravall, *Culture of the Baroque: Analysis of a Historical Structure,* trans. Terry Cochran (Minneapolis: University of Minnesota Press, 1986), 20. Obviously Maravall's notions are too Euro-centric to be applied in the context of the New World to any subjects

beyond the creoles, and then only with some care. It goes without saying that the Indians and the *morenos* came to realize that things were not going well at the moment when they were enslaved and forcibly deprived of their land by the forefathers of the European "individuals." Can resistance to conquest and enslavement emanate from anything but the realization that things could always be better? If we really wished to fix the origins of the modern individual in such a movement of consciousness and self-empowerment, we might need to trace it back to the first subjects of coloniality.

13. Sigüenza y Góngora, "Alboroto," 257. The entire passage reads: "But the blacks, the mulattoes, and all the commoners cried out: 'Death to the viceroy and to all those who support him!' and the Indians: 'Death to the Spaniards and to the *gachupines* (meaning the Spaniards from Spain) who eat all our corn!' and encouraging each other to be brave, since there no longer was a Cortés who could put them in their proper place, they came into the plaza to join the rest and to throw stones." (Pero los negros, los mulatos y todo lo que es plebe gritando: '¡Muera el virrey y cuantos lo defendieren!', y los indios: '¡Mueran los españoles y gachupines (son estos los venidos de España) que nos comen nuestro maíz!', y exhortándose unos a otros a tener valor, supuesto que ya no había otro Cortés que los sujetase, se arrojaban a la plaza a acompañar a los otros y a tirar piedras.)

14. Irving A. Leonard, *Baroque Times in Old Mexico* (Westport, Conn.: Greenwood Press, 1959), 42–43.

15. Carlos de Sigüenza y Góngora, *Infortunios de Alonso Ramírez*, in *Seis Obras*, ed. William G. Bryant, prologue by Irving A. Leonard. (Caracas: Biblioteca Ayacucho, 1984). The entire title of the descriptive account reads: *Misfortunes That Alonso Ramírez, a Native of the City of San Juan de Puerto Rico, Suffered by Falling into the Hands of English Pirates Who Kidnapped Him in the Philippine Islands and by Sailing Alone and without Bearings until he Reached the Coast of Yucatán, in This Way Having Traveled around the World.*

16. See Pratt, *Imperial Eyes*, 29–30.

17. For Sigüenza happiness was the inseparable companion of misfortune. See Sigüenza y Góngora, "Alboroto," 224.

18. See the foreword by Giles Milton to the 1998 edition. In William Dampier, *A New Voyage Round the World: The Journal of an English Buccaneer*, intro. Giles Milton (London: Hummingbird Press, 1998), i–x.

19. Milton, foreword, i.

20. Dampier, *A New Voyage*, 2.

21. Milton, foreword, iii.

22. Dampier, *A New Voyage*, 1.

23. Milton, foreword, viii.

24. For a defense of the text's debt to the picaresque tradition see Julie Greer Johnson, "Picaresque Elements in Carlos Sigüenza y Góngora's *Los Infortunios de Alonso Ramírez*," *Hispania* 64.1 (1981): 60–67. For the case in favor of the historical veracity of the work see J. S. Cummins, "*Infortunios de Alonso Ramírez*: 'A Just History of Fact'?" *Bulletin of Hispanic Studies* 61.3 (1984): 295–303. Álvaro Félix Bolaños criticizes this debate by stating that "it limits the *Infortunios* within two models of Renaissance discursive narrative," and he gives as examples the chronicles *(crónicas)* and the epics of chivalry *(libros de caballería)*, among others. See Álvaro Félix

Bolaños, "Sobre las 'relaciones' e identidades en crisis: El 'otro' lado del ex-cautivo Alonso Ramírez," *Revista de crítica literaria latinoamericana* 42 (1995): 133.

25. Giancarlo Maiorino, *The Cornucopian Mind and the Baroque Unity of the Arts* (University Park: Pennsylvania State University Press, 1990), 27.

26. Jean Rousset, *Circe y el pavo real, la literatura francesa del barroco* (Barcelona: Seix Barral, 1972), 32.

27. Perhaps the best example of such cavernous structures is the Church of Santa María in Tonantzintla, near Cholula.

28. One of the best solutions to this design problem in the Caribbean is the precious late Baroque Church of Santa María del Rosario on the outskirts of Havana.

29. The popular arts and the architecture of Puebla have always had a profound trace of Moorishness. The famous ceramic plates of Talavera, which can be purchased all over the city today, still conform to chromatic patterns, designs, and glazing techniques that are of Andalusi origin. What is more, the prevalent geometry of all design is still the eight-pointed Mudejar star. This should not be surprising, because Puebla was among the settlements that received the largest number of people from the former lands of al-Andalus when it was founded in 1532. Out of its 168 original inhabitants, 65 were from Andalusia, 39 from Extremadura, and 13 from Castilla la Nueva, for a combined total of 117, or 69.6 percent of the population. See Peter Boyd-Bowman, *Índice geobiográfico de cuarenta mil pobladores españoles de América en el siglo XVI* (México: Editorial Jus, 1968), vol. 1: xxvi.

30. "... peregrinación lastimosa." Sigüenza y Góngora, *Infortunios*, 7.

31. Sigüenza y Góngora, *Infortunios*, 8.

32. Jorge Fornet, "Ironía y cuestionamiento ideológico en *Infortunios de Alonso Ramírez*," *Cuadernos Americanos* 9.1 (1995): 200.

33. Sigüenza y Góngora, *Infortunios*, 38. "... títulos son éstos que suenan mucho y que valen muy poco, y a cuyo ejercicio le empeña más la reputación que la conveniencia."

34. "... un caso no otra vez acontecido, es digno de que quede para memoria estampado." Such was the sentence dictated by the censor of the Holly Office of the Inquisition, Francisco de Ayerra Santa María, on 26 June 1690. Ayerra Santa María, who was, like Ramírez, a native of San Juan de Puerto Rico, thought the book would also be of use on account of its valuable scientific data (mainly referring to winds and currents throughout the world of the flota). The words of the censor are recorded in the pamphlet edition of the *Infortunios* commissioned by the Instituto de Cultura Puertorriqueña. Carlos de Sigüenza y Góngora, *Infortunios de Alonso Ramírez* (Barcelona: Edil Española, 1967). 2. From now on this pamphlet edition will be cited as *Alonso Ramírez*. For the nature and effects of censorship dating back to the first laws of 1532, see Beatriz González S., "Narrativa de la 'estabilización' colonial," *Ideologies and Literature* 2.1 (1987): 7–52.

35. Here I differ from Nina Gerassi-Navarro, who finds the principal source of ambiguity in the text in "the play between the telling and the writing." See Nina Gerassi-Navarro, *Pirate Novels: Fictions of Nation Building in Spanish America* (Durham, N.C.: Duke University Press, 1999), 62.

36. Sigüenza y Góngora, *Infortunios*, 7. "Quiero que se entretenga el curioso que esto leyere por algunas horas con las noticias de lo que a mí me causó tribulaciones de muerte por muchos años."

37. Aníbal González, "Los infortunios de Alonso Ramírez: Picaresca e historia," *Hispanic Review* 51.2 (1983): 189.

38. Francisco de Ayerra was the son of Juan de Ayerra Santa María, a captain of the Spanish Army and veteran of campaigns in Flanders and Portugal, who in 1635 was named to the post of sergeant major of the Island and presidio of San Juan de Puerto Rico. See A.G.I., *Contratación*, 5789, L.1, F.199–200.

39. Sigüenza y Góngora, *Alonso Ramírez*, 1. "Así por obedecer ciegamente al decreto de V. S. [Vuestra Señoría] en que me manda censurar la relación de los Infortunios de Alonso Ramírez, mi compatriota, descrita por Don Carlos de Sigüenza y Góngora... como por la novedad deliciosa que su argumento me prometía, me hallé empeñado en la lección de la obra, y si al principio entré en ella con obligación y curiosidad, en el progreso, con tanta variedad de casos, disposición y estructura de sus períodos agradecí como inestimable gracia lo que traía sobreescrito de estudiosa tarea."

40. Sigüenza y Góngora, *Alonso Ramírez*, 1. "...y al laberinto enmarañado de tales rodeos halló el hilo de oro para coronarse de aplausos."

41. Laura Benítez Grobet, *La idea de la historia en Carlos de Sigüenza y Góngora* (Mexico: Universidad Nacional Autónoma de México, 1982), 124.

42. Lucrecio Pérez Blanco, "*Infortunios de Alonso Ramírez:* Una lectura desde la retórica," *Cuadernos Americanos* 9.1 (1995): 220.

43. "My name is Alonso Ramírez and my fatherland is the city of San Juan de Puerto Rico, the capital of an island that... separates the limits of the Gulf of Mexico and the Atlantic Sea" (Es mi nombre Alonso Ramírez y mi patria la ciudad de San Juan de Puerto Rico, cabeza de la isla que... entre el Seno Mexicano y el Mar Atlántico divide términos). Sigüenza y Góngora, *Infortunios*, 7. The "Seno Mexicano" encompassed what we today call the Caribbean Sea and the islands of Bajamar and Lucayes, or Bahamas. Then as now, Puerto Rico occupied a strategic position along the easternmost boundary of this archipelago, halfway between the Bahamas and Trinidad, between Saint Augustine and Port of Spain. This is the same geographic region that in the French version of Coronelli's map (1688) is described as the "Archipelague du Mexique."

44. For much of its history the inhabitants of San Juan lived in a constant state of siege, its frightened population conjuring images of heretical invaders coming to attack, pillage, and burn down the city. The first major attack of San Juan occurred a century before Ramírez, in 1595, when Francis Drake tried in vain to capture part of the treasure destined for King Philip II, which was being carried to Spain by ships that at the time where anchored in the harbor. Three years later George Clifford, Earl of Cumberland, was sent by Elizabeth I to avenge the defeat suffered by Drake's expedition. Cumberland took the city but could not hold it. He was forced to retreat in the most unheroic of ways on account of a terrible epidemic of dysentery that found his men carrying off the loot while unable to keep their pants on. As an omen of things to come, early during the expedition Cumberland had fallen from his horse in full armor and almost drowned in a lagoon on his way to attack the city. In 1625 the Dutchman Boudewijn Hendricks, leading a mercenary expedition for the West India Company, took San Juan by surprise and burned it to the ground but was unable to take the Morro castle and eventually had to retreat. A century after Ramírez's unfortunate adventures, San Juan would be attacked again. In 1797, after failing to capture the city, Ralph Abercromby complained that as an English

officer the only fault he could find in the defenses of San Juan was that they made the city unconquerable. It would take another century for the city to fall to those who inherited the English tradition of piracy in the Caribbean: in 1898 San Juan was bombarded by the Usonian fleet under Captain Sampson and later ceded by a defeated Spain to the United States as payment for damages inflicted upon the United States during the course of the Usonian pursuit of its war against Spain.

45. Note that, as in the map of Havana of 1567, the relationship between the soft forms of the urban conglomerate—here absent save for the delineation of its contours—stands in contrast to the sharp angles of the fortifications that rather aggressively check its growth. For a history of San Juan see the excellent book by Aníbal Sepúlveda Rivera, *San Juan: Historia ilustrada de su desarrollo urbano, 1508–1898* (San Juan: Carimar, 1989).

46. As in the case of Arcos de la Frontera or Jerez de la Frontera. *Frontera* means border; these were localities that at one time or another occupied the land that divided Christian from Muslim Spain.

47. I am paraphrasing the Spanish text where it states, concerning Puerto Rico, that "entre el Seno Mexicano y el Mar Atlántico divide términos." Sigüenza y Góngora, *Infortunios*, 7.

48. See José F. Buscaglia, "Puerto Rico 98: Architecture and Empire at the Fin de Siècle," *Journal of Architectural Education* 48.4 (1995): 250–59.

49. See the Gospel of John, 2:3. I am here borrowing from Maiorino, who correctly identifies this moment with the position of mystics like Sor Juana Inés de la Cruz, a personal friend of Sigüenza, with artists like Michelangelo, and with the idea of the Italian *discresce* (decrease) and of the *vivir desviviéndose* (to live longing for death) of Spanish religious mysticism. Maiorino, *The Cornucopian Mind*, 35–36.

50. Such is the depiction found, for example, in the exquisite Baroque silver sacrarium of the Old Convent of Saint Clare of Assisi in Havana, today at the Church of Santo Domingo in Guanabacoa, near Havana.

51. To this day Puerto Ricans are burdened with this duty, which is imposed upon them at birth. It is a demeaning obligation to be a first line of defense in the imperial master plan. The naval military base of Roosevelt Roads, which includes not just Puerto Rico and its territorial waters but also the U.S. Virgin Islands, is the biggest naval station in the world and the most important strategic position in the entire Atlantic Ocean. What is more, according to official colonial propaganda Puerto Ricans remain dutifully at their post. In fact, one of the most recurrent symbols of Puerto Rico, one that for the past century has been promoted by the colonial authorities, is the sentinel's garret or guard posts that punctuate the walls in all colonial fortifications, like the one that today greets cruise ships from atop the formidable Morro Castle as they enter San Juan's harbor. The sentinel's post is a homely place for the Puerto Rican, but one that, as I have pointed out before in relation to the one called the Devil's Garret, is also a site of desertion and escape in extraofficial discourse.

52. Sigüenza was mistaken on this point; the name of this island originally referred to the condition of the harbor where the capital city was placed, that is, it meant "good harbor" and not "rich port."

53. The Renaissance fortification certainly has a medieval air to it in its relationship and significance to the city it defended. In Havana, for example, where the Castle of La Fuerza occupies a similar contradictory moment of defense and

belligerence towards the city, the presence of the castle was not as ominous as in San Juan. This was of course due to geographic features—the castle of La Fuerza lies at the same level as the city. But it also had to do with the fact that early on Havana became a commercial outpost of major seasonal significance, while Puerto Rico remained, as it does to this day, an island-city whose principal importance was, almost exclusively, strategic and military.

54. At the time of Ramírez's birth San Juan was a city of women. Ramírez was ten years old when the census of 1673 reported a total of 1,136 women and only 627 men living in town. See Francisco Picó, *Historia general de Puerto Rico* (Río Piedras: Huracán, 1988), 98.

55. See A.G.I., *Contratación*, 5394, N.12.

56. Sigüenza y Góngora, *Infortunios*, 8. "Aunque ignoro el lugar de su nacimiento, cónstame, porque varias veces se le oía decir, que era andaluz."

57. A.G.I., *Justicia*, 838, N.6.

58. In her edition of the *Infortunios* Estelle Irizarry contemplates the possibility that Ramírez might have been the son of a crypto-Jew. See Carlos de Sigüenza y Góngora, *Infortunios de Alonso Ramírez*, ed. Estelle Irizarry (Río Piedras, P.R.: Editorial Cultural, 1990), 46–49. This seems highly unlikely since, as I have argued, it is almost certain that Alonso never met his father. Even less likely is the probability that, as Irizarry suggests, Alonso's father broke the news of their ancestry to his son when he was thirteen, just in time for his secret bar mitzvah. Simply put, given the conditions in San Juan, the man would have deserted the family long before.

59. Sigüenza y Góngora, *Infortunios*, 8. "Reconociendo no ser continua la fábrica y temiéndome no vivir siempre, por esta causa, con las incomodidades que, aunque muchacho, me hacían fuerza, determiné hurtarle el cuerpo a mi misma patria para buscar en las ajenas más conveniencia."

60. This term does not exist in Spanish and would thus be a neologism.

61. Sigüenza y Góngora, *Infortunios*, 8. "Confieso que, tal vez presagiando lo porvenir, dudaba si podría prometerme algo que fuese bueno, habiéndome valido de un corcho para principiar mi fortuna."

62. Carlos de Sigüenza y Góngora, *Libra astronómica y filosófica*. Sigüenza's exact words are "nuestra criolla nación." Quoted in Benítez Grobet, *La idea de la historia*, 127.

63. Sigüenza y Góngora, *Infortunios*, 8. "En la demora de seis meses que allí perdí, experimenté mayor hambre que en Puerto Rico."

64. Sigüenza y Góngora, *Infortunios*, 9. ". . . la abundancia de cuanto se necesita para pasar la vida con descanso."

65. Sigüenza y Góngora, *Infortunios*, 9. "Atribuyo a fatalidad de mi estrella haber sido necesario ejercitar mi oficio para sustentarme."

66. In 1677 Luis Ramírez de Aguilar was confirmed as *regidor* of Antequera in Oaxaca. See A.G.I., *México*, 195, N.15.

67. Sigüenza y Góngora, *Infortunios*, 10. "Desesperé entonces de poder ser algo, y hallándome en el tribunal de mi propia conciencia, no sólo acusado sino convencido de inútil, quise darme por pena de este delito la que se da en México a los que son delincuentes, que es enviarlos desterrados a las Filipinas."

68. See Camilo José Cela, *Diccionario secreto* (Madrid: Alfaguara, 1971), vol. 2, book 1: 116.

69. Some four hundred kilometers northeast of the island of Mauritius lay the Cargados Carajos Shoals, which bear a Spanish name given to this reef in the middle of the Indian Sea during the early days of the Age of Navigation, when it was a choice venue for leaving those who were sentenced by pirates to be cast away and marooned. In the Cargados Carajos barely a few small keys rise above the surface of the water, so it is one of those places where to this day the visitor truly feels as if he or she has arrived at the end of the world.

70. In Tagalog the expression is *karag.* See Cela, *Diccionario secreto,* vol. 2, book 1, 109.

71. Dampier, *A New Voyage,* 179.

72. Sigüenza y Góngora, *Infortunios,* 12. "Desengañado en el discurso de mi viaje de que jamás saldría de mi esfera con sentimiento de que muchos con menores fundamentos perfeccionasen las suyas, despedí cuantas ideas me embarazaron la imaginación por algunos años."

73. This is an architectural reference to the curve-countercurve motif that is so prevalent in Baroque architecture and decoration. Notable examples can be found in the façades of all the churches that followed the conventions set up by the Jesuits in their mother church, Il Gesu in Rome. The curve-countercurve is a prominent feature of these buildings and generally flanks the second level of a façade right under the pediment. I am here borrowing an idea that was initially Rousset's. See Rousset, *Circe y el pavo real,* 243.

74. Sigüenza y Góngora, *Infortunios,* 12. "Conseguí por este medio no sólo mercadear en cosas que hallé ganancia y en que me prometía para lo venidero bastante logro sino el ver diversas ciudades y puertos de la India en diferentes viajes."

75. Sigüenza y Góngora, *Infortunios,* 12. "Estuve en Batavia, ciudad celebérrima que poseen los mismos en la Java Mayor y adonde reside el gobernador y capitán general de los Estados de Holanda. Sus murallas, baluartes y fortalezas son admirables. El concurso que allí se ve de navíos de malayos, macasares, siameses, bugises, chinos, armenios, franceses, ingleses, dinamarcos, portugueses y castellanos no tiene número. Hállase en este emporio cuantos artefactos hay en la Europa y los que en retorno de ellos le envía la Asia. Fabrícanse allí, para quien quisiere comprarlas, excelentes armas. Pero con decir estar allí compendiado el universo lo digo todo."

76. Sigüenza y Góngora, *Infortunios,* 13. "Aún más por mi conveniencia que por mi gusto, me ocupé en esto, pero no faltaron ocasiones en que, por obedecer a quien podía mandármelo, hice lo propio; y fue una de ellas la que me causó las fatalidades en que hoy me hallo y que empezaron así."

77. Sigüenza y Góngora, *Infortunios,* 13.

78. Sigüenza y Góngora, *Infortunios,* 14. ". . . en busca de arroz y de otras cosas que se necesitaban en el presidio de Cavite."

79. Sigüenza y Góngora, *Infortunios,* 14. ". . . sin recelo alguno."

80. Dampier, *A New Voyage,* 179.

81. José Juan Arrom, "Carlos de Sigüenza y Góngora, relectura criolla de los *Infortunios de Alonso Ramírez,*" *Thesaurus* 42.1 (1987): 37.

82. For a good account of the entire period see William Lytle Schurz, *The Manila Galleon* (New York: E. P. Dutton, 1939).

83. Sigüenza y Góngora, *Infortunios,* 14. ". . . ollas llenas de varios ingredientes de olor pestífero."

84. Sigüenza y Góngora, *Infortunios*, 15. "... la más desvergonzada vileza que jamás vi. Traían las madres a las hijas y los mismos maridos a sus mujeres, y se las entregaban con la recomendación de hermosas a los ingleses por el vilísimo precio de una manta o equivalente cosa."

85. Dampier, *A New Voyage*, 183.

86. Sigüenza y Góngora, *Infortunios*, 16. "... no vivían mientras no hurtaban."

87. Dampier, *A New Voyage*, 187.

88. Sigüenza y Góngora, *Infortunios*, 16. "De éste cortó cada uno una pequeña presa, y alabando el gusto de tan linda carne, entre repetidas saludes le dieron fin. Miraba yo con escándalo y congoja tan bestial acción, y llegándose a mí uno con un pedazo me instó con importunaciones molestas a que lo comiese. A la debida repulsa que yo le hice, me dijo que, siendo español y por consiguiente cobarde, bien podía para igualarlos a ellos en valor, no ser melindroso."

89. See Peter Hulme, *Colonial Encounters: Europe and the Native Caribbean, 1492–1797* (New York: Routledge, 1992), 13–43.

90. Sigüenza y Góngora, *Infortunios*, 20. "Propusiéronme entonces, como ya otras veces me lo habían dicho, el que jurase de acompañarlos siempre y me darían armas. Agradecíles la merced, y haciendo refleja a las obligaciones con que nací, le respondí con afectada humildad el que más me acomodaba a servirlos a ellos que a pelear con otros por ser grande el temor que les tenía a las balas, tratándome de español cobarde y gallina y por eso indigno de estar en su compañía."

91. Bolaños, "Sobre las 'relaciones' e identidades," 140–41.

92. Concha Meléndez, "Aventuras de Alonso Ramírez," in *Obras Completas* (San Juan de Puerto Rico: Editorial Cordillera, 1970), vol. 2: 375.

93. Glissant, *Caribbean Discourse*, 23.

94. Sigüenza y Góngora, *Infortunios*, 23. "Para nosotros el día lunes era el más temido."

95. Sigüenza y Góngora, *Infortunios*, 23. "Era igual la vergüenza y el dolor que en ello teníamos al regocijo y aplauso con que festejaban."

96. Sigüenza y Góngora, *Infortunios*, 23. "... por no haber otro español entre ellos sino Juan de Casas." It is interesting to point out that there was another Spaniard aboard the ship. He was a Sevillian and a member of the pirate's society. Ramírez remembers him with particular despite because this Sevillian was a heretic and was also the one among the pirates who most enjoyed seeing pain inflicted on him and his crew. Who was this Sevillian, and why did he hate the Spanish so much?

97. Sigüenza y Góngora, *Infortunios*, 26. "... que a ellos, por su color y por no ser españoles, los harían esclavos y que les sería menos sensible el que yo con mis manos los echase al mar que ponerse en las de extranjeros para experimentar sus rigores."

98. Sigüenza y Góngora, *Infortunios*, 20. "Considerando la barbaridad de los negros moros que allí vivían, hincado de rodillas y besándole los pies con gran rendimiento, después de reconvenirles con lo mucho que les había servido y ofreciéndome a asistirles en su viaje como si fuese esclavo, conseguí el que me llevasen consigo."

99. Derek Walcott, "The Schooner Flight," in *Collected Poems, 1948–1984* (New York: Noonday Press, 1992), 346.

100. Sigüenza y Góngora, *Infortunios*, 26. "No se espante quien esto leyere de la ignorancia en que estábamos de aquellas islas, porque habiendo salido de mi patria

de tan poca edad, nunca supe (ni cuidé de ello después) qué islas son circunvecinas y cuáles sus nombres."

101. Sigüenza y Góngora, *Infortunios,* 28. "Considerando el peligro en la dilación, haciendo fervorosos actos de contrición y queriendo merecerle a Dios su misericordia sacrificándole mi vida por la de aquellos pobres, ciñéndome un cabo delgado para que lo fuesen largando, me arrojé al agua."

102. Sigüenza y Góngora, *Infortunios,* 31. "Abrazándose de mí, me pedían con mil amores y ternuras que no les desamparase y que, pareciendo imposible en lo natural poder vivir el más robusto ni aun cuatro días, siendo la demora tan corta, quisiese, como padre que era de todos, darle mi bendición en sus postreras boqueadas y que después prosiguiese muy enhorabuena a buscar lo que a ellos les negaba su infelicidad y desventura en tan extraños climas."

103. Sigüenza y Góngora, *Infortunios,* 32. ". . . cruelísimos en extremo."

104. Sigüenza y Góngora, *Infortunios,* 32. ". . . mi muchacho."

105. Cristóbal de Muros Montiberos is mentioned in a document of 1684 for his meritorious zeal as a priest in New Spain. See A.G.I., *Indiferente,* 205.

106. Ceferino de Castro y Velasco was named *regidor,* or alderman, of Campeche in April of 1689. See A.G. I., *México,* 198, N.50.

107. Quoted and translated in Leonard, *Baroque Times,* 193.

108. Fornet, "Ironía y cuestionamiento ideológico," 206.

109. Eugenio D'Ors y Rovira, *Lo barroco* (Madrid: Aguilar, 1964), 29. "El espíritu barroco, para decirlo vulgarmente y de una vez, no sabe lo que quiere. Quiere, a un mismo tiempo, el pro y el contra. . . . Quiere—me acuerdo de cierto angelote, en cierta reja de cierta capilla de cierta iglesia en Salamanca—levantar el brazo y bajar la mano."

110. See Cope, *Racial Domination,* 24.

111. Cope, *Racial Domination,* 49.

112. See María Concepción García Sáiz, *Las castas mexicanas: Un género pictórico americano* (Milan: Grafiche Milani, 1989).

113. García Sáiz argues that there is no doubt that the work is Magón's, even though none of the paintings are signed by him. See García Sáiz, *Las castas mexicanas,* 102.

114. "En la America nacen Gentes diverzas en color, en coftumbres, genios y lenguas." See García Sáiz, *Las castas mexicanas,* 103.

115. ". . . por lo común, humilde, quieto y sencillo" García Sáiz, *Las castas mexicanas,* 103.

116. See Cope, *Racial Domination,* 24.

117. In the *castas* system the *morisco* is the offspring of Spaniard and mulatto.

118. Isidoro Moreno Navarro, *Los cuadros de mestizaje americano: Estudio antropológico del mestizaje* (Madrid: Juan Porrúa Turanzas, 1973), 143.

119. Carl Linnaeus published his *Systema Naturae* in 1735. This was followed by *Philosophia Botanica* (1751) and *Species Plantarum* (1753). The works set up the basis for the classification of all life forms on the planet, thereby giving order to the perceived chaos of nature. For an explanation of the significance of Linnaeus's work, see Pratt, *Imperial Eyes,* 24–37.

120. The tradition of the paseo, which supplanted that of the alameda, became popular in Mexico during the early years of the eighteenth century after the Treaty of Utrecht (1712) resulted in the dynastic replacement of the Hasburgs by the

French Bourbons as monarchs of Spain. When Philip V became king, promenading down a boulevard, on foot or by carriage, became the most fashionable pastime of the elites. *Castas* were not considered *vecinos*, and as such they were there to serve and assist the Spaniards, not to promenade. Mexico City had several of these paseos, the most famous of which probably was the Paseo Nuevo or the Paseo de Bucarelli.

121. This is the "We, the People" of the creole, the *Nosotros* that Simón Bolívar would define in 1815 as "we who barely show signs of what once was and who, at the same time are neither Indians nor Europeans but a kind of intermediary specie between the legitimate owners of the country and the European usurpers: in sum, being as we are Americans by birth and entitled to the rights of Europe, we must dispute these with the natives and we must hold on to the country in the face of the invasion by the invaders [the Spaniards]" (mas nosotros, que apenas conservamos vestigios de lo que en otro tiempo fué, y que por otra parte no somos indios ni europeos, sino una especie media entre los legítimos propietarios del país y los usurpadores españoles; en suma, siendo nosotros americanos por nacimiento y nuestros derechos los de Europa, tenemos que disputar éstos a los del país y que mantenernos en él contra la invasión de los invasores). Simón Bolívar, "Contestación de un americano meridional a un caballero de esta Isla." [letter to Henry Cullen], in *Obras completas* (Havana: Editorial Lex, 1947), vol. 1:164.

122. García Sáiz believes this one might belong to the Andean School. See García Sáiz, *Las castas mexicanas*, 174–75.

123. García Sáiz, *Las castas mexicanas*, 250–52.

124. Pratt, *Imperial Eyes*, 205.

125. García Sáiz, *Las castas mexicanas*, 88–89.

5. Undoing the Ideal

1. "Informe de don Joaquín García (16 de marzo de 1874)," in Javier Malagón Barceló, *El Código Negro Carolino (1784)* (Santo Domingo: Ediciones Taller, 1974), 93–94. "... con respecto a las distintas clases de negros y sus descendencias, por razón de la trascendencia que tiene en la felicidad o perjuicio del estado la relación, conexión, inclinaciones, comunicación y abrigo ascendente o descendente entre los negros esclavos, los libertos, los libres más antiguos, y los mulatos de todas especies, quienes pensando y obrando con igual o muy poca diferente irracionalidad, flojedad y barbarie, son por sí solos incapaces de aspirar a otra felicidad que las de sus momentáneas urgencias, o apetitos; y por consiguiente son (sin tales reglamentos) la polilla del Estado, en lugar de útiles a la sociedad, y a sí mismos."

2. In 1783 the minister of the Indies in Madrid ordered the design and compilation of a code to govern the blacks of Santo Domingo. After reports from and consultation with planters and the highest authorities in the island, the Código Negro was put together in less than a year by Agustín Ignacio Emparán y Orbe, a royal functionary who had lived in Santo Domingo for three decades. The diligence of the colonial authorities was undermined by the abandonment to which the work was submitted when it got to Spain. Filed away in Madrid, Emparán's work was dusted off in 1788 and shipped by the minister of Justice and Ecclesiastical Affairs (Gracia y Justicia), Antonio Porlier, to Peru so that another royal functionary by the name of Antonio Romero could prepare a report on it in accordance with the king's

order to compile a Negro code that could be applied throughout his dominions. Porlier and Romero were as efficient as Emparán had been. A year later, in 1789, the king was signing a "Royal Decree concerning the education, treatment and occupation of slaves in all the Dominions of the Indies and the Philippine Islands" (Real Cédula de Su Majestad sobre educación, trato y ocupación de los esclavos en todos los dominios de Indias e Islas Filipinas). The implementation of the decree was resisted by the planters of Louisiana, which had been ceded by France to Spain in 1762 and where the French Negro Code of 1724 was still the law of the land. But it was most vehemently opposed by the planters of Havana and Caracas, who considered the code too favorable to the slaves. Consequently, the king's orders were thoroughly disregarded and the law was never followed. See Malagón Barceló, *El Código Negro*, lix.

3. See *Extracto del Código Negro Carolino, formado por la Audiencia de Santo Domingo, conforme a lo prevenido en Real Orden de 23 de Septiembre de 1783,* in A.G.I., *Estado*, 7, N.3, Anejo 1. The *Extracto* was the actual summary of the proposed Código Negro of 1874 that was prepared in 1788 by Antonio Romero at the bequest of Minister Porlier. "En èl se insinua la decadencia de la Isla Española, y de su Agricultura de dos siglos à esta parte, por los antiquados abusos de su constitucion, como numero de Negros, y Esclavos que posehe, ociosidad, independencia, orgullo, robos y excesos de estos . . . que se propone el sistema gobernativo de su reparacion y mejora." The entire *Extracto* is organized in paragraphs numbered 1 to 222. The quote is from paragraph 1.

I find the *Extracto* particularly fascinating as a document that, in accomplishing its mission to summarize, inevitably also reinterprets the Código Negro and reinscribes it within a larger frame of reference. In fact, I believe it is a more valuable document than the original Código because, although it is complementary to it, the highlights and omissions of the *Extracto* already respond to the concern for and acceptance of the fact that the independence and pride of the blacks and mulattoes was a universal phenomenon generalized in the Indies, the Philippines, and beyond.

4. See María Rosario Sevilla Soler, *Santo Domingo: Tierra de frontera (1750–1800)* (Seville: Escuela de Estudios Hispano-Americanos, 1980), 25–47.

5. Sevilla Soler, *Santo Domingo*, 67. By the end of the eighteenth century the free *moreno* population in the Spanish colonies of the Caribbean exceeded by far that of both slaves and whites. In the Greater Caribbean, the Viceroyalty of New Granada (present-day Panama, Colombia, and Ecuador) supported a population of 80,000 slaves and 420,000 free *morenos* in 1789, and in the cacao plantations of Venezuela a similar situation was evident, with 64,000 slaves and 198,000 freemen. By 1820, in Puerto Rico there were 22,000 slaves and 104,000 freemen, the latter alone outnumbering the whites. Herbert S. Klein, *African Slavery in Latin America and the Caribbean* (New York: Oxford University Press, 1986), 221–22.

6. Donald R. Horowitz's unpublished article "Color Differentiation in the American System of Slavery" is cited by H. Hoetink, *Slavery and Race Relations in the Americas: Comparative Notes on their Nature and Nexus* (New York: Harper and Row, 1973), 10.

7. See Arthur L. Stinchcombe, *Sugar Island Slavery in the Age of Enlightenment: The Political Economy of the Caribbean World* (Princeton, N.J.: Princeton University Press, 1995), 159–71.

8. B. W. Higman, *Slave Populations of the British Caribbean, 1807–1834* (Baltimore: John Hopkins University Press, 1984), 77.

9. As Hoetink explains, the most coveted reward, "manumission, especially that of an affective, non-economic type, was more often extended to Coloreds than to Negroes." Hoetink, *Slavery and Race Relations*, 56.

10. Saco, "La seguridad de Cuba," 142. "Si a este total formidable de 1,862,306 se agreaga la numerosa población de color esparcida en el litoral de la antigua Colombia, y los ciento setenta mil negros de las Guyanas inglesa, francesa y holandesa, y el Golfo de Honduras, la situación de Cuba se presenta un aspecto más alarmante. Y como si tanto no bastara, la república de Norteamérica, nos ofrece, en medio de sus libres instituciones, la dolorosa anomalía de tener reconcentrados en sus regiones meridionales, y como si dijéramos a las puertas de Cuba, casi tres millones de negros, de cuyo número yacen dos millones y medio en dura esclavitud.

"¿Quién, pues, no tiembla al considerar que la población de orígen africano, que circunda a Cuba, se eleva a más de cinco millones?"

11. Eugene D. Genovese, *Roll, Jordan, Roll: The World the Slaves Made* (New York: Vintage Books, 1976), 414.

12. What Genovese does not consider is how this phenomenon of mulattoization has affected the "white" population. Of course in a country like the United States the descendants of the light-skinned mulattoes might no longer be statistically relevant insofar as they were and are absorbed into the white population, whose members hold claim to being the "well-formed," which in Usonian lingo means not having one single drop of "black blood" running through one's veins.

13. *Extracto*, para. 26: "... los blancos, y civilizados sin exercicio, ni profesión, sinò lo es la del monopolio, y reventa de viveres de primera necesidad."

14. *Extracto*, para. 25. "... que esta parte de la Policia es muy importante en las Colonias, y mas en la Ysla Española, cuya media poblacion negra, y parda, ha adquirido con su libertad el derecho de vivir en el ocio, è independiente de todo yugo."

15. *Extracto*, para. 11. "... no siendo la mas severa disciplina y fuerza, capaces por sì à contenerlos en los excesos de sedicion, y fuga à que los convida lo inaccesible de las Montañas."

16. *Extracto* para. 12. "Es necesario desarraigar de su corazón tan vehementes inclinaciones, sustituyendo las ideas de lealtad al Soberano, amor à la Nacion Española, reconocimiento à sus Amos, subordinacion à los Blancos... y demas virtudes sociales."

17. Antonio Romero, *Dictamen sobre el sistema del Codigo*, in A.G.I., *Estado*, 7, N.3, Anejo 2, 7–8. "... teniendo presentes los principios y reglas que dicta la humanidad, compatibles con la esclavitud." And later: "... como los buenos Padres de familia lo executan con sus hijos."

18. As much was clear in Antonio Romero's *Dictamen*, or opinion of the Código, which starts by placing the blame for the underdevelopment of the island on the very low number of its inhabitants when compared to the neighboring French colony. Romero's conclusion was that "the shortage of field hands cannot be supplied by others but the blacks and slaves" (falta de brazos para su cultibo, que no pueden suplirse por otros, que por los Negros, y Esclabos). See *Dictamen*, 7.

19. Antonio Sánchez Valverde, *Idea del Valor de la Isla Española*, ed. Cipriano de Utrera (Santo Domingo: Editora Montalvo, 1947), 169. "¿Ignoran, por ventura, los colonos Españoles o Criollos quál es esta llave? No por cierto: bien saben que son las manos, principalmente, de los Negros."

20. Código Negro Carolino, chap. 3, law 1. See Malagón Barceló, *El Código Negro Carolino*, 168.

21. Código Negro Carolino, chap. 3, law 2. See Malagón Barceló, *El Código Negro Carolino*, 168.

22. In 1762 Luis Joseph Peguero included a curious addendum to his *Historia de la conquista de la Isla Española*, entitled "Treaty of the Nations That Arose on This Island." In it he describes the movement of going toward the black, labeling the union of a mulatto and a black as the *grifo* (from the Latin *gryphus* or twisted), and that of a *grifo* and a black as the *saltatrás*, literally the "jump-back-to." See Peguero, *Historia de la conquista*, vol. 2: 274–75.

23. Peguero, *Historia de la conquista*, vol. 2: 275. ". . . gracias a las introducidas pelucas, que con estas se ocultan los pelos naturales, que testifican de donde por Calidad venian los hombres."

24. Peguero, *Historia de la conquista*, 275. ". . . y no da lugar a que el Bulgo lo Geneologie."

25. Código Negro Carolino, chap. 4, law 4. See Malagón Barceló, *El Código Negro Carolino*, 176. ". . . aunque sea negro, o pardo primerizo pueda ascender de la cuarta generación de su estirpe a la jerarquía de los blancos."

26. Código Negro Carolino, chap. 4, law 5. See Malagón Barceló, *El Código Negro Carolino*, 176.

27. M. L. Moreau de Saint-Méry, *Descripción de la parte española de Santo Domingo*, trans. Armando Rodríguez (Santo Domingo: Editora Montalvo, 1944), 93–94. "Es también rigurosamente cierto que la gran mayoría de los colonos españoles son mestizos, que tienen todavía más de un rasgo africano que los traicionan luego."

28. Verena Martinez-Alier, *Marriage, Class and Colour in Nineteenth-Century Cuba: A Study of Racial Attitudes and Sexual Values in a Slave Society* (Ann Arbor: University of Michigan Press, 1989), 76.

29. García Sáiz, *Las castas mexicanas*, 107. "De Ynida y Calpamulato Gíbaro nace, inquieto de ordinario, siempre arrogante."

30. García Sáiz, *Las castas mexicanas*, 25. ". . . manchado de blanco."

31. See Benítez Rojo, *The Repeating Island*, 33–81.

32. Código Negro Carolino, chap. 3, law 3. See Malagón Barceló, *El Código Negro Carolino*, 168. "Siendo pues la clase primera la que por su excesivo número y condición y los ministerios a que se destinen debe formar, digámoslo así, el pueblo de la Isla Española; será la intermedia la que en cierta manera constituirá la balanza justa y equilibrio de la población blanca, con la negra."

33. Código Negro Carolino, chap. 3, law 6. See Malagón Barceló, *El Código Negro Carolino*, 171. ". . . las siniestras impresiones de igualdad y familiaridad."

34. chap. 3, law 6. See Malagón Barceló, *El Código Negro Carolino*, 172. ". . . desde sus primeros años en su corazón los sentimientos de respeto e inclinación a los blancos con quienes deben equipararse algún día."

35. Código Negro Carolino, chap. 3, law 9. See Malagón Barceló, Código Negro, 172.

36. Código Negro Carolino, chap. 3, law 3. See Malagón Barceló, Código Negro Carolino, 168. ". . . habiendo acreditado la experiencia en todas las colonias americanas no haberse mezclado jamás con los negros (a quienes miran con odio y aversión)."

37. I am referring to Francisco de Goya's *Saturn Devouring His Children* (1819–23), a canvas in the collection of the Museo del Prado belonging to the painter's later years. In a terrible denunciation of inhumanity, the painting depicts an old man frantically eating the body of a child.

38. Sánchez Valverde, *Idea del Valor*, 166. "La insolencia de Weuves y de otros Estranjeros no se ha contentado con insultarnos sobre la actividad y genio sino que ha tenido la habilatez de abrir nuestras venas y manchar la sangre, tanto de los Indo-Hispanos, como de sus Progenitores Europeos."

39. Sánchez Valverde, *Idea del Valor*, 166. "En una parte dice, hablando de los primeros: 'Si es que puede llamárseles Españoles a los Habitantes de Indias, cuya sangre está tan mezclada con la de los Caribes y los Negros, que es rarísimo encontrar un solo hombre cuya sangre no tenga esta mixtura.' En otra parte: 'No hay Colonia Española ni Portuguesa en que no se vean Mulatos poseyendo las Dignidades del primer orden. Por esta razón es que estas dos Naciones no tienen tal vez una gota de sangre pura, sea que hayan tomado esta mezcla de los Negros, sea de los antiguos Moros." See also Weuves, le jeune (the only name we have for this author), *Reflexions historiques et politiques sur le commerce de France avec ses colonies de l'Amérique* (Geneva: L. Cellot, 1780).

40. As a prebendary Sánchez Valverde was entitled to a monthly stipend derived from the revenues of the cathedral.

41. Quoted by Utrera from a document in the Archive of the Indies (A.G.I., *Santo Domingo*, 1106), in Sánchez Valverde, *Idea del Valor*, 10. "... tiene el genio muy vivo y emplea bastante libertad de lengua, y aun en el púlpito es ordinariamete muy libre en el hablar."

42. Sánchez Valverde, *Idea del Valor*, 27–28. "el sacrílego intento (perdone V.S. la propiedad de la expresión) de violar la immunidad de mi persona." In those days everyone, free or slave, who crossed the border in any direction was in principle entitled to asylum.

43. Utrera, in Sánchez Valverde, *Idea del Valor*, 37. "... cuyas palabras, enderezadas a persuadir una cosa, persuaden su contraria."

44. Sánchez Valverde, *Idea del Valor*, 28. "Yo no he ido a hablar sobre el gobierno, sobre el Despacho, sobre el Abasto, sobre las Elecciones, sobre los intereses particulares, etc. etc. ... gozaré de lo bueno con gusto y sufriré lo adverso con paciencia, como todos, sin dar motivo a quejas ni alborotos."

45. Sánchez Valverde, *Idea del Valor*, 167. "En España hay sangre tan pura como en cualquiera otro Reyno. Ninguno ha dexado de mezclar la suya con otros en las varias revoluciones que todas han padecido. Los Americanos, que han descendido de estas Casas, han procurado conservar su puereza en Indias más que los Franceses, cuyos Condes y Marqueses casan en las Colonias de Santo Domingo con Mulatas ricas."

46. Sánchez Valverde, *Idea del Valor*, 26. "Las señas de este eclesiástico son: estatura regular como de cinco pies y tres pulgadas, color moreno ... es regular vaya disfrazado."

47. Peguero, *Historia de la conquista*, vol. 2: 276.

> Por sierto Cosa de Riza
> de Alegria y de plaser,
> la blancura pretender
> sin blanca, y sin camisa:

la blanca plata, presisa
que se busque con Anelo,
pero blancura de cuero
que no llena la barriga,
es justa razon se diga
la locura de Juanelo.

Este Adagio tan fecundo
con que este discurso sierro,
nos esplica, sino Yerro
las verdades de este Mundo.
todo al fin es moribundo
blanco, y negro a mi ber,
y Yo soy del pareser
que en el mundo nobelero,
no es quien nase caballero,
solo quien lo sabe ser.

48. Peguero, *Historia de la conquista,* vol. 2: 275. ". . . porque no le abemos oido desir a ninguno desiendo de tal berdugo, de tal etiope, de tal moro, o ensanbeniato: ni tanpoco, soy Mulato, Mestiso, Sambo, Cabra o Grifo: luego dixe bien no abia ya solo blancos y negros."

49. Today, for example, both in Cuba and in Puerto Rico racial issues are for the most part dismissed by the authorities. Officially, racism has been abolished by decree in both countries. Unofficially, the further toward the white one might be along the socioracial continuum, the more racism is discarded as a subject of inquiry and the more racial distinctions are quietly enforced in the practice of everyday life. Such are the paradoxes of mulatto societies. One of the classic examples given by persons who propose such nonsense in Puerto Rico is that the term *negrito,* or little black boy—the equivalent of "boy" in the Usonian context—is the preferred and most "beautiful" term of endearment in the Puerto Rican lexicon. What these people "neglect" to see is that the term *negrito* is always used in an imperative form, as in "Negrito ven acá" (Come here, boy), "Negrito, házme un favor" (Do me a favor, boy), "Negrito cállate" (Shut up, boy), and "Negrito siéntate" (Sit down, boy). The use and abuse of the term gives a whole new meaning to the expression *mi negrito querido,* or my dear boy. There is no endearment here, but rather a malicious persistence of plantation politics, and the twisted memories not of love on the plantation but rather of love of the Plantation.
A similar term is frequently used in Cuba. Contrary to what one might think, the term *china* has nothing to do with the Chinese, but comes from the Quechua and means servant girl or, alternatively, someone with kinky hair. The *chino* was also a *casta,* referring to a third-generation hybrid who could be one of six possible mixtures but most commonly that of lobo (offspring of an Indian and a black) and black or Indian. (See García Sáiz, *Las castas mexicanas,* 26).

50. The *maréchaussée* was a militia or police organization that free mulattoes and free blacks were obligated to join. They were instrumental in the fight against the maroons.

51. Sánchez Valverde, *Idea del Valor,* 27. ". . . me ligaron los brazos junto con un mulato."

52. Arnold A. Sio, "Marginality and Free Coloured Identity in Caribbean Slave Society," *Caribbean Slave Society and Economy: A Student Reader,* ed. Hilary Beckles and Verne Shepherd (New York: The New Press, 1991), 151.

53. Rebecca J. Scott also holds a more complex view of the ambiguous and problematic role of the colored populations in Caribbean slave societies. Writing on Cuba, she notes: "Free persons of color constituted an uncertain element in the colonial equation. The Spanish administration had long sought to use them as a counterweight to the slave population, even to the extent of arming battalions of free Mulattoes and Blacks. In the 1840s, however, authorities suspected free persons of color of collaboration in a rumored general slave uprising and arrested, tortured, and executed members of Cuba's precarious free Colored middle sector. The Colored small-scale farmers, tenants, and squatters in the east, where in most districts they outnumbered slaves, were a similar unknown in the balance of power. As in virtually all slave societies, Mulatto free persons had often sought to distance themselves from Blacks in an effort both to avoid the 'stain' of shared slave ancestry and to assert the importance of differences in social status and gradations of skin color. At the same time, however, slaves and free persons of color had often been joined by ties of kinship." Rebecca J. Scott, *Slave Emancipation in Cuba: The Transition to Free Labor, 1860–1899* (Princeton, N.J.: Princeton University Press, 1985), 9.

54. Orlando Patterson, *Slavery and Social Death: A Comparative Study* (Cambridge: Harvard University Press, 1982), 257.

55. Everett V. Stonequist, "Race Mixture and the Mulatto," *Race Relations and the Race Problem: A Definition and an Analysis,* ed. Edgar T. Thompson (Durham, N.C.: Duke University Press, 1939), 261.

56. Esteban Montejo, *The Autobiography of a Runaway Slave,* ed. Miguel Barnet, trans. Jocasta Innes (New York: Pantheon Books, 1968), 22.

57. Montejo, *Autobiography,* 37–8.

58. Note that the *zambo* is akin to the *chino,* which, as I have discussed, is used in Cuba to this day, as is *negrito,* or boy, in Puerto Rico, to denote someone who is of lower and subservient status.

59. García Sáiz, *Las castas mexicanas,* 24.

60. Patterson, *Slavery and Social Death,* 96.

61. Stanley M. Elkins, *Slavery: A Problem in American Institutional and Intellectual Life* (Chicago: University of Chicago Press, 1968), 82.

62. C. L .R. James, *The Black Jacobins: Toussaint L'Ouverture and the San Domingo Revolution* (New York: Vintage Books, 1989), 171.

63. James, *The Black Jacobins,* 148. General Jean-Jacques Dessalines was L'Ouverture's right-hand man.

64. James, *The Black Jacobins,* 161.

65. Ibid.

66. James, *The Black Jacobins,* 188.

67. James, *The Black Jacobins,* 152.

68. James, *The Black Jacobins,* 125.

69. Ramón Emeterio Betances, "Alejandro Petion," in *Las Antillas para los Antillanos,* ed. Carlos M. Rama (Barcelona: Gráficas Manuel Pareja, 1975), 55. "Dicen que en sus últimos días, el prisionero negro no oyó sino una voz consoladora, la del mulato Rigaud, que gemía a su lado, en otro calabozo. Lección de la Historia; digna de meditarse."

70. James, *The Black Jacobins*, 181.

71. James, *The Black Jacobins*, 168.

72. Jamaica Kincaid, "On Seeing England for the First Time," *Transition* 51 (1991): 33.

73. James, *The Black Jacobins*, 123.

74. James, *The Black Jacobins*, 164.

75. Quintero Rivera, "Vueltita," 81.

76. Pamphile de Lacroix, "Mémoires pour servir à l'histoire de la Révolution de Saint-Domingue," in *La Révolution de Haïti*, ed. Pierre Pluchon (Paris: Karthala, 1995), 325. ". . . qui ne présentaient plus de résistance régulière."

77. Lacroix, "Mémoires," 327. "Les premiers boulets n'épouvantèrent pas les Noirs: ils se mirent à chanter et à danser; ils chargèrent à la baïonnette en criant: *En avant! Canons à nous.* Un bataillon de la 56ᵉ demi-brigade les attendit à bout portant, et fit un feu si vif, qu'en un instant ce qui n'était pas mort ou blessé fut en désordre."

78. Lacroix, "Mémoires," 328. "Les cadavres amoncelés présentaient encore l'attitude de leurs derniers moments: on en voyait d'agenouillés, les mains tendues et suppliantes; les glaces de la mort n'avaient pas effacé l'empreinte de leur physionomie: leurs trait peignaient autant la prière que la douleur."

"Des filles, le sein déchiré, avaient l'air de demander quartier pour leurs mères; des mères couvraient de leurs bras percés les enfants égorgés sur leur sein."

79. W. N. C. Carlton, *Pauline: Favorite Sister of Napoleon* (New York: Harper and Brothers, 1930), 75–76.

80. Lacroix, "Mémoires," 332. "Nous n'inspirons plus de terreur morale, et c'est le plus grand malheur qui puisse arriver à une armée."

81. Lacroix, "Mémoires," 332. "J'eus l'idée malencontreuse de croire que je pourrais aisément détruire par le feu l'odeur dont nous étions infectés."

82. Lacroix, "Mémoires," 332. "Soit que nous n'eussions pas rassemblé une assez grande quantité de bois, soit que les dégoûts de la putréfaction eussent empêché l'entassement rapproché des cadavres, notre opération de brûlement se fit mal. Une odeur plus insupportable que la première imprégna l'atmosphere; elle était si pénétrante, que je ne pus pointe parvenir à désinfecter l'habit que j'avais en présidant à cette pénible opération.

"Je conçus, par cette épreuve, la ténacité avec laquelle la laine garde les miasmes contagieux dont elle se sature."

83. Pyrrhus, king of Epirus, set out in the second century B.C. to emulate Alexander. At one point during his march, after the battle of Heraclea, he found himself in the unfortunate position of not being able to claim victory in its entirety even though the enemy had been defeated. Plutarch wrote that of the end of the battle: "It is said, Pyrrhus replied to one that gave him joy of his victory, that one other such would utterly undo him." Plutarch, *Plutarch's Lives*, Dryden edition (New York: Bigelow, Brown and Co., 1961), vol. 3: 31.

84. Lacroix, "Mémoires," 333. See also James, *The Black Jacobins*, 317. "Pendant que nous opérions l'investissement du fort, la musique des ennemis faisait entendre les airs patriotiques adaptés à la gloire de la France.

"Malgré l'indignation qu'excitaient les atrocités des Noirs, ces airs produisaient généralment un sentiment pénible. Les regards de nos soldats interrogeaint les nôtres; ils avaient l'air de nous dire: "Nos barbares ennemis auraient-ils raison? Ne serions-nous plus les soldats de la République? Et serions-nous devenus les instruments serviles de la politique?"

85. Lacroix, "Mémoires," 331. "Dès que nous fûmes démasqués, la redoute vomit tout son feu, et dans l'instant ce qui nous entourait fut renversé."

86. Jürgen Habermas, *The Structural Transformation of the Public Sphere: An Inquiry into a Category of Bourgeois Society,* trans. Thomas Burger (Cambridge: MIT Press, 1993), 8.

87. Habermas cites C. Schmitt's *Römischer Katholizismus und politische Form.* Habermas, *Structural Transformation,* 252, note 12.

88. Reinhart Koselleck, *Critique and Crisis: Enlightenment and the Pathogenesis of Modern Society* (Cambridge: MIT Press, 1988), 33.

89. Karl Marx, "The Eighteenth Brumaire of Louis Bonaparte," in *The Marx-Engels Reader,* ed. Robert C. Tucker (New York: W. W. Norton and Company, 1978), 613.

90. "... tel qu'il était au moment de sa mort."

91. "L'ami du peuple."

92. "Ne pouvant me corrompre, ils m'ont assassiné."

93. James, *The Black Jacobins,* 411.

94. Simón Bolívar, *Obras Completas* (Havana: Editorial Lex, 1947), vol. 1: 1091. "Yo no he venido a daros leyes, pero os ruego que oigáis mi voz: os recomiendo la unidad del Gobierno y la libertad absoluta, para no volver a cometer un absurdo y un crimen, pues que no podemos ser libres y esclavos a la vez."

95. Bolívar, *Obras Completas,* vol. 1: 1092. "No habrá, pues, más esclavos en Venezuela que los que quieran serlo. Todos los que prefieran la libertad al reposo, tomarán las armas para sostener sus derechos sagrados, y serán ciudadanos."

96. The Haitian proverb is quoted in Eric Williams, *From Columbus to Castro: The History of the Caribbean, 1492–1969* (New York: Harper and Row, 1970), 334.

97. See the excellent book by Alfonso Múnera, *El fracaso de la nación: Religión, clase y raza en el Caribe colombiano (1717–1810)* (Bogotá: El Áncora Editores, 1998).

98. "Informe de don Benito Azar al virrey don Benito Pérez," Mérida de Yucatán, 26 April 1811, in A.G.I., *Santa Fe,* 630. Quoted in Múnera, *El fracaso de la nación,* 186.

99. Múnera, *El fracaso de la nación,* 213.

100. Múnera, *El fracaso de la nación,* 161. "Su evolución muestra mejor que nada la debilidad y el completo fracaso del naciente discurso nacional."

101. In Sáiz, *Las castas mexicanas,* 103.

102. Such were the words used by Horrego Estuch to describe Plácido on the centennial of his assassination. See Leopoldo Horrego Estuch, *Plácido: El poeta infortunado* (Havana: Ministerio de Educación, 1960), 53.

103. Eugenio María de Hostos, *Obras completas* (San Juan: Editorial Coquí, 1969), vol. 9: 13–4. "Como el período de transición en que nació, Plácido era fisiológicamente una transición. Venía de la raza africana por su padre hacia la raza caucásica representada por su madre. Iba del negro al blanco.... Era ... de color indeciso entre el blanco y el mulato."

104. Hostos, *Obras completas,* vol. 9: 25. "La Isla de Cuba estaba, mientras Plácido cantaba las glorias de Isabel y de Cristina, en la peor de las situaciones en que puede estar un pueblo esclavo: estaba contento de su amo."

105. Hostos, *Obras completas,* vol. 9: 27. "Adulando lo que instintivamente maldecía, maldiciendo lo que acababa de adular con versos aduladores, era resumen viviente

del detestable momento de transición en que vivía, de la enferma sociedad que lo abortaba."

106. Hostos, *Obras completas,* vol. 14: 70. "Cuando se quiere una tortilla, hay que romper los huevos: tortillas sin huevos rotos o revolución sin revoltura, no se ven."

107. The contest between the Count and the Captain General was central to making Havana the monumental city that it is today since the rivalry of the two men and their respective interests was played out on an urban scale, both sides competing for the most praiseworthy public works, buildings and institutions of state beneficence. See Felicia Chateloin, *La Habana de Tacón* (La Habana: Editorial Letras Cubanas, 1989).

108. Besides Horrego Estuch's *Plácido,* see also M. García Garófalo Mesa, *Plácido, poeta y mártir* (Mexico: Ediciones Botas, 1938), and Jorge Castellanos, *Plácido, poeta social y político* (Miami: Ediciones Universal, 1984).

109. See Ángel Rama, *The lettered city,* ed. John Charles Chasteen (Durham, N.C.: Duke University Press, 1996).

110. Ramón de Armas, Ana Cairo Ballester, and Eduardo Torres Cuevas, *Historia de la Universidad de La Habana, 1728–1929* (Havana: Editorial de Ciencias Sociales, 1984), vol. 1: 312–13. "La joven dió a la figura del Alma mater un rostro dulce e ingenuo de bellos rasgos juveniles. La mujer ya hecha dio fuerza, vigor y esbeltez a la escultura."

111. Gabriel de la Concepción Valdés, *Poesías de Plácido* (Paris: Veuve de Ch. Bouret, 1904), 342.

> Lo que se me enseña canto,
> porque con mis trinos bellos
> aunque vierta oculto llanto,
> hago lo que me mandan ellos
> para no padecer tanto.
>
> Que le adulo, en la apariencia,
> piensa mi dueño y se hechiza;
> mas mirándolo en conciencia
> yo engaño al que me esclaviza,
> por conservar mi existencia.

112. Valdés, *Poesías de Plácido,* 341.

> Cuando por doquier se oía
> hablar los irracionales
> y el hombre los entendía
> (no es raro, pues en el día
> aun hablan los animales)....

113. Aldo Rossi, *A Scientific Autobiography* (Cambridge: MIT Press, 1981), 81.

114. Valdés, *Poesías de Plácido,* 342–43.

> Cuanto a ser esclavo... espera...
> te comprendo, y no te asombre:
> yo disculparme pudiera
> y al mismo tiempo te hiciera

la misma pregunta, *hombre:*
Haz cuenta que yo caí
en tus redes, y ansias vivas
no me salvaron de allí,
porque tú que me cautivas
eres superior a mí.

¡Mas tú que solo acatar
debes al sumo Hacedor,
y de un hombre a tu pesar
que no es a ti superior
te dejas esclavizar . . . !

¿Cuál es disculpa bastante
a tan loco devaneo?
¿Cómo quieres, ignorante,
encontrar en un pigmeo
más fuerza que en un gigante?

115.   Manuel Moreno Fraginals, *Cuba/España, España/Cuba: Historia común,* intro. Josep Fontana (Barcelona: Crítica, 1995), 167. ". . . un ídolo de la juventud criolla blanca de la época."

116.   Heredia's father, José Francisco de Heredia y Mieses, was the son of the captain and alderman of Santo Domingo. He fled his native city with his four sisters, an aunt, and a female cousin in advance of L'Ouverture's imminent attack in 1801. The ship, which was carrying about 150 creole women and children, was going to safe harbor in Puerto Rico when a storm took it all the way to Venezuela, running aground near Coro. It was in the midst of that veritable creole shipwreck that Heredia and his cousin, María de la Merced Heredia y Campuzano, who had previously dismissed his advances, decided to get married. A year later, with the news of Leclerc's capture of the city, they returned to Santo Domingo, but only for a short while. Once again the threat of the Haitian advance forced the Heredias to flee to Santiago de Cuba, where on 31 December 1803 José María Heredia y Campuzano was born.

When José María was only three and a half years old the family emigrated to Pensacola. They did not return to Cuba until the child was nine and then only for four months. Heredia would return to Cuba for little more than a year in 1817, and again for almost three years in 1821. The young poet died in his adopted country of Mexico in 1837.

117.   Horrego Estuch, *Plácido,* 19. "A la edad que Plácido comenzaba a probar el aliento de la enseñanza, Heredia traducía a Horacio y preparaba la publicación de varias poesías con el título de *Ensayos poéticos.*"

118.   See José Antonio Saco, "Exámen analítico del informe de la Comisión Especial nombrada por las Cortes sobre la exclusión de los actuales y futuros diputados de Ultramar y sobre la necesidad de regir aquellos países por leyes especiales," in Saco, *Colección de papeles,* vol. 3: 133. "¿Ni cómo podría de otra manera explicarse el fenómeno que presenta la confederacíon Norte-Americana, dando por una parte a los principios liberales el más completo desarrollo, y circunscribiendo por otra en algunos Estados los derechos políticos a sólo la raza blanca?"

119. Saco, "Exámen analítico," 136. "...semejantes hombres no están al alcance de los acontecimientos políticos de los pueblos, ni menos se hallan en circunstancias de apreciar los grados de más o menos libertad que a los cubanos puedan concederse."

120. Caudillismo is the rule of a strongman, or caudillo, the supreme political and military leader who figures as the representative embodiment of the creole nationalist state. The most prominent examples of caudillos in the twentieth-century Caribbean were Rafael Leónidas Trujillo, who ruled the Dominican Republic under the title of "Benefactor de la Patria" (Benefactor of the Fatherland) from 1930 to his assassination in 1961, and Fidel Castro Ruz, who has ruled as the "Líder Máximo" (Supreme Leader) of Cuba since 1959.

121. Saco, "Exámen analítico," 132. "Ellos saben que en aquellas islas hay una población heterogénea; pero su saber de aquí no pasa, pues ignoran la índole de sus habitantes, no penetran la tendencia de sus inclinaciones, no comprenden la fuerza de las antipatías y simpatías de las castas, ni menos perciben los resortes que se deben tocar para poner en armonía las piezas de una máquina que es sencilla cuando se conoce, complicada cuando no se entiende."

122. Valdés, *Poesías de Plácido*, 325.

> Negra deidad que sin clemencia alguna
> de espinas al nacer me circuiste
> cual fuente clara cuya margen viste
> maguey silvestre y punzadora tuna.
>
> Entre el materno tálamo y la cuna
> el férreo muro del honor pusiste;
> y acaso hasta las nubes me subiste,
> por verme descender desde la luna.

123. Valdés, *Poesías de Plácido*, 325–26.

> Si la suerte fatal que me ha cabido,
> y el triste fin de mi sangrienta historia,
> al salir de esta vida transitoria,
> deja tu corazón de muerte herido:
>
> Baste de llanto; el ánimo afligido
> recobre su quietud; moro en la gloria
> y mi plácida lira a tu memoria
> lanza en la tumba su poster sonido.
>
> Sonido dulce, melodioso y santo,
> glorioso, espiritual, puro y divino,
> inocente, espontáneo, como el llanto
>
> Que vertiera al nacer; ya el cuello inclino,
> ya de la religión me cubre el manto...
> ¡Adiós mi madre! Adiós.... *El peregrino*

124. Moreno Fraginals has noted that "the plantocracy never forgave him for his talent." Moreno Fraginals, *Cuba/España*, 182. "La sacarocracia no le perdonó su talento."

125. Valdés, *Poesías de Plácido*, 84.

Decía: "Dejo por heredero,
por mi última voluntad,
con tal que a ninguno pague,
a Don Fulano de Tal."

El heredero al oirlo
juró el mandato guardar,
y no saldar una cuenta
ni aquí, ni en la eternidad.

126. He is described as such in Mariano Torrente's report to the Spanish Council of Ministers in 1853. See Archivo Histórico Nacional (Madrid) (hereafter A.H.N.), *Ultramar*, leg. 3524, exp. 66, doc. 2. "...los dos hermanos mellizos D. Pedro y D. Ramón Santana de pura sangre española."

127. Spanish documents of the times describe Santana from the start as "Dictator of the Spanish part [of Santo Domingo] under the title of supreme leader" (Dictador de la parte Española bajo el título de gefe supremo). A.H.N., *Ultramar*, leg. 3524, exp. 7, doc. 2. They also speak of him as "a despicable fellow whose only aspiration is to steal and pillage, and who shifts allegiances with ease" (un canalla, sin otra aspiración que el robo y el pillage, y fácil a cambiar de bandera). A.H.N., *Ultramar*, leg. 3524, exp. 26.

128. *La Gaceta: Periódico Oficial de la República Dominicana*, 13 June 1854, 4. Santana had received this title after his defeat of Soulouque.

129. See Frank Moya Pons, *The Dominican Republic: A National History* (Princeton, N.J.: Markus Weiner Publishers, 1998), 188–96.

130. See, for example, the decree of 8 July 1857 that prohibits vengeful acts against Baez's former followers. A.H.N., *Ultramar*, leg. 3524, exp. 132.

131. Moya Pons states that in Santiago "most of the inhabitants were light-skinned but of mixed racial background." Moya Pons, *The Dominican Republic*, 207.

132. According to Mariano Álvarez, both cities had about the same population: Santo Domingo had eight thousand inhabitants and Santiago seven thousand. See Mariano Álvarez, "Memoria sobre la población y gobierno de Santo Domingo o La República Dominicana," in A.H.N., *Ultramar*, leg. 2775, exp. 16.

133. Decree of the Provisional Government of the Cibao, 11 July 1857, in A.H.N., *Ultramar*, leg. 3524, exp. 134, doc. 3.

134. A.H.N., *Ultramar*, leg. 3524, exp. 133. "El nuevo sistema de conquista puesto en practica hace algún tiempo en el Nuevo Mundo, conocido bajo la calificacion del filibusterismo; en que há alejado tal vez para siempre el largo reposo de la Ysla de Cuba, que incita y fomenta disenciones intestinas en todos los Estados debiles formados por la raza latina, se prepara a vuscar en esta República un atrincheramiento para intentar nuevas agresiones sobre estos mares. Acaba de estallar un movimiento insurreccionario en la rica Ciudad de Satiago de caracter bastante grave, movimiento que anunció publicamente en esta Capital y con tono de enfatica amenaza el Sr. Agente de los Estados Unidos de America."

135. In 1853–54, at the head of fifty mercenaries, Walker had tried to take Baja California and Sonora for himself. A year later, with a slightly larger force of eighty, he got himself invited to come to the aid of Nicaragua's Liberal elites. He then man-

aged to outmaneuver the Nicaraguans, naming himself president of the republic, a position he precariously occupied until 1857. In 1860 he was finally captured and executed.

136. Already in 1844 France was offering recognition to the new independent republic and also offering it military aid to defend it against Haiti in exchange for the entire peninsula of Samaná. (See A.H.N., *Ultramar,* leg. 3524, exp. 7, doc. 2.) A year later the United States sent General Cazneau aboard the frigate *Columbia* to negotiate Usonian recognition and to survey the Samaná territory. (See A.H.N., *Ultramar,* leg. 3524, exp. 76, doc. 1.)

137. This thesis is eloquently explained in Luis Martínez-Fernández, *Torn between Empires: Economy, Society, and Patterns of Political Thought in the Hispanic Caribbean, 1840–1878* (Athens: University of Georgia Press, 1994).

138. See Martínez-Fernández, *Torn between Empires,* 222–23.

139. "El estandarte de Castilla tremola ya en las fortalezas de Santo Domingo, merced á la espontaneidad e impaciencia con que este heroico Pueblo deseaba unir sus destinos á los de la magnanima nacion que por mas de tres siglos los rigiera tan dichosamente." A.H.N., *Ultramar,* leg. 5485, exp. 1, doc. 3.

140. Letter from the Spanish minister of state to the governor of Cuba, in A.H.N., *Ultramar,* leg. 5485, exp.2. "... para acudir a su socorro y evitar que el pueblo dominicano pudiera sufrir la menor disminucion en la integridad de su territorio, y el mas leve ataque en su independencia."

141. The list of proposed recipients of the Cross of Isabella the Catholic and of Carlos III can be found in A.H.N., *Ultramar,* leg. 3526, exp. 10, doc. 5. It bears upward of sixty names.

142. Moya Pons, *The Dominican Republic,* 206.

143. Letter from the minister of war and overseas possessions to the governor of Cuba, 1 August 1861, in A.H.N., *Ultramar,* leg. 5485, exp. 11. "Para que puedan desarrollarse los grandes elemetos de riqueza, que encierra la isla de Santo Domingo, es en primer lugar indispensable procurar el aumento de su población: por fortuna las condiciones del pais permiten esperar que la raza blanca llene esta primera necesidad."

144. A.H.N., *Ultramar,* leg. 3525, exp. 31, doc. 1. "Se recibió un parte del Señor Brigadier Primo de Rivera, fechado en Puerto Plata, en que se espresa que habiendo salido con su columna en direcciòn de Santiago de los Caballeros, hubo de retirarse al punto de su salida... sin que pudiese ver los enemigos ni hostilizarlos, por estar completamente ocultos y resguardados por la maleza."

145. I am borrowing the term "primitive rebels" from the excellent book by Eric J. Hobsbawm, *Primitive Rebels: Studies in Archaic Forms of Social Movement in the 19th and 20th Centuries* (Manchester, U.K: Manchester University Press, 1971).

146. Letter of the Provisional Government of the Cibao to the Queen of Spain, 24 September 1863, in A.H.N., *Ultramar,* leg. 3525, exp. 38, doc. 4. "Los cuarenta años de libertad civil y politica, la toleracion, en asuntos religiosos de que gozaba la poblacion bajo el gobierno republicano, juntos con nuerosas otras ventajas de las cuales se deben citar una representacion nacional y participacion en asuntos públicos, un derecho indispensable en una democracia, no se podian reconciliar bien con el sistema monárquico, y aun peor con el colonial." At the time, the captain general of Puerto Rico and that of Cuba, under whose orders the governor of the colony of Santo Domingo was now placed, ruled through the infamous *facultades omnímodas,* or all-embracing powers, conferred upon the office in 1833, which allowed

them to govern the colonies with the same absolute powers that a general would wield in a city under siege.

147. A.H.N., *Ultramar*, leg. 3525, exp. 38, doc. 4. "No obstante, este desastroso arreglo que hubiera causado una revolucion en cualquier parte del mundo, fué soportado aqui con la mayor resignacion; las unicas señales de dissatisfaccion de parte de la poblacion, eran suplicaciones ocasionales, lamentaciones y quejidos, como si dudase, aun que tan grandes faltas se podian haber cometido por la gente sabia de Europa, á quienes, gracias á nuestra modestia hemos considerado como nuestros superiores respecto á inteligencia."

148. Utrera, in Sánchez Valverde, *Idea del Valor*, 37.

149. A.H.N., *Ultramar*, leg. 3525, exp. 38, doc. 4. "La revolucion que estamos atravesando ahora es inminetemente popular y espontánea. . . . Ruegue á Dios que nadie informe á V.M. ál contrario, en la esperanza de que en abogar la continuacion de la Guerra pueda mejorar su posicion social!"

150. A.H.N., *Ultramar*, leg. 3525, exp. 38, doc. 4. "Nosotros hemos sido tratados de un modo ecsactamente igual."

151. Martínez-Fernández, *Torn between Empires*, 219.

152. "Santo Domingo," *Las Noveades*, 1 October 1863, 1. This is a quote from another periodical, the *Contemporáneo*, inserted into the article. "Las breves frases en que se da cuenta de lo ocurrido en Puerto-Plata, ofrecen á la imaginacion ménos exaltada un cuadro de horrores que hiela la sangre. Sabiéndose que los insurrectos son gente de color, se evoca el recuerdo de las terribles escenas que tuvieron lugar á fines del siglo pasado en la parte francesa de la isla de Santo Domingo, que hoy constituye la república de Haiti."

153. "Santo Domingo," *Las Noveades*, 1 October 1863, 1. "El peligro de lo que ocurre en nuestra nueva colonia es mucho mayor de lo que á primera vista parece. . . . Nadie ha olvidado que el año de 1844, y mandando en la isla de Cuba el general O'Donell, se tramó una vasta conjuracion, que afortunadamente se reprimió con rapidez. La muerte del poeta Plácido que causó tanta sensacion en Europa, y el número considerable de negros que vino á nuestros presidios del Mediodía, son evidentes señales de que no se comprimió aquella intentona sin haber tenido que apelar á medios de enérgica represion . . . el movimiento de la gente de color de Santo Domingo, ¿será síntoma de una conjuración general de la raza negra de nuestras Antillas?"

154. Valdés, *Poesías de Plácido*, 325–26.

6. Moors in Heaven

1. "Santo Domingo," *Las Noveades*, 1 October 1863, 1.

2. This was confirmed in a royal decree during the annexation process. Royal Decree of 24 June 1861, in A.H.N., *Ultramar*, leg. 5485, exp. 6, doc. 1.

3. Baez to the captain general of Puerto Rico, in A.H.N., *Ultramar*, leg. 3524, exp. 133.

4. A.H.N., *Ultramar*, leg. 3524, exp. 7, doc. 2. "Participa haber llegado á aquella Ysla un tal Ramon Levi procedente de Hayti hombre relacionado con los enemigos de nuestras colonias y que maquina contra la tranquilidad de ellas. Dice que es de calidad mulato y vecino del pueblo del Rincon en el 4° Departamento de esta Ysla donde tiene su familia, que en aquella está tratando de embarcarse en la Goleta

Matilde que se hacía á la vela para Mayaguez y que serà conveniente vigilar su conducta. Concluye espresando por posdata que de las indagaciones que ha practicado resulta que el espresado Levi es vecino de hormigueros ó de un lugar situado entre Mayaguez y Cabo-rojo."

Officially and unofficially, Puerto Rico played an important role in the events that took place in the Dominican Republic at this time. The governor of San Juan supplied intelligence and military support to back up Spanish interests in Santo Domingo while anti-Spanish partisans, primarily from the western regions of the island, did the same in support of republican causes. The links between this part of the island, which was farthest away from San Juan, and the peoples in the eastern part of Cuba and the northern country of the Dominican Republic had existed, as we know, from the earliest days of the colonies. Thus it is not surprising to find that in 1855 a man from the town of Cabo Rojo by the name of José Reyes Álvarez Peralta was in Santo Domingo acting as a double agent. He was there officially to deliver a copy of the treaty whereby Spain recognized the independence of the Dominican Republic. While there, Reyes Álvarez took the opportunity to make clear his admiration for the United States and to predict that Puerto Rico would gain its independence within four years. See A.H.N., *Ultramar,* leg. 3524, exp. 107, docs. 1 and 2.

5. Ramón Emeterio Betances, *Las Antillas para los antillanos,* ed. Carlos M. Rama (San Juan: Instituto de Cultura Puertorriqueña, 1975), xi. "Se ocupa de Haití, pero pensando en la libertad de la República Dominicana, lucha por Cuba pero pensando en la condición de la vida independiente de Haití, y ante todo se ocupa de todo pensando siempre en su Puerto Rico."

6. Betances, *Las Antillas,* vi. "Las Antillas para los hijos de las Antillas."

7. See Roberto H. Todd, "Ramón Emeterio Betances," in *Génesis de la bandera puertorriqueña: Betances, Henna, Arrillaga* (Madrid: Ediciones Iberoamericanas, 1967), 55. Todd is quoting from the testimony of the Puerto Rican writer Luis Bonafoux.

8. Hostos called Betances the "teacher, guide and friend" of Luperón, who was nine years younger than the Puerto Rican revolutionary. See "Luperón," in Hostos, *Obras completas,* vol. 10: 237.

9. "Proclamation of Quesada to the Puerto Ricans, 16 July 1874," in A.H.N., *Ultramar,* leg. 5113, n. 33, doc. 3. "Entónces os invitaremos á una sola sociedad para que nuestra divisa sea unidad en las Antillas." On the subject of the Cuban War(s) of Independence and the difficult relationship between racial and national ideologies in that struggle see the excellent work by Ada Ferrer, *Insurgent Cuba: Race, Nation and Revolution, 1868–1898* (Chapel Hill: University of North Carolina Press, 1999).

10. *Boletín Mercantil de Puerto Rico,* 11 June 1880, 2. Quoted in Félix Ojeda Reyes, *La manigua en París: Correspondencia diplomática de Betances* (Santo Domingo: Editora Corripio, 1984), 37.

11. Todd, *Génesis,* 55. "Queda, pues, bien entendido, que somos prietuzcos, y no lo negamos." Betances was consoling his sister, who had been eschewed by a close friend of the family when they had been mingling with people who, as he rightly described them, "deliriously" thought of themselves as blue-blooded. He was also pointing to the fact that this woman had repudiated his sister especially strongly because she was close to her in color, a typical action and one that I have described before in reference to people like Sánchez Valverde. Betances wrote to Demetria

Betances of her friend: "In your worldliness, you know how preoccupied people in certain circles are with [skin] color: and, I believe, being as you and I both are darker than the others, that was enough reason for her to stand away from you and for her to deny any relation to you among people whose favorite delirium is to think of themselves as being blue-blooded, especially when she is so close to you [in color]." (Tú conoces, teniendo mundo, la preocupación del color en ciertos círculos: y eso en mi sentir, bastó para que siendo tú y yo más prietos que los demás, esa persona se apartara de tí, sobre todo, que estabas más cerca de ella, y te negara en medio de gente, cuyo delirio preferente es el de ser azul.) Quoted in Todd, *Génesis*, 53. Betances always accepted the reality of his *mulatez*. That alone made him a revolutionary in the Caribbean context.

12. Antonio Maceo et al., "Protest of Baraguá," quoted in Aline Helg, *Our Rightful Share: The Afro-Cuba Struggle for Equality, 1886–1912* (Chapel Hill: University of North Carolina Press, 1991), 48.

13. See Paul Estrade, "La nación antillana: Sueño y afán de 'El Antillano,'" in *La nación soñada: Cuba, Puerto Rico y Filipinas ante el 98*, ed. Consuelo Naranjo Orovio, Miguel Ángel Puig-Samper, and Luis Miguel García Mora (Madrid: Doce Calles, 1996), 31.

14. Estrade, "La nación antillana," 35.

15. Helg's explanations are particularly enlightening on this point. See Helg, *Our Rightful Share*, 55–90.

16. José L. Franco, *Antonio Maceo: Apuntes para una historia de su vida* (Havana, Instituto Cubano del Libro, 1973), vol. 3: 239). "Yo creo que la práctica sincera de la democracia producirá sus saludables efectos cuando seamos libres."

17. Franco, *Antonio Maceo*, vol. 3: 240. "Nada se me ha participado de la suspensión de mi orden demandando auxilio."

18. See José Antonio Saco, "Exámen analítico," 133.

19. See Segundo Ruiz Belvis et al., *Proyecto para la abolicón de la esclavitud en Puerto Rico* (San Juan: Instituto de Cultura Puertorriqueña, 1969), 29.

20. Ruiz Belvis et al., *Proyecto*, 68. ". . . sería además un justo motivo para la intervención de pueblos extraños en la vida de las Antillas. . . . Este peligro es mucho mayor desde la última guerra de los Estados Unidos. Conviene repetirlo una y mil veces. . . . Los Estados Unidos, que no han desistido nunca de ser el pensamiento y la cabeza de América, no menos por esto que por ser lógico con su causa e interés, consagrarán sus fuerzas a la abolición de la esclavitud en los demás puntos del Nuevo Mundo."

21. Ruiz Belvis et al., *Proyecto*, 71. ". . . si semejantes perturbaciones del orden público son improbables en todas partes, en Puerto Rico son imposibles."

22. They spoke of the "dulzura de nuestras costumbres." See Ruiz Belvis et al., *Proyecto*.

23. Ruiz Belvis et al., *Proyecto*, 50. ". . . parecen constituir un solo elemento y una sola raza que marcha y se desarrolla en progresión sosegada y constante."

24. Ruiz Belvis et al., *Proyecto*, 102. "La población de color libre, tan numerosa en Puerto Rico . . . se ofrece como un eterno y brillante ideal a los ojos de la raza africana."

25. See Ruiz Belvis et al., *Proyecto*, 73. For a contrasting image see Guillermo A. Baralt, *Esclavos rebeldes: Conspiraciones y sublevaciones de esclavos en Puerto Rico, 1795–1873* (Río Piedras: Ediciones Huracán, 1985).

26. Betances, "Una biografía de Heureaux," in *Las Antillas,* 8. ". . . este hombre, que odia a los extranjeros porque son blancos, y a los negros porque él lo es."

27. Author unknown. Quoted by H. Hoetink, *Slavery and Race Relations in the Americas: Comparative Notes on their Nature and Nexus* (New York: Harper and Row, 1973), 101.

28. Hostos, *Obras completas,* vol. 9: 25.

29. See Melchor Fernández Almagro, *Historia política de la España contemporánea, 1897–1902* (Madrid: Alianza Editorial, 1968), 305–7.

30. Helg, *Our Rightful Share,* 105.

31. Glissant, *Caribbean Discourse,* 67.

32. Betances to Henna, in Betances, *Las Antillas,* 243. "Si Puerto Rico no actúa rápidamente, será para toda la vida una colonia norteamericana."

33. See Arturo Morales Carrión, *Puerto Rico: A Political and Cultural History* (New York: W. W. Norton, 1983), 152–72.

34. *San Juan News,* 14 February 1903, 7. ". . . por la pureza de sus ingredientes la Emulsión de Scott legítima destierra estos males de raíz y enriquece la sangre."

35. Advertising to Usonian audiences was also based on the fear of malnutrition and its fatal consequences. But there were no references to race or blood. In an 1895 postcard ad for Scott's Emulsion a color picture of a child wearing a sailor's suit is accompanied by a melodramatic Victorian inscription that reads: "Our boy, whose picture appears on the other side of this card, is a perfect type of health and beauty. It is a delight to look upon such a beautiful picture; but how sad to behold the suffering of the mother when her darling is smitten with disease, and his rounded, dimpled cheeks become pale and wan, and the bright eyes lusterless, and she sees day by day her little one wasting away. Unfortunately in every household some of the little ones are the victims of wasting disorder. For some reason their food fails to nourish them, and they finally fade and die." *Our Boy,* advertising postcard distributed by Scott and Bowne, New York, manufacturers of Scott's Emulsion, 1895.

36. Ironically, Scott's Emulsion had played a role as an indirect sponsor of Antillean independence. During the last decade of the nineteenth century the Puerto Rican creole Antonio Vélez Alvarado had made a fortune as the representative of Scott's Emulsion to the Spanish-speaking communities of New York City. With that income he financed *La Gaceta del Pueblo,* a separatist newspaper he edited that was the precursor of *Patria,* which was also published in New York by José Martí and the Puerto Rican editor Sotero Figueroa.

37. Murat Halstead, *Pictorial History of America's New Possessions* (Chicago: The Dominion Company, 1899), 542.

38. Halstead, *Pictorial History,* 512.

39. Halstead, *Pictorial History,* 580.

40. Halstead, *Pictorial History,* 680–81.

41. Halstead, *Pictorial History,* 681.

42. Ortega y Gasset, "How Castile Made Spain," 30.

43. Irving, *Life of Columbus,* 567.

44. Halstead, *Pictorial History,* 553.

45. Halstead, *Pictorial History,* 557.

46. Las Casas, *Historia,* vol. 3: 272.

47. Las Casas, *Historia,* vol. 3: 272. ". . . que no aprovechaba nada el solimán, sino para traer basura a casa."

48. Virgilio Dávila, "Redención," in *Patria*, in *Obras completas* (San Juan: Editorial Cordillera, 1964), 26.

> Queden, Patria, si es tu sino,
> Difamados tus varones;
> Tu albo manto hecho jirones
> En las zarzas del camino.
> ¡Y caiga el rayo divino
> Sobre el déspota triunfante!
> ¡Y sea maldito el instante
> En que te vio, entre ola y ola,
> El sabio marino, sola
> En medio del mar Atlante!

49. Dávila, "A la bandera americana," 47.

> Cuando, al ondular, agites
> Entre tus pliegues el aura,
> Que lleve a la "Unión" altiva
> La historia de nuestras lágrimas ...
> ¡Porque luego ocurrir suelen
> Metamorfosis extrañas!
> ¡Porque en lo moral, a veces
> El astro se vuelve mancha;
> El albor se vuelve sombra;
> La pluma se vuelve escama!

50. Irving, *Life of Columbus*, 567.

51. See, for example, John J. Ingalls, *America's War for Humanity* (New York: N. D. Thompson, 1898).

Index

Abbas, Ackbar, xv
Abû' Abd Allâh Muhammad XII
  (Boabdil): and "last sigh of the
  Moor," 3
Abû-l-Hasan 'Alî (Muley Hacén), 1
Acato pero no cumplo, 141, 156
Acosta, José Julián. *See* Junta
  Informativa
Act of faith *(auto-da-fé)*. *See*
  Inquisition, Holy Office of
Adoctrinamiento (indoctrination), 103.
  See also Enriquillo
Africans, 110, 113, 178, 179; as plague, 115;
  and Spanishness, 111; as threat to the
  indiano, 110; as wild dogs, 116. *See
  also* Blacks
Aguilar, Gerónimo de, 62
Al-Andalus, 28; social divisions in, 79,
  275n.74
Alarifes (master builders), 67. *See also*
  Santo Domingo de Guzmán
"Alboroto y motín de los indios de
  México" (Sigüenza): comparison
  with plagues in *Historia de las Indias,*
  130, 295n.8
Alhambra, 4, 36, 42, 44, 45, 74, 173;
  Alberca Court, 38–39; Court of
  Lions, 39, 37; Hall of the Kings, 40;
  halls of the Two Sisters and of the

Abencerrajes, 39–40, 136; *"wa-lâ
  ghâlibu illá'llâh"* (and there is no
  victor but Allah), 40
Allâh, 3, 40, 41, 52, 57
Almalafa (Moorish veil), 34, 58. *See also
  mantos*
Alma Mater (Korbel), 225–27; Franken-
  steinian character of, 227; and map
  of Havana in 1567, 227; and *Noble
  Habana,* 227
American. *See* Usonian America
Americanos, 199. *See also* Creoles
Haitian Revolution, 219; as a mulatto
  creole, 194. *See also* Spanish Negro
  Code
Amoriscados, 29–31, 41
Amoriscamiento, 31; and Sevillanization
  of the Indies, 58
Amo torna atrás (master comes back),
  193–94; analogical chain, 216; in
  analogical movement, 43, 73; in
  Dominican Republic, 239; regime of
  analogical conformity, 124; undoing
  the analogical principle, 127. *See also*
  European Ideal
Angiolillo, Michele, 253; meets with
  Betances, 253. *See also* Cánovas del
  Castillo, Antonio
Antelyes, Peter, 9, 12

323

Bonaparte, Pauline, 211, 214; as embodiment of Ideal, 212; as empress of the Plantation, 211–12; as Venus, 212

Borghese, Marie-Paulette. *See* Bonaparte, Pauline

Boyd-Bowman, Peter, 52, 58

Boyer, Jean Pierre, 218; reinstates the Plantation, 219

Bozales. See Slaves

Bréda plantation, 205, 207. *See also* L'Ouverture, Toussaint

Bryan, Williams Jennings, 259

Cabrera Infante, Guillermo, xv

Cairo Ballester, Ana, 313n.110

Campeche y Jordán, José, 143, 185, 250

Cannibalism, 160, 238; English as cannibals, 159

Canova, Antonio, 212, 216

Cánovas del Castillo, Antonio, 252; assassination of, 253–54, and Marat, 253

Cantar del Mío Cid, 30

Cap François, 211. *See also* Haitian Revolution

Carajo, 167. *See also* Irse al carajo

Caribbean confederation. *See* Antillean confederation

Caribbean Sea, 264; as black and mulatto sea, 189

Caribs, 129

Carrera de Indias (Route to the Indies), 54; stowaways in, 57

Cartagena. *See* Independent Republic of Cartagena

Casas, Juan, 163, 167; forced to eat excrement, 164–65. *See also* Ramírez, Alonso

Cassava, 94

Cassia fistula (golden-shower tree), 105, 109, 114, 291n.25. *See also Historia de las Indias*

Castas (caste) system, xxii, 130, 136, 150, 164, 172, 191; *albarazado* in, 175, 195; albino in, 174; as Baroque order, 175; and biracial Usonian system, 174; *calpamulato* in, 195; *cambujo* in, 174; *castas* described by Sigüenza, 130;

castizo in, 176; *chino* in, 309n.49; *español* in, 176; geometry of, 173; and gravitas, 175; as impossible project, 173; *lobo* in, 174; mestizo in, 173–74, 178; and moral character, 173–74; *morisco* in, 178; mulatto in, 180–82; *no te entiendo* in, 174; *tente en el aire* in, 174–75; *torna atrás* in, 175, 179; and *vecinos,* 304n.120; *zambo* in, 204; zoological nomenclature in, 174

Castas paintings, xxii, 173–82, 183; and creole will to power, 179; Matachine Indians in, 176; by Luis de Mena, 176–78; Paseo de Jamaica in, 176; plantains in, 178; role of women in, 176–78; still life in, 178; Virgin of Guadalupe in, 176. *See also Castas* paintings

Cathedral of Our Lady of Incarnation (Santo Domingo), 69; description of, 70–71; as expression of imperial claims, 73; horseshoe window in, 74–76; "imperfect" ribbing, 77–78; main façade, 71–73; West Indian Gothic, 78

Cattle raising, 118

Caudillismo, xxiii, 231, 235, 251, 253, 315n.120, 316n.127

Cela, Camilo José, 152

Cerrato, Alonso de, 117

Cervantes Saavedra, Miguel de, 35, 185

Chapel of the Rosary (Puebla), 134, 135; as luminous cave, 134; vertigo in, 136

Charles III, 186

Charles V, 36, 41, 44, 73, 94, 99, 107, 110

Chatelion, Felicia, 313n.107

Christians, new, 29

Christians, old, 34, 56

Christians: as pigs, 116

Chronicle of the Conquest of Granada, A, (Irving), 1–4; as unclassifiable text, 10

Church of San Lázaro (Santo Domingo), 76, 77

Cibao, 235, 240; economy of, 236; majority mulatto population in, 236. *See also* Vega Real del Cibao

Cimarrón, 61, 116; *negros cimarrones,* 117; from *símaran,* 278n.5; as wild dogs, 115. *See also* Runaway culture

Irving, Washington, xviii–xix, 47, 103,
163, 233, 260; and acquisition of
things Spanish, 11; and civilizational
insecurity, xix; 1492 as watershed for,
7; as Friar Agapida, 2–3, 6, 14, 20, 41;
as mestizophobic, 33; in Palace of
Charles V, 45; self-doubt in, 6, 27;
and Vanderlyn, 274n.57
Isabelino (Spanish Late Gothic)
architecture, 38, 69, 75, 285n.78
Islas, Andrés de, 181–82
Italian Renaissance, 36, 45, 278n.104. See
also Palace of Charles V

Jamaica, 246; Maceo in, 248; support
for War of Restoration in, 245
James, C. L. R., 205, 217; mulatto as
counterrevolutionary, 205, 209;
repulsion of wig-wearing, 209; and
self-mutilation in Rigaud, 208
Jefferson, Thomas, 188
Jesuits, 137, 198
Jíbaro, 195; allowed to carry arms, 195;
in castas, 195; as spotted with "white
stains," 195. See also Mestizo (as
almost-white)
Junta Informativa (project of Puerto
Rican delegates in), 250–51; demand
for abolition of slavery, 250; and
docility, 250; and movement toward
the white, 251; mulattoes as example
to African race, 251; Puerto Rico as
perfect colony in, 251; social peace
guaranteed by mulattoes, 251; warning of Usonian intervention, 250

Kincaid, Jamaica, xi, 209
Koselleck, Reinhart, 216

Lacroix, Pamphile, 210, 121, 214; on
fearlessness and savagery of Haitians,
211; French fear, 211; suspects some-
thing strange, 213. See also Crête-à-
Pierrot
Ladinos, 87; as tagarinos, 88
La Habana, San Cristóbal de. See
Havana

La Navidad fortress (Hispaniola), 107
Landing of Columbus in the Island of
Guanahani (Vanderlyn), 17–22;
and Columbus Doors, 22; and da
Vinci's Last Supper, 20; and Leutze's
Washington Crossing the Delaware,
21
La peregrinación de Bayoán (Hostos),
223
Lares Uprising (Puerto Rico), 247
Lascasian morality, 193, 195
Las Casas, Bartolomé de, xix–xxi, 51, 92,
102, 105, 109, 121, 130, 137, 146, 167, 171,
180–81, 183, 185, 195, 225, 261;
apocalyptic vision, 109; belief in
peaceful conversion, 96; as Bishop
of Chiapas, 95; colonization of
Cumaná, 95, 105; converso lineage
of, 93; defends indiano, 106; fear of
ultimate failure, 96; first conversion
of, 93; Indian as present, 93; as
indiano, 117; and introduction of
African slaves, 114; and Nuevas
Leyes, 95; as Procurador de los
indios, 94, 104–5; and project to
take European farmers to the
Indies, 98; second conversion of,
95; as soldier and slaver, 93; and
Suleiman, 110; and triumph of the
Church, 94; view of non-Christians,
93, 289n.1
La Yaguana (Hispaniola), 119;
destruction by Osorio, 122
Leclerc, Marie-Paulette. See Bonaparte,
Pauline
Leclerc, Victor-Emmanuel, 210;
embalmed in Egyptian manner, 211
Leonard, Irving, 131
Levi, Ramón, 246; of "mulatto quality,"
246
Lezama Lima, José, xv, 130; and
counterconquest (contraconquista),
xx, 184; and the imago, xv; and the
"metaphorical subject," xv; pleasure
of the unsuspected connections
(sorpresa de los enlaces), xvi, xx, 98
Liberty. See Independence

War of Restoration, xxiii, 240, 245;
creole power diminished in 240;
fought by peasant guerrillas, 240;
independence as function of
freedom, 240; letter to Queen
Isabella, 241–42; and *monte,* 241;
mulattoes as *plus ultra,* 243; and
mulatto intelligentsia, 241;
perceptions in Spain, 243; as
racial war, 240; radical practice of
freedom in, 241; Toussaint vs. the
queen, 241–43. *See also* Dominican
Republic
Weapons: in *banda norte,* 119; blacks
forbidden to carry, 119

Well-formed man. *See* Ideal
(European) Body
West Indian Gothic, 120. *See also*
Cathedral of Our Lady of
Incarnation
West Indian Hispanics. *See* Creoles
West Indies. *See* Antilles
Weuves, le jeune, 197
Weyler, José Valeriano, 252; and first
concentration camps, 252

Yesería (plaster reliefs), 38, 41, 134, 136

Zaharenian, 1; extremes, 20; story of
Zahara, 7; and *zahareño/a,* 1, 267n.2

José F. Buscaglia-Salgado is assistant professor in the Department of Romance Languages and Literatures and director of Cuban and Caribbean programs at the University at Buffalo.